Cavaliers
OF THE
DAKOTA
FRONTIER

WAYNE FANEBUST

HERITAGE BOOKS
2009

HERITAGE BOOKS
AN IMPRINT OF HERITAGE BOOKS, INC.

Books, CDs, and more—Worldwide

For our listing of thousands of titles see our website
at
www.HeritageBooks.com

Published 2009 by
HERITAGE BOOKS, INC.
Publishing Division
100 Railroad Ave. #104
Westminster, Maryland 21157

Copyright © 2009 Wayne Fanebust

Cover design by Scott Ehrisman

All rights reserved. No part of this book may be reproduced or transmitted in any form or by any means, electronic or mechanical, including photocopying, recording or by any information storage and retrieval system without written permission from the author, except for the inclusion of brief quotations in a review.

International Standard Book Numbers
Paperbound: 978-0-7884-4915-4
Clothbound: 978-0-7884-8151-2

This book is dedicated to the memory of my friend,
Aaron J. Munson
1944-2005

Table of Contents

Acknowledgement .... v-vii

Chapter I	Landmarks on the Plains	1
Chapter II	Speculators Arrive in the Great Minnesota Outback	13
Chapter III	The Delegate Question	55
Chapter IV	Adventures Along the Nobles Road	77
Chapter V	Yankton on the Missouri River Slope	99
Chapter VI	Pembina and the Ox-Cart Culture	131
Chapter VII	Inkpaduta	153
Chapter VIII	Trouble at the Town Sites	185
Chapter IX	The Squatter Government at Sioux Falls City	225
Chapter X	Steamboats on the Big Sioux River	261
Chapter XI	First Newspaper Fight in Dakota	273
Chapter XII	Dakota Territory at Last	291
Chapter XIII	The Great Dakota Stampede	327
Chapter XIV	Fate of the Cavaliers	363

Bibliography 407

Endnotes 413

Index 439

Acknowledgement

This is an "into the west" book. It is a book about dreaming and scheming on a grand scale in the mid-1850's and early 1860's, a time of widespread land speculation, when the national outlook was for massive immigration to the West. It is the story of three groups of speculators—from St. Paul, Dubuque and Sioux City—each of which maneuvered to locate town sites along the rivers and streams and other desirable locations in the wilderness everyone was calling Dakota. The way west was paved by the ambitions and blandishments of the town site speculators. While much of their promotion was exaggerated or false, they put many towns on the maps of the West, thereby providing the foundation for communities, many of which exist today, be they small towns, medium-sized or large cities.

I chose to call these speculators "Cavaliers" because they were a bold and reckless breed of men, engaged in a form of gambling, willing to take chances with their money, the money of investors and, of course, their lives. It was a game fraught with hazards, but they believed the odds were in their favor and the risks worth taking.

While lacking the glamour of the gunfighter or the dance hall girl, the speculators were no less important figures on the frontier. They should not be relegated to the basement of history or tucked away in a footnote. If this book accomplishes anything it will at least, insure that the story of the *Cavaliers of the Dakota Frontier* is given an audience.

It is often said that writing a book is a lonely experience. I find just the opposite is true. While working on this book and keeping an eye on the finished product, the relationships fell in line and friends came to the fore. First I thank my friend and colleague, Tom Kilian for his encouragement and support and for reading the manuscript in its early stages. I remember telling Tom some years ago and said that I was abandoning the project. Tom responded emphatically, saying "you finish that book." After that friendly admonition, quitting was never an option.

A book is not finished until an editor does a careful and thoughtful review of the manuscript. Every book needs an editor and, fortunately, I found a good one in Kathleen Marusak. "Kat" read each chapter carefully and meticulously. While she pointed out my dumb mistakes, it was her encouraging words in the margin that made me feel like a good writer. Her expertise and patience shows up in the finished product. I unhesitatingly recommend her to any writer who might be perusing this acknowledgment.

I thank my friend and fellow history buff Bruce Blake, for reading the manuscript and for hours and hours of conversation about the early days of Dakota. Fellow writer Maxwell Van Nuys from Colorado read and critiqued the chapter on Inkpaduta and offered many useful suggestions based on his expertise, and he has my thanks. My friend David Swan was always a willing listener and a provider of good ideas, and I thank him wholeheartedly.

Among the many public libraries that provided access to the secrets of the past, I thank those in Sioux Falls, Yankton, Pierre, Miller and Mitchell, South Dakota, Sioux City, Iowa and Luverne, Minnesota. Tina Irvine at the Sioux Falls Public Library deserves special thanks for handling the wide variety of inter-library loans requests that I tossed her way.

I especially enjoyed working at the Minnesota History Center in St. Paul and the South Dakota Heritage Center in Pierre. The same accolades go to the Center for Western Studies at Augustana College in Sioux Falls. All three are wonderful archives and are staffed by courteous and dedicated personnel.

My mother, Dorothy Fanebust, and my brothers and sisters have all contributed to this book in ways they don't realize and I thank them for their steadfast support and encouragement. Special thanks goes to my sister Connie Lilla for reading each new chapter and eagerly waiting for the next one.

No book of mine is complete until I thank my daughter Danae Howell, for her love, understanding and support. It was long ago as a little girl that she first came to understand just what writing means to me. And now that she has a joyful little girl of her own, Angelina, I have another source of love, happiness and inspiration.

Wayne Fanebust
Sioux Falls, SD
June, 2008

Chapter I

Landmarks on the Plains

"About midway in its course, the Big Sioux breaks through a remarkable quartz formation, and seems to have ruptured the massive wall of rock."
Jacob Ferris, 1856

The description of the Falls of the Big Sioux River by Jacob Ferris was not the earliest, but it was probably one of the most widely circulated. He described the Falls and other prominent features of the Northwest in his *States and Territories of the Great Northwest*, published in 1856. One might think he actually visited the Falls, but most likely his description was based on other eye-witness reports. The Ferris book was a combination guidebook and a manual for success in a frontier environment. It was one of many promotional works designed to encourage migration into the western wilderness. If Ferris and other promoters could turn the hostile wilderness into a land of enchantment, so much the better for America. These books were regularly served to a westward-looking market when America was afire with the fever of speculation along with the desire to explore and settle the West.

The success of this kind of publication, as well as any venture it inspired, ultimately turned on the quality and lay of the land, including its landmarks. It was one thing to write in enraptured terms about the Great Northwest; it was another to accurately report on natural phenomena so as to prepare people for the tests they faced. Landmarks, both natural and manmade, either encouraged or discouraged entrepreneurial forays into the wilderness. Landmarks were like pieces to a giant puzzle waiting to be pieced together and spun into an overall plan.

The Falls of the Big Sioux River was just one of many landmarks on the part of the Great Northwest that came to be called Dakota. Each river, lake and stream had its unique qualities and beguiling influence on the frontiersmen. There were great, oceanic expanses of grassland, some of it head-high and so vast that it, by turns, fascinated and overwhelmed. There were hills, mounds, rock formations, bluffs, buttes, badlands, woodlands and flatlands, all of which summoned both the muse and the muscle of man. These landmarks long served the native populations and the wild beasts of the plains, beings with an innate reverence for the land. While the non-indigenous people tended to see the utilitarian side of the wild, they were no less impressed with the beauty of the land and the possibilities offered by the wilderness.

Beginning in the 18th century, European-born explorers and mapmakers brought a sense of order to the Northwest, signaling an end to the mysterious aspect of the land. The unknown was becoming the known. In time the natural landmarks were joined by those created by man. This book is about those makers of unnatural landmarks and discoverers of the natural ones. These are the people this writer has chosen to call the *Cavaliers of the Dakota Frontier*. For good or for ill, they are the bold ones, the risk-takers, the few and the first. They were the speculators, town site promoters, political adventurers, buckskin entrepreneurs, boomers and materialist dreamers of all persuasions.

They studied maps, read books, formed companies and laid their money on the line. They listened to the enthusiastic accounts of those that wandered the West and lived to talk about it. They did some exploring on their own, but they were not explorers in the tradition of Merriweather Lewis and Robert Clark. Nevertheless, the Cavaliers moved beyond the relative safety of Minnesota and Iowa and planted their standards at selected sites on the hitherto untrammeled prairie.

In a time of "firsts," they laid out the first roads, operated the first ferries and steamboats; they turned the first furrows, built the first towns and forts and opened the first graveyards. The Cavaliers were interested in finding and harnessing waterpower, exploiting the soil, minerals, and other natural resources. While the Plains version of a "mountain man" was satisfied with an isolated cabin in the woods, or a dugout on a slope, the speculators wanted to raise cities. While they too may have enjoyed the solitude of the wilderness, they wanted it to come to a noisy end.

Having done some homework, the Cavaliers were sufficiently convinced that the land was good and the risks worth taking. They were optimists who believed that people would read their propaganda and follow the trails they blazed. They believed that raw land was wasted land; that the land was theirs to take, looking to civilization's unstoppable and unerring influence. Their government could be counted on to sanction and support their enterprises, and clear the paths of obstacles. They believed America would provide both the legal underpinnings and the human numbers needed to people their land. By the mid-1850's, they were ready to move into the Dakota wilderness.

Wilderness has always attracted free-spirited frontiersmen. Years before the speculators appeared, west-wanderers explored much of Dakota. One of the early-day adventurers who crossed the Big Sioux River was Philander Prescott. An explorer, trader, and trapper, he and his companions arrived in the fall of 1832, in search of beaver skins. They built a log house on the "Crooked," or Big Sioux River directly west of the Pipestone Quarries. Here they planned to spend the winter.

In December, Prescott went south to the Falls of the Big Sioux River from Minnesota, on a mission for the American Fur Company, with a "cart and two men and one horse and a small supply of provisions." This was the first recorded visit by white men at the Falls. They camped overnight and investigated the scenery, including the Falls.[1] Prescott saw the river and the Falls in winter, when the water was low. In his account, he makes no mention of seeing any sign of human habitations, native or otherwise, so it can be assumed that the area was in pristine condition. Seeing the Falls in an absolute state of nature was a privilege granted to men like Prescott, who came first.

Captain James Allen also visited this important natural landmark. In the summer of 1844, he led a company of soldiers on a western reconnaissance from Des Moines, Iowa Territory, into Dakota. They made their way leisurely to the Falls and were awe-struck by the immense water-power and the natural splendor of the ancient rock formation. After resting at the Falls, the expedition went twelve miles downriver and camped at the mouth of the Split Rock Creek. In his journal, Allen describes seeing herds of buffalo near the Falls of the Big Sioux River. The soldiers feasted on buffalo and the natural beauty of the land. They followed the Big Sioux River to its mouth, encountering small groups of Indians along the way.[2]

The confluence of the Big Sioux and Missouri Rivers constitute another landmark of great significance to the history of the Northwest. Two rivers coming together, both well timbered and navigable, could not fail to become a prominent feature on maps and attract strong men with ideas and ambitions. One such man was Theophile Brugier, a lithe and handsome Frenchman who was especially suited for life in the wilderness. He was the kind of man often described as having "powerful parts." He was imposing in his physical appearance, personality and intellect. A natural leader, the magnetic Brugier drew both Indians and white men to him and commanded their respect.

Brugier located at the mouth of the Big Sioux River in 1849, on the Iowa side. Iowa was a young state when he claimed about four and one-half sections of land and was the second resident of Woodbury County. He operated a ferry across the Big Sioux River, probably the first of its kind. Brugier married two daughters of his friend, War Eagle, a Chief of the Yankton Sioux, and fathered thirteen children, some of whom became frontier notables in their own right.

Living among many Indians and a large entourage of white retainers, Brugier carried on like a Lord of the Wilderness. He traded with the tribes and engaged in work for the U. S. government, supplying the military, growing rich from a steady stream of contracts. In time his sphere of influence moved up the Missouri River, where the regal Brugier became involved in land speculation and treaty negotiations.[3]

The Missouri River ranks as one of the most important landmarks on the Plains. This great river was as much responsible for drawing the speculators as was the Falls of the Big Sioux River. Early on it became an important artery of transportation, bringing men and supplies upriver from St. Louis to various military and fur trading posts. It was the time of the steamboat, a vessel particularly suited for the wild waters of the Northwest. While steamboats were far more expeditious than overland routes, the "Big Muddy" was often a terrible, deceptive and unforgiving river. Boats could move softly and swiftly over stretches of deep water and then suddenly be snagged by a tree trunk, or beached by a sandbar lurking in the shallows. The history of steam boating on the Missouri River is fraught with stories of wrecks, fires, sunken cargo and casualties. It was the uncanny skill of the pilots that made the difference between a completed journey and a disaster. The best steamboat captains became local legends. Among them Joseph M. LaBarge II stands out. He worked for the American Fur Company in St. Louis. In 1847, he piloted the steamboat *Martha* up the Missouri River from St. Louis, taking his wife Pelacie with him. This was the first trip up the Missouri River for him and for his wife—probably the first time a white woman appeared in the upper Missouri River country. He was the youngest pilot on record and lived to be the oldest.[4]

To the east of the Missouri River in Brule County, South Dakota, the traveler can see a ridge of hills in the distance. These are the Bijou Hills, a range of rugged, rock-studded hills, spread out over eight to ten square miles, once a nesting place for eagles. On August 25, 1801, Perrin DuLac, an explorer, visited the hills and planted a cedar post 20 inches square with his name, date and the words: "sitis cogoscenti deo naturea."[5]

The Bijou Hills were a familiar and conspicuous landmark to frontiersmen, and appear on some of the earliest territorial maps.

They were named after Joseph Bissonette, a Frenchman out of St. Louis. Like something that originated in the dark reaches of time, these hills were viewed with awe and mystery, and were somewhat romanticized by the early-day settlers and the press.

Bissonette was an early-day traveler in the Northwest. In 1812, he built and operated a trading post on the Missouri River, at the foot of the Bijou Hills.[6] As early as 1823, the hills bore his name.[7] It was believed that Indians used the hills as a place of refuge after attacking white settlements.[8] And it was claimed that Sioux City speculator, Henry W. Granger—who claimed the hills as part of a 250,000 acre Spanish land grant—was killed by Indians in the Bijou Hills.[9] These and other stories emanating from the famous Bijou Hills—the "mystery mountains," long ago, became a part of Dakota lore.

The Black Hills are, of course, the best known and most outstanding landmark in Dakota. And although these majestic mountains were a factor in the speculators' plans, they were too far to the west to be of immediate concern. Still the speculators were aware of the Black Hills, called them by that name, and believed the stories of gold and other mineral wealth, passed around by Indians and frontiersmen. As early as 1832, white adventurers penetrated the Black Hills in search of riches.

Among the landmarks created by man, the fur trading posts and military forts stand out for their influence on westward migration. Fort Pierre came about as a result of fur trade on the Missouri River. In the spring of 1832, the Chouteau Company, headed by Pierre Chouteau, built a 280-by-300 foot stockade. The Chouteau family, with roots in New Orleans, controlled much of the fur trade on the Missouri River that was centered at Fort Pierre. Among the early day visitors was the artist George Catlin who found the area to his liking.[10] From Fort Pierre, Catlin roamed the Dakota Plains, visiting Indian tribes, learning of their culture while painting the masterful works of art that today adorn the museum walls of America.

The federal government bought the fort from Chouteau in 1855, paying an exorbitant price. A contingent of soldiers under General William S. Harney used it as a base of operations against the Sioux Indians. Harney and his troops wintered at Fort Pierre in 1855-56, finding the place wholly unsuitable for the military. His soldiers agreed. They hated Fort Pierre, calling it "Fort Desolation," or worse.[11] They deplored the isolation and the bleak, hostile surroundings that made winter almost unbearable.

The army abandoned Fort Pierre in 1857, because of the lack of trees and hay for horses, but it continued to serve as a rendezvous for traders, trappers and steamboat travelers. Throughout the frontier era, Fort Pierre remained an important landmark and point of reference. Material from Fort Pierre was packed up, floated downriver and used to construct Fort Randall. This post was established in the summer of 1856 to protect the frontier from "roving bands of Indians." It was situated on the west side of the river, in what was then Nebraska Territory, on a plateau about a mile and a half from the right bank. An early day newspaper called the site "beautiful." Certainly, everyone liked it better than Fort Pierre.

Fort Randall was garrisoned by cavalry, infantry and artillery, with room for 600 men. It quickly became one of the leading military installations in the Northwest. It featured a commissary, a hospital, and commodious quarters for both officers and enlisted.[12] It was more than a military duty station; it was an entire community where civilians could earn money and purchase goods. A large chapel served as a place of worship, a library and a site for social gatherings. People felt both welcome and safe; the well-equipped post was a source of pride. The presence of Fort Randall, which over time became a town in itself, encouraged those speculators who wanted to establish town sites on the Missouri River.

There is another type of landmark that played an important role in attracting permanent settlements, namely, landmark events. Among these, treaties with the Indians stand out. And among the treaties, two offered an abundance of encouragement to those who would test the Dakota frontier. These are the Treaty of Traverse de Sioux, and its companion, the Treaty of Mendota. Together they opened up millions of acres in Minnesota Territory, which meant an absolute bonanza for the land and town site speculators.

The treaties were struck in 1851 after two years of work. More than any other man, Minnesota territorial Governor Alexander Ramsey was responsible for these treaties. Ramsey entered office as Minnesota's first governor determined to deal with the Indians for their land. He and his allies sensed they were in a position to convince the Sisseton, Wahpeton, Wahpekute and Mdewankaton Sioux to enter into a deal—land in exchange for money, goods and a reservation.

The whites bargained using an old formula: treat the Indians as "mere children," ignoring both fairness and honesty, while stressing the benign superiority of the "Great Father" in Washington, D. C. During the course of "negotiations," Indians were treated with a confusing mixture of flattery and contempt, threats and promises.[13] In the end the Eastern, or Santee, Sioux—divided into "upper" (Yellow

Medicine) and "lower" (Redwood) groups, ceded all their ancestral lands except for a narrow strip along the Minnesota River. They were to receive money, some of it paid immediately and some of it paid annually in cash and goods. But the biggest chunk was turned over to a group of traders who claimed they were owed money from the Santee. South Dakota Historian Doane Robinson said Ramsey conspired with the traders to defraud the Indians.[14]

While the entire process was corrupt, it was the trader debts under the Treaty of Traverse de Sioux that proved to be the most onerous part of the nefarious affair. The chiefs were tricked into signing the "traders' papers," thinking it to be merely another copy of the treaty itself. The debts were either greatly exaggerated or fraudulent altogether, allowing traders to cheat both Indians and the federal government, resulting in government subsidized fraud. All in all, it was an entirely one-sided and unsatisfactory treaty, which, over time worsened Indian-white relations, resulting in the terrible War of the Outbreak in Minnesota and Dakota.[15]

For a time, however, the treaties looked like a godsend and Governor Ramsey emerged as a very popular man, becoming one of the giants in Minnesota history. The Minnesota newspapers printed ecstatic articles in praise of the treaties. A St. Paul newspaper editor recognized the Treaty of the Traverse de Sioux as a landmark event, calling it the "greatest event by far in the history of the territory," for it meant "the red savage, with his teepees" would become a thing of the past.[16]

While the treaties made their slow progress through the U. S. Senate, settlers poured into Minnesota. After both were ratified and money was doled out to the Indians, St. Paul merchants were ready to sell horses and liquor to them. Town sites sprouted up on Mississippi Valley land soon after the Indians left for their reservation. Iowa benefited too. Encouraged by all this progress and new land, town site speculators in Minnesota and Iowa eventually developed far-reaching plans for the western wilds known as Dakota.

The newspapers were usually at the forefront of the westward movement, predicting the doom of native cultures and the success of white enterprise. That the Indians would disappear was taken as an absolute. That the lands along the Big Sioux and Missouri Rivers would be occupied by white settlers was also a certainty. "Destiny has willed it and it is right."[17]

Chapter II

Speculators Arrive in the Great Minnesota Outback

"I came here [Sioux Falls] in June, 1857. I was one of thirty-eight who were sent out by the Dakota Land Company to locate town sites with half-breed scrip."

Peter B. Burns, in the *Sioux Falls Press*
July 2, 1886

In 1857 the United States of America was moving inexorably toward the disastrous "War Between the States." Congress was struggling with problems of an unprecedented nature as the economic and cultural gap between the North and South widened. The newly formed Republican Party, with its anti-slavery attitude, was gathering supporters, grimly asserting itself in preparation for future political battles. But in Minnesota Territory, dominated by the much older Democratic Party, other, less doleful plans of conquest were afoot. Blissfully unaware of what was to lie ahead for the nation and themselves, an ambitious group of men were preparing to launch an invasion of their own sort. A peaceful one—one that they hoped would increase their personal fortunes and satisfy their political yearnings. They were about to embark on one of the nation's most ambitious town site founding expeditions.

Their firm, the Dakota Land Company headquartered in St. Paul, was encouraged by three successive years of town lot speculation on the Trans-Mississippi frontier.[1] From Minnesota south to Kansas, the way west was being staked out and paved by the noisy blandishments of the town site speculators. Taking advantage of a generous town site law passed by Congress in 1844, hundreds of towns were founded and platted, but most of them were barely identifiable as towns. Armed with finely drawn maps and lithographs, and little else, real estate hucksters made considerable sums of money selling lots to anxious immigrants. As this sort of business attracted swindlers who sold lots in "moonshine towns," many people were fleeced.

The men of the Dakota Land Company were interested in more than paper towns but they operated under a familiar formula with goals much like the other town site companies. They would locate desirable town sites, use scrip to get title to the land, convince people to settle there and reap healthy profits selling town lots. Looking southwest from St. Paul, they sought their bonanza in Minnesota Territory's unsettled and untested region, a vast tract of land that included the Big Sioux River Valley on the east, to the Missouri River on the west. The westward push by the land-hungry masses was seen as inevitable; the speculators only had to get there first and create towns.

In the spring of 1856, the national outlook was for massive immigration from the East to the West. A New York newspaper predicted an astounding 250,000 people would go west into the frontier, saying "never was there such excitement on the subject before," among all classes from cities and towns of all sizes.[2] In Dubuque, Iowa, then a launching point for speculators and immigrant parties, the newspapers were awash with advertisements by "land agents," all hoping to cash in on the coming bonanza.

People coming to the Northwest would be able to take advantage of an expanding network of railroads. By 1854 the eastern seaboard was linked with Rock Island, Illinois on the Mississippi River.[3] From that point to St. Paul, the rest of the journey was easily accomplished by steamboat. There was much talk about building a railroad from Dubuque to the new town of Sioux City, on Iowa's western border, to take advantage of the new markets sure to spring up in the West.

There was also bold talk in 1856 by a group of Minneapolis men, about forming a company to explore the Jacques or James River region, in far western Minnesota Territory, with a view of locating settlements. Since this was unceded land, inhabited largely by the Yanktonai Sioux and considered by the Indians to be great buffalo pasture, westward-looking whites began to urge the federal government to come up with another treaty to make the takeover legal. Still, the impatience of the speculators was such that everyone expected that the founding of town sites and settlements would precede a treaty. As one Minnesota newspaper proudly stated: "the steady progress of our settlements west cannot be staid (sp) by the lines of ceded land, nor the right of occupancy by the Indians recognized by our government."[4] Indian displacement was viewed as inevitable.

It was a time of hungry optimism driven by a healthy economy. St. Paul, created by the territorial legislature on November 1, 1849, was another gateway to the West. By the mid-1850's, it was buzzing with activity; parties of hunters passed through to hunt buffalo on lands bordering the Big Sioux River and the Red River of the North. Liquor flowed freely from crude, makeshift buildings called "rum-holes" that lined its narrow streets. Brothels operated openly and

St. Paul in 1857
(Collections of the Minnesota Historical Society)

profitably. Hotels, hammered together as quickly as possible, did their best to accommodate the large swarm of visitors and sightseers. On the edge of the Mississippi River, where it connected with the Minnesota River, St. Paul came off as uniquely western: rugged, optimistic, opportunistic and dangerous.

In the early 1850's St. Paul was called "Pigs Eye," after a tough old French-Canadian "voyageur," Pierre Parrant, whose squinty eye resembled a pig's eye.[5] He operated a crude groggery, selling whisky from a cave. Someone writing from his den called it "Pig's Eye" and the name stuck.[6] Parrant's joint was a frontier hovel and formed an inauspicious beginning of a city, but a proud newspaperman saw nothing ugly about St. Paul when he penned: "The ground from Pig's Eye to the Falls, I then will claim St. Paul for mine, the child of 1849."[7]

Most of its residents found St. Paul attractive, with its many fine mansions, gardens, fancy carriages and four and five-story brick buildings. The boomtown also had more than its share of prostitutes, gamblers, thieves, cutthroats, swindlers and the like, who "reveled to their hearts content—reducing vice to a science," and took pride in "the foul corruption that has marked their footsteps." Some measured the depravity of St. Paul against that of New Orleans—long considered as "the pandemonium of the country"—or San Francisco that was experiencing its lawless, vigilante days.[8]

On the whole, however, most people saw the good side of the restless city, heralding its prospects over its drawbacks. By 1855, with a population of 4716, steamboat trade was brisk and St. Paul's wide awake newspapers were all shouting the town's advantages from its muddy streets, false fronts and second-story windows.[9] In 1857 the *St. Paul Daily Times* predicted boldly that by 1867, St. Paul would have a population of 480,000![10] Boosters proudly proclaimed St. Paul was good enough to make people forget about California and its gold.

Fur trading was operating full blast. In fact, it was arguably the most important cog in the town's never ceasing wheel of business. Animals were killed and skinned in huge quantities as if they were supplied by some cosmic machinery blessed with limitless creative powers. Everyone, it seems, was prepared to do his part and strike a blow for profit and progress and silence some portion of the hostile wilderness. Someone was so anxious to eradicate loons and kingfishers on Lake Como, two miles from St. Paul, he advertised for hunters, offering to pay $3.00 per loon shot and fifty cents for each kingfisher killed.[11]

But nothing exceeded the zeal of the real estate speculators. Everywhere, someone was selling raw land and town lots. Buyers were equally enthusiastic, often paying exorbitant sums for land as if there would soon be no more to buy. An alarmed Minnesota newspaper editor wrote: "we have nearly as many town sites scattered over the country as farms...." [12] After observing the buying and selling frenzy, another man suggested that a few acres of land be reserved for farming before it was all gone.[13]

His tongue-in-cheek concern was well taken. The Land Office Department in Washington, D. C., revealed that in 1855, more land was pre-empted in Minnesota Territory than all the other states and territories combined.[14] In 1857 Minnesota Territory had land offices in eight towns, including Minneapolis.[15] From the signing of the Sioux Treaties in 1851, through 1857, the great speculative mania prevailed in Minnesota Territory.[16]

Henry M. Rice, a Minnesota pioneer and politician, cashed in big time buying and selling frontier real estate. He invested his money in a row of luxury homes in Washington City. The houses were occupied by such luminaries as Illinois Senator Stephen A. Douglas and Vice President John C. Breckinridge, and became known as "Minnesota Row." Rice was a lucky speculator and a smart investor.[17]

Outside of Minnesota there was growing displeasure with the state of affairs in western America. There were those who believed that the "rage to engage in real estate" was turning too many productive people into unproductive speculators. Calling it an "unnatural state of things," a Dubuque newspaper editor deplored the speculative mania that was causing so many to put aside their trades and professions and indulge in excessive land investment and paper town building. A man who worked diligently every day at his job or trade supported not only his family but also his community's economy, while a man who over-extended himself in land bought on credit was just a gambler, and gamblers were a liability. Dire consequences awaited all of America, the editor predicted, unless such people put a halt to their extravagant and irrational behavior.[18] But sober warnings went for naught as it was the time of the big grab and there were thousands of hands reaching for the pile.

Members of the Dakota Land Company were similarly inspired. The company was staffed by men of considerable all-around ability; some had political experience or useful connections with powerful men in high places. While most of them were not well-known, some of the key members such as lawyer Charles E. Flandrau and trader Joseph R. Brown were Minnesota pioneers of long standing—men of high intelligence who proved their mettle by handling successfully the hazards of frontier life.

Charles E. Flandrau, called the "Prince Rupert of the Northwest," was appointed the agent to the Santee Sioux in 1856 by President Franklin Pierce. A native of New York City, he was a tall, striking, well-educated man with strong eastern antecedents. His father was the law partner of Aaron Burr. The younger Flandrau was a good lawyer too, firm and decisive. He came to St. Paul in 1853 at age 25, and by 1857, he was an Associate Justice on the Territorial Supreme Court.[19] Yet he commonly dressed in buckskins and wore his hair long like the frontiersman he was.

More than 20 years after the town site experiment, the ambitious and talented Flandrau revealed candidly that his organization, the Dakota Land Company, plotted to "occupy" the new area, send a delegate to Congress, establish public facilities on its town sites and "make a good speculation out of the enterprise."[20] While he was not among the incorporators, Flandrau was a shareholder, and he was certainly one of those who provided vision, inspiration and direction to the venture.

Fellow speculator Joseph R. Brown was equally skilled and ambitious, and was an influential member of the Dakota Land Company, serving as its president in 1857. The son of a Maryland minister, Brown became a Minnesotan in 1819, when he ran off to Fort Snelling to serve as a drummer boy. He lived among Indians and fathered several children by a Sisseton woman, including Samuel F. Brown. He suffered an ax injury to his foot and as a result, his Indian name was "Siharota" or "Crooked Foot."[21]

The quintessential frontiersman, Joseph R. Brown balanced brain and brawn with a domineering yet genial personality—he habitually used the expression "by George," in a jovial, backslapping sort of way. He served in the territorial legislature with competence and partisan dedication. He founded the town of Henderson in 1857 and used his legislative skills to the benefit of his town. It was said of Brown that when he walked, "his face was ever turned upward toward the skies."[22]

In 1857 Brown was placed in charge of the Indian Reservation along the Minnesota River and immediately set about encouraging the natives to abandon their nomadic way of life and engage in farming. Religious authorities considered Brown an immoral man, unfit to exercise influence over the Indians, but he shrugged off the criticism and went to work with energy and commitment and the result was an explosion of Indian farmers living in log houses. While he was sympathetic with the Sioux, he was absolute in his belief that an adaptation to the white man's world was their only future.[23]

By sheer force of personality, Brown commanded and received a generous portion of respect from all Minnesotans—and over time, a fair measure of political enemies. He seemed to relish controversy and could hold his own with any opponent—Indian or white. And yet he looked for the good in men and was a kind and generous friend to all who came to his campfire or cabin. If Minnesota had mountains, Brown would have been a mountain man in the tradition of the mythical giants who roamed the Rockies. The Dakota Land Company could not have asked for a more inspirational leader than Joseph R. Brown.

Men such as Brown and Flandrau spent much of their time on the frontier, and yet wielded significant political power in the towns. They were dubbed "Border Ruffians" (to compare them to Kansas pro-slavery radicals) and "Moccasin Democrats" by their Republican adversaries who accused them of bringing Indians and mixed-bloods to the voting places. A St. Paul newspaper of Republican persuasion mockingly called them "slavocrats,"[24] because Democrats tended to oppose radical anti-slavery measures. While they had no desire to introduce slavery to the Northwest, they had other well-laid political plans. Joseph R. Brown, Charles E. Flandrau and their fellow speculators were about to find out just how much clout they had—and how much they would need to reach their goals.

William H. Nobles, a frontier road-builder and trailblazer of some renown, was connected with the Dakota Land Company, having lived in Minnesota since 1841. Heavily armed with Sharp's rifles and Colt revolvers, Nobles and his crew spent the summers of 1857 and 1858 laying out a U. S. government road on Minnesota Territory's vast outback, from Fort Ridgley on the Minnesota River to old Fort Lookout on the Missouri River. In 1856 Congress appropriated $50,000.00 and commissioned Nobles to build the road. Long-range plans called for the construction of a railroad to the Pacific Ocean through "Nobles' Pass" in the Sierra Nevada Mountains.

Another man strongly identified with the Dakota Land Company was Samuel A. Medary, governor of Minnesota Territory. He was appointed governor by President James Buchanan, replacing the outgoing Willis A. Gorman, also a Democrat. Medary arrived in St. Paul on April 22, 1857, in a "very Democratic" lumber wagon after the steamboat *Time and Tide* carrying him and his entourage met with an accident.[25]

Medary was an experienced politician and journalist from Ohio. Described by a contemporary as a "hard old nut,"[26] he had long served the Democratic Party with partisan loyalty and no expectation of receiving a political office. His appointment was the direct result of his friendship with Stephen A. Douglas of Illinois, who was the most popular and prominent Democrat of the 1850's.[27] It was said Medary accepted the position only to help out the Buchanan administration.[28] Furthering the goals of the political party he so fervently loved was reward enough for him, and if he did it in Ohio he could do it in Minnesota. His son Samuel Jr., also came to Minnesota and worked on the Nobles road as an engineer.

The elder Medary (or "Sammedary" as he was called in Ohio) was a staunch supporter of his friends, and to his enemies, especially Republicans and abolitionists, he was a fierce, unyielding adversary. When faced with a challenge by rival politicians, Medary quickly forgot his Quaker upbringing and came out swinging. Medary's newspaper, the *Ohio Statesman,* started in 1838, became one of the most powerful organs in that state and throughout the South, and it was through his influence that James K. Polk was nominated for President in 1844.[29] Before that he was a friend and supporter of President Andrew Jackson and over the years, managed and supported many a Democratic hopeful, including Buchanan and Douglas. He was said to have authored the phrase: "fifty-four forty or fight," in connection with the dispute with Great Britain over the Oregon/Canada border.[30]

Medary reportedly arrived in St. Paul in good health, ready to go to work, although he was among the invited dignitaries at the National Hotel in Washington, D. C., some of whom were victims of a mysterious poisoning that occurred at a state dinner party. The incident created a national furor as it was believed that the poisoning—possibly arsenic—was the product of a conspiracy to

Samuel A. Medary
(Collections of the Minnesota Historical Society)

kill newly elected President Buchanan, who was present, but did not eat or drink. It was reported that the president received an anonymous warning not to partake, so he was unaffected.[31] Most were not so lucky. While many eventually died from the strange malady, the tough old Medary suffered but survived the incident and continued west. Within a month after his arrival in St. Paul, he was leading the charge of the Minnesota Democratic Party and the Dakota Land Company.

The Dakota Land Company was incorporated by an act of the territorial legislature on May 21, 1857, during the peak of the town site boom. The incorporators included Byron M. Smith, Artemus Gale, Parker Paine, Thomas Campbell, Alpheus G. Fuller, Samuel F. Brown, N. R. Brown, James W. Lynd, Franklin J. DeWitt, and Frederick Freudenreich. The corporation was to "obtain title to...lands or other property east of the Missouri river," which "shall hereafter be offered for sale in this Territory, or future State of Minnesota..." Four hundred thousand shares of stock were to be issued at one hundred dollars per share.[32] Men hired as teamsters or to do other work, were given two shares of stock in the company and allowed to claim land next to a town site.[33]

To further benefit the Dakota Land Company, the legislature created seven counties in the sparsely populated southwestern part of the territory, namely Jackson, Martin, Nobles, Cottonwood, Murray, Pipestone, and Rock. The last two mentioned extended partly into what became Dakota Territory.[34] Affairs were moving rapidly, reminding men that just a short time ago, Minnesota Territory was experiencing the first groans of creation.

Minnesota Territory was organized in 1849 under the Whig administration of President Zachary Taylor. It was divided into several counties, including Wabashaw, which encompassed all of southern Minnesota Territory, extending west to the Missouri River. Its first governor was Alexander Ramsey, from Pennsylvania, a man new to the frontier, but eager to be a part of it all and exploit it for personal gain. He spent most of his four-year administration immersed in Indian affairs. The 1851 Treaty of Traverse de Sioux was one of his trophies.

After just eight years and three territorial governors, Congress deemed Minnesota ready for statehood and on February 26, 1857, a law was passed authorizing the people to write a constitution and set up a state government.[35] That summer a large delegation of prominent men of both parties was selected to meet in convention and write a constitution that would be acceptable to the Minnesota voters and to Congress. Unfortunately, the convention could best be described as a partisan brawl. After a stormy gathering, marked by threats, taunts, fist fights, angry walkouts and secret meetings, the organic document of the new state was somehow adopted.

Still Congress had to approve the constitution and admit the new state. While this was not automatic, most knowledgeable observers believed Minnesota would be admitted in short order. After that, all those who took title to land outside the new state would be in a position to control the political destiny of the new territory. As early as February of 1857, Congress was expected to create the "Territory of *Dakota*," from the "portion of the Territory of Minnesota west of the Sioux river and Red river of the north and that portion of Nebraska east of the northern chain of the Black Hills."[36] All the more reason for the Dakota Land Company to make haste for the vast and primal region people called Dakota or "Dacotah." Their name alone suggests their destination was known in advance of their expedition.

It seems that despite the optimism of the Dakota Land Company, many Minnesotans had a rather uncomplimentary opinion of the western and southwestern sections of their territory. While it was understood that the land east of the Big Sioux River was very fertile, it was believed that the vast tract lying west of the Big Sioux, all the way to the Missouri River, was broken, treeless, poorly watered and essentially valueless for agriculture. It was also "generally admitted," said a St. Paul newspaper, that there was a "deficiency of water power in the southern half of the Territory."[37]

The writer of this article obviously had no knowledge of the Falls of the Big Sioux River and its immense water power, but the men of the Dakota Land Company most certainly did. Not only that, they believed iron and coal deposits were present on the Big Sioux River in southern Minnesota.[38] It didn't matter that much of the land in the western reaches of the territory had been blackened by prairie fires in the fall of 1856.[39] The speculators were anxious to help themselves to that part of the territory, looked upon by many as inferior—land they expected to be cast aside when Congress passed legislation to make Minnesota a state.

So with appropriate fanfare, prayers and flag-waving, the Dakota Land Company eagerly launched its expedition into the untested territory on the very day the corporation was chartered. The *Daily Minnesotian* bade a sad goodbye to the "Big Sioux Falls Colony" along with "many sincere prayers and wishes for their success and safety... we have been promised news from the party at every opportunity."[40]

Clay Bryan, a reporter from the *Daily Minnesotian,* traveled with the hopeful pioneers.

The town site venture was complemented by a party of railroad surveyors going in the same direction. On May 24, 1857, two corps of engineers representing the Transit Railroad Company began a reconnaissance of the country in central and western Minnesota Territory, seeking out a route from Winona. Exploring the rivers, ridges and valleys of Minnesota proved uneventful, but when the teams hit the Big Sioux River, they "were compelled by the menacing bearing of the Sioux Indians, to abandon the survey further west." They turned back, but with the expectation that they would return the following spring and complete the survey of the road all the way to the Big Sioux River.[41]

The Dakota Land Company town site expedition was hoping for better luck and less resistance. It was entrusted to the leadership of Alpheus G. Fuller, who, after nine years of roughing it, became a prominent St. Paul gentleman, businessman and the builder of the Fuller House, one of the city's finest hotels. The party consisted of about 40 men with a sufficient number of teams and wagons to haul "sash, glass, nails, doors, furnishing lumber, agricultural and mechanical implements." The first leg of their journey, on the Minnesota River, was aboard the steamboat *Wave* that carried them as far as New Ulm.[42] According to the *Wave's* pilot, Captain Maxwell, the "Big Sioux Falls Colony" arrived at their destination "in good time and buoyant with hope."[43]

Their long, tedious trip after the New Ulm drop-off proved uneventful, although a report filtered back to St. Paul stating they were attacked by Indians.[44] When the truth was learned, it was met with much relief as just then folks were reeling from the blood and shock inflicted on a small settlement at Spirit Lake, Iowa, by a group of Indians led by the infamous Inkpaduta. Chapter VII of this book is devoted to Inkpaduta, who spread terror among whites, discouraging settlement while his reputation as an outlaw adventurer assumed great proportions.

From New Ulm the Dakota Land Company town site party moved overland in wagons. According to Peter B. Burns, a young man in it for the sake of adventure, and perhaps some land of his own, their first stop, other than for resting and eating, was at Lake Benton.[45] There they established a town site and called it Mountain Pass because the area had long been known as "Hole-in-the Mountain," a natural pass through the scenic *coteau des prairies* to the broad prairie to the west.

The correspondent from the *Daily Minnesotian,* who accompanied the "Big Sioux Falls Colony," sent a hastily written note back to St. Paul, by messenger, describing the new town site in glowing terms. He was especially impressed with the lay of the land, the presence of timber and water at "Mountain Pass, Dacotah," and cheerfully sent his findings back to the *Daily Minnesotian.* "We will start from here on our way to the Big Sioux River in a few minutes," wrote Clay Bryan.[46] The party continued west after leaving two or three men to guard the new "town."

After they crossed into what was to become Dakota Territory, they located another town, "Medary," on the Big Sioux River along the Nobles road. It was named after the governor, of course. According to Bryan, Medary was intended to be the capital of "this territory when Minnesota is divided." Joseph R. Brown maintained a trading post at the town site, which may have influenced the company to locate there. A creek that emptied into the Big Sioux River near the town site was also given the governor's name. Bryan praised the surrounding prairie, calling it good farming land.[47]

A few men were left at Medary and the remainder went further downstream until they came to another scenic spot on the Big Sioux River. It was deemed worthy of becoming a city so they staked off their acreage and called this one "Flandrau," after the young lawyer and agent of the Santee Sioux. Two important Democrats were now duly immortalized and the expedition continued on its way south to the area most coveted by the Dakota Land Company: the Falls of the Big Sioux River.

Apparently the Falls equaled or exceeded their expectations. It was said that members of the party from Maine went "halt mad at the first sight of the Falls."[48] Clay Bryan was also greatly impressed with this landmark, noting its immense waterpower and scenic surroundings. Using the bottom of a bread pan for a desk, he wrote prophetically: "The Red man of the West never trod a finer domain than this which we have just reclaimed from the wilderness and which in time will be a beautiful and populous, well cultivated region."[49] Bryan was one of those types who could stand in a campsite, look around at the wild scenery, and see a city—or at least write about it in a manner that would convince others to come and take a look.

The generally accepted view is that when the St. Paul men arrived at the Falls, they were surprised by the presence of another group of speculators. These men were members of the Western Town Company of Dubuque, Iowa, who arrived in May and were therefore comfortably encamped by the Falls when the St. Paul men arrived.

Byron M. Smith, an engineer, surveyor and explorer for the Dakota Land Company, remembered it somewhat differently. In an awkwardly written account of the expedition, Smith—who surveyed all of the company's town sites—said his company sent scouts ahead of the main party. And that on the first or second day of June, one day before the Western Town Company representatives arrived, James W. Lynd and an African-American man known only as Isaiah, appeared at the Falls. But in all likelihood, the Dubuque men arrived first and were merely absent when the St. Paul men showed up.

Whatever the case, there was land available for both town site companies, and the judicious course was probably uppermost in the minds of all concerned. In a hostile wilderness, the astute man sought peaceable relationships and safe havens. Pragmatism was another form of valor. When the advance party learned that the Dubuque people were on a mission similar to theirs, Lynd and Isaiah left to intercept the main party.[50] Lynd was a fur-trader and a political figure of some prominence, having served in the Minnesota territorial legislature, while Isaiah served the company as guide and interpreter.

The main party arrived at the Falls on June 6th. They made camp near the roaring cascades and two men were detailed to catch fish for the evening meal. Within one-half hour, the detail returned with "as many fish as they could carry." The next day, Sunday, was spent in washing and drying clothes on the rocks, and on Monday, they held a meeting with the Dubuque men. It was then they learned that the big prize, the Falls, had already been claimed by the Western Town Company.

This was undoubtedly a major disappointment, but not worth fighting over, so the St. Paul men immediately staked out 320 acres of land to the south, bordering on the Iowans' claim. They called their town "Sioux Falls City," the name Sioux Falls having already been taken by the Dubuque men. Then Lynd and five other men started downstream, and at a point east of Sioux Falls, where the Split Rock Creek meets the Big Sioux River, they located another town called "Eminija," a Sioux Indian name for the Split Rock Creek. Two men were left in charge of it.[51]

Two men were also left in charge of Sioux Falls City, according to most historical accounts, namely James McBride and James L. Fisk. Peter B. Burns was there too, although he is not mentioned in any of the histories. Many years later he told a Sioux Falls newspaper reporter that the company left him, along with Fisk and McBride, at Sioux Falls City with one month's provisions. They built a log house on the corporate property, an experience Burns recalled with particular fondness. When it came to creating a roof, they "bought a bark canoe from the Indians for $5 in gold, crossed to the island, and cut polls long enough to reach from one gable to the other, and then put brush and sod on top, which completed our cabin." But not before the canoe capsized and dumped Fisk into the river.[52]

The Western Town Company was the creation of a group of prominent Dubuque business and political figures, all happy victims of the town site mania. The company was incorporated by Henry S. Hetherington, president, William Churchill, vice-president, George P. Waldron, secretary, and directors Austin Adams, Dennis A. Mahoney, Dr. George M. Staples, W. R. Baird, J. W. Taylor, Jesse T. Jarrett and J. M. McKinley. Unlike the Dakota Land Company, it was a mixture of both Democrats and Republicans.

Of this group, Hetherington and Mahoney were the most

James L. Fisk
(Collections of the Minnesota Historical Society)

prominent. Both were partisan Democrats and both were active in eastern Iowa politics. Hetherington was a popular mayor of Dubuque, and Mahoney served as county treasurer and was connected with the *Dubuque Express and Herald,* a passionate, if not fanatical, pro-Democratic, anti-Republican newspaper. Austin Adams was a judge who later served on the Iowa Supreme Court. Dr. Staples, from Maine, specialized in surgery of the throat and lungs, having earned a medical degree from Harvard in 1855. Some Dakota historians concluded Staples was the instigator and leader of the group.

The Dubuque men quietly formed their company in October of 1856, apparently unaware of their powerful competitors in St. Paul. The Western Town Company was chartered for five years of existence—unless extended by the stockholders—and had a capital stock of $60,000.00, divided into five hundred shares at $125.00 per share. The "Notice of Incorporation" was proudly announced in the *Dubuque Express and Herald.*[53]

The men of the Western Town Company learned of the awesome and picturesque Falls of the Big Sioux River from a book entitled *History of the States and Territories of the Great West* by Jacob Ferris. They sent agents Ezra Millard and David M. Mills to locate a town at the Falls, as well as other locations, which they might find desirable.[54]

Millard and Mills left Sioux City, Iowa, near the end of October and arrived at the Falls after a trip of several days. In the name of their company, they claimed 320 acres that included the Falls and the wooded, eleven-acre island at the head of the Falls. Mills, a surveyor and veteran frontiersman, having joined the California gold rush of the 1840's, also took up a personal claim of 160 acres.[55]

The first annual report of the Western Town Company, issued in

1857, states that Milliard entered into an agreement with Mills, under the terms of which the latter was to "keep possession of said falls until the first of May, last." This suggests that Mills spent the winter at the Falls. If true, he must have built some kind of a shelter.

Accounts of the Falls of the Big Sioux River submitted by the Millard and Mills expedition were thought of as "so apparently extravagant" that the company directors were reluctant to believe them. Their curiosity piqued, however, another party of men led by Jesse T. Jarrett ventured to the Falls the following March to "take the place of Mr. Mills."[56] The party was also ordered to ascertain the "precise location of the Falls, and to give such a description of them as actual observation and survey would warrant." Jarrett, a reputable Dubuque surveyor and land agent, gathered information that corroborated the accounts of Mills and Millard.

News of the immense waterpower excited the speculators; the Falls of the Big Sioux River were judged the second best waterpower in the West, next to the St. Anthony Falls near St. Paul. The Dubuque men were also relying on the accounts of the French scientist and explorer Jean Nicollett, who explored the Northwest in the 1830's, and the report of a man named Adams who led a party of hunters to the Falls in 1856. For men who were accustomed to "Roughing it in the Bush," the Western Town Company heartily recommended Sioux Falls City, the coming metropolis.[57]

In May the Western Town Company sent a third group to Sioux Falls, consisting of John McClellan, Jesse T. Jarrett, Barclay Jarrett, James Farwell and Halvor Oleson, intending to maintain a permanent population there. These men became the companions of Fisk, McBride and Burns of the Dakota Land Company.

Enthusiasm for the joint enterprise was in high gear. The Western Town Company announced plans to bring in a steam sawmill from St. Louis, along with other machinery. They boldly proclaimed that some day Sioux Falls City, at the site of the "Great Sioux Falls," would be a prominent point on a "Great Trunk Railroad from St. Paul to Sioux City."[58] As evidence of their positive outlook, the company board of directors voted to increase the price of its stock by ten dollars per share, based on "information received from their Agent, Mr. Jarrett, as to the value of their property on the Sioux River..."[59] The *Dubuque Express and Herald* gave the enterprise a ringing endorsement, saying "there is scarcely a point in the North West, certainly no interior point that possesses more of the natural elements to make a city than does that of Sioux Falls."[60]

The Dakota Land Company had newspaper support too, primarily from the friendly *St. Paul Pioneer and Democrat*. But another Minnesota newspaper, the *Minnesota Free Press*, published in St. Peter under the editorship of W. C. Dodge, attacked the company and its plans. Shortly after Alpheus G. Fuller, "Baron" Freudenreich and party returned to St. Paul, following their town site locating expedition, the *Free Press* came out with an editorial that mocked the speculators' flowery and enthusiastic description of the Big Sioux Valley. The editor lectured his readers on Dakota and the Dakota Land Company and its exaggerated reports of "Hesperian gardens...on the Western borders of the earth, somewhere in the regions of sunset."

Claiming to see through a well-organized speculation scheme, the *Free Press* said that "the Dacotah Land Co., and other St. Paul Speculators, may have a chance to locate there the Capitol of another new Territory, and repeat the same swindling, plundering operations which they have performed at St. Paul. The good of the state has nothing to do with it." The speculators, according to Dodge, were in it purely for the money they could make for themselves. No one else would benefit.[61]

In another shrill article, Dodge claimed the Dakota Land Company was influential in establishing the western boundary of the state of Minnesota to suit its ambitions. Members of the company were not satisfied with the original version of the Enabling Act that set the western boundary from the southern tip of Big Stone Lake to the headwaters of the Big Sioux River, and thence to its junction with the Missouri River. Why would Joseph R. Brown and his friends want to change it "to an arbitrary cut across the naked prairie without a single landmark of any kind to mark its position?" he asked.

Then he supplied the answer: "The land east of the Big Sioux is all ceded land—the Indian title is extinguished. That west of it is not. The Dacotah Land Company, composed of St. Paul speculators, wanted that land to operate on. They desired to establish a tier of towns through it, along the new road, and to secure all available points upon the Big Sioux, before emigration could reach it, and thus secure the greatest field of speculation in the West!"[62] His breathless article screams of fraud and backroom maneuvering, and the insulting effect it had on the citizenry caught unaware.

One citizen, however, expressed a different opinion in a letter to the *Pioneer and Democrat*. Far from being self-serving, the speculators were doing the right thing. It was desirable for Minnesota and its people to have Dakota settlements near the western border of the new state, rather than many miles to the west on the Missouri

River. A white population to act as an economic buffer was better than having Indians as neighbors. Minnesota would benefit since the great immigration to Dakota would pass through its cities and towns. If settlement started on the Missouri River, Indians would be forced east toward Minnesota. This, however, was blocked by wise legislation, and "settlement in Dakota will necessarily commence on its eastern portion."[63]

Editor Dodge, however, would have none of it. He also had some unkind words to write about Nobles' road building enterprise, saying the "whole thing was a humbug speculation from the beginning." He charged Nobles, Brown and Medary with dishonesty in that they convinced Congress to appropriate a huge sum to build a "road" to "towns owned and located" by their company. Once again he declared that Minnesota would not benefit a bit from the appropriation or the road, and "the money will be found to be all used up, before the road ever gets beyond the sight of their towns." Dodge was convinced that Nobles had no intention of laying out a road to the Pacific, and the concern about Indians was simply an excuse to stop the work.[64] He saw the Dakota Land Company behind the "humbug speculation."

But the Dakota Land Company proceeded with its grand designs, as if newspaper opposition was merely another obstacle to be knocked down and conquered, not unlike the wild frontier that both beckoned and threatened. When there are worlds to conquer, there are always people willing to accept the challenge, risking ridicule and ruin—or worse.

In June of that hopeful summer of 1857, Peter B. Burns left Sioux Falls City and went to Medary for supplies, leaving the rest of the group for Indians to scare away. This was accomplished in a very short time. When Burns arrived at Medary, he found the place laboring under a siege mentality, having interpreted an Indian demonstration as threatening. Fearing the Sioux would pay a "professional visit" to their town sites, the Dakota Land Company sent word to Sioux Falls City in the person of a "negro interpreter," probably Isaiah, advising the settlers to evacuate at once lest they be killed and scalped. The Sioux Falls and Sioux Falls City men hastily organized and discussed their options, then decided to leave. Fisk and McBride went to Medary, and after a short time, it was decided to vacate that town site too. Some went to St. Paul, and others joined Nobles and his overland road crew.[65] McClellan and his associates also decided the Sioux Valley was too dangerous, so they loaded up their possessions in canoes and paddled downriver to Sioux City.

When news of the crisis reached Dubuque, it was reported that the speculators at "Falls City" barricaded themselves in preparation for an attack. After a lengthy council of the settlers, they decided to vacate, not for fear of the Indians, but because it would be too dangerous to try to bring in food and other supplies while they rode out the threat. The prudent course was to retreat rather than endure a siege and possible starvation. Before the white men departed, Indians destroyed one of their claim shacks.[66]

Chief Drifting Goose at the head of a group of Yanktonai Sioux has been credited with driving the whites from Sioux Falls, without bloodshed.[67] It would not be the last time he succeeded without force of arms. Skillfully using threats and intimidation, Drifting Goose kept the white man off-balanced and at wits end for the next twenty years. In 1857 he was already an important leader of his people, and after a series of decidedly unfriendly visits to the camps of the Sioux Falls colony, where hair-raising threats were uttered, settlers were convinced to depart. By late July, the Big Sioux River town sites were empty and quiet—but not quite dead.

While this crisis was unfolding, a party of Dakota Land Company agents left St. Paul with supplies and reinforcements. From New Ulm, they moved overland in wagons, on the "eastern section of the [Nobles] wagon road to the Pacific." The train consisted of thirty mules, twenty horses and fifty oxen, making the trip from New Ulm to Mountain Pass in seven days. The men ate well, as fish and waterfowl were in great abundance, and duck eggs were nightly fare around the campfires. The going was rough, however, as the streams and ravines were swollen due to recent heavy rains. They built crude bridges over some of the streams and sloughs making use of the long prairie grass. The large train of animals ground the prairie into dirt and mud, giving the road at least the appearance of a road.

They reached Mountain Pass, or Hole-In-The-Mountain, on Lake Benton, on July 2nd, and celebrated Independence Day there in the company of a number of men from Medary, who rode in on horses decorated for the occasion.[68] Then they learned that 100 lodges of "I-hank-toka," or Yankton, Sioux were encamped on the "Jacques" or James River, threatening to stop any further progress of Nobles' trans-continental road.[69] The Indians objected to the intrusion of the Nobles road crew because they feared the white man's activities would frighten off the buffalo, their primary form of sustenance.

This crisis undoubtedly instigated the evacuation of Big Sioux River town sites. It proved to be of no consequence, however, for within a short time, the town sites were again occupied and active, and Nobles continued on his way west. But the adventurous Peter B. Burns—who apparently didn't think of himself as a figure of historical importance—was not at either town site; following the scare at Medary, he returned to St. Paul and thence to Illinois, giving up whatever interest he may have had in the Dakota Land Company.[70] Perhaps the Dakota frontier was altogether more adventure than he cared to endure.

And yet the pioneering spirit was undiminished in the others. Take reporter Clay Bryan, for example. While on his way to Mountain Pass, he got lost and spent four days wandering the prairie with nothing to eat. Finally, he stumbled onto the Santee Sioux Reservation with feet so blistered that he couldn't walk for two days. And yet, when he wrote of his misadventures to the *Daily Minnesotian*, he emphatically declared: "I have been all over this country, and am well pleased with it; so must [be] all who come here..."[71] He wasn't ready to quit.

Others were similarly inspired. On August 27th, a well-supplied party of men from the Western Town Company arrived at the Falls. Happy to have reached their destination after a long, arduous journey, they let out a series of cheerful yells and pitched their tents on the big island.

They returned to their town site at the urging of company leaders in Dubuque, who encouraged them to get tough and defend the town at the point of a gun, if necessary. Build a fort, show some resolve and the Indians would back off.[72] One of the company leaders, director Dr. George M. Staples, made the trip to Sioux Falls to get a first hand look at the settlement.[73]

In addition to Dr. Staples, those who went to the Falls were Wilmot W. Brookings, Dr. Josiah L. Phillips, John McClellan, Smith

Kinsey, and company manager Jesse T. Jarrett and his wife Amanda, who insisted on accompanying her husband on the long journey from Dubuque. Amanda Jarrett recalled years later that her appearance at the Falls—which she claimed was the first by a white woman—was cause for rejoicing among the men of the settlement.[74]

None of new arrivals had been thoroughly tested by the frontier, but that was to change, and very soon at that. At the outset, however, while peace prevailed, they were concerned about improving their town site and put tools and backs to work. Among the implements and supplies they brought was a sawmill. Some of the men and Amanda Jarrett returned to Sioux City, and the remainder, six in all, immediately set to work cutting logs and stone to erect buildings necessary for survival that winter.[75]

Prominent among the first structures of the village was the Dubuque House, a crude hotel made of unfinished quartzite stone, quarried at or near the site. Built by the Western Town Company, it was intended to serve the traveling public, and was probably company headquarters as well. It was the first of many stone buildings to be erected in Sioux Falls from the immense supply of quartzite, and was a source of pride for its builders. Small in size, its rugged, pinkish exterior stood in stark contrast to the smooth, green prairie hills that seemed to roll on forever.

Staples appointed Brookings company manager in place of Jarrett[76] and returned to Dubuque, satisfied that the town site was in a prosperous condition and the "settlers are enjoying excellent health."[77] It must have appeared to Staples that the money invested by himself and his fellow speculators was well spent.

The season of activity along the Big Sioux River attracted the attention of outsiders. Among them, the editor of the *Sioux City Eagle* was especially curious and a bit skeptical. Without naming names, the editor of the *Eagle* said he was prepared to attack all those who tried to "gull the people with paper towns...or entice the unwary into buying corner lots situated in swamps...."[78]

There were some tense moments in store for the hardy speculators, but none that were caused by suspicious newspaper editors. On October 10th, while out exploring, Brookings and McClellan unexpectedly came upon a group of Indians. Instinctively, the two men turned around and ran back toward the Falls at top speed. When they had reached the hill above the settlement, they stopped and looked back only to see the Indians were running in the opposite direction.[79]

Later that evening the quiet of the town site was shattered by the sudden and noisy appearance of a band of Indians. In fighting regalia and war paint, the Indians rode down the bluffs, surrounded a pair of oxen and drove them off. It was probably more of Drifting Goose and his men. A detail of four men attempted to track the Indians but soon gave up and returned to camp.[80] The experience caused them to appreciate the precarious nature of their lives. Nevertheless, they were not ready to give up their town site.

The Dakota Land Company was also determined to hold on to and improve its claims, and prove to skeptics that they were doing more than making "paper towns." On September 21, 1857, a group of 21 men, led by Franklin J. DeWitt and Alpheus G. Fuller, departed St. Paul, bound for the Minnesota outback, which most referred to as Dakota. Eleven of the men got off at Medary, three at Flandrau, and the remaining seven went to Sioux Falls.[81] Among the latter were

James M. Allen, James W. Evans, James L. Fisk and James McBride. Once again they joined hands with their competitors and worked hard to make their colony comfortable for what all anticipated would be a long, hard winter, isolated and far away from the relative comforts of St. Paul and Dubuque.

That fall the real estate boom went "bust," following a financial panic back East. In New York and other eastern cities, banks fell like rows of dominoes. Money became scarce and often consisted of "wildcat" currency, meaning a fifty dollar bill could suddenly be worth less than the paper it was printed on, if the issuing bank went broke. In St. Paul—the "money mad" capital of speculation—hotels emptied out, forcing the Fuller House to lower its rates to $1.00 for a night's stay. Businesses failed, credit dried up and the city eventually lost about one-half of its population. The panic ruined the speculators' chances of making a quick profit from land sales.[82]

The Panic of 1857 was an economic disaster of national proportions, caused by over-inflation, too much credit, over-speculation and excessive railroad financing. As one wiseacre said: "the premature railroads of the west had fostered premature cities, teeming with premature traffic for premature populations."[83]

This slur could have been meant especially for the Dakota Land Company. But the company kept up its bold front and forged ahead, although officials were forced to assess each share $2.00 in September and another $2.00 in October. Company president, Joseph R. Brown, gave notice to all stockholders to meet at the Fuller House for the purpose of discussing matters "important to the interest of the company."[84]

This meeting took place in early October, not long after a friendly legislature passed laws incorporating the towns of Mountain Pass, Medary, Flandrau, and Sioux Falls City. Interestingly, the limits of the latter extended "one half mile above and below the Falls" and one mile east of the river, thus it included the claim of the Western Town Company.[85] The legislature also created Big Sioux and Midway counties with Sioux Falls City and Medary the county seats.

Despite the crash, the season was one of great political activity, caused in no small part by the St. Paul speculators. The growing popularity of the Republican Party gave the Democrats considerable unease, and the former looked to the southern tier of new counties to give them an edge in the fall tilt. Although these counties had little or no people, they were allowed delegates at the Democratic convention, at least three of whom were Dakota Land Company members.

The campaign that followed the selection of the candidates was fierce, if nothing else because Minnesota was on the verge of statehood and both parties wanted control of the new state government. With Medary not in the running, the Democrats wanted Henry H. Sibley for governor while the Republicans put up former governor Alexander Ramsey. October 13, 1857 was election-day. While the vote from older, better-established counties went to Ramsey, late returns from the southwestern counties turned the tide in favor of Sibley and he was elected by a small margin. William W. Kingsbury, the Democrat, was elected delegate to Congress over his Republican challenger. On appearances, it was another notch for the Dakota Land Company, for some of their towns supplied the winning vote.

Two historians writing in 1882 said "the returns of the wilderness precincts were unusually large...."[86] It was for that reason the

*Stock Purchase Receipt, Dakota Land Company
(Collections of the Minnesota Historical Society)*

Republicans cried foul, claiming voter fraud. The accusatory chorus was lead by the *Daily Minnesotian* of St. Paul. That newspaper insisted agents of the Dakota Land Company were involved in a fraudulent scheme for the purpose of electing Sibley.[87] Angry Republicans insisted there were few or no people living in the towns of the newly formed southern counties in which "voting precincts" were set up. They pointed out that in September, a busy Governor Medary had—by "proclamation"—set up a number of "election precincts," in faraway places like Pipestone in Pipestone County, and Oasis and Council City in Murray County, all Dakota Land Company strongholds, as well as in the far-North Pembina settlement. Republicans contended that mythical people voted in paper towns and as such, the vote should be thrown out.

They had a right to complain. Very few people—a handful of trappers and traders—lived in the southwestern counties in 1857, and yet a census report showed 173 people living in Cottonwood County in 1857. This report and others were signed by N. R. Brown, one of the Dakota Land Company organizers. He was probably Nathaniel R. Brown, a brother to Joseph R. Brown. This was the deceptive side of the company; it used expedient, illegal means to further its political and financial goals. Although many people saw through the scheme, the schemers got away with it and survived an election contest.[88] But a day of reckoning was on the way.

While the company was making enemies in Minnesota, it had a staunch ally in the *St. Paul Pioneer and Democrat*. Its fiery proprietors were die-hard, states-rights Democrats, but equally pro-union, and as time went on and the Civil War drew nearer, they found themselves on a particularly uncomfortable fence. But when it came to local politics and business, they had no problem in deciding who was right and who was wrong.

According to the columns of the *Pioneer and Democrat*, the Dakota Land Company was strictly legitimate, and Dakota Territory was an accepted fact. Although still a part of Minnesota, the newspaper treated Dakota as if it had its own political life, and everyone had the Dakota Land Company to thank for it. On November 29, 1857, the *Pioneer and Democrat* published a long, descriptive editorial entitled "Dakota Territory," describing the area in glowing terms.

"It seems highly probable that at the coming session of Congress, a Territory will be organized west of this State of Minnesota, comprising the large extent of territory cut off from the State...." The "cut off" area included the land from the western boundary of Minnesota to the Missouri River and north to Canada, or, as "prominent Dakotans" desired, a territorial mass that encompassed the Black Hills. This configuration would "create Dakota into a Territory of magnificent extent and resources." One gets the feeling that this is what the speculators had in mind all along.

The editorial continues at length, describing the bold new settlements that were muzzling the howls coming from that part of the wilderness. It estimated the population of Dakota to be about 4000, "giving 1500 to the Red River region and the remainder to the country, open to settlement, contiguous to the Big Sioux." At Sioux Falls City, there were "about 30 houses, a steam sawmill, and several stone buildings." A letter from that place said the mill was running "night and day, and that settlers were hauling their logs to the mill, and readily paying $20 per 1000 feet for sawing."

"At Eminija, a few miles below the Falls, and the head of

steamboat navigation on the Big Sioux, there are several houses." Flandrau, 40 miles to the north, had a "few houses," while Medary boasted "upwards to twenty houses, and probably as many families." Many settlers had taken claims along the rivers, including the Eminija (Split Rock) and Rock Rivers where they flow into the Big Sioux River. The soil was rich and "the entire valley is susceptible of the highest degree of cultivation, and will sustain a dense population." The lack of timber was, however, seen as a drawback that would tend to confine settlements to the rivers and streams, leaving the open prairies unsettled.

There was another, more serious problem, however. The only land that could be legally taken was that east of the Big Sioux River, as the Yankton Sioux still owned the area between the Big Sioux and the Missouri rivers. But most men expected that this obstacle, too, would soon be overcome. A treaty would be worked out between the Indians who were willing to sell their land, and the federal government, which, "as experience has demonstrated, seldom hesitates to deal in real estate." For these reasons and more, people could expect an "energetic attempt" by Congress to organize the new territory at the coming session.[89]

The facts and figures related by the *Pioneer and Democrat* smack of exaggeration, as the actual population of Sioux Falls City, for example, was a scant sixteen, all men. And at the beginning of winter 1857-58, this fragile population had built just three houses, one of stone.[90] This may not have been intentionally misleading. However the *Pioneer and Democrat* was probably printing information disseminated by the Dakota Land Company, which was simply carrying out its plan. It didn't matter that Republicans called them Southern sympathizers. The Company would gladly take all the publicity it was given. This would encourage further settlement of Dakota and materially benefit Minnesota's commercial interests.

By 1857 St. Paul was a comfortably established town in the Northwest, despite its financial woes. Sioux Falls City, however, was in its infancy and during its first winter, those living there had little to do except to find food and shelter, create ways to relieve boredom and dream about the great city they would build. Despite the imprisonment imposed by circumstance, this was no time to sit and wait. And with their Minnesota supporters leading the cheers, the Dakotans took matters into their own hands.

Chapter III

The Delegate Question

"At a recent election [in Dakota] held for Congressional Delegate, six hundred votes were polled in the Territory of which number A. G. Fuller, Esq., received over five hundred."

St. Paul Pioneer and Democrat
November 29, 1857

The "election" referred to above was held on October 13, 1857, although it was not an election in a true sense. When news of this "election" reached St. Paul, it drew friendly fire from a rival newspaper. While it meant no disrespect to Fuller, the *St. Paul Daily Minnesotian* thoughtfully pointed out that "Dakotah" was a myth. It existed solely as a "popular assumption without any law to authorize or sustain it." The writer of the article acknowledged the genuine need for representation in Congress by deserving people, but until Minnesota was admitted to the Union, the settlements in Dakota were merely a part of Minnesota Territory.[1]

Criticism came in from the East as well. The *Washington Union* in the nation's capital ridiculed the efforts of those who would create Dakota Territory. Calling them "Shriekers," the *Washington Union* said that folks throughout the land could soon forget about poor "bleeding Kansas" and its celebrated slavery controversy, for the "black Republicans" had found a new field for their labors. "Bleeding Dacotah and the rights of the Sioux will be as good a party cry as bleeding Kansas...."[2] Ah politics; it brings out the best in people. Even in its infancy, the territorial process was fully politicized.

It is doubtful that anyone connected with the Dakota movement cared about the observations of the *Washington Union,* the *Daily Minnesotian,* or any other rival newspaper. They carried on as if everything was on the up and up. And seven days after the mysterious "election," a "mass meeting" was held at Sioux Falls City. Next, settlers gathered at a "convention" at the "Dakota House" in Medary, on November 16, 1857. Those in attendance adopted high-sounding resolutions calling national attention to the fledgling settlements, urging Congress to provide them with territorial status. Although in Dakota for less than six months, the Dakota Land Company proudly floated its political plans.

The convention included an impressive list of names from Pipestone, Rock, Big Sioux, Brown and Midway counties—all of which were either located in the proposed new territory, or extended beyond the borders of what was to become the new state of Minnesota. James L. Fisk and Dr. Josiah L. Phillips of Big Sioux County were president and vice-president, respectively. Based on the newspaper account of this meeting, a strong sense of urgency and purpose emerges.

The goals of the settlers were stated in the preamble and resolution proposed by James McBride of Big Sioux County:

> *Whereas,* By the adoption of a State organization in Minnesota with boundaries which exclude a large number of the population of the Territory as originally organized, which population, equal to that of Minnesota when organized as a Territory, is left without any governmental organization, and consequently deprived

of many of the most valuable rights of American citizens, and whereas, this Convention has been called for the purpose of devising the best means of removing the evils to which the citizens of Dakota Territory, or that portion of the former Territory of Minnesota west of the State line now labors under, therefore,

Resolved, That a committee of one from each county here represented, be appointed by the chair to submit to this convention, such plans as may be deemed most proper and expedient to effect the early organization of a Territorial government, over that portion of the former Territory of Minnesota west of the present State line; and also such measures as will secure the speedy settlement and permanent peace and prosperity of the Territory.

It didn't matter that Minnesota had yet to be admitted to the Union. The handful of conventioneers carried on as if statehood was a certainty. A committee was duly appointed and went into a session of its own, while the rest of the convention engaged in "an animated discussion" (fistfights, no doubt) of various, diverging interests to individual members. When the committee returned, the issues were debated, a series of resolutions and amendments were adopted, and Congress was advised that: (1) it was urgent and necessary that a new territory be created, (2) that Alpheus G. Fuller was duly elected by the "voters of Dakota Territory as a Delegate to represent her interest in Washington...," (3) it was incumbent upon the federal government to "make an early purchase" of lands lying west of the Big Sioux River, from the Indians, so as to encourage immigration, (4) sufficient military protection be established to minimize Indian threats, (5) surveys of ceded lands be done most expeditiously, and (6) a "temporary seat" of the territorial government be established somewhere on the Big Sioux River, "leaving the permanent location to the Legislature or the people." Having completed their impressive wish list, the convention was adjourned, *sine die*.³

After firing off another contentious volley of words toward Washington, D. C., the settlers carried on as if they expected results. Governor Medary, apparently still collecting a salary as a federally appointed official, appointed the first officers for Big Sioux County. They were: James M. Allen, register of deeds; James Evans, sheriff; James L. Fisk, judge of probate; W. W. Brookings, district attorney; Josiah L. Phillips, justice of the peace; and William Little, James McBride and A. L. Kilgore, county commissioners.⁴

As the combined population of Sioux Falls and Sioux Falls City was a mere sixteen, it had one official for every two citizens but no one complained about a top-heavy bureaucracy. And it is noteworthy that men from both town site companies were chosen to hold office. These men took their offices in December, and as winter was in full swing, very little of a political or official nature was done. All the energies and efforts of the colonists had to be applied to surviving their first Dakota winter.

In St. Paul, where winter's ferocity had been blunted somewhat by minimal comforts, the *St. Paul Pioneer and Democrat* was warding off blows of a different sort, and taking a few swings at an enemy newspaper. The *Daily Minnesotian*, a staunch Republican newspaper and angry over the recent election outcome, criticized the colonizing effort in Dakota. By now the *Daily Minnesotian* was no longer a friendly rival, and having uncovered what it considered to be manifold voting fraud and forgeries, it weighed in heavily against its enemies including Governor Samuel J. Medary and Joseph R. "the Juggler" Brown.

Gathering all its indignation for a mighty blow, the editor of the

Daily Minnesotian exploded: "Outside of the Half-Breed Settlement of Pembina...there are not a dozen white men in the whole Territory!" But the angry editor was only getting started. "The meetings purporting to be held there, at which long proceedings are alleged to have been passed, are humbugs and fictions—manufactured here in St. Paul, for consumption by fools at Washington." The editor saw a scheming Governor Medary and his friend Joseph R. Brown behind these maneuvers. These "scoundrels" will "doubtless gull congress into passing an Organic Act; and Buchanan will be only too glad of an opportunity to reward a dozen or two hungry Democratic leeches with fat offices...where they will freeze in the winter from want of fuel and parch with thirst in summer upon its endless and waterless plains!"[5] Banish the villains to Dakota where they belong, and Minnesota will be purified!

The *Pioneer and Democrat* took the blow and fired back at *Daily Minnesotian* with its own brand of vituperation. Calling the charges a palpable lie, the editorial said the very fact that Sioux Falls City had about twenty houses and a sawmill proved that the territory had more than a dozen people. "Our policy as Minnesotians," rang the angry rebuttal, "is not to retard the settlement and organization of Dakota, but to aid in its settlement, prosperity, and success."[6] And besides, the charges of election fraud were just the rantings of a sore loser.

The *Pioneer and Democrat* was a strong supporter of the ambitious governor and his Democratic allies. But the *Daily Minnesotian* felt Medary belonged behind bars for his alleged electioneering antics, and when it learned that the governor was off to Washington, an article said he was going there to "reap the reward of his felonies...and to secure from Buchanan the appointment of

Governor of Dakota Territory."[7]

Actually, young Dakota's hopes for recognition and success rested not with Medary, but upon the ability of Alpheus G. Fuller, the leader of the Dakota Land Company's first town site expedition. Fuller had strong eastern antecedents, coming from a colonial family. He went west from Scotland, Connecticut in 1848, having been advised to leave the East due to poor health. He and a companion found themselves in St. Paul in October and Fuller became stranded for the winter when an early freeze stopped steamboat traffic. He settled in as best he could and grew to like the rough hamlet. On New Year's Eve 1848, Fuller wrote home, describing his "camp." It was "about fifteen feet square, a hole in the top for the smoke to go out, six poles set up to conduct the smoke out of log fire, and is as comfortable as you please." The ambitious young bachelor informed his family of plans to build a store, a warehouse and several dwellings in the spring.[8]

Fortunately he had sufficient money to get him through the winter, and come spring, he was joined by a younger brother, twenty-year-old David Luce Fuller Jr., who arrived in St. Paul "with financial reinforcements."[9] The ambitious brothers decided to stay in Minnesota Territory, hoping to prosper in the great Northwest. They established a thriving fur trading business and made long journeys into the northern reaches of the territory. In Minnesota Territory, Alpheus G. Fuller found more than a healthy climate.

In the years that followed "Alph" and David Fuller were joined by brothers Albert and George and sisters Elizabeth, Sarah, Jane and Abby. Alpheus was married during one of his eastern visits and brought his wife, the former Lilliore Richardson, to St. Paul. The

Fuller sisters were prolific letter writers eager to describe frontier life in graphic and yet charming word pictures. While many eastern women looked upon the wilderness as a damnable place, the Fuller girls were inspired by it. Their letters flit and ripple merrily with stories about boat trips on the rivers, wagon rides, partying with friends, camping in the woods, riding with Indians, going "strawberrying," eating "sanguishes" and fighting off "musquitos."

Although they were polite ladies with eastern manners and tastes, the Fuller girls were not the least bit intimidated by the sights and sounds of the "wild west." Rough men with guns, street fights, Indians in wild dress and the prevalence of wolves only seemed to pique their natural curiosity. While their brothers were off on some wilderness trek in the "up country," the pert and perky girls presided over the Fuller home. It was a fine mansion of brick, adorned by long white pillars, on Fort Street on a hillside with a fine view of the river from a rooftop observatory. Their vegetable garden grew on land now occupied by the state capitol building[10]

The Fuller brothers were instrumental in creating the town of Shakopee, named after an important Santee chief.[11] But it was in St. Paul that they made their mark as businessmen. Alpheus served St. Paul as an alderman. And on September 25, 1856, he celebrated the grand opening of the "Fuller House," a commodious five-story brick hotel in the heart of St. Paul, at the corner of Jackson Street and Seventh Street.[12]

In the bold, speculative spirit of the times, Fuller's goal was to build a hotel that would surpass all others in St. Paul, and he easily succeeded. He received a bonus of land and $12,000.00 to start the project.[13] When completed, the lavish hotel cost an astounding

$110,000.00, and was state-of-the-art with parlors and bathrooms, a piano, a bar room, a billiard room, suites, and a luxurious dining room presided over by an eastern chef. It was piped for gas and had running water. The furnishings for the Fuller House came from Philadelphia, New York and Boston, and were the best the market had to offer, costing more $40,000.00.

It had a commanding view of the Mississippi River and was conveniently close to the steamboat landing. From the beginning the patronage was more than sufficient to justify such a grand hotel located so close to the frontier. The Fuller House was compared to the Astor House in New York and the best Chicago had to offer.[14] Leased out to Stephen and Edward Long, the Fuller House became a social center for St. Paul and the traveling public, while Fuller continued his rise to prominence as a leader in the Dakota Land Company. Long after he completed his Washington, D. C. stint, Fuller was jocularly referred to as the "Minister Plenipotentiary to the Court at Washington."[15]

In 1857 A. G. Fuller, having been "elected" as "delegate" to Congress, dutifully went off to Washington, armed with an election certificate from the office of the register of deeds, Midway County, Dakota Territory, the "senior county." He was described by a contemporary as a man "whose ability and acquirements eminently fitted him for the position." He entered upon his onerous duties supported by letters of introduction from "conspicuous gentlemen in the West."[16]

Fuller was in Washington by December of 1857, ready for work. Governor Medary came in from Ohio. Congress was also ready to dig in, as there was much on their agenda, including the anticipated admission of new territories and states. Some observers believed that

Fuller House, St. Paul, Minnesota
(*St. Paul Daily Minnesotian,* December 22, 1859)

Dakota Territory would be organized, along with Arizona Territory, in a compromise measure. There was "strong influence" at "work in favor of both Territories."[17] In addition to Dakota and Arizona, Congress was expected to deal with the proposed territory of "Sierra Nevada" or "Columbus," a vast, amorphous tract of land between the Sierra Nevada Mountains on the west and the Rocky Mountains on the east.[18]

At the nation's capital, Fuller conferred with sympathetic congressmen and was allowed to appear in the House of Representatives as a "quasi-delegate." There he attempted to introduce a bill admitting Dakota Territory.[19] His efforts are reflected in a letter he addressed to the House, stating his claim to a seat as a "delegate" or "agent" for those people left outside the state of Minnesota. He pleaded on behalf of "10,000 to 15,000" people valiantly trying to make the wilderness produce in an area where there was "not the least shadow of law to protect them." There were "entire counties," formerly under the jurisdiction of Minnesota Territory, which were now "destitute of law," and at the mercy of the "savages."

Fuller's arguments were downright maudlin. In a long stream of consciousness, he wrote: "the steam engine is already at work there; the blacksmith, carpenter, mason and various other mechanics are at their daily avocations; the merchant has displayed his stock of merchandise; the farmer with his prairie team is busily engaged in turning the broad furrow, preparing the soil to receive the seed." Dakota, he insisted, had advanced far on its own and now only asked for Congress to reach out in friendship and recognition.

While his petition is thoroughly laced with outrageous exaggeration, why not make the assertion? Who was going to challenge his facts and figures? It was highly unlikely that anyone in Congress would have the evidence to refute his claim that "within the Valley of the Big Sioux River, large settlements have sprung into existence as if by magic, and scarce 20 miles can be traversed on its banks without passing a compact settlement."[20] It would be about 20 years before anyone could make that claim with any semblance of accuracy, but Fuller was only saying what his colleagues would say had they been chosen to impress and sway Congress.

After all, he was a speculator, a label freely applied to land gamblers in the 1850's. According to one old-timer speaking many years later, speculators were a wild, unwanted species that gave off an odor that made a polecat smell pleasant by comparison. He characterized a speculator as someone whose popularity at a land sale would be like that of a "Kluxer" at a camp meeting of black people.[21]

On the whole, Fuller aroused some concern and support, but he did not persuade. Nevertheless his presence there, along with delegate-elect William W. Kingsbury—who refused to relinquish his seat—was the cause for considerable debate. Both men were Democrats and both had the backing of some elements of their party. But why the Minnesota Democrats failed to unite behind one man is puzzling. It is probable that they were satisfied for having won control of the new state and were more concerned about the affairs of the state. In so thinking, they were willing to let the Dakota Land Company fend for itself in its struggle to control that part of old Minnesota Territory that had been excluded from the state of Minnesota.

Kingsbury—usually referred to as "W. W." Kingsbury—won his office handily, beating the Republican Charles McClure by a vote of 15,188 to 12,999, in the "real" October 1857 election. Still with several counties whose vote was not counted, he was not declared the winner until December 2, 1857. Kingsbury, the mystery man in these proceedings, was from Towanda, Pennsylvania where he was born on June 4, 1828. He came west to the Lake Superior country in 1855 and later made St. Louis County, Minnesota Territory his place of residence. Prior to his election as delegate, he served in the Minnesota territorial legislature and was a member of the Constitutional Convention.[22]

Kingsbury was allowed to serve during that short time when Congress was finalizing the admission of Minnesota, and as one historian observed, "to draw a tidy sum for mileage." Apparently he liked having his seat so well that after the Minnesota congressional contingent was admitted, he refused to leave. Because of this and Fuller's stubborn presence, the House swung into action, resulting in a little afterpiece of political comedy.[23]

The House took up the matter on May 27, 1858, when newly elected Rep. James M. Cavanaugh of Minnesota requested that Kingsbury's claim "as Delegate from that part of the Territory of Minnesota outside the State limits," be referred to the Committee of Elections. Cavanaugh wanted Kingsbury to go home. Next, Rep. Thomas L. Harris of Illinois asked that Fuller's memorial seeking the same office also be referred to that committee.

This set off a series of questions and responses by various members, all of which indicates most of them knew little about "that part of Minnesota lying without the new state." Still, they gave the matter close attention as if they believed there was something credible in either Kingsbury's election or Fuller's credentials. Should both men be admitted temporarily, while the matter is investigated? Are there other Minnesota territorial officers in limbo, or are they holding down their offices? What is the population of the "rump territory"? Who received the most votes outside the new state? One seemingly bewildered congressman wondered out loud if they were dealing with a "pretended organization of the inhabitants of Minnesota," or an "organization in Dacotah?" Such questions and others resulted in the matter being handed over to the Committee on Elections.[24]

On June 2, 1858, the matter was back on the floor of the House of Representatives, with Rep. Harris taking the lead. Another uninterested congressman tried to squeeze in some discussion on a bill benefiting widows and orphans, but Harris would not yield the floor. "I wish to take up the case of the Delegate from Minnesota Territory," he said, resolutely.

Next, the majority report from the House Committee on Elections was read into the record, followed by the minority report and Fuller's documents. Soon congressmen were digressing along differing lines of thought, seeking a solution to the dilemma.

The minority, headed by Rep. John A. Gilmer of North Carolina, pointed out that there were two elections on October 13, 1857: one inside the proposed new state of Minnesota, and one on the outside. The "outside" people elected Fuller, not Kingsbury. The latter received no votes from the people outside the new state. Gilmer's report further noted that the residents outside the proposed state held a separate election "in anticipation of the organization of a new territory under the name of Dacotah." Further, there was some precedent for allowing Fuller to serve. In 1802, Ohio Territory was allowed a representative, and again in 1849, H. H. Sibley was permitted to represent Wisconsin

Territory under similar circumstances.

The majority report concluded that W. W. Kingsbury, a Democrat, had been duly elected. The report states: "There is no Territory of Dacotah" and therefore no authority for it to send a representative to Congress. But rather the "so-called territory of Dacotah is the Territory of Minnesota," and that territory already had a representative in Kingsbury.[25] Kingsbury had a certificate signed by Samuel A. Medary, the governor of Minnesota Territory. This should have wrapped it up, but members couldn't resist more debate, especially about who voted, where they voted, and just what kind of frontier organizations were on the agenda for consideration.

Harris, who took the lead in the debate, was now convinced that the majority report was paramount and should be accepted. To bolster this position (and after he was called a liar on an unrelated matter), he caused to be read into the record two additional letters, both of which seemed to answer the question of whether Kingsbury received votes from outside the new state.

The first letter was from Edward M. McCook,[26] the personal secretary to Governor Medary, who had also acted as secretary of the board that counted the votes for delegate. According to McCook's recollection, about 200 votes from Pembina were cast for Kingsbury, along with some votes from "precincts on the Missouri River." He could not, however, recall an exact number.

The second letter was from John B. S. Todd, leader of a group of Missouri River speculators who were progressing toward creating a town at the site of the Yankton Sioux Indian village. Todd's group opposed a territory organized under conditions favorable to the Dakota Land Company. In his letter Todd said, "I have the honor to state, such an election was held on the Missouri River, at the precinct of Kennerly, on the 13th of October, 1857, at which I was present...." He went on to state that Kingsbury received all the votes cast for delegate, including his own.

There will be more about Todd and the "election" on the Missouri slope later, but at this point in the House debate, the tide had shifted toward Kingsbury. Still, the waters were not clear, and other members got into the fray. William H. Kelsey of New York wanted to know if there were actually two separate elections, and if Fuller really opposed Kingsbury. Harris said it was irrelevant. Kelsey persisted, asking which candidate received the most votes outside of the new state.

Harris tried to change the subject, harkening back to the question of whether the creation of the state of Minnesota annulled the position of delegate from the territory left behind. Additional wordy discourses followed, including one by Rep. Washburn of Maine. He stated there were "organized precincts and organized counties outside of the State limits, containing, I believe, in all, a population of something like fifteen thousand souls...." He insisted that Kingsbury should be allowed to represent these people, because Fuller could not prove how many votes he received except for those at Midway County. Washburn had no faith in Fuller's certificate.

Rep. James Wilson, who signed the minority report, believed Fuller's certificate was genuine. He insisted that there were two legitimate elections and Fuller received a majority of the votes cast in the five counties left out of the new state, according to a certificate he possessed. His colleague Gilmer, who had met with Fuller and agreed to present his case as a personal favor, was satisfied that Kingsbury received no votes from outside the new state.

Finally, Rep. James Hughes of Indiana launched a detailed dissertation that seemed to embody the general confusion shared by all. His choice for delegate from "Minnesota Territory," was Fuller. Yet despite having won all the votes on the "outside," Fuller had no right "just to walk in here and take his seat upon this floor, although there is precedent [H. H. Sibley] for it." Why so, some wondered? Well, it was because the "Territory of Dacotah" existed in name only, like some mythical place. It was largely unknown, unorganized, and there was nothing to indicate that it would be organized in the near future. Better, perhaps, to unite this enigma with Nebraska Territory, he suggested. After all, no one really knew how many people occupied the new land. Once senses a room full of congressmen with puzzled expressions and shrugged shoulders.

"I am not in favor of hot haste in admitting men to this House before the people of a territory have fairly asked for a Delegate," said Hughes. Then someone handed him a piece of paper that he immediately read into the record. The paper was headed: "Medary, November 23, 1857," and was signed by the same men who certified Fuller's election certificate. It went on to state that five counties outside of the new state of Minnesota cast 100% of their votes in favor of Fuller. There was no mention of Kingsbury or any other opponent. Instead, "Midway County, Medary precinct," gave 103 votes to A. G. Fuller, and "Big Sioux County, Sioux Falls City precinct," gave 97 votes to Fuller. Big Sioux County had two other "precincts," namely "Emaneja" and "Summit City," which gave Fuller 51 and 29 votes, respectively.

If members of the House were looking for something that would settle the question, they had it but entirely missed it. For these figures were clearly false and indicate just how poorly informed Congress was about political affairs on the Dakota frontier. It went right over their heads and into the record. Shortly after that, the House of Representatives adjourned without reaching a decision.[27]

When they resumed the next day, some of the same ground was covered, as members, new to the debate, asked questions about the location of elections, numbers of votes cast and for whom. In response a seemingly exasperated Rep. Harris insisted it was "entirely unnecessary to inquire into the number of votes Mr. Fuller received, because he received no votes cast in conformity with any existing law." He was unimpressed with Fuller's paperwork, including a crude seal of "Dacotah Territory, or a picture representing it." "There is no such Territory as Dacotah," he said, and then repeated it as if for emphasis. Dakota was made to seem ethereal and faraway, like a dream, like a faint echo coming from a strange place.

Rep. Clark B. Cochrane, who had not been a major player in the debate, suggested that in view of what had been revealed, "all the Federal officers of the Territory of Minnesota might go back to the wilderness, organize a new government, and hold their respective offices." That suggestion found no support. However, after some additional discussion, an amendment by Hughes was put forth stating that the admission of the state of Minnesota, by operation of law, dissolved the Territory of Minnesota and left it without any "legally organized government," and therefore, "the people thereof are not entitled to a Delegate in Congress until that right is conferred upon them by statute." It passed by a vote of 102 to 80.[28] Both Fuller and Kingsbury were ousted.

Joseph R. Brown was in Washington when the vote was cast. As he fully expected the formation of a new territory, Brown was keenly disappointed. In a letter to his former newspaper, the *Henderson Democrat,* Brown said the setback "will be deeply felt by Dakota." Its worthy citizens were let down by their government and left without a "single soldier to protect the interests of the settlers in that territory...." With no law to build upon, they were "thrown entirely upon their own resources for protection and government."²⁹

When news of the vote reached the western media, one newspaper couldn't resist getting in a dig or two. The *Omaha Nebraskan* quoted Congressmen Harris thusly: "And for Mr. Phelps (did he mean Fuller?) to claim a seat as a delegate from Dacotah, when no such territory was recognized as such, was a piece of presumption and impertinence which ought not be tolerated for a moment."³⁰ Oh really? For a reporter to misspell a namely so badly is a form of carelessness not to be taken lightly. But what could those early Dakotans expect from a newspaper that called the Big Sioux River the "Big Blue River"?³¹

The *New York Tribune* couldn't resist poking fun at the two rival candidates for the office of congressional delegate to a non-existent territory. Calling it a "family affair" because both Kingsbury and Fuller were Democrats, the *Tribune* pretended to commiserate with "disinherited" Dakota, all by itself in the wilderness and looked upon with disdain by the newly minted state of Minnesota and its proud people, all "wrapped up in their dignity and selfishness...." It seemed so hopeless. Then suddenly, "from among the decapitated there emerges all at once the champion of the Dakota cause..." in the form of Mr. Kingsbury. But hold on and not so fast, for the "civilized populace of Dakota" needs a better man, responded Mr. Fuller. What followed was an artful bit of sparing by two farcical and pretentious candidates that, in the end, fooled no one, and resulted in the "stay of the organization of the Territory."[32]

While the contest was a small matter for a New York City newspaper, congressional concerns were at least a bit more substantive. And after considerable debate and careful thought, it seems the Congress couldn't decide which man had the better claim to a seat in the House, so both were rejected. In doing so, they were not forced to choose one pack of lies over another. Fuller's figures were over-inflated beyond the point of absurdity, and Todd's letter about an election on the Missouri River was false.

In October of 1857, there was but a handful of white men camping along the Missouri, all of whom were licensed government traders or their employees, none of them necessarily "citizens" of Dakota. The area was still controlled by Yankton Sioux Indians who dealt with the traders. No "precincts" could have been set up and no lawful voting could have occurred. Finally, the election in Minnesota that resulted in a Kingsbury victory was tainted by inflated vote counts in newly formed and thinly populated southwestern counties.

Aside from these concerns, there were those who opposed the organization of Dakota because of a general hostility toward the idea of admitting new territories. Recalling the struggle over the admission of Kansas, many congressmen wanted no part of another bitter and partisan fight over adding another territory, knowing the questions about states rights and slavery would come up again.[33]

When all was distilled, the big loser was the Dakota Land Company. Had Fuller and his congressional supporters succeeded in organizing Dakota Territory in 1858, the Dakota Land Company could have depended on a friendly Buchanan administration to name one of the Big Sioux River town sites the capital city and dispense the best offices to its members. But it was not to be.

Washington was a hostile place and Fuller was a disappointed man, but far from ready to quit. While he was praised by the *St. Paul Pioneer and Democrat* for bringing the interests of the Dakota settlers into focus,[34] he was hammered by newspapers that were hostile toward the Dakota Land Company and the Democratic Party. He returned to the West bearing bad news for his friends. Their campaign of misrepresentation and exaggeration had failed. While he did manage to get a post office for Sioux Falls City, the big prize eluded him.

Fuller was back in Washington during the winter of 1858-1859, writing letters as the "Delegate-elect from Dakota Territory." He and his allies were sticking with their original plan of bringing about the creation of a new territory formed from "five organized counties on ceded lands, together with a large Indian tract within the limits of the former Territory of Minnesota," extending west to the Rocky Mountains. He gave a ringing endorsement to the "enterprising, bold and hardy frontiersmen...willing to endure the hardships of pioneer life."

While Fuller confessed there were forces in Congress waiting to defeat the territorial organization, he was certain that people living there were overwhelmingly in favor of it. He wrote: "Having resided in the Territory since May, 1857, and having during last summer and fall visited each of the organized counties, and met the citizens in mass meetings, on their farms, in their workshops and at their homes...I am convinced that more than nine-tenths of them will entirely approve the [territorial] limits designated by the Committee on Territories."[35] Whatever can be said about his lack of candor, he certainly had a flair for effective dramatization.

But his antics apparently did not sit well with his family. In a letter to her younger brother Frank, Abby Fuller expressed keen disappointment over brother Alpheus' Quixotic persistence. She wrote, "Alpheus is over in Dacotah & it makes me ache to see how he has left his things suffering here [St.Paul]." She also commented on Kingsbury, saying, "Mr. Kingsbury got into town today and spent an hour or two with me. He has been just such another fool and I told him I thought they had better both, when they met in Dacohtah (sp), shake hands and quit."[36] Her words, although sincere, were like spit in the wind, for her brother Alpheus had the blood and bone of a frontiersman in him. He had written off Minnesota in favor of Dakota.

For Fuller and his fellow Dakota pioneers, there was much work ahead and the two camps—Sioux Falls and Yankton—were up to the challenge. The Dakota Land Company refused to let Fuller's loss put an end to their plans for territorial dominance. John B. S. Todd's role in this frontier drama will be explained in another chapter. Suffice it to say at this point, he and his Yankton allies had been, in part, responsible for defeating Fuller and the Dakota Land Company. All would be heard from again as the opposing groups struggled for control of Dakota's political and economic destiny.

Chapter IV

Adventures Along the Nobles Road

"A bigger humbug than his [Nobles'] Pacific Road expedition and the Dacota (sp) Land Company's operations, has never been before the public of Minnesota."

Minnesota Free Press, November 18, 1857

The creation of the Dakota Land Company followed by its highly publicized town site founding expedition caused it to loom large in the public mind and in the Minnesota press. Controversial from the outset of its operations, the company became a magnet for criticism and its leaders were suspected of deception and greed. They were speculators in a time of great and outrageous speculation, but their plans were huge by comparison to others of similar ambition. A surveyor for the company said it was an "association resembling in power and resources the East India Company."[1] But in the eyes of its detractors, it was far less important, and it was a St. Paul company, the city that was synonymous with wasteful speculation. As such the Dakota Land Company drew the ire of rival politicians and their newspaper allies both inside and outside of St. Paul.

The loudest, angriest and most persistent voice of dissent came from the *Minnesota Free Press* of St. Peter. The newspaper's Republican editor, W. C. Dodge, attacked the Dakota Land Company almost from its inception, focusing on its questionable political maneuvering and speculative bent. While Dodge regularly slammed Democrats Joseph R. Brown, Charles C. Flandrau and Samuel Medary, his primary point of attack was William H. Nobles and the Fort Ridgely and South Pass wagon road. Dodge loudly proclaimed it to be a fraud, a "humbug" and a hoax, a made-up enterprise designed solely to soak up public funds and benefit—if there was any good to it at all—the Dakota Land Company.

But newspaper publicity wasn't entirely bad and Nobles had some support from the third estate. Among the supporters, the *Henderson Democrat* headed up by Nobles' friend and colleague, Joseph R. Brown, praised the efforts of the road-maker. During the long and cold winter of 1856-57, Brown's newspaper reported that Nobles was "working like a badger" toward getting congressional approval for the extension of the road from Fort Ridgely to the South Pass and beyond.[2] Always seeing the "big picture," Brown's newspaper emphasized that roads were fundamental and beneficial, even if the benefits were not evenly distributed. They were needed to open the frontier to settlement, and men like Nobles—whose interests were devoted toward progress and advancing civilization—were anything but selfish. Only a nay-saying crank would deny the usefulness, practicality and inevitability of roads.

It was a time of great westward road building activity, and Congress and the Secretary of the Interior were busy trying to decide which roads to support for the sake of immigrant transportation. One such road started from Independence, Missouri on its way to California, by way of a more central route.[3] W. M. F. McGrath was the superintendent of this project. A northern route was proposed after gold was discovered in the Fraizer River in western Canada in 1858.

These trunk routes would complement the Nobles road, each getting its share of traffic. The creation of wagon roads coincided with robust talk about building a trans-continental railroad—a subject that had great public support.

Joseph R. Brown—whose exploring instincts equaled those of Nobles—provided his readers with some background information on Nobles that made him out to be almost heroic. Long before he was commissioned by Congress to lay out his Pacific Road, as it came to be called, Nobles was known as an explorer "who has spent much time and money in his travels and researches among the Rocky Mountains." He was a "true son of the prairies and the wilderness," bold and energetic and yet a real gentleman and a leader with a dominant personality, ideally suited to direct a frontier enterprise. His goal, "the great object so long near his heart," was to create an immigrant wagon road through the Rocky Mountains, "the passage through which has been the cause of so much suffering and so many deaths." [4]

In 1849 Nobles went to Shasta County, California, to look for gold and stayed in that country until 1852. While in the far west, he discovered the pass through the Sierra Nevada Mountains that shortened the route to the Pacific by 500 miles. For his efforts, a group of grateful California people presented Nobles with $10,000.00 in cash.[5] He had discovered his true calling: exploring and path-finding, and came back to Minnesota to live and to promote and build roads.

Nobles spent the $10,000.00 in private funds to explore the route for his road out of Fort Ridgely to the far west. He drafted the wagon road bill that eventually passed both houses of Congress, after he provided the push needed to get passage, no thanks to the "old fogies" from "down east." It was a matter of great personal pride, recalled

Nobles, of his accomplishment. "No one can imagine the amount of good feeling that I entertained toward all mankind...."[6] Nobles' western star was shining brightly, just then.

Nobles was born in New York state in 1816. A machinist by trade, he went west in 1841, stopping at St. Croix Falls, Wisconsin, where he worked as a millwright in the lumber industry. Two years later he was in Stillwater, Minnesota Territory, making him one of the early arrivals in the territory. In 1848, he moved to St. Paul and commenced business as a wagon maker and blacksmith in a small shop on Robert Street. He made the first wagon in the territory, for Henry H. Sibley, out of wood and steel, doing all the labor himself. He was inventive and versatile and assisted in the surveying of St. Paul, carrying the "first chain."

After his California experience, he settled in St. Paul and served two terms in the territorial legislature during a time, he said, "when laboring men had some chance...." Nobles, along with congressional delegate, Henry M. Rice, became a determined lobbyist in favor of road building. He firmly believed that a trans-Mississippi road, beginning in Minnesota, would benefit the people and settlements of his territory on the verge of statehood. He argued to Congress that his northern route was shorter, the climate more favorable and the supply of wood much greater than a central route. Nobles' attractive arguments gained supporters throughout Minnesota Territory, and for the years 1854 through 1856, the territorial legislature topped all other lawmaking bodies in the promotion of road building.[7]

The *Pioneer and Democrat* called him a "highwayman," a label with mixed meanings but a title he was willing to wear with pride. For it was in road building that he made his mark, having been involved in founding the "first highway from Stillwater to St. Paul," way back when "St. Paul was a little beyond the creek." Nobles declared his respect and affection for the man who made an "honest living by the sweat of his brow."[8] Always a hard worker, he bore up well under the hardships of frontier life.

How could such a hard working and stable man become the target of editorial wrath? By associating with the Dakota Land Company, according to Dodge, and engaging in activities that, on the surface, may have seemed to be practical and in the public good, but were, in fact, self-serving. Dodge warned people not be fooled by this man's outgoing and friendly exterior. Then, while Dodge was hound-dogging Nobles, a series of ugly events on the frontier caused his name and reputation to be sullied.

Things got off to a favorable start in the spring of 1857.The Secretary of the Interior, Jacob Thompson, authorized Nobles to commence creating his road. Congress dedicated $50,000.00 to the Pacific Road project and Nobles began spending it on supplies and equipment. He opened up an office at the American House in St. Paul, and went about forming his company, essentially a government party consisting of 75 men and a number of officers. Among the latter were: W. H. Nobles, Superintendent, Locating Engineer and Assistant, Samuel A. Medary (the territorial governor's son), Construction Assistant Captain William Davier, Commissary, A. J. Whitney, Physician, J. D. Goodrich, Clerk, Ross Fish, and Wagon Master, Joseph Beusamy. Heavily armed with Sharp's rifles and revolvers against a possible Indian attack, the party went west by way of New Ulm, in the spring of 1857, to find a road.[9] Their train consisted of twenty-five mule-drawn wagons, heavily loaded, along with twenty horses and fifty oxen.

    A correspondent from the *St. Paul Pioneer and Democrat*, another supportive newspaper, followed along and reported back on the happy progress of the expedition. The wagon train followed the Cottonwood River for several days and the crew built bridges over sloughs and marshes as was necessary, using "long rank grass." The road builders met with a party of adventurers headed by Congressman William Grow of Pennsylvania, out hunting buffalo on the prairie, near the Big Sioux River. The two groups joined forces and celebrated the Fourth of July in fine style, including a feast of ham, meat pie, pudding with whiskey sauce, and beans. They were joined by a number of Dakota Land Company men from Medary and another group bound for Sioux Falls City. Grow, called a "gentleman of the first water," gave a speech to the gathering at Hole-In-The-Mountain, now a Dakota Land Company town site.[10] The road crew had a fiddler among them and, with a group of curious Indians looking on, the night was spent dancing and singing.

    Nobles and his men learned that a hundred lodges of Yankton Sioux Indians were waiting for them on the Big Sioux River, with a view of halting the westward progress of the road crew. But this seemed to have no effect on the men. One of the men was quoted as saying, "they [the Indians] will have a fine time of it, if they undertake it." Young Sam Medary was sent back to Fort Ridgely to fetch a mountain howitzer and 150 rounds of shot to back up the warning. It was even reported that a son of Inkpaduta—the Wahpekute chief responsible for the slaughter of settlers at Spirit Lake, Iowa—was among the Yanktons. And lucky for him that the road crew didn't know of his presence with the Yanktons or "he would now be dangling upon one of these trees."[11] Brave words indeed, but as it turned out there would be no contact with the son of Inkpaduta and the crew's restive attitude would be directed at others.

On July 15th, the Nobles party arrived at a point 25 miles west of the Big Sioux River and were met by a large party of Yanktons who bade them go no further. Nobles engaged in numerous councils with the Indians but could not convince them to allow his party to continue working westward. The chiefs would not permit the intrusion onto their hunting grounds because "they would frighten away the buffalo, their sole means of sustenance." Nobles was greatly outnumbered and his supply of ammunition was low, so the road-building party retreated back to the Big Woods on the Cottonwood River and went into camp.[12]

While his crew was engaged in building a bridge over the Cottonwood River, Nobles and Fish made a trip back to St. Paul by way of the Yellow Medicine Agency. Along the way Nobles paid a surprise visit to editor Dodge of the *Minnesota Free Press*. The St. Peter meeting was apparently cordial and Dodge made an about-face. He was satisfied that the road-building had nothing to do with the Dakota Land Company, and further that Nobles and Medary were made members of the company without their knowledge. Dodge stated mildly that he was "glad to learn…the appropriation may be applied in good faith to the object for which it was intended." Nobles, he concluded, was an honest and honorable man and the "great thoroughfare" he was creating would pass through St. Peter on its way to California. It would "assist in making St. Peter the largest and most important inland town in Minnesota."[13] Take that, St. Paul.

So it appeared that Nobles succeeded in turning an enemy into a friend, or at least blunting Dodge's lance a bit. But another newspaper in faraway Washington, D.C. was not so easily convinced of Nobles sincerity. The *Evening Star* noted Nobles' return to St. Paul after his incident with the Yankton Sioux. An editorial in the *Evening Star* took the position that the Yankton Sioux impediment would be used by Nobles as an excuse to stop the progress on the western road. "We place little reliance on any such plea," said the editorial, "because we anticipated long since that the expedition would fail to perform the work allotted to it...." The editor was of the firm belief that Nobles had already spent the $50,000.00, and would soon show up in Washington, asking for more money.[14] The matter had become a minor scandal, drawing in many leading newspapers.

Despite the swirl of controversy and exchanges of accusations, Nobles went west again and met with the Yankton chiefs in mid-August, on the Big Sioux River, and emerged with permission to continue the project over unceded land. According to the *Henderson Democrat*, a domineering and forceful Nobles convinced the Indians that resistance would be futile. He essentially ordered the Yanktons to search for and find Inkpaduta, and if the effort were not made, "every Indian party...between the Big Sioux and the Missouri, would be treated as an enemy." [15] He claimed this threat had a pacifying effect on the Yanktons and caused them to re-direct their anger and energy.

The Indians were not the only obstacle for the tough-minded Nobles. He feuded with the Secretary of the Interior and fended off criticism from suspicious Minnesotans. His status as the superintendent of a historic undertaking caused him to take on feelings of excessive self-importance. Once, in the heat of an argument with ex-governor

Willis A. Gorman, Nobles could take no more. He struck Gorman, knocked him down and gave him a public thrashing in a St. Paul street.[16] It was Nobles' way of saying beware of my wrath when you stand in the way of my ambition, the great object of my life.

Despite the feuding and fighting, work on the road continued throughout the summer, the crew partially completing it to a point on the east side of the Missouri River opposite old Fort Lookout. On September 1, 1857, Nobles and his crew started east again. He accompanied the crew back to the Big Sioux River, and then went on to Henderson, by himself, on urgent business. While there, he granted an in depth interview to the *Henderson Democrat* and provided the reading public with some important details on the summer's work.

The road extended a distance of approximately 240 miles on an "airline" from Fort Ridgely to the Missouri River. The road followed the Cottonwood River from Fort Ridgely in a southwesterly direction, then turned westward until it came upon Lake Benton. There it passed through the nature-made gap at Hole-in-the-Mountain, over the *Coteau des Prairie* until it crossed the Big Sioux River about two miles below the town site of Medary. After that it proceeded almost due west until it met and crossed the James River, a few miles north of Sandy Hill. From that point it went straight west to the Missouri River, where it branched off in two directions, both of which ended at the east bank of that great river.

Nobles bragged that water was good and plentiful all along the road to the Missouri River. "A horse cannot travel two hours without finding water" from among the many lakes, streams and springs. But he warned that it would be dangerous to stray too far to the north or south of the road because water was scarce and of poor quality.

It was also an easy ride for heavily loaded wagons as the grades were not too high. And it would be necessary to build just two bridges along the way, both over the Cottonwood River in Minnesota. Crossing the Big Sioux and James Rivers was easily accomplished by fording the streams over the rocks placed in the riverbed to pave the way. Swamps and lowlands were avoided. In general the land was described as good, rolling prairie and its potential for grazing cattle in the James River valley was also good. But for the most part the land was without trees for shade or landmarks, or to break up the monotony of the slow miles, until the traveler reached Missouri River.

The road was about 30 feet wide. While there was, of course, no actual paving or grading done, mounds three to five feet high were constructed at the road's edge for the entire distance of the road, at intervals of a quarter or a half a mile, or closer, if it was considered necessary. This was the most labor-intensive part of the work as almost 2500 mounds were piled up between Fort Ridgely and the Missouri River.

While a road builder of the 1850's was not expected to create an actual road, but rather to find and mark a trail of least resistance that would eventually become a road, Nobles was proud of his effort and that of his trailblazing crew. They reached their goal for the season: to complete the road to the Missouri River. He spoke highly of his men, bragging that "not a single case of sickness has occurred, nor an accident of serious character." Morale was high in the ranks and tasks were "promptly and faithfully executed."[17]

For Nobles, the best way to prove his good intentions and silence his critics was to do the work he pledged himself to do. By doing so, he stripped the project of all political innuendo. The result was a road: a simple fact of life. A public road created with public funds was a road that anyone could use. What could be more disarming to critics like Dodge?

Dodge seemed to be satisfied. He published an article acknowledging the completion of the "Pacific Road to the Missouri River." Nobles had marked the road with mounds, bridged the streams and swamps, making a passable artery of transportation available to the public through a fine stretch of prairie.[18]

As fall approached, everything seemed to be working well for Nobles, having put in a good summer's work and pacified an enemy editor. Then one Tuesday in October, a man named John A. Jacques walked into the office of the *Minnesota Free Press*, and when he left, Dodge changed his tune; Nobles was once again a bad man. Dodge had a sensational scoop and with it, another chance to fire away at Nobles, the Dakota Land Company and the Democratic Party.

Jacques was righteously indignant, claiming to have been the subject of mob-bullying at his claim on the Cottonwood River, about seven miles from New Ulm, where he lived with his wife, a small child, a brother and his father. He had a run-in with a quarrelsome neighbor, A. Tuttle, whom "the Democrats recently nominated for legislature." (Dodge never missed an opportunity to take a shot at the Democrats.) The Jacques' had been in engaged in a long-running feud with Tuttle who had threatened to run them off their land. Tuttle, whose fishing racks in the Cottonwood were destroyed by some friends of the Jacques, warned them that if they did not leave voluntarily, he would "raise a crowd and hang them." And according to Jacques, Tuttle knew exactly where to find his "crowd."

Jacques poured his angry heart out to a more than willing listener, and Dodge took copious notes. He produced a long article that told of a fight in which Jacques' brother whipped the older Tuttle, thus exacerbating an already volatile situation. The brother turned himself in to the authorities in New Ulm and paid a fine for getting his licks on Tuttle. That failed to appease the latter who paid a visit to the Jacques house with a "mob of about forty men, consisting principally of Nobles' company," armed with Sharp's rifles. Jacques was unloading potatoes when he saw the riders approach. After he sent his father to find his brother who was at work about a mile away, Jacques went inside the house, fearing violence.

The riders stopped at his door and demanded that he come out. Jacques asked for their authority to make such a demand. A loud hand slap on their guns was their collective reply, while they proclaimed "here is our authority." Shots were fired through the window, one of which passed through Jacques' shirt but did not hit him. Another bullet struck the wall of the cabin where Mrs. Jacques had been standing only moments earlier. Some of the men shouted, "Burn the house!"

At this point, Jacques stepped out to confront the mob in hopes of securing the safety of his family inside. "If you wish to kill me, here I am, but spare my family."

One of the riders inquired about his brother, saying that they had not come to kill Jacques. But when one of them revealed a rope, Jacques felt his time had come, thinking they would take him into the timber, find a tree and string him up. After some further discussion, about 20 of the riders started off in the direction of Jacques' brother's claim. Jacques was taken along with them.

Not far down the road, they met Jacques' father driving an ox-team. When asked about the brother, the old man simply said he was gone. This brought an angry response of "shoot him!" But once again, it was just a threat. Instead, ten of the men took John Jacques over to Tuttle's residence. When he saw his hated enemy, Tuttle shouted, "That is one of the dammed villains! Shoot him! Shoot him!" Two riders aimed their guns at Jacques who, once again, feared for his life. And once again, they did not shoot. Instead they took him to the Nobles camp where he was advised, in no uncertain terms, that he and his family and neighbors had until Wednesday to leave the country. Feeling a great reluctance to leave their improved claims, they went to Fort Ridgely for protection but were told by an officer that he had no authority in the matter. Hearing this they made arrangements to stay elsewhere while they sought justice.

It is interesting that Jacques would stop at a newspaper office instead of going to see the Brown County sheriff, but if he was seeking sympathy, support and publicity, he got what he wanted. (And probably knew just where to go.) Besides, Dodge said, it would do no good to go to the Brown County authorities, hinting that they would be sympathetic to Tuttle and Nobles' men.

Feeling he had more than enough ammunition to do some damage, Dodge published his article on October 28, 1857, under the caption: "Lynch Law in Brown County--Daring outrage by a Gang of Villains!" The article rages with anger and indignation; he used no restraint and was careful to point out that only Nobles' men had Sharp's rifles so it must have been them who fired the shots into Jacques' cabin. Jacques claimed he could identify the men if he saw them again as they had frequented the area.

Dodge noted that Nobles' men were due to be paid off and "disbanded in a few days." He warned that unless the governor took action, the villains would be gone and therefore escape punishment. He demanded action and the most "severe punishment" for the gang of bullies. "Such outrages as these must not be allowed to pass unpunished, or the life and property of our citizens will become the sport of any crowd of drunken rowdies who choose to act thus."[19]

Dodge had another reason to be upset with Nobles' and his men. Just before the recent election, they were encamped on the Cottonwood River, in Brown County, seemingly hanging around with nothing constructive to do. But, Dodge said, they had a reason for being there; they were needed to add votes to the Democratic column in Nicollet County, where the vote was expected to be close and a Republican had a real chance at winning an office. So they stayed, got drunk and voted and helped to elect a Democrat. Because of the illegal voting and the bullying of the Jacques, Dodge's anger at Nobles, his men and his fellow Democratic speculators had reached a new level.

He promised more scathing editorials and lethal articles exposing the crime and corruption of the Minnesota Democratic Party, an organization desperate enough to intimidate, cheat and lie, openly in the light of day, in order to stay in power. Nobles' party of thugs might escape official punishment, and avoid criticism from St. Paul newspapers, but the vigilant Dodge would give them no cover or rest. Foreshadowing future attacks, he said: "A bigger humbug than his [Nobles] Pacific Road expedition, and the Dacota (sp) Land Company's operations, has never been before the public of Minnesota."[20] Dodge used the incident not only to re-politicize the road-making venture, but also to show that Nobles' government crew was no better than a gang of outlaws.

Nobles fired back. In a hard-hitting letter dated December 4, 1857, printed in the *St. Paul Pioneer and Democrat*, he explained his position relative to the Jacques-Tuttle feud. He went into a history of the fight over the fish traps, claimed John A. Jacques was a bad man from Wisconsin or Ohio, and was exceedingly unpopular and greatly feared by his neighbors. And it was the neighbors, not his men, who wanted to lynch the Jacques brothers, noting also, that it was a fate they richly deserved.

Nobles said Tuttle was the victim of threats, bullying and a terrible beating at the hands of Jacques' brother. That is to say, the "Hon. Mr. Tuttle" was the victim. The "murderous assault," the "unparalleled outrage excited the honest indignation of all of my men." Nobles said that his men simply went to Jacques' house to order him out of the country, not to burn him out or string him up. He said the fire that destroyed the Jacques residence was set by Jacques' father and Nobles' men actually tried to extinguish the blaze.

He took his critics (including Dodge) to task for the unkind and libelous remarks about the Pacific Road. There was no "humbuggery" going on, just honest hard work which thoughtful people understood and appreciated. "The best evidence of the usefulness of the road is already demonstrated, from the fact that the Cottonwood valley and Big Sioux valley are being well peopled along the line of said road."

He closed his letter by addressing his supposed association with the Dakota Land Company and handled the question by saying flatly, "I have nothing to do with the Dakota Land Company." After all he had selected his route "long before the Dakota Land Company was dreamed of." But if the company created cities along his route, so much the better, for he would be complimented.[21] So with several bold strokes of his pen, William H. Nobles slammed his newspaper and political critics with a vigor and vituperation equal to the abuse they heaped upon him.

Outrageous excuses and lies, replied Dodge, who used Nobles emotional explanation to further entrap him in a web of deception and crime and erode his credibility. Dodge said he never intended to take the position that Nobles participated in the acts of violence directed at Jacques, but rather that he plainly condoned such acts and by failing to take corrective action, ratified them. Such a man as Nobles, Dodge wrote, "is not fit to be a government mule-driver." He was certainly not qualified to build a road, which, of course, he didn't do despite his claims and all the surrounding publicity. The road—the "humbug"—was a "nice fat job" for Nobles and done primarily to "benefit the Dacotah Land Co.!"[22] Dodge promised more revelations.

Dodge was clearly out of control and on a vendetta, but there is evidence that the Dakota Land Company and allies had more than a passing interest in Nobles' road. In the spring and summer of 1857, Nobles was accused by the Department of the Interior of overspending and unauthorized spending. He was hammered for buying provisions from an unapproved source that turned out to be a member of the Dakota Land Company. Since that organization was out on the frontier planting towns, it was only logical that the success of the road would enhance their chance to profit from real estate speculation.[23] At any rate the connections looked too cozy and gave Dodge more editorial barbs to toss at Nobles.

About a week after raking Nobles and with Christmas just around the corner, the feisty editor was at it again. Sometimes a frontier editor had to dig for dirt and other times the desired dirt was thrust upon him. And so it was that Dodge got lucky. His next anti-Nobles, anti-Dakota Land Company diatribe was handed to him courtesy of another drunken act of aggression by a member of the Nobles' party, namely, Captain De Vere.[24]

Someone from St. Paul, who apparently knew that Dodge had an insatiable appetite for salacious news on Nobles and his men, sent him a letter outlining the details of an incident at the American House, a St. Paul hotel. The letter writer was visiting the hotel when he saw De Vere insult one of the servant girls, apparently by making an indecent proposition. When De Vere was repulsed he left, but returned with a pistol and threatened to shoot someone if "his wishes were not complied with." De Vere continued with the foul and abusive language and only shut up when the hotel proprietor stepped in and stopped it. And wouldn't you know it, a scolding Dodge told his readers, not only did Nobles fail to restrain De Vere's outrageous behavior, he encouraged it.[25]

The holidays came and went and as was typical on the northern frontier, the harsh winter weather imposed itself on friend and enemy alike. The flow and energy of news reporting slowed to the point of freezing. At any rate, Dodge seemed to relent. Maybe he was satisfied that he had made his point; perhaps he had no fresh information, or decided that nothing he could say or write would result in punishment for Nobles' bad boys. An emotional and politically charged man such as Dodge believed that corruption from the enemy was so widespread and powerful, that only a thorough and convincing political victory by the Republicans would save the state. He had taken the fight to the

Dakota Land Company, the Democratic Party and several newspapers that he didn't like. There seemed to be no end of the parade of enemies to attack. He did his part proudly so he could look back and say, "I fought the good fight." It was a struggle that he endured, for the most part, by himself.

Nobles was equally determined to finish what he started, come spring. But in February of 1858, he was removed from his road superintending duties, without notice, and replaced by William McAboy, from Ohio. Nobles was charged with "unnecessary delays" and "useless expenditure of public money" by someone in the Interior Department. Upon investigation, however, he was restored to his superintendent position by the Secretary of the Interior, and cleared of all charges.[26]

Despite the bitter harangues of his political enemies in Minnesota, Nobles had strong support in Washington. With that support he emerged from the controversy in a stronger position, having been named the disbursing agent as well as the superintendent. His friends now expected him to ask for and receive an additional appropriation of money.[27]

Nobles was free to resume his duties on the frontier. He could pack his field desk and maps and move on despite criticism from men like Dodge, understanding that the barbs he took from them were more political than personal, and that a newspaperman from St. Peter lacked the power to do much more than aggravate. He saw the bigger picture, the grander West, and its potential for adventure and personal gain. He understood that he and his colleagues were in a fight to hold their edge in the Minnesota legislature, and at the same time, hope that the Democrats held the White House and Congress.

For without that source of strength, their town site plans would be greatly weakened, if not destroyed altogether.

A careful and thorough study of Minnesota road building by historian W. Turrentine Jackson ties the project to the Dakota Land Company speculators. He reveals that when the Dakota Land Company was chartered, Nobles and another man were granted 20-year charters to operate ferries on the Big Sioux, James and Missouri Rivers. The ferries were, naturally, located along the Nobles road where a ferry operator might make some money in times of high water. Professor Jackson concludes that "from the outset" the road was a front for plans cooked up by certain congressmen who were looking to make money from land speculation.[28] By implication, Nobles, the unnamed congressmen and the Dakota Land Company officials were all in it together. Thus Dodge received some latter-day vindication.

Dodge must have suspected some kind of a sweetheart deal, but he was probably motivated more by his desire to bring down a sworn enemy. So with a determination unique to an 1850's newspaper editor, Dodge kept hammering away, trying to convince an audience that Nobles, "has not built a mile of road, except in a few places, where the *Dakota Land Company wanted it fixed for their benefit!*[29]" It was just another in a series of Quixotic uppercuts, and just as ineffective. Some people objected to Dodge's stubbornness and grew tired of his rant, but no one complained about a free press.

The incident involving John A. Jacques was soon forgotten. After all, it was primarily one angry man's word against that of another angry man. The authorities and other newspapers ignored it and the people forgot about it. Jacques and Tuttle went somewhere and got lost and remain a footnote in history. They were, after all, just fodder in a newspaper fight over politics, power and money, and quickly became irrelevant. What mattered to Dodge was maintaining his sense of editorial integrity.

What mattered in the long run to Nobles and his friends was commitment to the town site enterprise, the ability to keep working and continue in the belief that something good would emerge from the hard, dirty struggle. Wagon roads, railroads and enduring town sites—names on maps of the West that would remain long after all traces of the Nobles' road were gone—would be the best evidence of the Dakota Land Company's sincerity, vision and long-term commitment toward developing both Minnesota and Dakota.

A secret deal notwithstanding, that Nobles sincerely believed in his South Path road there can be no doubt. No amount of criticism could sway him from his belief. After all, he borrowed money to get started when government funding was slow in arriving. He purchased clothing for his men on his own account, and despite accusations that he squandered the funds appropriated by Congress. Nobles said that "far from being a defaulter to the Government for over $20,000.00, the government so far is a defaulter to me in the sum of $5000.00 at least." He claimed that $19,000.00 out of the original $50,000.00 appropriation was spent on men who were hired to "watch my movements." So if the clerks in Washington wanted to give the public a clear picture of expenditure and accomplishment, they could announce that Nobles "built over two hundred and fifty miles of good substantial Wagon Road," for "less than $31,000.00...."[30] When the smoke cleared from the commotion caused by accusations, lawsuits, investigations and angry newspaper articles, Nobles was awarded $8,199.99.[31] A fighter to the end, he didn't leave the ring empty handed and he undoubtedly felt vindicated.

A Nobles quote in the *St. Paul Daily Times* sums up his views and ambitions in terms that his fellow Cavaliers could understand. "The West is becoming so powerful already that it matters but very little whether the older States assist much or not. From this great framework of navigation, railroads will be built, and telegraphic lines will be established, if not altogether upon our own sail, but little north of us...and these lines will be extended to the Pacific."[32] Just like his road—all the way to the Pacific Ocean. It was a dream worth dreaming and an ambition worthy of a man who loved the West and willingly embraced its challenges.

Chapter V

Yankton on the Missouri River Slope

"Our belief is that it (the capital of Dakota) will be at the mouth of the James River...."

Sioux City Eagle
September 19, 1857

Almost from the moment the town of Sioux City, Iowa, first breathed life, some of its citizens had their eyes on the land people were calling Dakota. Looking from the edges of the bluffs onto the vast prairie wilderness, they envisioned town sites, farms and profits. They saw settlements on the banks of the Big Sioux, James, and Missouri Rivers, and a railroad connecting all this with Sioux City. Iowa had long been a "theater of speculation," and men could not be faulted for expecting the same to happen further west.

From among the potential town sites, one spot was coveted above all else: the village of the Ihanktonwan, or Yankton Sioux Indians on the Missouri River near the mouth of the James River, under the leadership of Chief Struck By The Ree. For some men of the speculative bent, this was the big prize, and the most desirable place to build a city—even better than the Falls of the Big Sioux River. According to at least one historian, a Sioux City man named Ben Stafford was the first to advocate the building of a town at the Yankton village site, after a visit there in 1857.[1]

Why this particular site when the Missouri slope stretched out for hundreds of miles? Why did the future town of Yankton inspire so much scheming, risk-taking and dogged competition? Many of the personal reasons lie among the dead, but there are some sources that can be examined, and this chapter will attempt to answer the intriguing question.

The Western Town Company, as we have seen, drew considerable attention to Dakota, bringing the first Iowa settlers to the new land. The Dakota Land Company did the same for Minnesotans. By late 1857, Nebraskans too were casting envious eyes beyond their northern borders. An Omaha newspaper called Dakota the "garden spot of the Northwest," a place of unparalleled beauty and fertile soil that was destined to prosper.[2]

The Native Americans who claimed the land by tradition had a similar love for it. The Yankton people of the great Sioux Nation had lived there for generations. In addition to their ancestral village, their homeland was approximately 12,000,000 acres, bordered by the Big Sioux and Missouri Rivers, extending north to a line drawn roughly from Fort Pierre east to the Minnesota border. The Yankton people maintained a generally non-hostile attitude toward whites, having mingled with French trappers and traders since the days of Lewis and Clark. They readily accepted those things from European and American cultures that were of benefit to them.

The Yanktons were generally looked upon by the white man more favorably than the Tetons and Santees. "The Yanktons are said to be the most intelligent and peaceful, the noblest formed and best behaved Indians in the Sioux Nation," reported the *St. Paul Pioneer and Democrat* in 1859. They were ready to be "schooled in the arts of civilization."[3] Indians thus "advanced" would be more easily dealt with by the government, or so it was believed. But toleration of the alien, European-born culture went only so far. As long as they refrained from squatting on Indian land and torturing the earth with their plows and roads, white visitors were tolerated, even welcomed. A government trail from Sioux City to Ft. Randall passed by the village, and was used regularly to carry mail and supplies. And occasionally groups of men would gather in Sioux City, cross the Big Sioux River and hunt buffalo in Dakota, without incident. But in August of 1857, when a group of whites attempted to settle west of the Big Sioux River, they were driven out by the Yankton Sioux.[4]

In 1857 no one would argue that the immigrants had any legal right to settle on Yankton land. But the white man knew how to create that right by creating a treaty. As early as 1856 plans were in the works for an agreement between the federal government and the Yankton Sioux, and the speculators were in the thick of it. Conspicuous among them was John Blair Smith Todd, who coveted Yankton land as much as any white man.

Todd was already in his middle years when he decided to try on Dakota. Born in 1814 in Kentucky, Todd was groomed for a military career. He graduated from West Point in 1837, although he received failing grades during his final year.[5] He served with military distinction in the Florida Indian Wars. During the Mexican War, Todd fought bravely at Vera Cruz and Cerro Gordo. For his exemplary service, he rose to the rank of Captain.

In 1855 he served under General William S. Harney, and participated in the punitive raid against a village of Brule Sioux at Ash Hollow, Nebraska Territory. Many women and children were

John Blair Smith Todd
(Collections of the South Dakota State Archives)

among the dead, but this failed to sour Todd on western ways. Like the military man he was, he simply moved on, accompanying the Harney expedition north to Fort Pierre where he and 1200 fellow soldiers spent a most miserable winter. In the summer of 1856, Harney—a notorious, hard-headed Indian-hater—led his troops away from the awful place they called "Fort Desolation," to a new site further south where they established Fort Randall.[6] The new fort was a part of the government's plan to establish a defense perimeter on the upper Missouri River to halt Indian "aggression."

It was at Fort Randall that the tall, dapper, smooth-talking Todd decided a career change was in order. He resigned his commission and became the post trader, or "sutler," at Fort Randall. He obtained a government license to trade with the Indians, a piece of paper that made many a shrewd man wealthy. For a skillful and cunning trader could turn a license to trade into a license to steal.

With his flashy, silver-headed cane always in hand, the domineering and talkative Todd moved among rough frontiersmen and Washington society ladies with equal ease. Although a Democrat, he was a cousin of Mary Todd Lincoln, wife of the future president, and his political connections were strong. Abraham Lincoln liked the Todd clan and in a joking reference to his in-laws' aristocratic airs, said that while God was satisfied with just one "d," the Todd's added another to their name since one was not enough.[7]

From his headquarters at a Sioux City store, a proud and confident Todd made plans and allies. Todd believed he could profit by dealing with the Indians and then profit some more by dealing them out.

In the summer of 1856, he teamed up with David M. Frost from St. Louis, who had operated D. M. Frost and Company, a trading firm since 1853. Todd and Frost had served together in the Mexican War, a military relationship that apparently formed the basis for a business partnership. Together they established trading posts at desirable locations on the upper Missouri River, taking in furs in exchange for supplies and trinkets. Todd handled the "political end" of the company as it grew to become one of the wealthiest businesses of its kind in the Northwest.[8] Frost, Todd and Company served trading posts on the Missouri River as far away as Fort Union.

Frost, Todd and Company, however, had loftier ambitions in mind—-goals similar to those of the Western Town Company and Dakota Land Company. While they went about the business of establishing trading posts, their real motives soon became known. They wanted to create a town on the site of the Yankton village called *Shado Otunwahe*, or Red Clay Village, then occupied by about 2600 people.[9] This was the principal Yankton village. Over the years, the Yanktons met there in council and yearly received white visitors who came by steamboat, bringing messages and presents from the "Great Father."[10]

The ground at *Shado Otunwahe* sloped gently upward from the bank of the Missouri River, forming a broad plain that caught the attention of the speculators. The lay of the land was suited for building. Nearby was another Yankton village under the leadership of Chief Smutty Bear, respected by his fellow tribesman for his abilities as a hunter. As this village skirted the water's edge it was known as "Smutty Bear's Bottom."[11] Together, the two villages were looked upon as prime town site property by Todd and his associates.

Knowing that others might have similar designs, Todd and Frost established a trading post at the Yankton village in May of 1857.[12]

Construction of the post was supervised by William P. Lyman, from Pennsylvania, who also established a ferry on the James River under a government license at the military trail crossing.[13] Agents Frank Chapel, George Presho and George D. Fisk were placed in charge of the trading post while Lyman operated the ferry.[14] As Todd was a licensed trader, he and his men were permitted to stay on unceded land, trade with the Indians and bide their time.

They did quite well. In one week during the summer of 1857, Todd, Frost and Company, shipped to Sioux City 7567 buffalo robes, 729 beaver skins, 32 elk skins, 14 bear skins, and the hide of one moose.[15]

In October of 1857, Todd was elected mayor of Sioux City, but declined to serve because of what he called an "unfair" election.[16] Be that as it may, it seems Todd had more onerous duties to attend to. He spent much of the winter of 1857-1858 in Washington D. C., with a group of Yankton Chiefs. In the relative comfort of the nation's capitol, he and others hammered out a treaty of great historical importance. Due to concerns over Indian unrest, and the belief that the frontier would be safer if Indians were confined to reservations, the office of Indian Affairs wanted another treaty with the Dakotas. After the first attempt failed, Todd was selected to be the negotiator.[17] It was a responsibility he was more than willing to undertake.

Todd was a shrewd man with considerable experience in dealing with Indians—and much of it from the barrel of a gun. He and his allies needed someone with a different kind of influence over the Indians. Someone who could persuade even the most stubborn chief, and make him put his "X" on the parchment. They found their man in Charles F. Picotte.

Charles F. Picotte was a man of mixed blood and, some would

say, of confused or divided loyalties. He had the unique distinction of having sentiments in two cultures, a logical product of both the city and the frontier. His father was a wealthy Frenchman, Honore F. Picotte, and his mother was Eagle Woman Who All Look At, a sister of Chief Struck By The Ree.[18] The elder Picotte was connected with the Columbia Fur Company and occupied much of his time traveling up and down the Missouri River, living and working at the forts and trading posts. He had a white wife in living in aristocratic comfort in St. Louis and four Indian wives on the frontier. At Fort Tecumseh, near the mouth of the Bad River, in the remote Northwest wilderness, Charles was born on August 30, 1830. His Indian name was Itekeca, meaning "Shaggy Face."[19]

When he was about eight years old, Charles was sent to Missouri to be educated. It was said that Father Peter De Smet, the legendary Jesuit missionary among the western tribes, took the boy to St. Louis to begin his education.[20] The boy's father lavished money on him, under the belief that Charles was suffering from consumption and would not live long. Believing he was doomed, Charles spent money freely and took to drinking. He did not die, however, and returned to his people when he was about twenty years old, in good health, having done well in his studies. When Joseph R. Hanson met Picotte in 1858, the latter was "the most perfect specimen of physical man I ever knew." They became good friends.[21] Hanson was one of many friends that Charles would cultivate among the white population.

Picotte married a woman of the Teton Sioux and after she died, took a wife from among the Yanktons. Far from scorning him for taking on the white man's ways, the Yankton people accepted Picotte. He also proved useful to the U. S. government, serving as

Charles F. Picotte
(Collections of the South Dakota State Archi)

an interpreter for General Harney in 1856 at Fort Randall.[22] Harney anointed him "Head Chief of all the Sioux Nation."[23] In connection with this outlandish proclamation, in 1857, his services were sought out by those who wanted another treaty.

When he got wind of the proposed treaty Picotte was not optimistic, for he knew the chiefs were opposed to it and apparently immovable. Picotte nevertheless went to Fort Randall where the treaty-makers were in deliberations. There Picotte advised the Indians to ignore the treaty and leave for their annual fall hunt—then he went to Fort Pierre. Soon after, he received an anxious, if not angry, order to return to Fort Randall.[24]

At the outset Todd disdained the services of Picotte, believing him to be in sympathy with his Indian blood. Treaty talks, however, bogged down, so Todd relented and Picotte was summoned.[25] The impatient treaty-makers sensed it was time to seize the day. With Fort Randall on the west, well staffed with soldiers, and settlements to the north and east, the Yanktons were hemmed in and under pressure. Like ripe fruit ready to drop softly into a basket, another great real estate bonanza was at hand.

Although Picotte thought it unwise to impose treaty talks on the chiefs, Todd thought otherwise, and after about a week he convinced Picotte to prevail upon the chiefs. Picotte believed the chiefs were ill prepared to make the long journey so late in the year, but nevertheless changed his mind and agreed to help. He convinced his fellow tribesmen to make the journey to see the Great Father in the person of President James Buchanan. On December 11, 1857, Todd, Picotte, Zephyr Rencontre, Theophile Brughier and a contingent of 16 Yankton men including four Chiefs set out for Washington, D. C.

The journey over land in lumber wagons was fraught with difficulties due to rough roads and cold weather. Todd took a keg of whiskey along, ostensibly because he feared the Indians would "sicken" from drinking ordinary water.[26] Most likely, all hands dipped into the vessel in order to relieve the monotony of the long trip.

The wagons got stuck and broke down repeatedly. Picotte recalled the time when a wagon tipped over and its contents, including the whiskey container, fell on him. As he crawled out of the mess, men were yelling, "where is Charlie?" He stood up and held up the keg, telling the others to "take that and they would find me, next to it." As Picotte said, "we tried to get some little fun out of the great annoyance."[27] Finally, after a week of misery, the party arrived at Iowa City. There they boarded a train for the rest of the trip.

Among the party was Padaniapapi, or Struck By The Ree, perhaps the best known of all the Yankton chiefs. Born about 1800, he was already an old man when he went to see the Great Father. Often referred to as "Strike The Ree," and "Old Strike,"—and on at least one occasion "Struck The Three"—the venerable old chief had long inclined to reconcile himself to the white man. It was said that "no white man's blood had stained his hands."

Indians and whites alike considered him a shrewd man, and his influence with his fellow chiefs was counted on by Todd and Picotte.[28] Historian George W. Kingsbury, who knew Struck By The Ree, described him as a man "too wise to oppose it [the treaty] by force, and wise enough to make the best of it."[29] The pragmatic Struck By The Ree resigned himself to accepting the treaty, explaining to his fellow chiefs that "the white men are coming like maggots. It is useless to resist them." He understood that in sheer numbers alone, the whites were too powerful for Indian resistance.[30]

For many years a story circulated among Indians and whites about Struck By The Ree and the Lewis and Clark discovery expedition. It was said that when the famous explorers visited the Yankton village in 1804, the young Struck By The Ree was presented to them. They wrapped him in an American flag and declared to all present that the boy would grow to be a great leader of his people and a loyal friend of the white men.[31] While the story is part of oral tradition, Struck By The Ree became a great leader of his people, in large part because of his intelligence and ability to persuade. He was a great orator who could mesmerize listeners.

While Todd, Picotte and Struck By The Ree were laboring in Washington, Todd's business associates formed the Upper Missouri Land Company in February of 1858.[32] In so doing, they were able to stay ahead of rival groups with similar designs. Among Todd's entourage were a number of Sioux City men, including Samuel "Old Spot" Mortimer, Lewis H. Kennerly, Edward Atkinson and Enos Stutsman. Their objectives were twofold: consummate the treaty and establish trading posts at desirable points that in time would become town sites.

Others from Sioux City formed their own coalitions. One such group was led by W. P. Holman and his son C. J. Holman, and was backed by a number of Sioux City men, including Ben Stafford. In March of 1858, they made a colonizing foray at the Yankton village. They canoed up river from Sioux City and stopped on the Nebraska shore, at a place called La Neer, about six or seven miles south of the village. All but the elder Holman crossed the river. On the Dakota side, they crossed the James River and worked their way through a long stretch of water and ice-covered flood plain in order to reach their prize. Everything seemed to go well; no other person was in sight when they arrived. Satisfied, Holman pitched a tent. It was a modest beginning.

Several days later, the Holman party was greeted by George D. Fisk and "Old Spot" Mortimer, who put up their own tents close by. Soon they were joined by a group of angry Indians who ordered Holman's party to leave. Having accepted for the moment that they were trespassers, Holman and his men retreated to the Nebraska side of the river.

In early May, the Holman party heard about the treaty. Believing the treaty was signed and in effect, a group of men rafted logs across the river, laid out twelve sets of foundations and began the construction of a log cabin near the bank of the Missouri River, where present day Pine and First Streets intersect. Their work attracted the attention of the pro-Todd element and at Old Spot's behest, the Indians led by Dog's Claw attacked the cabin. The Holman group, not willing to give up easily, engaged the Indians in a vigorous fistfight. (Lucky for all, they left their guns on the Nebraska shore.) Holman's men prevailed, or at least made a good showing, for their cabin survived. In time it was finished and the crude dwelling is credited as being the first permanent white habitation in the town of Yankton.[33] They did not occupy their cabin, however, but instead set up camp on the Nebraska shore and waited.

Not long after the completion of the Holman party cabin, agents from Frost, Todd and Company began the construction of a cabin near Rhine Creek, not far from the headquarters of their competitors. Members of the Holman party stealthily carried away the logs intended to build the Frost and Todd cabin and cut them up for firewood. Not to be outdone, however, the Todd agents completed a cabin near the river bank at the foot of present day Walnut Street. Yankton now had two dwellings.[34]

On April 19, 1858, the treaty with the Yankton Sioux was signed by the chiefs and Charles M. Mix, Commissioner of Indian Affairs. It was no easy negotiation as many of the Indians, including Smutty Bear, were strongly opposed to selling their land. After a considerable period of time, their resistance was worn down by Picotte, who urged the Indians to sign and get the best deal they could. He convinced them that the unstoppable whites were certain to come in great numbers. Picotte negotiated with a sense of urgency, believing he had obtained the best for both worlds. Picotte was quoted years later as saying "we [the Yankton Sioux] would have been the first Sioux to fight the whites, instead of the Santees, if it had not been for that treaty." [35]

Yankton oral history concludes it was a swindle. According to Yankton tradition, handed down for generations, the resistance of the chiefs was worn down by alcohol. They were told the hotel water would make them sick, and ordered not to drink it. Instead they were given liquor to drink. Alcohol, combined with pressure applied by skillful and intimidating negotiators in a purely alien setting, negated all resistance and the government won the day.[36]

By the terms of the Treaty of 1858, the Yankton Dakota relinquished control and ownership of a tract of land variously described as eight million to twelve million acres. In exchange the Indians retained a 400,000-acre reservation upstream on the Missouri

River, across from Fort Randall. They were to receive $1,600,000.00 in annuities, spread out over fifty years, and perpetual access to the sacred Pipestone Quarries in Minnesota. The government retained the right to build roads and forts on the reservation.

When Todd and the treaty-makers returned to the West, they were hailed as heroes. The delegation was warmly received at Sioux City, whose citizens saw big money in the works. Todd's star was rising fast. He was opening the West, freeing up land for others while securing his own political and economic future. He was a strong supporter of a plan to make the upper Missouri River region a "white farming" society.[37]

When the chiefs returned to Dakota with news of the treaty, many Yanktons felt betrayed and sold out. Although Smutty Bear signed the treaty, he did so under protest for he disliked it intensely. He became a rallying point for Indian discontent. Struck By The Ree and Picotte, who pressured him into signing, bore the brunt of the criticism. The former was threatened, humiliated and even shot at, but as he was always protected by his followers and the American military, the worst he got was a bullet that ricocheted off his heel. He lived to regret deeply signing the Treaty of 1858.

Picotte got rich. For his part, he was awarded 640 acres of land, part of which was situated on *Shado Otunwahe*. Indians derisively referred to it as "Charlie's Town." No matter though, for it was his land to do with as he pleased, and in 1861, he left the reservation and moved to Yankton to enjoy his largess. Picotte, a member of the frontier *nouveau riche,* frequently used a rolled up twenty-dollar bill to light his cigars.[38]

Todd and his allies were also big winners. They and "all persons…

residing within said ceded country by authority of law" were allowed to enter 160 acres at the rate of $1.25 per acre.[39] Todd selected a quarter section adjoining Picotte's on the west that became the town site of Yankton.[40] His company also was permitted to claim 160 acres at each of its trading posts. After Dakota Territory was created, a new county was formed, named Charles Mix to honor the commissioner. It contained the Yankton reservation that was frequently called the Greenwood Agency.

For the government, the treaty was a real estate bonanza, having acquired so much rich land for so little compensation. About 13.5 cents per acre, according to the *Sioux City Eagle*, whose editor called it a "pretty good price for Uncle Sam to pay."[41] Still there were some people who thought the government was overly generous. The editor of the *St. Paul Pioneer and Democrat* said the Indians benefited from a farsighted government that doled out the sale price in payments, rather than a lump sum, so the Indians wouldn't "squander" the money "on useless trinkets." Instead the Indians would receive stock and agricultural equipment to "promote their industry and civilization."[42]

Another treaty-watching St. Paul newspaper was unimpressed. The *Daily Minnesotian* was disappointed that much more land was not ceded, especially the area that included the headwaters of the Big Sioux, Jacques (James) and Minnesota Rivers. This newspaper saw in the treaty a scheme to benefit speculators of the Democratic stripe. Because all the ceded lands were to the far southwest of St. Paul, its businesses would not benefit from immigration.[43]

As the treaty had to clear the U. S. Senate, it would not take effect for many months after the names and marks were affixed to the document. In the meantime, the Yanktons stayed on their land and angrily kept the tide of settlement at bay. Doing so required constant vigilance, for a growing body of white men, women and children waited anxiously, ready to move onto the land reputed to be fertile and productive. Speculators from Sioux Falls City and Sioux City, settlers from other parts of Iowa and beyond, all were ready to move out when it was "official." For many it was their first chance to have land of their own, and so much of it too—almost impossible to fathom for those who came to America from crowded conditions in Western Europe.

In July of 1858, a group of wide-eyed settlers showed up in Sioux City, explaining to a reporter for the *Eagle* that they were bound for Dakota.[44] It seems they were mistakenly told that the area would be open for settlement by autumn. Where they ultimately went was not reported.

What one gleans from the press, however, is a sense of urgency, as if huge numbers of people were ready to rush in at the moment the government gave its permission. Sioux City newspapers were eager to let the world know that parties were in town, "bound for Dakota," the land of promise, where buffalo still roamed in large numbers and wolves "made the night hideous" with their howling.

The *Sioux City Register* estimated that "over a thousand people in Iowa alone" were waiting to rush in to the "country bordering upon the Missouri river, and extending upwards from the mouth of the Big Sioux." Furthermore, they were desirable people; "hardy pioneers who are ever ready to shoulder their axe and rifle and assume the position of a vanguard in the onward march of civilization."[45]

While the *Register's* figures are exaggerated, there was some temptation to make a run for Dakota, creating an urgency of another kind. From the time the treaty was consummated, the situation was tense and potentially dangerous, as there were those who couldn't wait until the Senate approved the treaty. The government-sanctioned squatters of the Todd organization and the Indians did their best to keep the invaders out.

In August of 1858, a third group of town site speculators arrived at the Yankton village of Struck by the Ree. This group consisted of Joseph R. Hanson, Horace T. Bailey, John Patterson, Kerwin Wilson and Henry and Myrom Balcom. They soon learned that they were unwelcome and like Holman's party, departed for the Nebraska side of the river, where some of them eventually took up land and settled.[46] Hanson was determined to settle on the Dakota side, and became one of Yankton's prominent citizens and historians.

Holman's party was equally determined, but in September or October of 1858, Indians again attacked their cabin and destroyed it completely. The following day, a contingent of soldiers from Fort Randall, under the command of Captain Charles S. Lovell, arrived with orders to destroy any unauthorized habitations and evict all trespassers. Lovell and Indian Agent Alexander H. Redfield confronted Holman and in no uncertain terms, ordered him and his men to leave the area. His cabin destroyed by angry Indians, and the U. S. Army threatening arrest, Holman and his men gave up their long siege and retreated to Sergeant Bluffs, near Sioux City.[47] Todd and his associates were left alone on the field with the big prize within their grasp.

According to the *Sioux City Eagle*, the Indians destroyed more than one cabin, reporting that an entire group of squatter shacks were burned down. Noting the squatters were unharmed, the *Eagle* downplayed the danger imposed by Indians and instead, predicted trouble from among the town site contenders.[48] But Holman's group had given up, sensing the futility and danger of bucking Frost and Todd and their Indian allies. It was a devastating defeat for the Holman party as they had opened a claim book and members of their organization—most of them from Sioux City—had laid claim to more than 100 locations of 160 acres each, surrounding the proposed town site.[49]

Soon after, a group of Iowa men, "armed to the teeth," set out for Dakota. Apparently not associated with the rival town site groups, they were determined to make a portion of it their own. They were unwilling to wait for the government to act. However, about a week after they left Sioux City, the party returned, exhausted and hungry, and with a sad tale to tell. They got lost on the prairie, a mule died, and they went four days without food. Their failure was, however, assigned to ordinary misfortune, not to the Indians, or rival speculators.[50]

Meanwhile, Lovell and A. H. Redfield, the agent assigned to the Yankton reservation, continued their mission, hunting for illegal settlers along the Missouri slope. Those encountered were forced to flee as their cabins were burned. The squatters were indignant and outraged at the conduct of the soldiers. How could they, people demanded to know, favor Indians over whites? The soldiers, of course, were doing no such thing. They were following orders. It was believed the punitive measures were preferable to an all-out war against the Indians.[51]

The winter of 1858-1859 passed quietly along the Missouri

slope, with the Yanktons staying at their villages and the white man staying away. Only Todd's men were allowed to remain, and they busied themselves with hunting, trapping and staying alive. The severity of winter on the Plains was, by itself, enough to stop all but the most adventurous pioneers. Had the government declared the area open for settlement, in the dead of winter, few, if any, would have made their move.

The treaty was approved by Congress on February 17, 1859, thereby becoming the law of the land. Not long after, settlers began moving in, in small numbers, settling in timbered areas near the rivers and streams. Todd's group had eight town sites occupied, covering all bases, trusting that the capital of the new territory would surely land on one of their sites.[52]

The Yankton town site, however, was the main attraction, and in early March, the number of squatters there was increased substantially. Enos Stutsman, Charles L. Tackett, Henry C. Ash, Obed Foote and F. M. Ziebach left Sioux City, taking their ambitions to Dakota.[53] Ash built the first hotel in Yankton; his wife was the first white woman in the settlement. Many a weary traveler enjoyed a dinner of catfish and molasses at the Ash Hotel. It was the start of a long and fruitful life in Dakota for the Ash family.

Charles L. Tackett was a rough, disreputable character from St. Louis who had worked as a tinsmith at Fort Pierre. He later operated a "ranche" or trading post along the stage route on Chouteau Creek between Yankton and Fort Randall.[54] His liquor establishment attracted all the riff-raff of the frontier including freighters, soldiers, outlaws and prostitutes, and Tackett presided over his operation as a sort of "justice of the peace," like a Judge Roy Bean character.

Drunken brawls, shootings and summary hangings were common at Tackett's station, making it a fearful place for stage drivers to stop. They avoided the place if at all possible, for the same reason that Tackett's Indian wife ran from him out of fear. He was a man of violence living as he pleased on the lawless frontier. It was said he cut a notch in a large tree for every man he hung.[55]

A much more civilized, but no less determined, F. M. Ziebach gave up the editorship of the *Sioux City Register* for the untamed Missouri River slope. But it seemed a logical choice, for Ziebach was a true political adventurer, and all those who knew him saw another newspaper in the offing.

His friend Enos Stutsman was equally political with intellectual capabilities strong enough to overcome his great physical shortcomings. While he had considerable strength in his well-developed upper body, his lower body was terribly deformed. He had but one leg, and that was a mere stump. He scuttled about on short crutches that could never carry him as fast as his mind wanted to go. Still, what he lacked in ordinary mobility, he more than made up for in brainpower, wit and humor. Speculator, lawyer and natural entertainer, Stutsman was one of the great wits of the frontier, born to be the life of the party that was sure to erupt in his presence.

An eccentric James "Limber Jim" Witherspoon was no doubt an attendee at those early day soirees. He first came to Yankton in 1858 and managed to get in on the Todd land bonanza. His claim was contested, however, and according to Witherspoon, he walked all the way from Yankton to Washington, D. C. to argue and win the contest.[56]

Another lively soul who cast his lot in the "far off lonely land of Dakota," was Moses K. Armstrong, who left behind a large number of friends in southwest Minnesota. In a letter to a Winona, Minnesota, newspaper, Armstrong cheerfully chronicled his many hardships on the prairie, and then urged his friends to write him at "Yancton, near Jame's River Ferry, Dakota Ter., *via* Sioux Falls City, Iowa."[57] Armstrong, Stutsman and their fiercely ambitious companions were to become the "Founding Fathers" of a new city. For many years it would more than hold its own in its competition with its rival at the Falls of the Big Sioux River.

Although Yankton was not yet ready for lot sales and construction, the *Sioux City Eagle* predicted a rush of new settlers, eagerly moving onto the newly ceded land. Large parties of "emigrant wagons" were passing through Sioux City on their way to Dakota.[58] As the Indians had yet to leave for their reservation, the settlers—including Todd's allies—faced constant danger. Bad feelings erupted in violence as bands of Yanktons occasionally destroyed habitations and threatened the settlers. Once again Picotte intervened and convinced the Indians that they must inevitably give up their land and live on the reservation.

As the time came for the Yankton people to leave their ancestral home site, Smutty Bear, who stubbornly objected to the treaty, threatened to take control of the tribe from Struck By The Ree. Opposing groups sent messages back and forth as tensions mounted. Todd's men—Stutsman, Presho and Chapel—feared for their lives and hid inside their cabin behind boarded windows and doors. Soon after, however, the Indians settled their differences and bloodshed was averted. Instead of fighting, Smutty Bear and Struck By The Ree held counsel and a feast. Smutty Bear was persuaded to give up his resistance.

Before they departed, however, all the Yankton people gathered in one last, grand encampment at *Shado Otunwahe*. "Limber Jim" Witherspoon, who witnessed the gathering, claimed that as many as 3000 Yankton Sioux were concentrated at the site that would soon become the town of Yankton. Twenty years after the event, when Yankton was in full bloom, Witherspoon told a newspaperman that the "camp was in the form of a circle, the teepes (sp) being placed around the base of the bluff range west and north of town and extending thence towards the Missouri about where Capital street now runs...." There was tension among the Indians and Witherspoon recalled seeing "thirty-six painted warriors" mounted and riding around the teepees, "indulging in a pantomimine (sp) which probably contained something of importance to the Indians...."

When the symbolic show of force subsided, some old women of the tribe walked to the top of a hill where "a couple of dead Indians were laid away on scaffolds." They reverently and tenderly gathered the bones and buried them. The next morning, July 17, 1859, the native Yankton people dismantled their teepees and with their belongings lashed to poles, began their "march over the western hill toward their new home."[59]

The native Yankton people left for Greenwood, most of them on foot, following the steamboat *Carrier* that carried agent Redfield and the first allotment of provisions to the agency. It was a long, sad goodbye as a despondent and heartsick people left their beloved homeland, surrendering control over it, forever.[60] Doubtless many felt that the value of their lives was reduced in proportion to the amount of land they had left.

Soon after the Indians departed, Todd's men met and dissolved

Struck By The Ree
(Collections of the South Dakota State Archives)

the Upper Missouri Land Company. They immediately created the Yankton Land and Town Company with Todd as president.[61] To quote Witherspoon, "the few white men left upon the townsite (sp) of Yankton were monarchs of all they could squat upon."[62]

The happy squatters immediately surveyed the new town site and named it "Yankton.", On occasion it was also spelled "Yancton." As there was no law to turn to in the event of a dispute, they formed a "Claim Club" to protect their claims.[63] Each member took a vow to come to the aid of anyone whose claim was threatened by outsiders. Todd's claim was adjacent to that of Picotte and formed the heart of the new town. Having made mighty strides toward their goal, they continued squatting, plotting and waiting for a government survey to make it official.[64]

The Yankton settlers were visited by representatives from the Dakota Land Company out prospecting for town sites.[65] The rival groups met peacefully, treating each other with respect although, no doubt, also with suspicion. The St. Paul men returned to Sioux Falls City, believing that they too, had benefited from the treaty that opened up countless miles of shoreline for new towns. But it was Todd's group that had reason to celebrate. They were the big winners on the Missouri River and saw the major portion of their plans come to fruition. *Now* the settlers could come and feel welcome.

By mid-August, word that the Yankton Sioux were gone was well circulated. As if giving a signal, the press announced that whites were welcome—and safe. *The Dubuque Herald* proudly stated: "This new territory is now open for settlement." In the same article, the *Herald* revealed that a large party of prospective settlers left Dubuque for "Dacotah Territory," all believing there was "not the least danger of being annoyed by savages."[66] It was a hearty send-off to a confident group of speculators, the kind of publicity that fit neatly into the experimental plans of Todd and Frost and their allies.

The plans, however, were nearly given a thorough shredding. In 1860, discontented Yanktons living at Greenwood staged a minor revolt after it was discovered that agent Redfield was engaged in a swindle. Picotte was pulled into the matter after a council. He went to Redfield and confronted the agent with "glaring facts of fraudulent dealing on his part." An angry and upbraided Redfield ordered Picotte out of his presence. Picotte—with his Sioux blood boiling—refused to leave, insisting on his right as a chief to stay and be heard.

Not to be outdone, Redfield ordered "seven or eight of his employees" to take hold of Picotte and toss him out. The men refused to do as ordered. But their refusal only made Redfield more obstinate, so he drew his revolver and pointed it at Picotte's chest. Unafraid, Picotte opened his shirt and dared Redfield to shoot him. Redfield turned away, walking out on the porch.

Tom Redfield, son of the agent, "seized a goblet...and struck me on the side of my head and face, inflicting two or three severe wounds, and knocking out one of my teeth," said Picotte. While a doctor was attending to Picotte's wounds, warriors—who believed he had been mortally wounded—began shooting at the agency building from "the hillsides in every direction." Only after Picotte sent word that he was not dead did the shooting subside. He emerged from the fray with a considerable loss of blood and a badly scarred cheek.[67] Picotte also had his fill of the reservation and returned to Yankton where excitement of another kind was in the making: politics and town building. He found this more to his liking and feely indulged in the happy sport.

Dakota had yet to become a territory with a functioning government but all knowledgeable people believed it was only a matter of time. Todd and his friends knew they had to muscle up politically in order to take control once Congress acted. Thus far everything had gone their way. They got the treaty, the town site and were a step or two ahead of their rivals. In short, the experiment was proceeding quite well.

The Yankton experiment was similar to that of Sioux Falls and other Big Sioux River town sites. The speculators used the government to leverage their companies into a position to realize their goals. Their frontier enterprises were largely subsidized by the federal government. The government gave away land or sold it cheap; it financed territorial government; it provided offices and income; it licensed and protected traders; and it funded military posts and built roads, providing both protection and additional money-making opportunities. Through treaty provisions, the government doled out money to Indians that was often and easily diverted to the accounts of the speculators, traders, or other federal appointees. And of course, the government was there to fight the Indians when treaties, trickery and trinkets failed to placate them.

In short, this was not the pure, private enterprise one might expect of "rugged individualists" on the western plains, unfettered by regulations. But no one at the time was concerned about outright paternalism. It was not recognized as such. Besides, they still had to work hard and take risks. They employed a tried and true formula for success and used it for all it was worth. Although Washington often balked, scoffed, or dragged its feet, it consistently supported the westward movement in Dakota and elsewhere. "Manifest Destiny" was more than a political shibboleth. It was material progress and moral authority, moving forward together like a beacon, bringing mankind out of the dark and into the light of civilization as it peeled away layers of the wild frontier. Civilization was the strong, invincible and invisible ally to white men of European antecedents, second only in importance to God. Nothing else was needed for inspiration or rationalization and no right-thinking person would object.

Chapter VI

Pembina and the Ox-Cart Culture

"...The Red River half-breed has a story as curious as any which while away the winter nights...."

St. Paul Pioneer and Democrat
July 30, 1858

Those who occupied the extreme northeast corner of Dakota were, indeed, the most unique of all the early day people. Rooted deep in the past, long before the territorial days, their story has a far away flavor to it. Colorful and wild in appearance and behavior, these people—most of them mixed-bloods—stood out among the Cavaliers of the Dakota Frontier. Many years before the town site founders forged their way into the southern regions of Dakota, their northern counterparts were well established at such places as Pembina and St. Joseph, in the northern-most part of the valley of the Red River of the North. Here, these spirited Huns of the Plains lived a semi-nomadic life, hunting, trapping, trading, farming—doing whatever was needed to stay alive. They did quite well.

By the late 1850's, when Sioux Falls City, Medary and Yankton began booming through the influence of speculators, Pembina was an old settlement with a population much greater than the new towns to the south. Historian George W. Kingsbury places the first "white" settlement at Pembina in 1780.[1] This probably refers to a trading post operated by French-Canadians.

Following a long and profitable connection with St. Paul, Pembina was able to leverage itself into the political games begun by the Dakota Land Company and Frost, Todd and Company. Quite often the southern Dakotans carried on as if they were the only people of consequence. Yet the most astute among them knew that Red River men would not be kept forever in the dark with their colorful, though primitive, ways. After they were jolted away from their days of innocence, Pembina people showed they had the stamina and the will to compete and contribute to the economic and political life of Dakota.

The Red River of the North has one very unusual characteristic: it runs north. Starting at Lake Traverse, in northeastern South Dakota, it flows almost straight north into Canada, emptying into Lake Winnipeg. It was long associated with both the French and English, and their competing fur-trading businesses. French and French-Canadian explorers dominated the area in the mid-18th century, living and trading with the native population. From 1670, the British-owned Hudson Bay Company claimed much of the land around the Red River of the North. Although they were rivals, the French and English were able to get along. That ended when a prominent British subject had other ideas for the Red River region.

In 1805 Thomas Douglas, Lord of Selkirk and Earl of Angus from Scotland, a member of the Hudson Bay Company, decided to found a permanent settlement on the Red River of the North. Lord Selkirk, as he was normally called, was an impractical visionary with grandiose plans and the willingness to take great risks with his money and other folks' lives. He believed with all his heart that British possessions in the New World should be peopled by British subjects, if only to keep them from moving to America. Believing he had found his portion of paradise in the British Northwest, he sought to share it with others.

In 1811 Selkirk obtained a grant of land from the Hudson Bay Company for use as a settlement. The land grant contained 74,000,000 acres spread over 116,000 square miles. He called his domain Assiniboia.[2] The deal was made without regard to Indian claims to the land. It also ignored potential American claims. Some of this land bordered, and even slightly overlapped, the Louisiana Purchase. As a further complication, the international border with Great Britain had not yet been established.

To people this land, he gathered a number of his fellow Scots from the Highlands of northern Scotland and some Irish as well, and sent them sailing to the New World.[3] These folk were not especially adapted to life on the prairies and forests. Most had fishing backgrounds and no experience in farming or hunting. Many were ne'er-do-wells looking for that one big break, and still others were eager youths, naively anxious to shoulder guns to hunt buffalo and fight Indians. They were all essentially homeless, having been evicted from the northern Scotland estate of the Duchess of Sutherland.[4]

One writer concluded that Selkirk never intended to create a colony of "civilized men." Rather he sought to form a society consisting of the natives, the Hudson Bay Company's "old servants" and their "half-breed" descendants. He brought over fresh European immigrants simply to "diffuse a spirit of industry and agricultural knowledge among these children of nature."[5] But new Europeans brought more than industry and thrift, and they soon found themselves caught up in a cultural conflagration that none of them could have anticipated.

This combustible mix of people established their first foothold where Winnipeg, Canada, now stands, calling their settlement Fort Douglas. This was to be the primary settlement. Then in the spring of 1812, they arrived in the wooded valley of the Pembina River, where it joined the Red River, and built a wooden enclosure, calling it Fort Daer. This was the very beginning of the town of Pembina.[6] It was on the west bank of the Red River, about 70 miles to the south of Fort Douglas. In time, the Selkirkers, as they were called, located other forts and settlements along the Red River of the North.

While Lord Selkirk's domain was empire-like, the settlement at Pembina is the focus of this chapter. The founding of Pembina marked the beginning of a very tragic episode in Dakota history. The tragedy combined familiar elements: two opposing business ventures and sedentary, farming people at odds with clans of hunters and gatherers.

The French-backed Northwest Fur Company was formed in 1783 in Montreal. Fur-bearing animals were plentiful so the enterprise thrived and encouraged a large number of French-Canadians to move into the Northwest. Led by Captain Alexander Henry, the Northwest Fur Company came to the Red River Valley in 1799. The following year, Henry established his headquarters at an unoccupied post in Pembina.[7] The jovial and flexible Frenchmen met and mixed with the Indians, mainly the Chippewa, resulting in offspring referred to in many works of history as the "Red River Half-Breeds."[8] These mixed-race people played major though contradicting roles. At first they opposed the Selkirkers—those who would create a permanent, agricultural settlement. And yet in the end, their hardiness, experience and industry helped to establish the first towns in the region.

With the appearance of the Selkirkers, the Northwest Fur Company became a fierce rival of the much older Hudson Bay Company. The French company objected to a permanent agricultural settlement in the area, and contested the propriety of the sale. The "half-breeds," or *Metis*, as they were more politely called, were convinced by Northwest Fur Company leaders that the Selkirkers were interlopers, taking land that was not theirs to take. They must be driven back to the Hudson Bay, by force if necessary.

The Selkirk colonists persisted, despite their fear and distrust, doing their best to make the new land their home. There were great herds of buffalo and other wild game to feed on and good soil for crops. While they were disappointed with their lot and upset with Lord Selkirk for selling them on the place, they held forth quite well against the elements, despite more than the usual frontier hardships.

They were, however, less successful in dealing with the agents of the Northwest Fur Company. The Selkirk colonists were kept under constant duress by the hostile fur men and their *Metis* associates, who lost no opportunity to harass and intimidate. Over time, houses were burned, livestock was killed, stored food was destroyed, and lives were threatened by "bands of drunken half-breeds."[9] Still, the colonists refused to quit and the settlements actually grew in population and structure, as a second and third wave of immigrants from Europe came into the Red River Valley.

The Northwest Fur Company, however, was equally determined to drive them out. And to that end, a large force of men attacked the colonists near Fort Douglas, on June 19, 1816.[10] The governor of the colony and some twenty others were killed by the savage rabble at what became known as the "Massacre of the Red River." This resulted in the evacuation of the Valley and the destruction of the houses and other property left behind. But the murderous vandals were not content with a mere victory. They pursued the retreating Selkirkers, inflicting further punishment, and capturing some.[11]

An alarmed and outraged Lord Selkirk intervened as best he could. He returned to Canada, freed some of the prisoners and arrested some of the killers. He also procured military protection for those exiled colonists who could be persuaded to return and try again. Meantime, Selkirk worked vigorously to prosecute the guilty and rebuild the settlements.

While getting the settlements on the mend, Selkirk became mired down in deals with dubious frontier characters. Among them, fellow Scot, Robert Dickson, turned out to be a liability if not an embarrassment. Dickson, a British agent, operated a series of fur trading posts in what later became Minnesota Territory. He had his headquarters on the eastside of Lake Traverse, near the camp of his Yanktonai Sioux brother-in-law. Dickson had considerable influence among the Indians and was known west of the Mississippi River as the "red-headed trader." During the War of 1812, he recruited Indians, including some Sioux, to fight against the Americans.[12]

Behaving like a little Caesar of the Plains, Dickson also claimed the Red River Valley. He was, however, willing to support Selkirk's claim in return for his Lordship's promise to engage in mutually beneficial trade. This would serve the wishes of both men, as all of the Red River Valley would become a British colony.

Selkirk went even further. He convinced the Cree and Assiniboine chiefs to relinquish their claims to both the Red River and Assiniboine River valleys. This deal was to become one of the strongest arguments in favor of the Selkirk claim. It also proved to be equally detrimental. The combination of Selkirk and Dickson, and their followers, drew the suspicion of the United States government. Congress saw a potentially troublesome conspiracy at work. And in 1818, the United States established the international boundary with the British, at the 49th parallel, from the Lake of the Woods west to the Rocky Mountains. Plans were also set in motion to defeat Selkirk's claim to land on the American side of the border.[13]

Lord Selkirk met with opposition everywhere, as the power and influence of his opponents increased. He came to the stark realization that his grand experiment, however nobly conceived, was a failure and a waste of his fortune. Finally, broken in spirit and disappointed to the core, the philanthropic Lord Selkirk returned to Scotland in the fall of 1818. He was far from finished, however. In Switzerland he unfolded his plans for a New World utopian community, hoping to convince some Swiss to leave their mountains and come to the Red River lowlands and make new homes.

Selkirk published notices throughout Switzerland in both French and German, making exaggerated if not outright false promises in an effort to induce another group of unsuspecting Europeans to migrate to North America. It worked. Much of Europe was laboring under enormous economic and social problems as a consequence of the disastrous Napoleonic Wars. In Switzerland, especially hard hit, Selkirk gathered together a large group of young families who were anxious to leave their wretched lives behind and take up the good life in Canada.

In the spring of 1821, the colony of over 200 people sailed away in good spirits. After a long and arduous journey across the

Atlantic, the Swiss arrived in Canada and made their way through snowstorms and high winds to Fort Douglas, getting lost repeatedly along the way. While they were welcomed with open arms at Fort Douglas, they were sadly disappointed at their prospects. Spring rescued them from winter, but locusts destroyed much of the summer crop. When winter set in again the food supply was low, not nearly enough to feed everyone. This is not what the new people expected; this was not utopia.

Faced with life or death choices, it was decided that a group of about 75 of the youngest and strongest settlers would go south to Pembina and spend the winter where they believed survival was possible. They were informed that buffalo and elk were in good supply and that other food could be obtained from the Indians. Winter was full upon them when they arrived at Pembina and set about to build huts for shelter. Too inexperienced to hunt buffalo with any efficiency, they ate poorly, devouring anything edible. That they survived at all is a tribute to their tenacity and adaptability, as the temperature often fell to 40 degrees below zero.

This was far more than any of them cared to endure, and feeling they had been grossly misled by Lord Selkirk, most of the Swiss settlers left the following year, making their way first to Fort Snelling on the Mississippi and thence to St. Louis. They had had quite enough of the great Northwest. For them it was a no man's land, so isolated and remote that mapmakers and geographers ignored the region. The memories of that awful winter were indelible, especially for those who froze their extremities for lack of warmth.[14]

In the meantime Selkirk died in the south of France in 1820, where he had gone to improve his failing health. He would no longer dabble in nation building or inflict undue hardship, however unintentional, on the very people he so ardently wished to help. His estate carried on the fight against his adversaries until 1836, when the Selkirk descendants sold Assiniboia—minus that part in the United States—back to the Hudson Bay Company.[15]

His investment of time, effort and money was not all in vain, however. Many of the Europeans did stay and the settlements did somehow survive. The area around Fort Douglas was renamed Kildonan, after a town in Scotland. By 1823, some 600 people were living in Pembina, despite the exodus of the Swiss. Most were mixed-bloods, but many were original Selkirkers and their children.[16] On August 8, 1823, the American flag was raised at Pembina for the first time. Up to that time most folks believed they were living in a British colony. When they were assured they were on American land, many of those with strong ties to Britain moved further north, beyond the international boundary.[17]

By 1823, the settlers on both sides of the border were looking back on more than a decade of hardships. They endured terrible suffering during the winter of 1817, only to have their promising crops destroyed by grasshoppers in 1818. The next year, the insects returned in larger numbers. Piled several inches deep, the layers of rotting grasshoppers put forth an awful stench—just another challenge for the settlers. The threat of human marauders, however, was gone. The rival companies—weary of the bloody competition, merged, securing the peaceful occupation of the settlement.[18]

Nature, however, was not through. In the winter of 1825-26, a terrible blizzard struck the Northern Plains. The following spring, a great flood caused the Red River of the North to overflow, covering a vast area on either side with water. Barns and houses were inundated, and along with dead livestock and other debris, made their way toward the Hudson Bay causing settlers to flee to higher ground. Adding strangeness to disaster, observers watched as a house floated by in flames.[19] By June the water retreated, allowing people to resume normal activities. The northern settlements then enjoyed a long series of relatively unimpaired years, leading into the early 1850's.[20]

The people of the Red River of the North learned to live off the land, and live with one another. French Canadians, Indians, *Metis* and Selkirkers all looked away from a violent past and turned to hunting and trapping on a large scale to supplement their crops. In this endeavor, the Selkirkers found themselves at a distinct disadvantage, for they lacked hunting skills. As such, they were forced to travel with the hunting parties, acting as mere servants to the hunters, including the Indians.

In time, all became successful hunters, cleaning the vast prairies of most of the wildlife, while supplying the seemingly insatiable markets to the East. Making all this possible was a small, unpretentious vehicle, made entirely of wood, usually oak, and a bit of rawhide, called the Red River ox-cart. First appearing about 1800, it was a simple, open-box resting on an axle and two wooden wheels, pulled by a pair of horses or oxen. Other than this, the cart's identifying feature was the loud, incessant squeaking of each wheel as it trundled awkwardly, but reliably toward its destination. Despite its shortcomings, the Red River ox-cart was a more versatile and useful form of transportation than the canoe, travois or dog-sled. With a little improvement over time, this humble, creaky wagon

Red River Ox-Carts from Pembina
(Collections of the Minnesota Historical Society)

revolutionized buffalo hunting and aided in the extinction of the great herds like another high-powered rifle. It also became the central artifact in the flamboyant Red River culture.

Between 1821 and 1840, it is estimated that 650,000 buffalo were killed on the Northern Plains.[21] Throughout the 1850's immense herds roamed the eastern Dakota prairies, ranging from Pembina south to the Big Sioux River valley. It was common for excited observers to bear witness to the land, "black with buffalo." And then, strangely, sometimes hunters would ride for days without seeing a live buffalo.

For many years the Red River Valley was prime hunting ground, attracting not only Pembina hunters, trappers, voyageurs and Indians, but also parties of well-to-do and titled men from the East. People acted as if this hunter's paradise would last forever. Then the ox-cart entered the northern hunt.

With the Red River ox-cart, hunters, in increasing numbers, roamed the vast prairies from Lake Traverse to Pembina, sweeping both east and west. While snooty people called them "primitive vehicles," the ox-carts were amazingly adaptable, for drivers could negotiate rough, hilly, dry terrain and wet sloughs with equal agility. Hunts were often grand affairs with dozens of families, numbering in the hundreds, joining together. While the Selkirkers tagged along in "homespun clothing," subsisting modestly, the "aristocracy of the plains," consisting of "officers, traders, clerks at the posts, and the buffalo hunters," took with them luxury items such as fine liquors.[22]

As the years progressed, more carts joined the hunting parties. It was possible to kill and dress up to 1000 buffalo a day, and transport the meat to markets without the need for waterways.[23] A hunt in July of 1840, near the Cheyenne River in present day North

Dakota, netted 2000 buffalo.

Flintlock rifles used in the great hunts were imported from England and were designed for the fur trading business. Over time, the Red River hunters acquired great shooting skills. Some could shoot accurately while riding at a full gallop among the herd, with a mouth full of balls for reloading. Well-defined rules of the hunt were established and followed to the letter. For example, it was illegal to run a buffalo on the Sabbath, and no person—regardless of the day—was allowed to run a buffalo until the general order was given There were graduated penalties for violating the rules, including a flogging for a third offense.[24]

While the tongue was invariably cut from the buffalo and eaten, the principal food of the hunters was a Red River concoction called "pemmican." It was made of buffalo meat dried with wild berries such as cranberries. It was easily preserved in great quantities and made a tasty nutritious trailside meal. The popularity of pemmican spread far and wide throughout the Northwest, becoming a signature staple of the Red River culture and another marketable commodity.

Another type of hunt was conducted by "sportsmen" from all over America. These were grand, often expensive expeditions, planned and carried out with showy extravagance. On one such hunt, a large party gathered at the Winslow House in St. Anthony, Minnesota in August of 1859. Before heading west into the Red River Valley, "and the plains beyond," for a four-week buffalo hunt, the *St. Paul Pioneer and Democrat* noted they were well-equipped and thoroughly "liquored," expecting to have a jolly time. They were given a rousing send-off.[25]

On another occasion, a number of Southern ladies joined a group of three men on a buffalo hunt. In the fall of 1860, the men and five bold, ante-bellum women, including the daughter of General Albert Sidney Johnston, departed Minneapolis in the direction of Devil's Lake. At Fort Abercrombie on the Red River, they were given a fifteen-man military escort and joined by another contingent of Southerners. Enchanted by the sheer grandeur of the vast prairie, they indulged themselves, drinking in all the natural pleasures of a once-in-a-lifetime adventure. But they shot no buffalo, taking back with them only a bear, a raccoon, a crane and hundreds of prairie chickens. They could also tell their friends that Indians stole two of their horses.[26] That they returned at all is probably more attributable to luck than skill.

St. Paul became the chief beneficiary of the great Red River hunts. Beginning in 1844, the ox-cart "trains" made annual treks to the Mississippi River, carrying meat, buffalo robes and skins and furs of many animals including mink, muskrat, marten, fisher, bear, fox, wolverine and lynx. Each year the trains were larger and by 1854, five years after Minnesota Territory was created, 1500 squeaky ox-carts made their showy appearance in St. Paul, the capital city. The long journey usually started in late June, taking about a month to reach St. Paul.

The ox-cart market trains were as impressive as the hunting expeditions. For example, an 800-cart train might include some 1300 men, women and children, making it a family event that was enjoyed by all. Often a priest would be among the travelers, providing spiritual comfort. Indeed, in these halcyon days, the Pembina people were arguably the happiest anywhere on the western frontier. With furs, hides, pemmican, ox-carts and well-fed families, life was complete.

The trains proceeded at a slow pace—about 15 to 20 miles per day, but spirits soared, in spite of the wilderness journey that often included crossing numerous swollen streams. The trains moved crisply, like an army, each with a "governor" to keep discipline. One skilled driver could control up to four carts. While the cart took its name from the oxen that pulled it, one Minnesotan recalled seeing tame buffalo hitched to the traces.[27]

The leaders of the train traveled in high style, bringing with them many luxury items such as wines and cheeses. At night the carts formed tight circles, enclosing the travelers and their possessions. Around campfires families ate pemmican, dried beef and whatever wild game was shot that day. All joined freely in the singing, dancing, drinking and merry-making that lasted well into the night.[28]

Another interesting feature was the "lady of the train," the wife of the "commander-in-chief" of the expedition. She could be Indian or "half-breed", but she always traveled in style in a covered cart and she was looked upon as a person of "wealth and authority." The "lady of the train" was also highly respected by the St. Paul merchants who catered to her desires to buy trinkets or a dress.[29]

When at last they arrived in St. Paul with their wares, they made a most impressive entrance. The men sported the wildest plumage, typically bright blue hooded coats, adorned by brass buttons, beads and sashes. Furs and deer-skinned moccasins were also part of their costume. These confident longhaired, well-armed bravos drew out all of St. Paul to greet them. They were warmly welcomed, although some folks tied up their dogs.

In time their fame traveled to other cities on the Mississippi, bringing groups of tourists to St. Paul. The arrival of a Red River ox-cart train became an annual event not to be missed. It can be compared to the joy inspired by the arrival of a traveling circus, as hundreds of curious visitors flocked to the ox-cart camps to savor a foreign flavor. The cry, "Wait for the Red River Carts," was a familiar refrain on St. Paul streets.[30] The merchants waited for the lucrative entertainment, as the ox-cart celebrities always seemed to have money, even after the financial crash in 1857.

A contemporary, who was on hand when one cavalcade arrived, said the noise from the wheels was loud "enough to drive a Christian mad."[31] During a church service one Sunday at St. Anthony, the minister paused mid-sermon when he heard the first, faint sounds of the squeaky wheels. He immediately closed his Bible and said "to be continued next Sunday...." He knew better than to try to talk over the noise that would soon fill the streets and the fascinating and fun-loving Red River people would detract even the most steadfast of believers.[32]

Another visitor, J. H. Beadle, who lived in Minnesota in 1859, recalled seeing ox-cart trains arrive in St. Paul. He listened with curious interest to the incessant squeaking from miles of greaseless wheels. On one occasion, he recalled seeing a cart of more than ordinary pretensions.... Shielded from the elements by a "rude awning," it contained a couple of white men whom he presumed to be men of some importance, connected with a fur company. Beadle, a traveler and writer, said it was common for one or more trains to arrive daily for several weeks during the summer.[33]

The impact of the trains on the Minnesota Territory economy was substantial while it lasted. The St. Paul traders eagerly bought their pelts and hides for resale. The merchants were even more grateful for the vast array of items that the Red River people ordered to take back to Pembina. This included food, clothing, and just about any kind of building material. The friendly exchange made many a St. Paul merchant rich. It is no wonder that the annual appearance of the Pembina people was waited for with such great anticipation.

Prosperity from the Red River trade fueled speculative fever in St. Paul. Beginning about 1850, land sales took off. Prices for lots assumed astronomical figures. Every man became a real estate dealer with town site maps and brazen claims. As we have seen from Chapter II, the Dakota Land Company was among the many town site companies formed during these hectic days. Farming was ignored in favor of the desire to make a quick profit. Although St. Paul had avoided the troubles caused by violent men who frequented the frontier, crime was rampant and food became scarce. Then the bubble burst in 1857, and after reeling in shock for a time, St. Paul moved forward at a sane pace, relying, as ever, on the Red River trade.

The ox-cart trains hit their peak in 1858. By then the value of the trade to Minnesota was estimated to be $250,000.00.[34] The following year, steamboats on the Red River of the North began carrying freight formerly hauled in the ox-carts. But the supply of raw material—hauled by ox-cart, steamboat, or railroad—could not keep up with the demand. Like an insatiable maw that wanted more and more of the meat, hide and blood of the Plains, the market swallowed up wildlife with great rapidity. The buffalo steadily diminished in numbers, and by 1870, the great herds were gone from the Red River Valley, driven into disappearance by prolonged and wasteful hunting.[35] By that time the Red River ox-cart was thought of as a cultural landmark, a relic of a bygone era.

With most of the animal life sucked out of the region, it was, indeed, the end of an era, and not any too soon for some. For despite the vast wealth carried into St. Paul from Pembina, the Red River folk were looked upon, at best, as only "semi-civilized," and the sooner they were relegated to the past, the better.[36] St. Paul businessmen were more than happy to pocket the profits from the trade, and just as eager to turn their backs on their trading partners when advancing technology and other markets opened avenues of opportunity that would keep the hordes of half-breeds out.

While their welcome gradually wore thin in St. Paul, the Pembina folks—both *Metis* and whites—provided some political punch after the creation of Minnesota Territory in 1849. Indeed, it was the Red River enterprise that got the territory off to a good start. Some of the seasoned Red River politicians were "Moccasin Democrats," and they contributed mightily to the strength of their party in its running battle with the Republicans in the 1850's.[37]

When territorial Governor Alexander Ramsey took the helm in 1849, he was greatly impressed with Pembina and St. Joseph. Pembina County was one of eight counties created by the first territorial legislature. In 1851, when Ramsey visited Pembina, it had a population of 1134 people, mostly *Metis*. They had homes and business places, and about 2000 acres under cultivation.[38] This made them a potential voting block that could not be ignored. As one condescending observer noted in 1850, they were "honest, simple-hearted...citizens qualified to vote and hold office."

This didn't seem to satisfy everyone. It was typical for the newspapers of the day and later-day historians to treat the *Metis* with a mixture of amazement and contempt. They were seen as a curious people produced by the "well-known affinity of the French men for the Indian women."[39] It is also a fact that there were not many white women around to take for mates. As a result, it was estimated that the "half-breed" population of the Red River region, including Manitoba, amounted to about 3000 people.[40]

Although they were a peaceful, friendly, bilingual people, and successful as parents, pioneers and entrepreneurs, mixed blood was their fatal liability. It was generally believed the *Metis* inherited the wild and savage ways of their Indian mothers and very little, or none, of the good in their European fathers. As such, their accomplishments, which none could deny or refute, were minimized and viewed as oddities, entirely out of place in the natural scheme of things.

So they remain adrift in history, like an anonymous faceless mass, for historians have been content to dismiss them as merely nameless "half-breeds." And yet they were among the earliest permanent settlers in what became Dakota Territory. While the prominent white settlers in those far northern environs are remembered by name, the early history of Pembina is more closely associated with the forgotten Red River *Metis*. Significantly, however, the farms, towns and trading posts of *all t*he people of the Red River of the North were in an advanced state of affairs, fueling the economy of Minnesota Territory and beyond, long before the town site companies began banking on the shores of the Big Sioux and Missouri Rivers.

Among the eastern press, the Washington City *Evening Star* made it known that the sturdy Pembina settlements were at the heart of the "inchoate Territory of Dacotah," and would likely form the basis of "official" territory. In June of 1857, before the Dakota Land Company made national news, the *Evening Star* recognized Pembina and related Red River communities as civilized settlements of long standing. Since they lay west of the proposed boundary of the new state of Minnesota, it was believed that these settlements would soon be given territorial status by Congress. "Everything seems to conspire to stimulate progress in the remote West." [41] In a way that any newspaperman could understand, the people of the Red River of the North had been doing that sort of thing for a long, long time.

Chapter VII

Inkpaduta

"We hope that...the dread of a visitation from Ink-pa-du-ta will not hang over our frontier settlers the coming winter."

St. Paul Pioneer and Democrat
September 10, 1857

Of all the people on the Dakota frontier of bad or dubious character, none other stands out as a man of violence like Inkpaduta, a Wahpekute Sioux Indian. Feared and hated by the whites, and distrusted by many Sioux, Inkpaduta became a symbol of evil throughout much of the Northwest during the 1850's and 1860's. The bizarre and the bloody attached itself to Inkpaduta—one of the few Indians called by contemporaries and historians by his native, Dakota name. In frontier times, to pronounce his name was, for some, to arouse the demons from down under and awaken a devilish image. For in those early days, no other man on the Dakota frontier inspired fear as much as the dreaded Inkpaduta.

Like other men of violence, and on the run, much of Inkpaduta's life is a mystery. Therefore, the historical record is often incomplete, or in conflict on the subject of this man. When he does come into sharp focus, it is because of the atrocities blamed on him and his band. It should be cautioned, however, that the evidence does not always support the conclusion, and we can never be certain that he was responsible for all the evil laid at his feet. And in assigning blame, we must consider that everyone is influenced by forces over which we have no control.

In the late eighteen-fifties, bloody deeds attributed to Inkpaduta and his band caused his name to be known throughout northwestern Iowa, southern Minnesota and in Dakota, as far west as the Missouri River. Doubtless many a prayer included an urgent and earnest request to be saved from the awful ravages of this man. His destructive acts and bad reputation discouraged settlement and tested the nerve of even the bravest of pioneers.

Inkpaduta, meaning "Scarlet at the Top," or "Scarlet Point," was born about 1800 on the Watonwan River in Minnesota, according to Thomas Teakle, author of the excellent book, *The Spirit Lake Massacre*.[1] His birth date is not a settled matter, however, and another source says he was born in 1815.[2] He was the son of Wamdisapa (also spelled Wamdesapa), or the Black Eagle, of the Wahpekute tribe of the Santee Sioux. Inkpaduta was born near-sighted, a condition that worsened as the years passed.

Wamdisapa was reputed to be a man of cruelty, who headed an outcast band of his people.[3] This group was forced to wander the prairies and plains, forever in exile, without a permanent home, as if bearing some awful curse. The Black Eagle band ignored treaties and boundaries, and were constantly at odds with other tribes. When they were not on the move, they could usually be found on the Missouri River, close to where the town of Vermillion, SD, was later located.[4]

Upon the death of Wamdisapa, Inkpaduta inherited control over the band of Indian outlaws. He assumed the aggressive policies of his father, only more ruthless and with greater ambition. From 1836 to 1857, numerous incidents of violence in Iowa and Minnesota were attributed to his "Red Top" band, so named for the red cloth tied to their lances.

Deserving or not, by 1848, Inkpaduta had a reputation for savagery that was known throughout the region. The murder of popular Chief War Eagle That May Be Seen and his band of 17 Wahpekutes was attributed to Inkpaduta's band.[5] There was even some speculation that he planned the murder of his own father.[6] "Evil," "savage," and "blood-thirsty," are just some of the harsh words used by writers to describe Inkpaduta. His bad reputation followed him into the 1860's and 1870's, and because he escaped capture, death or serious injury in so many battles and skirmishes, some Indians believed he lived a charmed life.

Inkpaduta was a large man, over six feet tall. His hard facial features were given further definition by smallpox scars, making him ugly, or as some would say, even demonic in appearance. White settlers remembered him as sullen, morose and mysterious. It may have suited him, however, for this grim reaper of the Plains seemed to thrive on his reputation for evil and survived by skillfully avoiding capture, thereby becoming a larger than life figure. Having been rejected by his tribe, and set to wandering, only made him more determined to survive.

Inkpaduta wasn't always at odds with the whites. In the early 1850's, as his band ranged up and down the rivers of Iowa, he often camped near the cabin of Curtis Lamb, near present day Sioux City. He and Lamb forged a solid friendship over the years based on trust and fair dealing.[7] Among other Indians, Inkpaduta's band was welcome in the camps of the Yankton Sioux on the James River, and had some connection with the Omaha tribes.

While his erstwhile Wahpekute kinsman were living on a reservation, as little more than captives, Inkpaduta's rag-tag band wandered throughout northwestern Iowa and southwestern Minnesota Territory. They frequently traveled the banks of the Des Moines, Big Sioux and Little Sioux Rivers, camping here and there. They were outcasts, small in number, but they were free. Still they often helped themselves to annuities passed out pursuant to the Treaty of Traverse de Sioux. And in 1856, Inkpaduta's gaunt wanderers showed up at Fort Ridgely, Minnesota Territory, and asked to be included in the distribution of treaty annuities. But this time they were denied and driven off by other Wahpekutes, as if to signify their lowly status.

Insulted, poor and hungry, the vagabond band returned to Iowa. When winter came, they were camped near the new settlement of Smithland, close to Sioux City. Early in December, the northwest was struck by a terrible three-day blizzard that set the tone for the entire winter, one of the worst of the 19th century. The desperate Indians depended on their skill as hunters and the generosity of their white neighbors. The Smithlanders, numbering about twenty-five, however, were ill prepared to handle nature's cruel demands. What supplies they had, they wanted to keep for themselves and therefore, grew tired of Inkpaduta's intrusive band of beggars.

By February of 1857, the desperate whites decided it was time for the Indians to leave. They organized in military fashion, and in a show of force, surprised and disarmed Inkpaduta's band, and ordered them to depart Smithland. Caught off guard and overtaken, Inkapduta tried to reason with the Smithlanders but failed. Disheartened and defeated, the band trudged away from Smithland with the cruel specter of winter at their backs.[8]

That winter was especially hard on man and beast. Many settlers, especially newcomers who were ill prepared for the extreme cold, lost their way on the prairie and froze to death. The snow was so deep in southern Minnesota Territory that in some places, groups of deer became bogged down and were unable to move. Those hunters lucky enough to come across snow-trapped deer only had to get close enough to cut their throats, and they had fresh meat.[9]

Trapped by intense cold and deep snow, Inkpaduta and his followers, with meager provisions, struggled to survive until spring. It was the kind of winter that instilled a special discontent, which only the threat of starvation can impose upon living things. Inkpaduta's desperate people kept moving, plodding through the prairie wilderness in a bold, animal attempt to stay alive. Pity anything that crossed their path.

At this point, Inkpaduta's band had dwindled down to about eleven warriors, including his twin sons Roaring Cloud and Fire Cloud, and a son-in-law, Rattle Strike. The remainder consisted of a number of women and children. Years of living like outlaws had taken its toll. And yet, due to their reputation, it was generally believed the band numbered 500 to 600 warriors. At top strength, however, it consisted only of 50 or 60 people.[10]

Inkpaduta may have had plans to attack the settlements in northwest Iowa.[11] He was heard to say that he would make war any time he saw fit since he was not a party to the Treaty of Traverse de Sioux, and couldn't draw annuities.[12] One thing seems certain: after the Smithland incident, Inkpaduta felt an intense hatred toward whites and he did nothing to conceal it. In February of 1857, his hungry band made its way north, toward Spirit Lake, in search of white habitations.

Spirit Lake, Lake Okoboji and the many smaller lakes and ponds associated with the area, had long been sacred territory to the Sioux. Many great myths and legends arose from those beautiful, mysterious waters, weaving their way into Indian culture. Spirit Lake was believed to be haunted by spirits of the dead, and no Sioux dared to cross it in a canoe.[13] The lakes were a mecca to the Sioux, a gathering place second only in importance to the Pipestone Quarries. And yet, through a series of treaties from 1825 to 1851, the Sioux people surrendered all of their Iowa paradise.[14]

This angered wild Indians like Inkpaduta, who considered the lakes his personal domain. For wherever the white men set their plows and built their cabins, the game disappeared, making it harder for the Indians to find food. Reservation Indians also resented the movement of settlers onto their hereditary lands, especially considering the miserly and dishonest manner in which annuities were distributed under the treaties. As an aggrieved Indian, Inkpaduta was certainly entitled to those sentiments. As an outcast among his own people, seething with a desire for revenge, he was doubly resentful and extremely dangerous.

As his band worked its way north, they harassed settlers, wrecked cabins and killed or stole livestock. They had yet to kill any people. But that was soon to change. As they got closer to the lakes, game was more plentiful and spring was approaching. The Indians were able to eat. When they reached the lakes on March 7, 1857, they celebrated with a war dance near the cabin of Rowland

Gardner, located along the south edge of West Lake Okoboji. The Gardner family was part of a settlement of about 40 people who arrived at the lakes the year before.

At first, the Gardners seemed unconcerned with the appearance of the Indians. Either the Gardners were unable to recognize Inkpaduta, or they were unfamiliar with his reputation. In any case, the Indians were seemingly ignored, and no one seemed at all curious or cautious about the war dance. Like many white Iowans, the Gardners probably felt that because of the treaties, the threat of an Indian attack was very minimal, for the Indian menace had been displaced to the distant plains.

If so, they were very wrong. The next day, the Gardners were suddenly attacked and the entire family killed except for fifteen-year-old Abigail "Abbie" Gardner, who was taken captive. Then the Indians moved on to other cabins, killing settlers randomly and indiscriminately. The first day's killing netted 20 victims. They were able to move freely and leisurely, among the scattered home sites, isolated and far from any protection. Isolation had its scenic side but more importantly, perhaps, a very dangerous feature. Living near the peaceful, wooded lakes, the settlers were romanced into a dangerous level of comfort. They were at home with this strange mix of peace and peril, and it was the perilous aspect that rose with the dawn on March 8, 1857.

On March 9th, the band continued its bloodletting, killing more settlers and taking two additional captives, Mrs. Alvin Nobles and Mrs. Joseph Thatcher. The killing spree was concluded on March 13th, at Spirit Lake, when the cabin of William Marble was attacked. He was killed and his wife Margaret Ann was taken prisoner. A thousand dollars in gold that Marble had belted to him was also stolen. Through reconnaissance, stealth and deception in seemingly well planned attacks, a total of 32 people were killed at the lakes by Inkpaduta's band.[15]

This was the terrible "Spirit Lake Massacre." In its time it was burned into the memory of Iowans, Minnesotans and Dakotans. It is known to this day as one of the seminal tragedies in frontier history. It became the historic yardstick by which other tragic and horrible events of the Northwest were measured.

Knowing that word of the slaughter would reach other settlements in time, the Indians left the area with their grieving and suffering prisoners in tow. For the rest of her life, Abbie Gardner lived with the memory of the mangled bodies of her family, and the sight of her mother's bloody scalp dangling from a warrior's belt.[16]

They traveled at a casual pace, heading northwest. At Lake Heron in Minnesota Territory, about 30 miles from Spirit Lake, they stopped and prepared for an attack on the settlement of Springfield (now Jackson, Minnesota), fifteen miles from Lake Heron.

Meanwhile, news of the Spirit Lake massacre reached authorities in Minnesota and Iowa. Charles E. Flandrau, agent of the Santee Sioux, was informed of the incident. He was familiar with Inkpaduta and his reputation. Flandrau immediately set out for Fort Ridgely on the Minnesota River, to organize a relief expedition. Within a short time, Captain Bernard E. Bee was placed in charge of 48 men assigned to find and punish the perpetrators, and lend aid to their victims. Joseph La Framboise, a mixed blood interpreter, Flandrau, and his personal interpreter, Philander Prescott, went along. Both La Framboise and Prescott were seasoned frontiersmen.

The rescue party endured great hardships as they trudged slowly through deep snow, hauling cumbersome loads, at a pace far too slow to catch the Indians. As such, they were helpless to stop the attack on Springfield. Flandrau later admitted he was infuriated at the army's lame effort. He complained they were "equipped in about the same manner as they would have been in campaigning in Florida, their only transportation being heavy wheeled army wagons, drawn by six mules."[17] Springfield would have to fend for itself.

Fortunately, Springfield had also learned of the massacre at the lakes and had time to prepare for a fight. Although there were several casualties, the citizens held off the attack and the Indians left without destroying the entire settlement. But the damage was severe, and by the time Bee's party reached Springfield, all they could do was aid the suffering.

News of the Spirit Lake massacre, compounded by the attack on Springfield, caused near panic in southern Minnesota Territory. While settlers were preparing to unite and fight or leave the territory, a report of the excitement circulated in St. Paul and set off another round of fright. While there was no danger to the capital, a large group met at the courthouse, formed committees and laid out plans for self-defense. Not everyone, however, was ready to form ranks and fight, and one of St. Paul's newspapers—the *Daily Minnesotian*—scoffed at those who attributed so much power to a relatively small band of outcast Indians.[18]

Inkpaduta's party continued their flight after the setback at Springfield. From March 26th to April 10th, they were constantly on the move. At one point, they saw the soldiers approaching and concealed themselves for an attack. Fortunately for all concerned, the soldiers failed to see the Indians and didn't get close enough for a fight. Inkpaduta then turned his band west, in all haste, toward the Big Sioux River, while the soldiers returned to Fort Ridgely. The close encounter was cause for alarm and the fugitives traveled non-stop for two days and nights.[19]

The forced march was especially hard on the women captives. They had to carry heavy burdens and trudge through slush and snow. They were subjected to mistreatment by their captors. Food ran short and they, along with their captors, had to eat skunk and muskrat, sometimes uncooked. Sometimes the captives had nothing to eat but duck feathers, singed by the campfire. Many of the horses, stolen at Okoboji and Springfield, were not fed so they starved to death. This was lucky for the hostages, however, as they at least had horseflesh to eat. Finally, after a two-week march, the fleeing party reached the pipestone quarries. Here they tarried for a day, making pipes, before resuming their westward journey. After leaving the quarries, the Indians slowed their pace. Apparently feeling more secure, they camped and rested to suit themselves.

Finally, they reached the Big Sioux River and prepared to cross. There was a natural crossing on the river where the town site of Flandrau was to be laid out only a few months later. The crossing had been used for generations by the Indians on their pilgrimages to the pipestone quarries. At this point, the river was normally wide and shallow. But it was now springtime and the water was high due to melting snow. The Big Sioux River was a flood stage and dangerous to all who dared attempt to cross it.

Mrs. Thatcher had suffered more than the other women. She had phlebitis that developed into blood poisoning, and as such, it was with great difficulty that she kept up with the others. When she approached the ford on the swollen Big Sioux River, she sensed her life was about to end, and made this known to the others.

At first Mrs. Thatcher was permitted to make the crossing—on fallen trees—without her pack. Then as she was making her way across the tree-bridge, an Indian tripped her, causing her to fall into the raging river. Despite the current and her weakened condition, Mrs. Thatcher managed to make it to the bank. Then, as she struggled to pull herself out, she was shot and killed. Her body sunk beneath the icy, turbulent waters and was lost to all but the elements. After she died, the Indians claimed the river was haunted by the "spirit of the white woman in the water."[20]

Abbie Gardner was struck by the natural beauty of the area, and the terrible irony of the experience was not lost on the teenager. The winding river lined with maple, elm and oak, the lofty summits, the rich, rolling prairie, seemed to her a picture of natural perfection. "Had we been in a mood to appreciate it, we surely should have enjoyed this beautiful picture."[21] That she was able to extract some sense of beauty from the horrible circumstances is truly amazing and is testimony to her exceptional will and strong character. As she crossed the Big Sioux River that day, Abbie's terrible suffering was at least mitigated by some pleasant thoughts.

The rest of the party made it safely across and went into camp for a short time, before continuing westward. The loss of Mrs. Thatcher was borne by the surviving captives with great sorrow, for they saw in her death the fate that they believed awaited them too. Still there was some relief in that her terrible suffering was over. Burdened with these mixed feelings, they painfully made their way across the prairie, hoping against fading hope, for rescue.

As the group traveled westward, they met other bands of Indians that greeted Inkpaduta in friendship. This suggests that the band frequented the region and was on good terms with other Indians. These Indians were probably Yanktons or Yanktonais.

On May 5, 1857, the band reached Skunk Lake, or what the Indians called M'da Chan-Pta-Ya Tonka, meaning "Lake with a Grove of Trees." According to Teakle, this was Lake Madison in Lake County, South Dakota.[22] Others, including Abbie Gardner, said Skunk Lake was actually Lake Herman located quite close to Lake Madison.[23]

Skunk Lake was at the edge of the great buffalo range and game was plentiful. It was one of Inkpaduta's favorite campsites. Doubtless the Indians felt some relief as they set up their lodges by the lake. It was spring and they had evaded capture and were beyond the reach of winter. Here they could hunt, eat and rest; here they were a safe distance from the soldiers at Fort Ridgely. They stayed there for five days, just long enough for a rescue party to find them.

Unknown to Inkpaduta and his men, a plan to rescue the hostages had been underway for some time, led by Charles E. Flandrau, under the direction of Minnesota Territory Governor Samuel A. Medary. It was decided almost immediately against sending troops, or for that matter, any white men, after them. Flandrau was certain that any "hostile demonstration" would result in the deaths of the white women. It would be better, he thought, to send two or more scouts in the direction of the Big Sioux and James Rivers, to locate the band and ascertain Inkpaduta's intentions as to the hostages, and then send a rescue expedition.[24] While engaged in formulating such a plan, two Indians, whom Flandrau referred to as "my Indians," brought in Mrs. Marble, one of the captives. She was presented to Flandrau and informed him that two others were alive, when last seen.[25]

Margaret Ann Marble's rescue was fortuitous. The two Indians referred to by Flandrau were brothers named Sounding Heavens and Gray Foot. They were Christianized Sioux and lived at the Yellow Medicine Agency in Minnesota. They were out hunting near Skunk Lake when by chance they came across one of Inkpaduta's hunters. From this man they learned that Inkpaduta was holding some white women prisoners. Feeling sorry for the women, they felt an attempt must be made to free them, even if this meant haggling with the domineering Inkpaduta.

After a trip of about 30 miles to the west, they came upon "Red End's" camp near a lake. Before they reached the lodges, they were confronted by armed men who questioned them, and having found their explanation to be acceptable, the two men were allowed to see Inkapduta. The first night was spent listening to tales of the massacre and the next morning Sounding Heavens and Gray Foot proposed to buy one of the hostages.[26]

Inkpaduta proved to be a shrewd negotiator. Finally, after many hours of determined bargaining, he allowed them to take one of the prisoners to show some good faith. Gray Foot, whose Sioux name was Si Ha Hota, said that Inkpaduta was finally persuaded to give them one captive after they told him that the powerful white authorities would make all Indians suffer, should they not bring back at least one of the women. Convinced, Inkpaduta said take one woman or none at all.[27] Believing they cut the best bargain under

Charles E. Flandrau
(Collections of the Minnesota Historical Society)

the circumstances, they did not hesitate.

The Christian Indians selected Mrs. Noble, but distrusting them, she reacted angrily. Rejected, they then chose Margaret Ann Marble who went willingly.[28] They obtained Mrs. Marble's freedom in exchange for one gun, some blankets, a keg of powder, and some trinkets. It was a risky venture for them, as Inkpaduta was suspicious because they were converts to the white man's religion.[29]

The shrewd "Christianized" rescuers demanded $500.00 each for their efforts. They insisted that they receive cash, not $500.00 in horses, or guns or ammunition, but cash. While Flandrau thought the sum was rather large, he nevertheless paid it, thinking generosity on the part of the government would encourage further cooperation among friendly Indians.[30] In 1860 Si Ha Hota was given a special written commendation by the Superintendent of Indians Affairs, for his work in rescuing Mrs. Marble.

Margaret Ann Marble had survived nearly three months as a tormented and humiliated captive, much of it on the harsh, wintry prairie. After a journey of 15 days in the custody of her rescuers, she arrived at Lac Qui Parle and then was turned over to missionaries Stephen R. Riggs and Dr. John Williamson at Yellow Medicine, where she was met by Flandrau. After a brief stay she arrived safely in St. Paul on May 30, 1857.

It was at this time that the Dakota Land Company of St. Paul launched its town site expedition into the Big Sioux Valley, an area Margaret Marble came to know all too well. It is almost certain that the speculators were aware of Inkpaduta's bloody work in Iowa, and that he had retreated toward the Big Sioux River. But as we have seen in Chapter II, they went merrily on their way west, armed with some sweet sense of purpose.

The Nobles' South Pass wagon road crew was bound for the far frontier too. Governor Medary—understanding the urgency and perhaps feeling some pressure from the public—called on Superintendent W. H. Nobles to "use such means as are in your power to rescue the two remaining captive white women...." Medary knew that Nobles' expedition was headed directly into "the Indian country" and would be in a position to find Inkpaduta's place of retreat. He appealed to Nobles' sense of humanity, stressing the need to free the frontier of murderers and outlaws for the benefit of all. The governor confessed that the territorial treasury lacked the money to fund a full-scale effort to both rescue the remaining captives and punish the Inkpaduta band.[31]

Flandrau, a member of the Dakota Land Company like Nobles and Medary, threw his energies and influence into the game. He knew there were still two women to rescue, as Margaret Marble had told him of the death of Mrs. Thatcher and the probable location of Inkpaduta. Flandrau chose three other Christian Sioux to attempt a rescue of the remaining two. Those selected were Paul Mazakutamani, John Other Day and Che-tan-maza, or Iron Hawk, all of whom Flandrau trusted.

Mazakutamani, also spelled "Mazakootemani," was highly regarded by the whites as he had converted to "civilized" ways to an extent that far exceeded most Indians. He had great leadership and diplomatic skills, thought to be wholly inconsistent with a wild race. Having converted to Christianity in 1841, it was said that he was "... born an Indian and died a white man."[32]

Flandrau "charged his men positively to let no obstacle discourage them, or no difficulty turn them back; to exercise their best judgment in negotiating for the prisoners, but to give everything they had rather than fail."[33] They gave their promise to Flandrau and agreed to find Inkpaduta and negotiate for the release of the women. They were given $889.12 worth of goods for bargaining purposes that Flandrau purchased on credit. The Minnesota territorial legislature, in special session, appropriated $10,000.00 for the rescue effort, so Flandrau had a sizeable purse to work with and could expect to be reimbursed for his own expenses. And on May 23, 1857, the three Indians went west in search of Inkpaduta's camp and to earn their share of the appropriation. It was a dangerous mission.[34]

Having implemented his rescue plan, Flandrau hurried to Fort Ridgely and discussed a punitive raid against Inkpaduta with Colonel Alexander, the commanding officer. This offensive was to be launched as soon as the other women were rescued. It would have given Flandrau and his fellow Minnesotans great pleasure to annihilate Inkpaduta and his people. The plans were abandoned, however, when the soldiers were ordered to Utah to deal with rebellious Mormons.[35] Dakota was spared what might have been a bloody battle, for Inkpaduta was not alone.

Inkpaduta broke camp after Margaret Marble was released. He and his band headed northwest to the James River Valley. After traveling about two weeks, they encountered a party of Yankton Sioux under the leadership of a one-legged chief named End of the Snake. After a short visit, End of the Snake purchased Abbie Gardner and Mrs. Noble from Inkpaduta, intending to re-sell them at a later time at one of the Missouri River forts. Both bands of Indians continued north to the "Earth Lodges."[36]

One night while in camp on the eastside of the James River, Mrs. Noble was pounded to death by Inkpaduta's son, Roaring Cloud, because she refused to vacate the tent where she and Abbie were to spend the night. Now the youthful Abbie was truly alone, fearing she would eventually meet the same fate. Leaving the body of her friend behind, she was taken by the Indians further into buffalo country, recalling later that she saw immense herds of the beasts roaming across a vast, treeless prairie.

Two days after the killing of Mrs. Noble, the Indians crossed the James River not far from the location of the future town of Ashton. Here they joined an encampment of about 190 lodges of Yankton Sioux. Abbie didn't know it but rescue was at hand. For the three Christianized Indians rode into the camp, dressed in white man's clothes and ready to bargain for Abbie's release. They had followed Inkpaduta's trail all the way from Lake Madison.[37] On the way, they discovered and buried the body of Mrs. Nobles after wrapping her in a blanket.

Flandrau's men found Inkpaduta's people in the company of a large party of Yanktons, encamped on the west side of the James River, where it was joined by Snake Creek.[38] On May 30, 1857, after five days of tough negotiating, Abbie was "purchased for two horses, 12 blankets, two kegs of powder, 20 pounds of tobacco, 32 yards of blue squaw cloth, 37 and 1/2 yards of calico and ribbon, and other small articles."[39] She was sent away with her purchasers in a wagon piled high with buffalo skins and meat.

After a long but safe and relatively comfortable journey, Abbie Gardner arrived at the Yellow Medicine Agency on June 10, 1857.[40] From there she was taken by steamer to St. Paul, where her arrival at the wharf was cheered by a crowd of curious well-wishers. The sense of relief must have been incredible. While she was still a captive, a story was floated about that Abbie had been stood up on the side of a hill and used for target practice by her captors. It was said that she was shot in both legs and left to die.[41]

Happily for all, the story was a canard. Two out of the four captured women were rescued, an improbable feat under the circumstances. It was believed that Mrs. Nobles might have been saved had she made it as far as the Yankton encampment. They were within a day's trek from it when she was suddenly killed.[42]

While Abbie was still on the frontier, Margaret Ann Marble was given a fine reception at the Fuller House in St. Paul. Governor Medary was in attendance, along with other dignitaries and the members of the public who came to honor her for her amazing strength, and for surviving against such great odds. She stayed at the Fuller house for some time in a destitute condition, with no friends or relatives to help her. A $1000.00 sum was raised for her by sympathetic folk. Governor Medary gave her $150 cash and put the rest in a bank account.

Margaret Ann Marble went on to Washington, D. C., and visited the Commissioner of Indian Affairs. She described her terrible suffering at the hands of Inkpaduta and asked the government to indemnify her for her losses on the frontier caused by the Indian invasion of the Spirit Lake settlements.[43] She could have used the help because the money she received from sympathetic Minnesotans was lost when the bank failed following the financial Panic of 1857.[44] And yet one wonders if she ever really missed it considering the magnitude of her loss while a captive in the wilderness. She eventually moved to California.

Abbie was also given the star treatment at the Fuller House, in the company of Governor Medary, Agent Flandrau and a number of other men and women. The gallant, young heroine—her skin burned brown from her wilderness adventure—was toasted and praised for her perseverance and courage. The men who rescued Abbie spoke about their experience, telling those in attendance that they were acting at the direction of Flandrau, whom they addressed as "Our Father." Flandrau followed with some kind, fatherly words, lauding the Indians for having done their duty. Concluding, he said, "Your Father [meaning himself, of course] will start immediately on a journey to Washington where he will see your Great Father [meaning the president] and be enabled to explain your part in these matters personally to him."

Then a solemn Governor Medary addressed the Indians, saying: "My Red Children, I am happy to meet you here, because you have been performing a worthy and humane act. You have brought us back this young white girl who was taken by those whose conduct you disapproved of." He went on to thank them for their bravery and unselfishness and closed by stating it was his wish that this occasion could help create an atmosphere of peace and understanding between the races.[45]

Both Medary and Flandrau took pains to point out that there were "good Indians" and "bad Indians"—the former consisting of those who assisted their fatherly figures. In an overbearing display of paternalism, both white men treated the Indian rescuers as if they were, in fact, children, incapable of independent judgment and naturally dependent upon their "fathers" for guidance and supervision. To read the newspaper articles on this event is to see two condescending white men, stiffly and pretentiously lecturing to red men as if they were mere artless beginners, looking up in awe from the bottom rung of the cultural ladder.

According to Stephen R. Riggs, however, the efforts of the rescuing party, under the leadership of Paul Mazakutamani, was nothing less than heroic and brilliant. In a letter to the *Minnesota Free Press,* Riggs pointed out that the mission was very dangerous and its success depended upon timing and careful, skillful negotiating, made even more difficult by a "message which preceded them from an Indian on the Coteau." This message advised the Yanktons to take a hard line in the bargaining because "capital might be made of Miss Gardner."[46] It seems the message served its intended purpose.

Unconcerned over the cost of her rescue, Abbie Gardner made no speech at the affair—not even to thank her rescuers; she was basking in the wonderful realization that she had survived and was now safe. That she survived at all was considered a miracle by those present, and was a testament to her great courage and inner strength. Whatever rewards she would gain in the future, she earned many times over in the recent past. Just as they did when Margaret Marble was honored, the public came to see a miracle in the flesh, a newly minted celebrity. Abbie, like Margaret, embodied everything that was special about pioneers. Set to wandering on foot, in the dead of winter, grief-stricken, under-fed, ill treated and poorly clothed, they overcame all these terrible deprivations and emerged with their dignity and sanity intact. It was an example even the hardest man could appreciate. It was teary-eyed living proof of the righteousness of their cause backed by their religious faith; it was evidence of their success, as pioneers, against overwhelming odds.

The outpouring of public support for Abbie, still a girl, was warm, sincere and wonderful. The governor was even willing to adopt her into his family in the event she was unable to locate her kin. But Abbie was ready to move on, and after sitting for an ambrotype picture, she left St. Paul. Medary escorted her to Dubuque, Iowa, where she found her sister and in a sweet, tearful reunion, both were swept away by an emotional tidal wave that most certainly surpassed anyone's ability to understand.[47] She also had relatives in Steuben County, New York, where she was expected to go.[48]

While she may have sought privacy, Abbie Gardner—America's new heroine—was not soon forgotten. Before the year 1857 was over, a 48-page booklet (that misspelled her last name, Gardiner) about her terrible ordeal on the wild, Indian-infested frontier, was published and on sale for 25 cents a copy. A portion of the proceeds was to be given to Abby for her education.[49]

With two out of four hostages safe within the bounds of civilization, there remained the matter of punishing the villains who were still at large, presumably in Dakota. Medary pumped up public spirit by pledging to rid the Northwest of Inkpaduta. He organized the St. Paul Light Cavalry, appointed officers and issued orders to be prepared to "protect the frontier from the Indians, should hostilities ensue."[50] Medary was no doubt pleased when word came back to the settlements that Flandrau's party of Indians had killed Inkpaduta's son, Roaring Cloud, near the Yellow Medicine Agency.[51]

While Flandrau was pleased with this too, he was very upset over the U. S. Army's lack of interest in pursuing Inkpaduta. Still he and others would not let the matter fade. And if soldiers couldn't be persuaded to go out onto the distant frontier on a worthy mission, other means would have to be obtained. A scheme was formulated to get agency Indians to do the dirty work.

In June of 1857, about 6000 "annuity" Indians gathered at the Upper and Lower Agencies in Minnesota to receive their goods and money. Among those gathered were a large number of Yanktons and Yanktonais. Payments under the Treaty of Traverse de Sioux were ordinarily paid in June. Only this time the Indians were disappointed.

They were addressed by William J. Cullen, Superintendent of Indian Affairs, at the Upper Agency. Another "father figure," Cullen told them bluntly that they were responsible for the crimes of Inkpaduta, "for the lawless characters of their nation...." Therefore unless some of their warriors embarked on an expedition to punish Inkpaduta, no annuities would be paid. Hunt him down and you will get your due, or stay home and stay hungry.

Angry Indians went into council and returned with an answer: no, they would not do as the superintendent demanded—unless U. S. troops accompanied them. It was a rather bold ploy, probably intended to force Cullen to reveal exactly what was expected of them. The reply was immediate and unequivocal: no troops were available; the Indians would have to go by themselves.[52]

A stalemate was at hand, and much of Minnesota waited uneasily. The Indians were upset and threats were made. Whites became alarmed, fearing an attack on the settlements. Some even departed for eastern safe zones. Then Little Crow, chief of the Mdewakantons, came forward and agreed to lead an expedition into Dakota to find and punish Inkpaduta.[53] Cullen was pleased as Little Crow's influence and popularity among the eastern Sioux had grown considerably in recent months. Little Crow said he would do it in order that his hungry people at the agency received food.

An Iowa newspaper suggested that food was at the heart of the matter. Superintendent Cullen insisted that Inkpaduta had requested and received annuities for eleven people in the fall of 1856. This is why Cullen was so adamant in his demand that the Santee leaders select a delegation to go out and bring the outlaw back—dead or alive. For despite his reputation for independence and ferocity, Inkpaduta was an "annuity Indian" and it was up to other "annuity Indians" to go after him to earn more annuities.[54]

The awful events at the Iowa lakes made news back east, as one would expect, but with much less impact. One eastern newspaper, the *Evening Star* from Washington D.C., was convinced that reports of the tragedy were greatly exaggerated and made for the purpose of enhancing town site speculators' plans of personal enrichment. Looking at dispatches sent to Washington by Flandrau, the *Evening Star* saw in them, "tricks and connivance" by speculators who were spreading horror stories in order to keep competitors out of the region they sought to dominate.[55]

For people on the frontier—both red and white—the matter was one of seriousness if not desperation. And on July 22, 1857, a group of 106 Indians, led by Chief Little Crow, four "half-breeds" and interpreter A. J. Campbell, set out from Yellow Medicine Agency to find and punish Inkpaduta. On the 27th, they reached the "Crooked (Big Sioux) River" and the next day, they arrived at Skunk Lake. There they found six lodges of Inkpaduta's band—but no one in camp. Their quarry was tracked for about twenty miles, and as darkness fell, Little Crow's men spotted their targets and opened fire. In a short time, however, it was too dark to shoot with any accuracy.

The light of morning revealed that they had killed three men and wounded another. Two of the dead were Inkpaduta's grandsons. Inkpaduta, himself, was nowhere to be seen—dead or alive.[56] The escape artist had escaped again.

Little Crow's Indians returned to the agency and made their report. They decided against pursuit after learning Inkpaduta and his followers had joined a party of Yanktons at Snake Creek. There were too many, according to Little Crow, and the risks were too high. They brought back three prisoners—two women and a boy, not the kind of finish Superintendent Cullen was expecting.[57]

Cullen was very dissatisfied but the matter ended. The Indian volunteers gave it their best effort, and the army showed no inclination to mount a serious pursuit of the elusive Inkpaduta. The respite gave him time and opportunity to simply disappear, which he did, remaining in seclusion for about five years. It was believed he went far to the west of the Missouri River.

As could be expected, the Minnesota press followed the Inkpaduta matter very carefully and with great interest. After the return of Campbell and Little Crow, it was reported that a party of 33 Sissetons were on the trail of Inkpaduta, vowing to bring him in. This was viewed with considerable skepticism. The press and the white people were growing impatient.

Then came the report that the Sissetons had wiped out Inkpaduta's entire band, with the exception of one man. This of course, proved to be false. The terrible Inkpaduta was still out there—alive.[58] Anxious and fearful white folks looked for someone to blame.

The army was given a good roasting for its disinterest and ineptitude. In September it was learned that about 100 infantrymen were scheduled to "finish up the Ink-pa-du-ta business." Fine idea, said a writer for the *Pioneer and Democrat*, but he raked the officer in charge for looking in all the wrong places. In a pointed article, he insisted that to anyone "familiar with the haunts of our celebrated subject, it will appear clear that the troops could not have selected a *better* route to avoid a meeting with the gentleman."[59] Once again people felt the U. S. Army let them down.

The press got some satisfaction from one of the Indian women taken prisoner by Little Crow, who spoke to authorities through Campbell. From her it was learned that when Inkpaduta's band was attacked at "Big Driftwood Lake," they panicked and several dashed into the water. In an attempt to escape, a number of women and children were drowned. She also revealed the names of those in Inkpaduta's group, explaining that the raid reduced it to about nine people.[60]

This was good news to the Minnesotans, and the press issued praise accordingly. People were relieved to learn that the once mighty Inkpaduta was reduced in power, and on the run like a beaten dog. Cullen was commended for sending Indians out to punish other Indians. This accomplishment was seen as a major turning point in the white man's struggle to subdue and destroy Indian culture. It would have a "most happy effect upon the Sioux, and meets with decided approval upon the frontier." If a "portion of the Sioux nation has consented to act as agents of the government, in the destruction of their own brethren," then the "idea entertained by the Indians, of their own invincibility" is destroyed.[61] The *Pioneer and Democrat* advised everyone to breathe a little easier. While the main culprit remained at large, he was greatly weakened, and the white man had gained a moral victory.

But the notorious Inkpaduta was soon heard from again, this time in connection with a report that five hundred soldiers were slaughtered on the plains by Teton Sioux. This shocking news made its way to the border cities by way of a young Sisseton from Big Stone Lake. In the fall of 1857, the young man happened to be encamped on the Missouri River with a party of Yanktons, and had the occasion to sit next to Inkpaduta at a feast. There he was told of the terrible slaughter of white soldiers, "Long Knives," who were surrounded and killed in the night while they were preparing to bed down at their camp near the Missouri River.[62] While the story turned out to be unproven hearsay, it adds to the Inkpaduta legend. Who would not expect his name to be connected to such a large and tragic event?

In 1861, rumors were afloat that Inkpaduta was back in Iowa, leading a group of "prowling" Indians, getting too close to settlements, including those at Spirit Lake.[63] And in 1862, when the War of the Outbreak swept across Minnesota, and into Dakota, Inkpaduta was in the thick of it. It was said that he teamed up with his erstwhile enemy, Little Crow, and was a strategist and leader in attacks on white settlements. It was even believed, but not proven, that Little Crow sought out Inkpaduta's help in the war.[64] It was in war that Inkpaduta found allies and earned respect from other Sioux for his leadership and courage under fire.

Once again the authorities were after him. On July 27, 1862, it was learned that Inkpaduta was camped on the Yellow Medicine River in Minnesota. Lt. T. J. Sheehan was ordered to take 10 or 12 men, and with utmost secrecy, apprehend the Indian outlaw, or kill him if necessary.

These plans went awry, however, as sympathetic Indians learned of the expedition and warned Inkpaduta, sending him "flying toward the western wilds."[65] Once again the wily warrior escaped, finding refuge on the Plains, a region whose harshness was a perfect match for Inkpaduta and more than a match for most other men.

The remarkable Inkpaduta was seemingly everywhere, with far ranging murders blamed on him or on others acting under his direction. It was said that other Indians blamed their killings on Inkpaduta to avoid retribution.[66] Dakota historian Doane Robinson wrote that Inkpaduta was "everywhere from the Canadian line and the Bad Lands down to Nebraska and central Minnesota...."

In November of 1862, Inkpaduta was in possession of the burned out town of Sioux Falls, along with "about 40 braves, stragglers who had gathered about his forlorn standard."[67] (The destruction of Sioux Falls is explained in detail in Chapter XIII.) In May of 1863, he murdered a man near New Ulm, Minnesota. And two weeks later he, or his men, killed a man at the ferry on the James River in Dakota.

Inkpaduta got blamed for massacring the children of Hansen Wiseman, whose cabin was on the Nebraska side of the Missouri River, across from Yankton.[68] He engaged General H. H. Sibley in battle at Stony Lake, Dead Buffalo, and Big Mound in northern Dakota.[69] But these incidents occurred in late July of 1863, and not even the powerful and ubiquitous Inkpaduta was capable of being in two places at the same time.

After he fought against General Alfred Sully in the battle of Whitestone Hill, near present day Oakes, North Dakota, he retreated to the northern Dakota Bad Lands and continued to battle Sully at Killdeer Mountain. Once again the aging warrior survived. He was an old man and stone blind when, on June 25, 1876, he was in charge of a division of Sioux at the battle of Little Big Horn.[70] By this time he was leading by sheer force of personality and with a reputation earned by a life of violence and success against the white man. He must have been quite a sight at Little Big Horn, amid the gunfire and chaos, assisted by his twin grandsons. Of course, he survived to share in the greatest Indian victory in their long struggle against the white man.

Inkpaduta was with Sitting Bull when that great Indian leader took his followers into Canada, after the battle at Little Big Horn. He died there and appropriately, perhaps, the date of his death is an unsettled question. Most likely he died between 1879 and 1882.

Throughout his life, he fought against the white man, resisting civilization by brute force, as if denying its very existence. As if bearing some awful curse and with nowhere to turn to for comfort and peace, his life was one of constant conflict with his enemies, always on the move, in a struggle for survival. In a lifetime of violence and warfare, he showed no mercy or tolerance for he understood neither. He practiced compromise only when it was absolutely necessary to do so.

The charismatic Sitting Bull broke down and surrendered and became a pitiful caricature of his former self by appearing as a tame, clownish Indian in Buffalo Bill's Wild West Show. Americans enjoyed seeing wild beasts perform after they were de-clawed. The bold and defiant Crazy Horse gave up and was murdered while in custody. Both were beaten and starving when they reached for the sky to surrender; both became reluctant, unforgettable celebrities. Not so, however, for the mysterious and far less famous Inkpaduta. Of the many great Sioux chiefs who struggled so valiantly to keep

Indian land and save Indian culture, he remained free and at large until the very end of his life, a proud, wild man to the last. And it should surprise no one to learn that he died totally unreconciled with his enemies.

Chapter VIII

Trouble at the Town Sites

"The settlers, for several miles each way, were warned of the danger, and they fled...leaving nearly everything behind to be plundered and burnt by the Indians."

On the burning of Medary,
St. Paul Pioneer and Democrat,
June 24, 1858

Eighteen fifty-eight dawned brightly over the scattered Dakota town sites. Although the settlers had but a weak hold on the land they claimed, there was sufficient tenacity and cooperation among them so that the towns were never abandoned. When news reached the outlying areas that several Yankton Sioux chiefs were on their way to Washington to talk treaty with the "Great Father," hopes soared. In those days the world was so big and man was so puny, and yet the possibilities seemed endless. To have an additional 12,000,000-plus acres available for speculation must have pumped up even those whose sense of adventure had long since been drained away by the cruel demands of nature.

Winter cut off much of the contact between Sioux Falls City and the newspapers of St. Paul, Dubuque and Sioux City. It was as if nature put up an impenetrable barrier, making communication and traffic impractical or dangerous. Town site officials situated in the relative comfort of St. Paul and Dubuque could only wait and wonder about their investments and their fellow speculators somewhere out in the wilderness, bearing the awful brunt of a cold winter. But isolation and boredom breed discontent among men who are accustomed to action, and on occasion, parties from Sioux Falls inevitably set out for parts known and unknown, braving the elements as only pioneers could do.

As a result one bit of news reached Sioux City in February—coal had been discovered at Sioux Falls, and a specimen brought in to the office of the *Sioux City Eagle*. It was examined approvingly and pronounced a "good article of coal."[1] Operations were expected to commence without undue delay, to determine whether coal mining would be profitable. To people unaccustomed to frontier hardships, a find such as this had to be uplifting. At least they would have something to burn to keep warm.

If there was a coal deposit at the Falls, investment capital might be encouraged to move in and develop it, thus giving the village a better chance at survival. That was good news. On the frontier, however, newspapermen were all too often explaining and rationalizing misfortune and tragedy. For several months, the towns on the Big Sioux River—although always in a precarious condition—had escaped the imposition of tragedy. But that all ended when W. W. Brookings came rushing into Sioux Falls City one morning in early February, exhausted and near death due to exposure to the cold. The colony was forced to deal with its first real emergency.

It all started when Brookings, who was managing the affairs of the Western Town Company, left Sioux Falls City on horseback one February morning along with Smith Kinsey. It was an ill-timed move, for Brookings could have easily frozen to death on the prairie or died at the town site. As it was it left him disabled for the rest of his life.

News of the tragedy first came to light on April 24, 1858, when the *Eagle* staff learned of Brookings' plight by way of a messenger from Sioux Falls. The *Eagle* then reported that Brookings, "well known to the most of our citizens, was in a very critical and deplorable condition, having frozen his feet while attempting to visit Sioux City, in February last." According to the *Eagle's* source, Brookings and Kinsey left Sioux Falls in the early part of February, and upon reaching the Rock River, found the "stream so swollen that they were unable to cross and Mr. K being taken sick, they resolved to return to Sioux Falls, a distance of about fifty miles."

When they got to within about fifteen miles of Sioux Falls (near the town site of Eminija), they tried to cross the Big Sioux River and take a shortcut to town. Night was falling, it was extremely cold, and Brookings fell off his horse into about four feet of icy water. Once ashore, they tried to kindle a fire but were unable, and as he was facing death by freezing, Brookings decided to make a run for Sioux Falls. But first he "fixed his sick companion as comfortably as possible to pass the night on the prairie, and started on foot for the Falls." One can only assume that their horses got away from them or were disabled.

Showing amazing stamina, fortitude, and a Herculean will to survive, Brookings raced toward Sioux Falls City, crossing the prairie hills, leaving painful and memorable footprints in the snow. He stumbled into the speculators' camp the next morning. To the utter shock of his friends, his feet were frozen so solidly that his boots had to be cut away to expose his lower limbs. His suffering was intense and it was readily apparent that his condition was critical. Brookings was made as comfortable as possible in his dirt floor cabin. A doctor from Sioux City was dispatched to render care. Kinsey returned to Sioux Falls the following day, having survived the frozen interlude without undue suffering.[2]

If there was the slightest hint of a silver lining in this sad incident, it came in the presence of Dr. Josiah L. Phillips, a friend and colleague of Brookings'. Phillips was also young and adventurous and was awarded his medical degree in 1857, from Chicago's Rush Medical College. Although he lacked the desired surgical tools, Dr. Phillips cut off both legs of his friend, about four inches above the knees.[3] It was done as a last resort to save his life. The amputation was performed with a large butcher knife and a small tenon saw while the patient lay on a bed of buffalo robes in his small cabin.[4] Afterwards Brookings was confined to his cabin for several months, during which time his friends feared he would die. They cared for him as best they could.

In one long, nightmarish experience, the life of a bright young man was changed drastically. Just three years before, he and his friend Phillips were students at Bowdoin College in Brunswick, Maine. Brookings, a Maine native from the Atlantic shore, graduated from Bowdoin College in 1855. Two years later he was admitted to the Maine bar, an accomplishment that would have satisfied most men. But he was a restless lad with some seafaring experience under his belt, and wanted more adventure. On June 29, 1857, he started for Dubuque where he planned to open up a law office. After a month's time he was a member of the Western Town Company, driving an ox team on his way west to the Falls of the Big Sioux River, to make his fortune. Had he done nothing more than pull through the winter of

1857-58, with his hardy companions, he would have been worthy of the title of "Cavalier of the Dakota Frontier."

Something rather cruel and strange emerges from Brookings' awful ordeal, because of inconsistencies in the record. A biographical sketch says that Brookings and his companion were on their way to the Yankton village on the Missouri River, hoping to stake a claim to that land in the name of the Western Town Company.[5] It was due to their misfortune, as related above, that their mission wasn't accomplished. If true, and had they reached their destination safely and secured a town site at the Yankton village, then Dakota politics may have unfolded with different wrinkles and scars.

Another biographical sketch printed in the Bowdoin College newspaper after Brookings' death tells a different story. After explaining that Brookings settled in Sioux Falls City, the article goes on to say that "during his first winter, there was an Indian uprising, and while on a 50-mile ride to warn another settlement, Mr. Brookings was lost in a blizzard; and while crossing a river his horse fell through the ice, wetting him to the skin."[6] While there was trouble with the tribes as will be explained later in this chapter, it would be wrong to characterize the events as an "Indian uprising." This version is simply incorrect.

In 1879 his fellow speculator, Byron M. Smith of the Dakota Land Company, said that Brookings was on his way to "jump" the site of Eminija, owned by the St. Paul company at juncture of the Big Sioux and Split Rock Rivers. While so engaged, he fell into a creek below the Falls, which was later named "Slip Up" because this was where Brookings "slipped up" in his plan.[7]

While it is likely that Brookings and Kinsey were on a town site

Wilmot W. Brookings
(Collections of the South Dakota State Archives)

mission for their company, Smith's assertion is ludicrous. A plan to stake out a town site at or near the Yankton village seems like something ambitious Sioux Falls men from both companies would conceive and attempt to carry out. But it is a stretch into the realm of wild imagination to conclude that Brookings wanted to "jump" Eminija. While it was nicely situated and well watered, there were many miles of riverfront land waiting to be claimed; Brookings didn't have to alienate his fellow speculators to get good land. Besides, it is clear from the record that the both the Western Town Company and Dakota Land Company treated each other with respect hoping that out of their joint effort, success aplenty awaited all.

It is possible, however, that Brookings and Kinsey left Sioux Falls in secret, hoping to get to the Missouri slope before it was reached by the Dakota Land Company. They, too, had their sights set on the Yankton village, believing that a treaty between the United States and the Yankton Sioux would soon be reached. It is likely the men of the Western Town Company had ambitions approaching those of their comrades from Minnesota.

Both town site companies persisted in the belief that if they stayed and built, others would join them. Their beliefs were given substance by news that the U. S. Senate passed the Homestead Act that would give 160 acres of land to the settler who lived on it and improved it. While some viewed this as a give-away, and a disaster to creditors, the land hungry saw it as timely deliverance during a depression. And while the House had yet to act in favor, the prevailing opinion held that it would do so.[8]

As such, immigration from the East was expected as a matter of course. While there was considerable land available in western Iowa and southwestern Minnesota, there were, inevitably, those who wanted to try their luck a "little bit further west." A mail carrier said that he saw "not less than 60 teams" on the road between Faribault and St. Peter, whose destination was Dacotah, the "new land of promise."[9]

And those folks who did travel a "little bit further," and decided to visit Sioux Falls City in the spring of 1858, were probably greeted with something approaching pure joy. One can easily imagine the sentinels on the hills as they scanned the eastern horizon for the sight of wagons. And seeing the slow moving caravans, they galloped into the campsite and told their friends to prepare to welcome new people. On the frontier loneliness impressed itself heavily upon the mind, like a glacier inching its way across a frozen landscape; but it could be shattered in an instant, like the thinnest glass, by the sudden appearance of unfamiliar faces.

Among those who arrived in Sioux Falls City the spring of 1858 was a man named Goodwin, his wife Rebecca and their hired man.[10] Shortly thereafter, Charles White, his wife and three-year-old daughter arrived. The little girl was said to have been the first white child in Sioux Falls City.[11] A visitor to town site, Frederick P. Leavenworth, a surveyor, noted in his diary in October of 1858 that it "snowed all day" and that he "saw Mr. and Mrs. White and Goodwin, the only two women in the Sioux Falls colony. Saw Henry Masters and William Little of the Dubuque and Dacota Land Companies."[12]

The population of Medary increased measurably too. Franklin J. DeWitt—who assumed control of the town site for the Dakota Land Company—was joined by a group that included a carpenter, a bricklayer, a speculator and some settlers.[13] Mail service was another welcome improvement. A U. S. mail route was established from New

Ulm to Medary and from there, to Flandrau, Summit City, Sioux Falls City, Eminija and Sioux City, Iowa. Another line was extended from Medary to Fort Randall in Nebraska Territory.[14]

On March 30, 1858, the Dakota Land Company published a notice to all shareholders that their stock had been assessed $2.00 per share. All shareholders were advised they had six weeks to visit the Fuller House in St. Paul and pay, or forfeit their stock in accordance with the corporate charter.[15] In view of their success and the favorable outlook, it was the opportune time to bring in some additional capital. The company officials were feeling confident; they liked the look of spring upon their town sites and took advantage of fair weather to boast about their accomplishments and frontier assets.

The Medary people apparently came through their first winter at the town site in good shape. On March 12th, the settlers staged a two-mile ice skating race on the Big Sioux River. The winner was awarded $50.00.[16]

Come spring, immigrant trains on the Nobles government wagon road were arriving daily, and the new people settled in Medary or somewhere along the Big Sioux River, picking out the best sites. Several parties stopped at Medary, stored their provisions, and sent scouts as far west as the James River. Other groups of the land hungry were taking steamboats up the Missouri River as far as the mouth of the Big Sioux, where "there is a small class of steamers ply as high as Emanesia, (Eminija) a flourishing little town some 12 miles below the Falls...."

Sawmills were running "day and night, and yet not half the demand for lumber could be met." Those not building with logs were building houses of stone. Still others were living in tents, waiting for the availability of lumber so they could build houses. A correspondent of the *Pioneer and Democrat* said the scene at Medary, "at a distance of a tent-skirted town, reminds one of old camp-meeting times." Crops were in and seemed destined to outstrip those planted in central Minnesota. If we are to believe their reports, then indeed, prosperity was blooming like wildflowers on the prairie.

Wild game was everywhere and fish was easily taken from the river in great quantities, so folks had a variety of meat on their tables. Hunting buffalo had become quite a sport, as large numbers of the beasts had been driven east by Indian hunting parties. "Herds of these famous 'prairie rovers' are seen nearly every day, grazing on the opposite banks of the river from this site (Medary) and parties on the chase are as often seen." If we are to believe the reports and propaganda, then the new Dakotans were indeed, living off the fat of a generous land.

Buffalo were blackening the prairie further north too, in great numbers. Governor Medary, Vice President John C. Breckinridge and a Turkish admiral, along with other dignitaries were planning to hunt the beasts near the Red River of the North.[17] It was a great, blood-stirring sport, an excitement peculiar to the times, as the lumbering bovines were the largest mammals in North America.

When it was learned that Vice President Breckinridge and distinguished guests were coming west for a buffalo hunt, the fledgling town of Medary, Dakota, offered to accommodate the party, if they were "really desirous of having a buffalo hunt...." The emboldened town site entrepreneurs were ready to host them without the least fear of appearing uncivilized.[18] After all, some said Medary was destined to become the capital of a great new territory, and under such auspicious circumstances, could not fail to impress even a Vice President.

Sioux Falls City was making as much noise as its neighbor to the north. Crops were in a promising condition. Aside from the usual garden items, sorghum and tobacco were planted. W. W. Brookings was convalescing as comfortably as could be expected and was looking forward to resuming his duties as the manager of the Western Town Company. As he was near death, his recovery was considered nearly miraculous and his desire to stay on the frontier was viewed as inspiring. Guided by this shining example of inner strength and sense of purpose, his fellow citizens boomed their town site, causing the *Sioux City Eagle* to chime in with praise. No longer a skeptic, the editor opined: "we think the Falls is a good location and in a few years we doubt not, will see quite a large town there. Success to it."[19]

Then trouble started threatening the stability of the town sites. Although the Yankton Chiefs had signed a treaty in Washington, on April 19, 1858, relinquishing all but 400,000 acres of their land in Dakota, the agreement had not yet been ratified by Congress. As such, the whites had no right to enter Indian land west of the Big Sioux River. Also, a number of Yankton and Yanktonai people were upset with the treaty and unwilling to tolerate white trespassers under any circumstances.

These tribes were closely related although the Yanktonais were wilder and considered more "warlike." The Yanktonai Sioux roamed most of what is now northeastern South Dakota, a good buffalo range. Their primary village was located on the Elm River in what is now the northern portion of Brown County, South Dakota. They had a winter village called the "Dirt Lodges" in southern Brown County, where Mud Creek joined the James River, very close to the boundary with present day Spink County.

The Yanktonai Sioux watched with growing bitterness as whites gathered at the town sites along the Big Sioux River, or crossed the river on scouting or hunting forays further west. Finally, the disgruntled Indians would take no more and decided to drive the white people back into Iowa or Minnesota. Among the leaders of the dissenting element was Chief Smutty Bear of the Yankton Sioux, who, despite signing the treaty, wanted no part of its enforcement.

Medary, the pride of the Dakota Land Company, was their first and primary target. A large band of Yankton and Yanktonai Sioux, traveling in the direction of the Pipestone Quarries, rode into Medary on June 12, 1858. When they left the settlers were gone, the town was in flames and the corporate assets were laid to waste. Some weeks before, a delegation of Sioux had appeared and told the settlers to leave, but the warning was ignored.[20]

In fact, several days before the razing of the town site, Medary hosted visitors from Philadelphia. Samuel Fisher Corlies and two young friends, Evan Randolph and Daniel Neal, arrived by way of Hole-in-the-Mountain, having come west for the sake of adventure, to see the wild frontier and, of course, hunt buffalo. They arrived in Medary on May 21, 1858, and Corlies noted in his journal that the "house" was "fortified in expectation of being driven off by Yanktons in a short time." He further described the house as "bullet proof" and very "frontier" in appearance. Two days later the party of adventurers left Medary in a rainstorm, in the direction of Sioux Falls, happily exploring and hunting buffalo. Corlies' journal entries reveal no fear or anxiety on the part of him and his friends. They left

Medary not because of fear of Indians but rather to continue their high adventure.[21]

The assault on Medary did not, however, come without warning, which may have saved many lives. Rev. S. R. Riggs of Hazelwood, Minnesota, wrote a letter to the *Henderson Democrat* describing the movement of a large band of Yanktonai Sioux. These "wild" Indians, about 1200 lodges strong, with cannons taken from soldiers, were in the valley of the James River, moving toward Minnesota. It was rumored that Inkpaduta was among them, and that the Indians were set on making war against the whites, if they were not compensated for lands illegally taken during the 1851 Treaty of Traverse de Sioux.

Whatever their motives, Riggs was certain the angry Yanktonais were coming to Minnesota and their presence among the reservation Indians would mean chaos and loss of progress on the reservation. While Riggs was suspicious of the war rumors, he smelled trouble and pleaded with officials to take the initiative, meet with the Indians somewhere well to the west of Minnesota, discuss their grievances and secure peace by quieting their claims to the disputed lands.[22]

Then on May 29th, Dr. Thomas S. Williamson, a well-known and well-respected Presbyterian missionary, wrote to the people of Medary advising them that a large contingent of Indians were headed their way, determined to drive them out and burn the town. Williamson, who worked many years among the Santee Sioux in Minnesota, advised the settlers to make no resistance; instead, display every peaceful intention and offer the Indians a feast. Williamson claimed the information came from a reliable source, Hisayu, an Indian who would be with the Yanktonais when they arrived.[23]

The Indians arrived in Medary in an ugly frame of mind, on the very day the settlers got Williamson's letter. Fortunately, most of the town's residents were away visiting Sioux Falls City. The rest had retreated to Medary's blockhouse when the danger was known. The blockhouse was no doubt the rough frontier house noted by Corlies in his journal.

As tension mounted the town site leader, Franklin J. DeWitt, stepped forward on behalf of the colonists and tried to appease the Indians. He had no success. He was told that the Sioux resented the advancements made by the whites over the past year and were upset because they had not been paid for the land taken up by the Nobles' government road. The anxious settlers offered coffee and hard bread, but the Indians were not in a conciliatory mood. Even as DeWitt and others pleaded with the Indians, many among them were at work, taking what they wanted and destroying the rest.[24] They were determined to wipe away every trace of the white man's progress. It was said that DeWitt favored a fight but was outvoted.[25]

The events of the day were also remembered by another man, H. L. Back. He was a member of an immigrant party who rode into Medary from Cottonwood Lake, sixteen miles to the east, after it was learned the town was in trouble. He and companions arrived in time to see 1500 Indians confronting DeWitt and sixteen other men. DeWitt talked to the leaders through interpreters. The Indians were armed with bows and arrows and looked "wild and woolly" in their buffalo robes. Many had never seen white men before and with their rough costumes and equally harsh manners, they were a frightening spectacle to the handful of whites present. While Lean Dog and Smutty Bear made speeches, the women dug up and ate potatoes from a twelve-acre field that had been planted a short time before.

Franklin J. DeWitt
(Collections of the South Dakota State Archives)

Back remembered seeing a small, red-headed lad about twenty years old, who refused to be intimidated, and challenged to fight not one, but six Sioux warriors. Fortunately for all concerned, the warriors merely smiled at his audacity. The settlers were given four days' supplies and ordered off the premises. As they left that evening, some to Yankton, some to Sioux Falls, and others to Minnesota, they were forced to watch the flames destroy their town and all the possessions they left behind.[26] When a census was taken in 1860, Medary had but one resident, a hunter named Francois LaPaire, down from the Hudson Bay territory.[27]

As Medary was a focal point for immigrants coming into Dakota, a considerable amount of goods was stored there while the settlers searched for claims. Years later it was revealed that the settlers buried some of their possessions, at or near the town site, including Byron Smith's tongs and a homemade flag. The cached items were recovered in 1907 and donated to the South Dakota State Historical Society, as mementos of the destruction of Medary.[28]

One of the displaced settlers, who called himself "Dakotah," wrote a letter from the pipestone quarries to a Minnesota newspaper, describing the sad event. He blamed the aggression on two sons of Inkpaduta, who enticed members of the Sisseton and Teton Sioux to "rob the whites." He also said the Indians were in a starving condition, so desperate with hunger that they needed no encouragement to pillage the settlement. He placed part of the blame on the government that failed in its promises to the Indians.[29]

About a week after the event, DeWitt told a reporter from the *St. Paul Minnesotian* that the Indians had set fire to all nine of the town's cabins and made off with a number of horses. All outlying claims were visited and their buildings burned or destroyed.[30] To the south, Flandrau was destroyed and its citizens driven out.[31] An angry DeWitt was in St. Paul trying to drum up military support for his displaced comrades and to seek compensation from the federal government for their property losses.

It was, indeed, the high tide of both excitement and disappointment for the hopeful settlement of Medary. The settlers lost everything to the hated Indians and were forced to bid a tearful goodbye to the town they were building—the little community that, for a short span of time, promised a lifetime of rewards. A dejected settler expressed his feelings in writing after "a fatiguing retreat march of nearly 40 miles," saying "at the moment we were ordered to leave, the torch was applied to every building in the town, and every claim cabin round about, which, in our retreating steps we witnessed fall to the ground—the toil of our hands were heaps of ruins, the pioneers' homes were beds of ashes, to be scattered again to the prairies."[32]

The Medary settlers were fortunate that they lost only their possessions. For according to Williamson, in a letter to the *St. Paul Daily Times,* the Sioux intended to kill the men, but decided against doing so because of the presence of some annuity Indians. The angry Sioux also warned that they would return again next year, "and make a clean sweep of all they found there...." Williamson was clearly sympathetic to the Indians' grievances while at the same time, deploring the losses of the settlers. He called for the federal government to intervene and strike a balance between the rights and safety of both parties. He also concluded that it would be foolish for the settlers to return to Dakota Territory, until the "government shall have made some satisfactory arrangement with those who burnt, Medary...."[33]

News of the destruction of Medary reached St. Paul, where many believed that the frontier was about to erupt in widespread warfare. Governor H. H. Sibley, a Democrat, sent a message to the legislature asking for volunteers to protect the frontier and $10,000.00 to fund the emergency military enterprise. There were renewed fears that Yanktonai warriors were moving east into Minnesota, and would attack the Upper Sioux Agency. Part of the Medary refugees gathered there and assumed a defensive posture, determined not to retreat another inch. Learning this, the alarm was sounded by the *St. Paul Pioneer and Democrat*, calling for immediate action by the state of Minnesota and the federal government.

An editorial in the *Pioneer and Democrat* said the aggression should have been anticipated. When the 1851 Treaty of Traverse de Sioux was consummated, only the Sissetons and Wahpeton bands of the Santee Sioux gave up land to the government. The Yanktonai people also claimed the land east of the Big Sioux River, and they were not represented at the negotiations. It should have surprised no one that these Indians would view as trespassers, all settlers who settled along the Big Sioux River. Since the settlements were destroyed and others threatened, the prudent course was to invest money in military protection. The editorial blamed "a long series of newspaper hoaxes and exaggerations" for lulling the public into thinking the frontier was safe.[34]

This was not the opinion of all Minnesotans, however. Others were skeptical of reports of "Indians on the warpath," and saw in the incident, evidence that the speculators were anxious to make people believe in imminent danger where none existed: in other words, a hoax of a different color. The *Mankato Independent* calmly asserted that "it appears that efforts are being made to get up another Indian panic by interested parties at St. Paul," namely the Dakota Land Company, solely for the purpose of protecting their vested interests in town sites. The *Independent* and others with investments in the new state of Minnesota were concerned about negative public opinion, and how it might curb the tide of immigration and investments from the outside. They questioned whether the Dakota Land Company had a superior right to the land than did the Sioux. Men with no interest in remote town sites didn't want public funds spent to protect the air castles of speculators.[35]

The St. Paul *Daily Minnesotian*, a newspaper that regularly opposed the *Pioneer and Democrat*, and downplayed the goals and accomplishments of the Dakota Land Company, took a similar stance. It ridiculed the governor's request for volunteers and money. It rejected the possibility of an all-out Indian war and sneered at the misfortune of the St. Paul speculators. The *Daily Minnesotian* declared that town site speculators were responsible for wildly exaggerated claims of an imminent Indian attack. It was their way to siphon public funds into their pockets.

Long after the Medary excitement subsided, the *Daily Minnesotian* discovered and quoted from an article in the *Winona Republican*, a newspaper that interviewed W. J. Duley, a Minnesota settler who had toured much of Dakota in the summer of 1858. Duley downplayed the significance of the losses at Medary and Flandrau. He said Medary had only one habitable building and that was occupied by men from the Dakota Land Company. These men, he said, had claimed the best lands surrounding Medary and they were simply waiting, like vultures, to "prey upon immigrants." The town of Flandrau, he said, consisted of a single log house that the Indians destroyed.

The dramatic story of the "sacking and burning" of towns was merely a frontier yarn, according to Duley.[36] This suited the *Minnesotian* quite well and it used the information in its ongoing battle with the Democratic Party, the *Pioneer and Democrat* and the Dakota Land Company. The *Minnesotian* readily accepted Duley's story that the only losses at Medary consisted of a "shanty," four barrels of flour and one barrel of pork.

The *Minnesota Free Press* from St. Peter was even more nasty and direct when it was known that the Dakota Land Company sought remuneration from the federal government for its losses at Medary. This newspaper was suspicious of all speculation, especially when it originated in St. Paul. It lambasted the Dakota Land Company and its claim for damages, calling it a "Nice Little Game." At most, the loss was about $5,000.00; the rest of the claim was a "rascally fraud." The land belonged to the Indians and the whites "had no business there." Nevertheless, the *Free Press* conceded that with influential men like Brown, Nobles and Medary making their case before Congress, that the "appropriation will be made" (just like the Nobles road) and used to benefit the Dakota Land Company. But a day of reckoning was coming, trumpeted the *Free Press*. Yes, "surely the day of the *humbugs* is at hand—and among them, the Dacotah Land Company is not the least."[37]

A less political and more sober stance was taken by the *Monticello Times,* whose editor downplayed the danger while cutting through the palaver. Refusing to join those who were playing politics with the Dakota Land Company, he saw something more fundamental. The Indians were simply destitute and the attack on Medary was not an act of war but the theft of food by hungry people, "the startling antithesis to the bread riots of the old world capitols." He placed the blame on the federal government and its inability to deal fairly with the tribes.[38]

A vigilant and angry Franklin J. DeWitt would listen to no criticism or explanations and joined in the demand for the protection of the frontier. In a smartly worded letter to the *Pioneer and Democrat*, DeWitt claimed that $50,000.00 worth of property was destroyed at Medary, most of which belonged to the displaced settlers. He slammed the *Daily Minnesotian* for downplaying the incident, accusing the editor of insensitivity and intentional misrepresentations. He insisted that people were not asking for punitive action against the offending Indians, but rather wanted the government to offer some kind of protection to see that it never happened again. The people affected, said DeWitt, were on ceded land and were doing nothing wrong, and therefore should not be subjected to editorial ridicule and official indifference.[39]

The *Minnesota Free Press* seemed to gloat over the losses of DeWitt and his associates, saying, "the state of affairs is peculiarly unfavorable for the Dacotah Land Company and their nice little speculations." The *Free Press* reminded its readers that some men connected with the company committed "outrages" against the Jacques family the year before, and then threatened to "tear down our office," for publishing the story of the crime.[40] Bottom line, the St. Paul-based company got what it deserved and it had no right to expect any public sympathy. Speculators are gamblers and gamblers often lose.

While the Dakota Land Company was no doubt simply trying to protect its investments and long range plans, rival newspapers of the Republican stripe, with axes to grind, were unrelenting. They never passed up the chance to slam the Democrats, and they distrusted speculators in general and the Dakota Land Company in particular. They had no interest in the grand designs of visionary (or greedy) town site founders and painted a sorry picture of the Dakota experiment. Those who read their columns probably believed that people were giving up on Dakota.

Samuel Fisher Corlies and his two friends were having the time of their life in Dakota in the spring of 1858, as they hunted and explored their way to the Falls of the Big Sioux River after leaving Medary. On May 25, 1858, they woke up after a terrific storm to find hail six inches deep around their camp site about 30 miles north of Sioux Falls City. Undismayed, they continued their journey on horseback and arrived at the town site about 7 P.M. that night and "dined." They spent a comfortable night at the "suttler's house." Corlies made no effort to describe the town site or its people in his journal.

The next day they visited the Falls and Corlies attempted the inevitable description of the natural wonder, concluding the "beautiful waterfalls" would be "romantic" if there were more trees as an enhancement. They tried their luck fishing at the Falls but "owing to the rise, caused by late rains, caught nothing but a few catfish."

Corlies and party departed Sioux Falls City for the next town site that he called "Emmerson," no doubt a terrible misspelling of Eminija. After a pleasant three-hour ride they arrived at the "Shantee" and took supper with some town site men whom he does not name. They spent some time walking about that evening and made note of a "number of mounds nearby, supposed to be Indian graves." The next day they left, crossing the Split Rock River on their way south to the Rock River, through country "totally destitute of timber," apparently unaware of a crisis that would soon threaten Sioux Falls City.[41]

DeWitt believed that Sioux Falls City was safe from depredations, as he thought the Indians would not carry their wrath to the southern end of the Big Sioux Valley, after destroying Medary. Still it was his opinion that the settlers at Flandrau and Sioux Falls City should gather at the Falls and "prepare for defence."[42] After a messenger arrived in Sioux Falls City with news of the wholesale destruction to the north, the town was immediately thrown into a state of high excitement. After a sense of comparative calm was restored, some life and death decisions were made.

First, the settlers sent two riders off toward Medary to be certain that there was a real emergency. Not long after, the riders came back saying they spotted a large contingent of Indians thirty-five miles north of Sioux Falls, moving south. The emergency was real. Now it was either stand and prepare to fight, or leave.

The Dakota Land Company had recently constructed a one-story-and-a-half stone house on the riverbank, called the "Dakota House." This served as their headquarters and a sort of all-purpose gathering place. Each floor had one room about fifteen feet square; the upper story was reached by climbing a ladder. While it was one of the more imposing structures in the settlement, it was not considered big or strong enough to hold off an attack. Something more was needed.[43]

It was decided that there were enough people at the town site to make a stout defense and fight, if necessary. Next, they decided to build a fortification around the Dakota House, using the heavy sod, which the men believed was thick enough to stop both arrows and bullets. They decided against trying to fortify any of the houses of the

Western Town Company, as they were located too close to the bluffs, whereas the Dakota House was on the river bottom, affording a clear view in all directions.

Walls seven- to eight-feet high were built, enclosing an area of about 100-feet square, including a spring of good drinking water. Portholes were dug out of the sod for shooting and observing. The gallant, makeshift militia rigged up an alarm system in the form of a "pendant circular saw," which chimed when beaten.[44] They even dug a "deep ditch" around the base of the walls, and fenced off three acres of adjacent land for their livestock.[45]

All the Sioux Falls and Sioux Falls City settlers, taking with them their movable property, gathered inside the cozy structure that was aptly named "Fort Sod." Rebecca Goodwin converted some of the mens' shirts and one of her skirts into an American flag that was proudly flown from the lonely battlements. One of the besieged, James M. Allen wrote a letter to his father from the confines of Fort Sod, on June 17, 1858. In it Allen describes the conditions and morale of those thirty-five men and one woman who "unanimously determined to remain and defend ourselves and our property." They were all good shooters, Allen wrote, including Rebecca Goodwin, who could "shoot a gun as well as anyone."[46] Luckily for historians, Allen's letter was saved and made a part of the historical record.

Allen's "Fort Sod" letter has long been treasured because it sheds light on an incident that has fascinated and intrigued Dakota historians and history buffs for generations. It has been written about, discussed, interpreted, quoted and footnoted over and over again. Allen's letter, however, was not the only surviving document from Sioux Falls during those dangerous times. Smith Kinsey also wrote a "Fort Sod" letter that found its way to the *Dubuque Daily Times*. Since it has not received the attention given to Allen's letter, it is set forth below in its entirety.

"Sioux Falls, June 17, 1858

My Dear F.—There has been an exciting time here for three or four days past, about the Indians. The town of Medary, fifty miles above here, has been burned and the settlers driven off by Indians. Mr. Dewitt, agent of the Dackota (sp) Land Company sent us word by a half-breed to leave. We have made up our minds not to go. We have forty settlers here now. We held a meeting immediately and went to work and built a fort 100 feet square out of sod, with walls four feet thick. No Indians have come here yet, but if they do, we are prepared for them. We will fight if they come and commit any depredations. We have moved most of the Town Company's property into the Fort. There are 125 Indians in the party but they may not come at all. The settlers have joined together and moved all their property into the Fort. We are all in fine spirits.

Yours, etc., SMITH KINSEY."[47]

Both Allen and Kinsey wrote from the heart about the expectancy of danger that never came. The settlers never had to fire a shot in defense. And luckily for them, for had the Yanktonai warriors in sufficient numbers descended upon Fort Sod, it is likely that the settlers would have been defeated or eventually starved out by overwhelming odds. As it was the Indians made an appearance, but did not launch an attack. According to Rebecca Goodwin, the Indians stayed and watched for three days and then departed.[48]

The settlers were relieved but apparently not yet willing to leave the relative safety of Fort Sod. According to Allen, they stayed in and around their earthen confines for a total of six weeks, all the while totally isolated and utterly alone. And yet, news of the siege may have reached Sioux City, where two companies of troops were sent to Fort Randall, with two more expected. Their mission: "prevent Indian incursions which have been annoying the frontier...."[49]

No troops came to Sioux Falls City, however, and after a nervous month and a half in and around Fort Sod, their provisions were very low, having only musty flour to eat along with fresh fish taken from the river. They had grown "poor in spirit and weak in flesh." No doubt they were also bored and tired of the same old faces. Then DeWitt and a man named Brown (probably Joseph R. Brown or one of his family members) showed up unexpectedly in a horse and buggy, bringing with them fresh provisions and good news. The gallant defenders happily marched out of Fort Sod to greet their friends, in "battle array, rivaling Falstaff's army."[50] The long siege was over.

The good feelings were short-lived, however, as the close brush with disaster convinced many of the settlers that Dakota was unsafe and would remain so for a considerable time to come. Some left never to return, thus cutting deeply into the small population. News of the Indian trouble on the frontier retarded further settlement. The trouble at the town sites seriously eroded the large ambitions of the speculators.

Still the by-word was optimism; not everyone was scared away. At Sioux Falls City, a man named H. Duley (probably W. J. Duley) gave a stirring Fourth of July speech, quite likely within the walls of Fort Sod.[51] Letters making their way back to St. Paul speak of hope and success, as if those who stayed were able to shake off the horrors of that summer. The Western Town Company claimed and laid out a new town called Nicollet, south of the Falls, on the Big Sioux River at the mouth of the Rock River.[52] They were ready to sell lots.

Their reports sent back to Dubuque in the summer of 1858 were anything but downcast. Dr. Josiah L. Phillips wrote on behalf of the Sioux Falls settlement in glowing terms, as if the Fort Sod incident never happened. After giving obligatory information about the good crops, he said "the alarm about the Indian depredations has kept away for a time many who had intended...to locate in our vicinity. This excitement has now quite passed away so far as we know." The only Indian Phillips felt worthy of mention was the "old Indian Chief, who...was supposed to have led on the savage hordes, came over with part of his family and made us a friendly visit...." Phillips' advice: "don't let the fear of Indian troubles disturb you." Instead he preferred to write about the things the colony had and what it needed, such as a variety store and a post office.

He also rambled on about the fabulous buffalo hunts near Sioux Falls City, when immense herds of the great beasts were seen east of the Big Sioux River. Phillips wrote with praise about a magnificent bull that gamely withstood the hunters' guns until eight bullets finally brought him down. "So you see," he wrote, "we have many excitements of life and much to amuse even at Sioux Falls City."[53]

Phillips' upbeat sentiments fit nicely with the goals of the Dakota Land Company. Always trying to put a positive face on the news, directors of the company emphasized their accomplishments, and downplayed their losses. At their annual meeting in August of 1858, stockholders were given an upbeat report by Secretary Joseph Gay. He readily acknowledged that the company "suffered heavy damages and losses in the sacking and burning of the towns of Medary and Flandreau," but peace had been "restored on the borders," and the federal government was certain to pay for damages caused by the Indians. Their treasury was low and money scarce, but shareholders were dutifully paying assessments so a shortfall would be avoided.

On the positive side, 2640 acres of scrip had been purchased from the government to claim and buy six towns, two in Minnesota and four in Dakota. Heading the list was Saratoga, Minnesota, 60 miles west of New Ulm, where the company claimed 640 acres. Next there was Mountain Pass, Minnesota, at the shores of Lake Benton on the Nobles government road, also 640 acres.

In Dakota, 25 miles west of Mountain Pass on the Nobles road, was Medary, 240 acres. Although it was totally in ruins, the company had no plans to abandon it. "Flandreau," now spelled with an "e," the "county seat of Nobles County," 15 miles south of Medary, where the Coteau Percee Creek joined the Big Sioux River, the company claimed 640 acres. It, too, was considered a viable town site although deserted.

Sioux Falls City, the county seat of Big Sioux County, "and the recognized capital of the Territory," 320 acres, was not surprisingly considered the prize asset. The secretary's report said it was to be the terminus of "the Transit Railroad west." And of course it had the mighty Falls of the Big Sioux River. Twelve miles below it was Eminija, the highly touted but rarely heard from town site. It was the "County seat of Vermillion county—at the mouth of the Split Rock River and Pipestone Creek—on the Big Sioux," and "at the more practicable head of navigation for large class steamers, 640 acres." The company had yet to do very much at Eminija.

The aforementioned six towns were paid for and it was said that the company would refuse an offer of $200,000.00 for any of the six.

In 1858 the company also located the town sites of Lynd, Redwood and Redwood Centre, Great Oasis, in Minnesota, and Renshaw (20 miles north of Medary), and Commerce City (at the great-bend of the Big Sioux River, half-way between Sioux Falls City and the Missouri River), in Dakota. In October of 1858, the company sent a party headed by Joseph Gay and Byron M. Smith out to investigate and survey the boundaries of all six town sites, and prepare the needed plats and papers. Then all six were properly entered at the land offices with jurisdiction over the sites.[54]

All of this looked good on paper, but in reality, the company made much less real progress. Of the four Dakota towns begun in 1857, only one, Sioux Falls, had any people left. The troubles of 1858 had taken a heavy toll.

The remaining settlers focused their attention on Sioux Falls after the destruction of Medary and Flandrau. It seems as if Sioux Falls was just too beautiful a place to desert and leave to nature or the Native Americans. Even at that early stage, the little town site resembled a resort, with its many small stone houses built near the river, surrounded by hills, adjacent to an attractive, wooded island, and within listening distance to the peaceful and melodious Falls.

Sioux Falls City settler Samuel J. Albright—about whom the reader will learn much more in another chapter—was enamored with the area. Writing to St. Paul he said, "Sioux Falls, where we are now encamped, is the most romantic spot I have ever seen." He described the Falls as "truly beautiful, consisting of six or eight distinct leaps of water, in the distance of a quarter of a mile." He was especially entranced by the somber presence of a "square column of rock, about twelve feet through and some thirty feet in height, entirely disconnected from any surrounding object. The entire mass bears the appearance of having passed through an ordeal of fire."[55]

Albright's strange attachment to this natural wonder mirrored the experiences of many others who came before and after. It was the legendary Falls that brought them here and once under their magic, made the mere thought of leaving extremely disagreeable. Like others who were overwhelmed and charmed by the wild, symphonic magnificence of the Falls, he summoned the muse in him and tried his best to render the one perfect description, but no doubt he turned away feeling he had failed.

There was a non-poetic side to living in a northwestern paradise and the determined people of Sioux Falls City worked the rest of the summer and into the fall, trying to put in place the foundation for a permanent community. In the next chapter we will learn something of their political schemes, but equally important, and more immediate, was the need to protect their property. Precious livestock disappeared from time to time, keeping folks on edge. The animals could have strayed away on their own, but most thought otherwise. It was believed that Indians were watching the town site, and by stealth at night, ran off horses and cattle.

Search parties went out but were unsuccessful. An angry Albright announced that "in view of the numerous outrages and thefts committed hereabouts of late," the citizens were "organizing a company of fifty mounted rangers, for their own protection; and my word for it, with fifty such specimens of sharp shooters as I have within the past few weeks in the Sioux Valley, well mounted and armed, it would be hard with six times their number of Yancton braves should they come together on the prairie." Albright was certain that Indians were the culprits and that they would be dealt with summarily, if caught.[56] Brave words, but one tends to wonder where a community of less than 50 people would get the fifty horses for their "mounted rangers."

All these things, however, made sense to the men of the *St. Paul Pioneer and Democrat*. According to popular opinion, as reflected in that newspaper, the red race was moving, steadily and inevitably, toward extinction. And it wasn't the whites who were doing the killing; it was civilization, a force larger than all races, one which operated in sync with a grand designer, beyond mortal control. A *Pioneer and Democrat* editorial reasoned thusly: "Before that civilization the Indian must disappear and the more rapidly the better." Extinction was always the fate of those deemed inferior, by those who presumed themselves to be superior.[57]

The settlers at Sioux Falls City must have believed civilization was working its will for them. Word reached St. Paul reporting crops yielded quite well that year, despite inattention during the growing season. Men were smoking cigars made of Sioux Falls tobacco, which was held up to be as good as Cuban. Autumn brought other benefits too; the Indians left the area for their winter grounds on the Missouri River, except for "a few stragglers who still linger around the corn and potato fields, and pick up what has been left in gathering in."[58]

A St. Paul newspaper reported that a survey crew from the Transit Railroad Company laid out a line from New Ulm to a point on the Big Sioux River near Sioux Falls. The optimistic view was that this railroad would ultimately connect St. Paul with the Pacific coast and benefit all those stops in between.[59] Working during the winter of 1858-59, the Transit crew completed over 50 miles of grading in Minnesota on its way west toward the Big Sioux River.[60] Members of the Transit party visited Eminija and Sioux Falls, and were suitably impressed with the town sites and waterpower at the Falls.⁶¹

There was more good news. Mail service from Sioux City was re-established thereby reconnecting Sioux Falls to the outside world. A man carried mail on horseback between the two towns, covering the distance in about twenty-four hours.⁶²

With the resumption of mail, and a proposed railroad in the offing, Sioux Falls City looked like a good place to settle despite the 1858 summer of trouble. But those settlers who chose, or were chosen, to stay for the winter, would most certainly have the place to themselves, with only the howl of the wolf and other unsettling sounds of nature to remind them that there was something out there that wouldn't wait until spring.

W. W. Brookings was one of those who went back East in the fall of 1858, but not to avoid another winter on the frontier. He traveled by ox-drawn wagon and rail to Philadelphia to be fitted with artificial limbs. He returned to Sioux Falls in January of 1859, and was seen about the town site, "walking steadily and firmly, using only one cane."⁶³ His physical recovery from the effects of the tragedy of February of 1858 was as complete as it would ever be, and he was ready to resume his involvement in business and political affairs.

Some time after his return to Sioux Falls, W. W. Brookings was called on to defend his brother S. D. Brookings, in a mysterious murder case. The killing took place on S. D. Brookings' claim on the Big Sioux River on the Iowa side. The accused brother was arrested and incarcerated in Sioux City, where a preliminary examination was conducted. W. W. Brookings appeared for his brother but was not successful in getting the charges dropped. Some time later, S. D.

Brookings escaped from jail, disappeared and was never tried.[64]

The troubles of his brother did nothing to tarnish the reputation or ambition of W. W. Brookings. He was a fighter and a leader, imbued with a single-minded belief in his own personal destiny. By example alone, he had more than convinced his fellow settlers of his abilities. Brookings was eagerly and warmly accepted in his community, as frontier people were always pleased to rally around their leaders. To keep company with the fearless took the edge off of fear.

Smith Kinsey must have been one of those inspired by Brookings' example. Less than a year after he shared the hardships of Brookings' tragic winter adventure, he and another man, Frederick Haseloh, set out from Dubuque, in December, with a "heavy wagon on runners, with a year's stock of provisions on board, and every implement of husbandry needed in farming." Hooked to the wagon sled was a house, also on runners.

The two men lived and cooked in the house as they moved slowly across the snow-covered Iowa prairie toward Sioux Falls. Drawn by three yokes of oxen, the unusual vehicle contained a dog, a cat and a half dozen hens. The spirit of adventure and enterprise was ablaze in the two young men of the Western Town Company, facing the risks of a January journey and fully expecting to reach their colleagues at the Falls.[65]

They fared much better than three men who set out for Medary in January of 1859, carrying supplies. The party was overcome by a snowstorm causing all three to freeze their hands and feet before they could find shelter.[66]

But despite stories of suffering and hardship that made news, Dakota was favorably noticed in faraway places, although it had yet to achieve territorial status. A "Sioux Falls correspondent," to the *Washington Union* urged the "sons and daughters of the east, of the middle, and southern sates..." to push "out into the undressed garden of the sunset land." In a piece that could have been taken from a Dakota Land Company minute book, he called Dakota a land of "salubrious clime," with "rich and inexhaustible soil." He predicted that in a "year or two hence," America would see on "the upper Missouri, and the Big Sioux and James Rivers, fleets of lofty steamers astonishing the natives with their shrill whistles, and filling up the land with people and merchandise."[67]

That kind of optimism was grossly overstated. In May of 1859, the Western Town Company announced it would sell its Sioux Falls town site for cash, to the highest bidder. The sale was scheduled for June 18th, at the company office in Dubuque. The company was selling a complete package, including "a claim cabin, blacksmith shop and tools, store house, steam mill and engine of 18 horse power, two yokes of oxen, two wagons and one (sp) poney...." Interestingly, there was no mention of their hotel, the Dubuque House. But they were offering to sell their claim of 160 acres opposite Sioux Falls called "Lowell," and the Nicollett town site in Sioux County, Iowa.[68]

The once hopeful party of investors was "reaching for the sky just to surrender."[69] Some months previous the Board of Directors served notice on shareholders to report and pay their fines or face increased fines and forfeiture of stock. It would appear that the troubles of 1858 made shareholders nervous, causing many to cut their losses rather than pour more money into the company. Nevertheless, some of the Western Town Company members— including Phillips, McClellan and Brookings—stayed in Sioux

Falls, along with their colleagues from the Dakota Land Company. They were willing to take more risks.

The Dakota Land Company wasn't about to quit, but its leaders were also searching for more operating capital. The secretary, Joseph E. Gay, announced that at a January 11, 1859, meeting of the Board of Directors, all shares were assessed an additional $2.00 per share. Shareholders were advised to make payment to the treasurer, G. G. Walker, by February 22, 1859, or watch their stock forfeit back to the company in accordance with its by-laws. While some of the original shine may have worn off the company logo, its principals were still optimistic.

News from the East was promising. It was reported from Philadelphia, that President Buchanan appointed an Indian Agent for Dakota Territory, because it was anticipated that territorial status would be granted at the next session of Congress. Mr. B. Schoonover and two assistants were preparing for the long trip to Dakota with the expectation that they would make their headquarters at Sioux Falls City, until a permanent location for an agency was established. In the same article it was revealed that the army would send four companies of troops to Dakota, to be stationed at Lake Preston, erroneously said to be located "2 miles west of the Big Sioux and 30 miles north of Medary." The military presence was expected to ease the transition of the land from the Yankton Sioux to the federal government under the terms of the treaty. With the treaty implemented and the troops in place, no further disturbances were expected from the wild "Yanktonais of the North."[70]

As it turned out, 1859 was a reasonably peaceful and prosperous year for Sioux Falls City and the other, mostly deserted town sites in the Big Sioux Valley. The *Central City* (New York) *Courier* said Dakota contained some "two thousand five hundred miles of navigable rivers," and "some dozen or twenty flourishing towns...."[71] According to another report, Sioux Falls City had 30 to 40 farms in close proximity to the town site, each with five to sixty acres under cultivation, and crops looked just fine.[72] These reports were, of course, greatly exaggerated, but the Dakota promoters would take the publicity.

Good news came from the *Democrat*, a friendly newspaper in Winona, under the lead line: "Emigration to Dakota." The article notes that the steamboat, the *Favorite,* was carrying Dakota Land Company freight, bound for Sioux Falls City, including "quite a party of emigrants, supplies, horses, oxen, cows and farming implements." The same article said that another steamboat, the *Jeannette Roberts*, was hauling freight and people toward Sioux Falls City, the "Capital City."[73] This was the stuff of settlement and progress. What better way to respond to critics?

When critic Moses K. Armstrong arrived in Sioux Falls on October 1, 1859, heading for Yankton, he was not overly impressed. Writing to the *Democrat*, he described Sioux Falls City as a "small town on the Sioux river, containing five cabins, one saw mill, blacksmith shop, two white women and twenty-three white men."[74] He wrote about a hard, waterless journey from Hole-in-the-Mountain to Sioux Falls, calling the land in between a "waterless and woodless desert." He did admit, however, that Sioux Falls had one valuable feature—the Falls. Armstrong spent some time talking to the settlers before moving on to Yankton where he was allied with that town's political and economic interests.

James M. Allen, a prominent Fort Sod veteran and letter writer, had a far more positive perspective. Taking to his pen again, this time writing to the *Cleveland Herald,* his hometown newspaper, Allen boasted of the great potential that Dakota held out to the hopeful emigrant. He emphasized the beauty and the power of the Falls and proclaimed that the fertility of the Dakota soil was such that it "might bear respectable comparison with the banks of the Nile...."[75] Since Allen survived the Fort Sod siege, the flame of optimism burned bright in him and many of his colleagues.

And for good reason too, for there was no repetition of the trouble of 1858. As we have seen, the Yankton treaty was ratified in February of 1859. In July, the Yankton Sioux accepted the inevitable and sadly departed to their 400,000 acre Missouri River reservation. This undoubtedly caused the Sioux Falls City people to feel safer. Indians' visits were expected to be much less frequent and less confrontational in nature, and travel between Sioux Falls City and the mouth of the James River on the Missouri was expected to increase. By the summer of 1859, a well-marked road existed between the two sites.[76]

The Dakota Land Company anticipated this, and in June of 1859, sent an expedition out to inspect the Missouri slope for possible town sites. A group headed by D. F. Brawley and Byron M. Smith left Sioux Falls City by canoe and "planted the flag of the Dakota Land Company on such valuable sites as may be found from the mouth of the Sioux to Old Fort Lookout on the Missouri...."[77] They were moving into territory dominated by Frost, Todd and Company, as if heading for some final showdown for control of the political and economic destiny of Dakota.

The company held a meeting in St. Paul at Parker Paine's office on September 27, 1859, and the mood was decidedly upbeat. Despite the break-up of the Western Town Company, the St. Paul men put forth some bold proposals. Samuel J. Albright addressed the group and spoke in favorable terms about the "enviable conditions of the settlers...." Resolutions were passed directing the board of directors to purchase materials for a "commodious Hotel" and a "Capitol building, to be erected immediately" for use by the next legislature. Bold talk, indeed.

New officers were elected, including the selection of a Republican to a key post, thus indicating that the company was not strictly Democratic in makeup and political outlook. This suited the *St. Paul Daily Minnesotian*, as it was taken as a sign that in the Dakota Land Company hierarchy, "politics can hold no sway in the company."[78] It appears that the company stalwarts were trying hard to bounce back from the losses of 1858, and in a bi-partisan way, press on with their goal of creating and building towns that would provide lasting benefits for themselves and for those who would come to live there.

Chapter IX

The Squatter Government at Sioux Falls City

"A new star has been born into the milky-way of Territories, with no thanks to Uncle Sam...."

St. Paul Pioneer and Democrat
October 29, 1858

On the wild frontier the need to feel safe and secure can hardly be understated. While a church was often the first institution to be established in a pioneer settlement, putting together some form of government was also an important priority. Town site speculators had to convince settlers that their towns were safe and orderly, and soon after their plat maps were laid out with parks, streets and avenues, the business of setting up local government was given prompt attention.

We have seen that the Minnesota territorial officials supplied their remote frontier towns with a rudimentary government. This, however, was neutralized when the state of Minnesota came into being on May 11, 1858. The "north and south" line was used to define the new state's borders, leaving the Big Sioux River town sites outside the veil of protection. While this was no surprise to the St. Paul speculators—in fact it is what they expected and wanted—it did leave them with a problem: there was no legal authority for them to build upon. Without government, their plans for the rapid settlement of the area were endangered. Storekeepers, blacksmiths and farmers, the sturdy folk they were looking for, wouldn't come to live in a lawless place.

When Alpheus G. Fuller returned to the Big Sioux Valley with news that he lost his bid for a seat in Congress, his fellow speculators were discouraged. But they weren't ready to quit, having survived a long winter in the prairie wilderness amid great deprivations. Besides, they were still confident that Congress would see things their way, and make them a territory. They were encouraged by the number of new people coming into the Big Sioux Valley. But things were changing in Washington, D. C., and if the St. Paul men were to realize their goals, they had to work hard and fast.

In Dakota, they went about setting up their own government. They used a method similar to the "town meetings" utilized long ago by the original thirteen colonies. All those concerned simply met and decided that for the good of all, they would establish their own governing authority. Since Congress had, by statute on June 3, 1858, dissolved all former territorial laws over what had been western Minnesota territory, the people thereby affected felt they had no choice but to go forward on their own.[1]

As might be expected, the Dakota Land Company led the way, and it is at this point that their long-range goals become clear. In addition to planting towns and selling real estate, they wanted to control the location of public institutions such as colleges, county seats and prisons, and secure for themselves the key political offices that would be filled by the president. They counted on a friendly Democratic administration to give them an edge.

With their attention on the men on the Missouri River slope

who were eyeing the Yankton village with a town site in mind, the Big Sioux Valley speculators—led by Sioux Falls City men—went about the business of establishing law and order. As they had no legal authority to do so, their creation was referred to as a "squatter" government. As it turned out, it drew both derision and praise.

An important first step toward this end was the establishment of Dakota's first newspaper: the *Dakota Democrat*. The Dakota Land Company hauled in a printing press with a storied past, from St. Paul, installed it in a small, stone building near the Big Sioux River and were ready to publicize their work. In order to pressure the federal government, the squatters had to project a determined image. A newspaper was sure to make a good impression and disseminate information as well. Stockholder Samuel J. Albright, a seasoned newspaperman, eagerly left St. Paul in favor of Sioux Falls to serve as the editor of the *Dakota Democrat*. He was given a hearty sendoff by the *Pioneer and Democrat*.

As if Dakota Territory was just moments away from congressional recognition, the St. Paul newspaper said, "a party consisting of Messrs. A. G. Fuller, S. J. Albright and Mr. DeWitt...left this city yesterday (August 27, 1858) for the new Territory of Dakota. They take with them a printing press and the other necessary material for the publication of a 'Western paper, devoted to Western interests,' at Sioux Falls City, a new town started last summer under the control and supervision of the Dakota Company."[2] It would have been more accurate to say the newspaper would be devoted to the interests of the Dakota Land Company, whose ambitions were now fully politicized.

The arrival of a press in Sioux Falls City made news in Sioux City,

Iowa. Its newspaper, the *Sioux City Eagle*, learned that "great efforts" were in the offing to make Sioux Falls the capital of "Dacotah," thus explaining the printing press. In an article which smacks of rivalry and competing interests, the *Eagle* declared: "we are of the opinion it can't be done," as the rightful place for the capital was on the Missouri River, and "we think it will be there."[3]

And yet the squatters to the north had other ideas that were aired at a "mass convention" at Sioux Falls City on September 18, 1858. According to one source, all areas of the territory were represented,[4] but most likely the convention was dominated by men from the Big Sioux River town sites. Several men made speeches on matters touching their land and lives. They argued that a temporary organization was necessary as Dakota was "fast attaining the unenviable notoriety reached by Texas in its early days: as the resort of thieves and outlaws." The population, they insisted, had already reached the point where disputes between men had arisen and courts and laws were necessary for resolving them.[5]

For these reasons and others equally important, resolutions were drafted and a memorial was addressed to Congress, demanding the speedy organization of Dakota Territory. They also wanted the military to establish and staff a post in the Big Sioux Valley. Before adjourning, the delegates voted to hold an election on October 4th, to elect a legislature.

According to Albright, the convention reflected a "degree of intellect and sound reasoning on political questions" to an extent which he "scarcely expected to find in a country so lately settled."[6] The convention turned into a celebration or "jubilation," as the settlers met on "Jarrett's Hill" above the Falls to view the vast and scenic valley below. They fired their guns and offered loud, hearty cheers for the president, the Queen of England and the laying of the Atlantic Ocean telegraph cable. Truly, they saw a bright future ahead and felt fortunate to have chosen such a beautiful place to live. Despite their isolation, they were not alone and helpless; they believed they were an integral part of a dynamic world, and would soon bring themselves and their communities fully within its exciting orbit.

An official notice of the convention was printed on the press owned by the Dakota Land Company, and is probably the first document printed in Dakota. It was reported that Albright, using Yankee ingenuity, prepared the document with a "planer" on a "barrel head."[7] It was a small piece but it was written with a great sense of pride and purpose. The outside world was advised that as a consequence of a "Mass Convention of the people of Dakota Territory, held in the town of Sioux Falls, in the County of Big Sioux," Dakotans would choose a legislature and make laws to suit themselves.

As was explained in Chapter VIII, Medary had been evacuated and then destroyed by Yanktonai Sioux earlier that summer. Flandrau suffered a similar fate and Eminija was little more than a paper town. As such, Sioux Falls City was designated the capital city of their territory. Because of the trouble at the other town sites, it is likely that only men at Sioux Falls City voted, if indeed there were any actual polling places and the casting of ballots. Since they had no rules but their own rules, and no one to watch over them, they could do what they wanted to do.

One historian, who had access to some of the squatters, explained their voting process as it was told to him. On the morning of the election, the settlers divided up into three or four parties. Each had a team and a wagon and each headed out in a different direction. "Every few miles they would stop to rest, an election precinct would be established and an election held." (They probably popped a cork or two.) Those in charge of the "precinct" would vote not only for themselves, but for their uncles, cousins and other relatives, until a suitable number of votes were tallied.[8]

Whatever the case, the squatters managed to at least create the appearance of an election, and it was treated by the *St. Paul Pioneer and Democrat* as an established fact. A governor, nine members of the House of Representatives and five members of the Council (the upper house of the legislature) were reportedly elected. The president of the Council, Ephraim Pierce, was a member of the last Minnesotan territorial legislature.[9] Other officials were appointed and the group swung into action as if all Americans were watching.

A letter from "Sioux Falls, D. T.," to the *Pioneer and Democrat* happily revealed that "the stars and stripes were unfurled from a flagstaff in front of the building used as a Capitol..," followed by thirteen volleys fired by the "Dakota Rifles," and "cheer upon cheer by those who assembled to witness the inauguration of their Territory."[10] The date was October 12, 1858.

The man selected to be the governor of the squatter government was Henry Masters, an erudite and worldly man from Bath, Maine, who was living in Brooklyn, New York, when Sioux Falls City was founded.[11]

One might ask why Samuel A. Medary wasn't selected. After all, he had prior experience and was an acknowledged leader of the Dakota Land Company. A St. Paul newspaper asserted that Medary aspired to be the first governor of Dakota, and toward that end, engaged in illegal acts in concert with other Democrats.[12]

Medary served as the Minnesota Territory governor until May 23, 1858, at which time there was, of course, no longer a need in the new state for a territorial chief executive. He left St. Paul quietly, but under a cloud. By the summer of 1858, Medary was in Kansas where he again found work as a territorial governor.[13]

For many, including some Democrats, the departure of Medary would only benefit Minnesota. After observing Medary's governing style, it was clear that he did not come to officiate but was rather "on a tour of speculation."[14] When the results of speculation were not to his liking, he left, and after a short stint as the postmaster in Columbus, Ohio, he landed in Kansas, a hotbed of ante-bellum sectionalism.

Back in Dakota things were far less crowded and volatile when "Squatter Governor" Henry Masters took charge. He was associated with the Western Town Company and came to Sioux Falls City from Dubuque early in 1858. He liked what he saw and sent for his wife and three children. The Masters' "luxurious outfit" included a piano, something entirely out of context in the rough settlement.[15]

"Governor" Henry Masters was roughed up a bit by an unfriendly Minnesota newspaper editor, who saw a scheming bunch of land speculators lurking behind all the high-sounding talk about laws and elections. *The Democrat* from Winona, no friend of the Dakota Land Company, mocked the handful of settlers at the Falls and their little election. Declaring that the "mass" convention consisted of a "few members of the Dakotah Land company," *The Democrat* said snidely that "Alpheus G. Fuller, Henry Masters his clerk, one (S. J.) Albright and the Cook" gathered together to elect the first officials. "Mr. Fuller aspiring to a higher or more lucrative office, Masters was elected Governor, although the contest was warm between him and the cook. Fuller voted for Masters and Albright for the cook. After dinner, however, Albright's appetite being satisfied, his affection for the nameless cook diminished and turning for Masters, the day was decided." Masters was the governor and the defeated cook was relegated to the job of directing the "Dakotah Rifles."[16]

"...We feel it is our duty as a public Journalist, to expose this trick of scheming *Land Agents,*" crowed the Winona editor. Sinking to the "depths of lowest depravity," the Sioux Falls settlers intentionally publicized false election returns, ignoring the large vote from the Pembina settlements. *The Democrat* then went on to reveal that only four men voted in Sioux Falls (apparently the aforementioned four), while a total of 2001 men voted in the far north precincts, none of whom voted for Fuller or Masters.[17]

The *Minnesota Free Press* of St. Peter also ridiculed the "election" and belittled the "elected officials." It had established itself as the number one nemesis of the Dakota Land Company and used the squatter election to launch another blast at one of its favorite targets. Editor W. C. Dodge made St. Peter a fierce rival of St. Paul. He generally took the position that anything that came out of St. Paul smelled of speculation, or was associated with the Democratic Party or the Dakota Land Company and was, therefore, corrupt.

Dodge called the Sioux Falls squatter election part of the "same grand political stealing operations that have been carried on in St. Paul during our Territorial existence." While he had no knowledge of Albright, he said Pierce was well qualified for "any duty or dirty work that may be required." The angry editor summed up his assessment of the squatter effort by saying, "no better men could have been sent there to manage such a nice little piece of Democratic

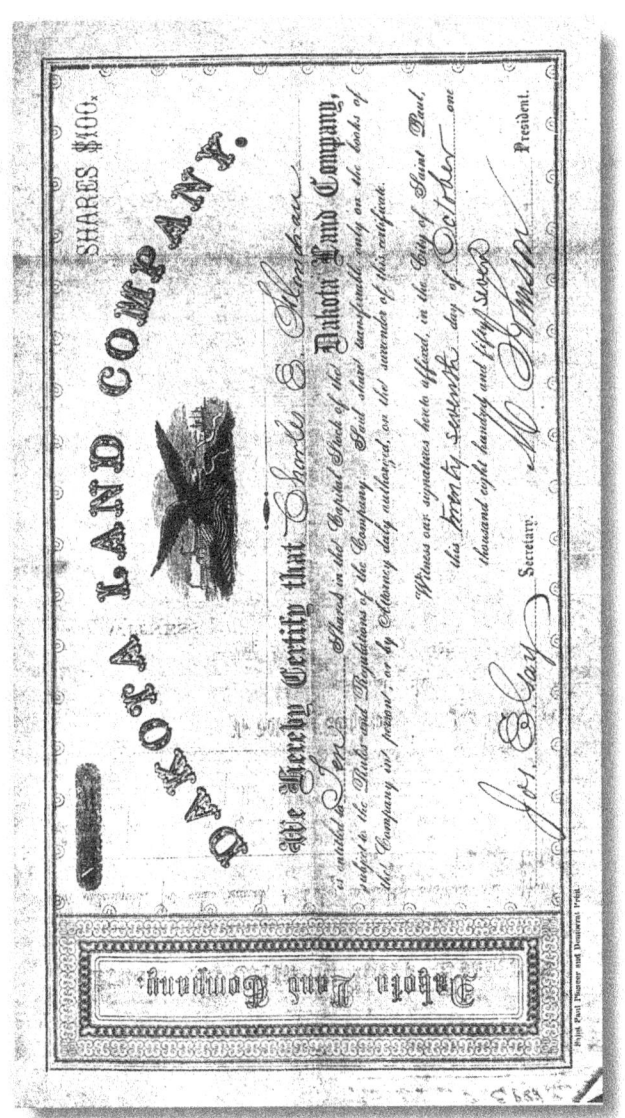

Dakota Land Company Stock Certificate
(Collections of the Minnesota Historical Society)

skullduggery, than those engaged in it."[18]

If "Governor" Masters ever saw the articles slamming or poking fun at him and his fellow speculators, he probably just laughed it off. For he was a genial man of words; an articulate, sermonizing Spiritualist, and a sometime poet who wrote a poem about the Falls of the Big Sioux River.

Spiritualism was all the rage in America during the 1850's, drawing both devoted adherents and staunch critics. Started in 1848, it was a Christian religious sect inspired by the young Fox sisters of Hydesville, New York, who heard strange rappings in their home that were interpreted to be messages from a ghost. Since the ghostly rappings were heard when one or both girls were present, the Fox sisters—Maggie and Kate—attracted the curious, and the suspicious, in droves.

People anxious to believe seized upon the event, and the new religion spread across America like a wind-blown virus. The Fox sisters became touring celebrities. Spirit "circles" sprang up in several eastern cities including New York. Many prominent people were drawn to the mysterious movement including newspaperman Horace Greeley, abolitionists Frederick Douglas and Cassius Clay, and writer James Fennimore Cooper.

Spiritualists believed that contact with the dead was not only possible but could be readily accomplished through mediums and nighttime seances. They believed the dead remained in close proximity to the living, in a realm of the spirit where they regularly sought the company of friends and family who had not yet departed. People who attended séances wrote about seeing bright lights, disembodied hands, levitating furniture and hearing beautiful music punctuated by loud noises. Raising the dead was a lively business. Although mediums were hounded by critics from the press and many were exposed as frauds, by the late 1850's—finding sanctuary in a country that guaranteed freedom of religion—Spiritualism seemed unstoppable. Henry Masters was a devotee of the new religion.

What it was that summoned Masters from the woods of Maine to the rolling, open prairies of Dakota, is a question that is likely to remain unanswered for all time to come. Was it religious inspiration or more secular motives? Perhaps he found something there that reminded him of where he had been. Was he searching or running? We can only speculate. Nevertheless, in those days of great distances and large barriers, the change from Maine to Dakota was akin to stepping from the living dimension into the beyond, a transition that was uniquely Spiritualistic.

His poem about the Big Sioux River was published in the first issue of the first newspaper in Dakota—the *Dakota Democrat*—on July 2, 1859, making it the first literary effort in what was to become South Dakota. Entitled *Sioux Falls,* the dreamy, first verse reflects Masters' free-flowing, romantic inclinations:

> "Thou glidest gently, O thou winding stream,
>   Mirroring the beauty of thy flowery banks,
> Now yielding to our soul's Elysian dreams,
>   For which we offer thee our heartfelt thanks."[19]

While he may have had goals similar to his fellow speculators, it seems that Masters was more interested in the Falls as an enduring natural wonder, and far less concerned with exploiting it to serve industry.

The articulate, dreamy and sophisticated Masters—whose personality and talent were more like those of a college professor than a frontiersman—emerged as a leader, and his popularity catapulted him into the governor's chair, such as it was in that remote and isolated venue. There he could leisurely cast his poetic metaphors into the pure, rippling waters of the Big Sioux River, and wait for an answer. After all, he had very little to do as there was very little to be done under the circumstances. And yet, as we shall see, he undertook to handle these few duties with a sense of purpose and urgency.

Albright, who had been the chief clerk in the most recent term of the Minnesota territorial legislature, was named the "Speaker of the House." He contributed some practical and political experience. Committees were formed and then the squatter legislature, which preferred to be known as a "provisional" body, passed a number of laws and memorials pertaining to local matters. They adopted the 1857 Minnesota Code of Laws as the official code of Dakota Territory. The squatters were guided by a book on parliamentary procedure brought from Minnesota by Albright.[20]

On October 17, 1858, the governor delivered a message to the legislature and the following day, they adjourned. "All their proceedings were conducted with the utmost propriety and the body itself for dignity and decorum might serve as a model for some Legislatures much farther east."[21]

While little of substance is known about the squatter legislature of 1858, Governor Masters' address was printed in the *Pioneer and Democrat*. Thus preserved, it provides some insight into the man himself and the legislative body that he headed. Most historians make mention of the squatter legislature and then quickly dismiss it as trivial or nominal. While it is true they acted out of self-interest and were unlikely to attract much attention, the handful of settlers saw themselves as worthy of respect. They wanted to be taken seriously as they were earnestly engaged in serious business. Civilizing a howling wilderness was never a laughing matter, although the Dakota Cavaliers employed humor, as needed, to ease their fears. Looking to a similar course plotted by California and Oregon, the Sioux Falls City men believed they had precedent on their side.

Masters' message is a carefully crafted and eloquent document, worthy of notice. First he thanked those who placed in his hands the responsibilities of chief executive, and he humbly expressed his sense of unworthiness at such a great honor. Then he praised the rich soil and salubrious climate of Dakota, and went on to speak about issues important to pioneers, such as agriculture, roads, bridges and courts. He emphasized the need to establish schools as soon as possible, saying, "We must not forget the important fact that we have minds to cultivate, mental seeds to be sown...." He urged the legislators to take their duties seriously, even though there would be those who would pronounce their efforts a waste of time. But after all, the squatters were only doing what others in their place would do.

He had a broad view of religion and advised the new Dakotans to be tolerant, and respect the great diversity of religious faith that was uniquely American. The Constitution, Masters said, was "wisely framed by the venerated sages of a past age, who so happily and justly incorporated into that model charter of human liberty, the invaluable doctrine of liberty of conscience, that there seems nothing further for me to say upon the subject of religion, than to express my desire for your concurrence in the toleration of every religious sect however widely they may differ in and forms of worship...."[22] One senses that here was an extraordinary yet little-known man, expressing universal views in a remote setting, like someone facing the dark unknown armed only with logic, perspective and a dreamer's flawless optimism. For a man like Masters, there was always a bright light somewhere.

It was a short speech before a limited audience, directed at men whose efforts were destined to be little more than a footnote in history. Still, in terms of eloquence and intellectual content, it must rank as one of the best speeches ever made in Sioux Falls. We can be certain that those who heard it remembered it, each in his own way. While envisioning what Sioux Falls might become over time, Masters and his fellow pioneers experienced the village in its wild, primitive shape, the way we can only dream of seeing it.

Just like a real governor, Masters declared November 18, 1858 a day of public thanksgiving in Dakota. His "proclamation" was as smooth and eloquent as was his speech to the legislature. He gave thanks for the blessings bestowed on the small, fragile colony, saying it "is present to witness the happiness expressed in such a circle brought together on the return of this day." Then in a prayer that barely concealed his Spiritualistic beliefs, he reminded his people of a higher "thanksgiving day of souls" and that everyone could look forward to a reunion with family and friends in another "sphere." Signed, Henry Masters, Governor at Sioux Falls, Dacotah Territory, on October 30, 1858. Politics and culture on the southeastern Dakota frontier were off to an auspicious beginning.

Anyone reading Master's moving proclamation might think it emerged from a utopian community. Of course that's what he allowed people back East to think. A prayer by and for contented people was good propaganda, especially when it is laced with praise and written with conviction. In merely explaining his beliefs, Masters was good advertisement for Dakota. Masters was telling people everywhere that he and his companions were here to stay.

Bad advertisement came from other sources. The *St. Anthony* (Minnesota) *Express* made light of Masters and the squatter legislature. Pretending to quote from the "Dakota *Journal,"* a weekly newspaper published in the "constellation Gemini," the *Express* revealed that a "member of the Dakota Senate," introduced a law for the protection of buffalo on the plains between the Big Sioux and Missouri Rivers.

Upon a "third reading," the following bill was passed:

"Be it enacted by the Legislative Assembly of Dakota:
That so much of this State as is embraced in the district of country bounded on the East by the Big Sioux, on the South and West by the Missouri, and on the North by the Yellow Medicine, be and the same is hereby set apart as a reservation for the exclusive use and habitation of the buffalo; provided the Federal Government does not permanently locate the Indians on the same, and

Be it further enacted:
That if any member of the Dakota Land Company shall make or cause to be made any paper towns within the district embraced in the above boundary, it shall be lawful for the aborigines to extirpate and confiscate the same; and any person or persons who shall organize parties out of the state and come within its jurisdiction to hunt buffalo, shall be guilty of a misdemeanor."[23]

No one should interpret this to be a sincere attempt to protect the buffalo and its wild environment, and no one should think for a minute that this self-serving satire contains any concern over the rights of the Indians. This second "provision" can, however, be interpreted to be a biting criticism of what many believed to be an exaggerated claim by the Dakota Land Company for the losses at Medary and Flandrau that past summer.

A settler in Sioux Falls City, known only as "G. L.," took exception to the finger pointing and criticism. In a letter to St. Paul, G. L. gathered his indignation and said: "The people of Dakota are not a set of scheming speculators and itinerant vagabonds." He made it known that Dakota was being settled by the "sons and daughters" of America, honest people with good motives, coming in from all directions, seeking out permanent homes on the healthy and luxuriant Dakota prairie.[24]

Henry Masters remained a happy part of the Dakota experiment. He became the unofficial correspondent to the *Dubuque Express and Herald*. Although his correspondence was infrequent, it was written with passion. His columns about his adopted town were lavish in their praise, describing the Falls and its "laughing waters" as a romantic wonderland that he and his companions had all to themselves. He rambled in a heartfelt and poetic manner about a special place where men feasted easily off the best of nature. They were the first and they had everything, including a variety of fishes, an abundance of game, fur-bearing animals, stone and wood for building, exceedingly rich soil, and the celebrated Falls, whose lyrical sound and impressive flow entranced all those who would stop, listen and reflect.

To Masters, the consummate sojourner, it was nature's masterpiece, created to keep him satisfied. Aside from this, he had but two suggestions: "Another mill is much needed, and there is also a good chance for a suitable person to engage in tavern keeping."[25] It seems we can surmise that something was lacking after all.

The stirrings in Sioux Falls City were apparently given serious attention in *Sioux City*. The *Eagle* observed that "the good people of Sioux Falls in Dacotah Territory have established a territorial government to suit themselves—appointed a Governor and are now jogging along at a prosperous rate." The *Eagle* article called Masters "energetic and efficient," and his speech to the legislature first rate, "abounding in practical suggestions and happy thoughts."[26] Master was known and respected in Sioux City and his presence at the head of the squatter government gave it credibility where it could do some good.

Far to the north of Sioux Falls City, the citizens of St. Joseph and Pembina in Pembina County took their own shaky, extra-legal steps. They too, had been cut off from Minnesota, where they had enjoyed a long and successful relationship with St. Paul businessmen. Now they were on their own, like their counterparts to the south, without laws to guide them. They met in convention and passed a proclamation, in both French and English, which set out a direction for their people and communities. While they disdained a local, squatter organization, they wanted to do something to remind the powers that be that there were people out there unwilling to be ignored. Since the federal government had decided to leave them without laws, they declared it was the wise course to hold an election to choose a delegate to Congress. This man would represent their interest "until officers are appointed and a proclamation issued for a new election under such organization." It was signed by H. S. Donaldson, President.

On the 18th of October, an election was held at St. Joseph, Pembina, Lane Wama on the *Coteau des Prairie* and Big Stone Lake. When news of the election reached St. Paul, remarkably, all the voters from St. Joseph and Pembina (434 total) had cast their votes for W. W. Kingsbury, the same man who had so recently fought A. G. Fuller for the right to be Dakota's delegate to Congress. The other two polling places had not been heard from.²⁷ These men were apparently acting totally independent of the Sioux Falls City people, although both groups were undoubtedly aware of each other's towns and ambitions.

Kingsbury's "election" was characterized as a joke by a letter writer to the *New York Tribune*. The writer—who used the *nom-de-plume* "Dakota"—noted that Kingsbury arrived in New York City from Pembina, on his way to Washington, D, C,, "with face flushed and whiskers frosted by the breath of winter." Kingsbury was carrying a bag of votes cast by "half-breed and full-blood Indians," along with election certificates signed by "Indian traders." "Dakota" invited everyone to laugh at this latest muscular exercise of the franchise, and sneer at the victory by a man who never set foot in Dakota, the "territory" he claimed to represent.²⁸

Most assuredly, the northern election fell victim to the same credibility problems as did those held in Sioux Falls City or Yankton during the pre-territorial days. All the extra-legal, squatter elections suffered from the lack of verifiable data, conflicting newspaper accounts and, most glaringly, wildly exaggerated vote totals "certified" by self-serving men posing as "election judges." And yet one of the groups, or perhaps a combination of all three, did have a positive impact on Congress.

In February of 1859, Alpheus G. Fuller was in Washington, still claiming to be Dakota's delegate, and trying to pump new life into the territorial movement. At this time it was learned through various newspapers that the chairman of the committee on territories had introduced legislation to create "Dacotah" Territory. The bill, prepared by Rep. J. M. Cavanaugh, a popular Minnesota Democrat, outlined the boundaries of a huge new territory that extended all the way west to the territories of Oregon and Washington. It established a legislature consisting of thirteen members of the House of Representatives and seven from the Council. The first election was scheduled for the first Monday in September of 1859. Representation in the legislature was to be as follows: two councilmen and four representatives from Big Sioux and Pipestone counties; three councilmen and five representatives from Medary, Stephens and Rock counties; and one councilman and two representatives from Vermillion and Yankton.

"Free white" males, excluding military personnel, who were at least 21 years of age and actual residents of the territory, were allowed to vote. The fugitive slave laws were expressly made to apply to Dakota, meaning blacks were not welcome. This expressed the influence of Southern Democrats, who were riding high following the passage of the Kansas-Nebraska Act. This law repealed statutes barring slavery in the new territories north of latitude 36 degrees, 36'.

Significantly, the bill stated that "when admitted as a State the said Territory shall be received into the Union with or without slavery as their constitution may prescribe at the time of their admission." Truly, this was a pro-states' rights, "popular sovereignty" Democratic measure designed to placate the South.

Section 13 of the bill made Sioux Falls City the capital, at least for the first session of the legislature. After the legislature met for a third time, the capital site could be changed by the legislators and the governor. And in a surprising and sweeping statement, the bill made legal the work of the squatter government. Section 18 stated: "...the laws passed by a recent legislative assembly of said Territory held by the authority of the people thereof, not inconsistent with this act, be, and the same are by declared to be in force in said Territory...." [29]

This was as much (or more) as the Dakota Land Company could hope for, but the bill "was laid on the table," leaving the squatters in legal limbo. While the proposed organic law seemed only just and fair to the people affected by it, political realities in Washington doomed it to failure. This was clearly a Democratic measure. But 1858 saw the new Republican Party and disgruntled, anti-Buchanan Democrats roll up major successes in the House of Representatives.

Many of these new men were of an anti-slavery bent, and were unwilling to establish states and territories that threatened to spread or strengthen that odious institution. The collapse of the economy following the Panic of 1857 also contributed to the defeat of the territorial legislation.

The old-line Democrats and those hanging on to the party, such as the Dakota Land Company, felt the sting of defeat at the hands of the new men. Although there is nothing in the record to suggest that the Dakota speculators were counting on slaves to do their hard work, their plans were damaged nevertheless.

The Dakota Land Company was also weakened by the defection of one of its leading members. James W. Lynd angrily denounced the Democratic Party in his newspaper, the *Henderson Democrat*. With some well-chosen parting shots, he said his party had strayed away from the path of honesty. He accused the Democrats of plotting to use "bogus returns" in the upcoming election to trump up votes in the "out of the way counties." Blaming his former colleagues, Lynd said the Democratic Party of Minnesota was "corrupt and depraved."[30] Whether he meant to or not, Lynd struck a blow in favor of the Missouri River speculators. Dakota was thrust into the great debate over slavery that threatened to swallow up even the most laudable of plans.

The squatters, however, refused to give up. The economy had bounced back nicely after a two-year hiatus. A large immigration was expected in 1859, and Sioux Falls City was within reach. From the northeast, immigrants could travel to Sioux Falls on the New Ulm, Minnesota, road that passed through Medary. There was a trail from Sioux City, and a well-traveled road from the mouth of the James River to the Missouri River.[31]

James M. Allen, the "Secretary" and "certificate maker" of Dakota, made it known that Sioux Falls City fully expected to grow in the coming year, as he had received many letters of inquiry from the East.[32] More people were on the way. If the speculators' modest accomplishments in 1858 were insufficient, then a bigger noise was needed, and with increased population, they would be ready to sound off. There was no quit in this bunch.

In 1859, they held another convention, formed another legislature and pounded out another round of legislation. Interestingly, we know a great deal more about the second squatter legislature of Dakota.

On September 3, 1859, a small group of settlers met in "convention" in Sioux Falls City at the Dakota House, to discuss the advisability of setting up another squatter legislature.[33] By this time they undoubtedly knew that the treaty with the Yankton Sioux had been approved by Congress, thus opening up more than 11,000,000 acres of land between the Big Sioux and Missouri Rivers. This meant they could expand their base of operations and locate town sites on the James and Missouri Rivers. This also meant that rival town site companies could move in to the new area and threaten the political supremacy of the Dakota Land Company.

The political activity of the summer and fall of 1859 was recalled by Samuel J. Albright in an article entitled "The First Organized Government of Dakota," written in 1898, for the Minnesota Historical Society. While his account does not square in every way with other records, it does provide information the others do not. Albright says that there was something like a territorial-wide election in 1859, which included Pembina and the newly arrived speculators on the Missouri slope. He recalled a "warm rivalry" between the Yankton and Sioux Falls men, with each group "puffing itself up for the capital site." Albright apparently didn't think too much of the Yankton men, calling them "plodding rivals" of the Scandinavian persuasion. They were no match for the Yankee pluck and energy of the Eastern-born and -bred colonists who were "all Americans with the persistence and push incident to their nativity."[34]

The Sioux Falls City men viewed the political situation with more urgency than did their "plodding rivals." With big plans in the works, they were anxious to hold an election to elect a representative to Congress, a governor, secretary of the territory, a full slate of councilmen and members of the House of Representatives, and a number of local officials in Big Sioux County. They were: a judge of probate, district attorney, sheriff, register of deeds, county treasurer, coroner, two justices of the peace, two county assessors, two constables and three county commissioners.[35] As there were probably about forty people (mostly men) living in Big Sioux County, the high number of local officials meant that there was about one official for every three people, and a chance for every man to win an office.

Election-day was September 12, 1859.

For delegate to Congress, Albright recalled that the first choice was Alpheus G. Fuller, again.[36] But as editor and proprietor of the *Dakota Democrat* in 1859, Albright refused to endorse anyone, asking only that the voters "select the man who you may judge best qualified..."[37] According to sworn statements following the election, the voters selected Jefferson P. Kidder, a popular politician from St. Paul. Henry Masters was named to serve another term as squatter governor, although there is no record of how many votes he got, and who, if anyone, opposed him. But there is more information on the delegate question.

In his essay, Albright says that the Yankton men put up John B. S. Todd for delegate, but he was defeated by Kidder with the help of the Pembina vote which he (Albright) controlled through a friend in that settlement. The result was the "defeat of Todd and the success of the Sioux Valley ticket carrying with it the location of the capital at Sioux Falls City."[38]

Albright's assertion conflicts with a number of documents later collected and published in the South Dakota Historical Collections. According to "Secretary of Dakota Territory" James M. Allen's "Certificate of Election Returns," signed almost six months after the election, those counties that voted were Big Sioux (two precincts), Vermillion, Midway, Rock and Pembina. No votes were reported from Yankton. Using wildly exaggerated vote totals, Allen concluded that Kidder beat Fuller by 1938 to 147. Todd's name is nowhere mentioned on Allen's certificate.[39] W. W. Brookings lodged two certificates in support of Kidder, one as "Acting Governor" and the other in the capacity of "Governor Ex-officio." [40]

The efficacy of the "certificates" was undermined by Moses K. Armstrong, a dyed-in-the-wool Yankton booster who passed through Sioux Falls City not long after the so-called election. A Sioux Falls resident told Armstrong that the 23 men living at the town site managed to poll 187 votes at one of the "precincts" of Big Sioux County.[41]

Armstrong apparently came away from his visit believing that Fuller was chosen to be the delegate to Congress again, but he was misinformed. In a letter to DeWitt from the Yankton agency, where he was spying on the men of the new settlement, Fuller pledged his support for Kidder. He made it clear he had no desire to return to Washington and buck the tide. "The great object I had in view at the time of the election has been accomplished, that was to prevent a delegate from being elected in the southern portion of the territory." Fuller was satisfied with Kidder and seemingly more satisfied that he lost the election, as he would decline the honor "under any circumstances." He would remain at the Yankton agency "on the lookout," until "all political wires are pulled and then go east" to Washington, to assist Kidder in any way possible.[42] .

Fuller's revealing letter is housed in the archives of the South Dakota Heritage Center and its burned edges indicates that someone tossed it in a fire to destroy the evidence and then, changing his mind, quickly pulled it out of the flames. The scorched letter is significant in that it corroborates Albright's statements regarding a rivalry between the Yankton and the Sioux Falls City men. It makes it clear that the Dakota Land Company was worried about competition to the south that could influence the formation of the new territory and the selection of the capital. Fuller's letter also points out that he believed the men under Todd's leadership were something more than "plodding rivals."

Then there were unanticipated problems for the Sioux Falls City men. The community was shocked by the sudden and unexpected death of Henry Masters, a man counted on to serve as governor and preside over the legislature again. It was first reported—and often repeated—that Masters was seemingly in good health on the morning of his death, attending to work at his farm that included what is now the southeast corner of 8th Street and Duluth Avenue in Sioux Falls. Then later in the day, September 5th, he suffered a stroke (then called apoplexy) and died with his son, Henry Jr., present. It was the first known death of a white man at the Falls.[43]

The loss of any person in a struggling, isolated settlement is serious, but the death of a man of Masters' stature was immeasurable. It was the soul of a poet that winged its way into the cosmos that September day. The saddened and diminished colony had to start a cemetery and replace its governor. Henry Masters was buried on his own farmland, on a bluff overlooking the Falls that he so loved.

After Masters' death, Albright was named governor, but he refused the honor, preferring to remain the Speaker of the House. Soon thereafter, Brookings assumed that easy responsibility. And it was Brookings—his disability notwithstanding—who acted as governor, *ex officio*, during the second session of the squatter legislature. Unlike Masters, Brookings made no address to the legislature—or none that was published. Nevertheless, this small honor proved to be the first in a long line of political successes for him.

According to Albright, the legislature lacked a suitable public facility to meet in. "There was no domed capital to open wide its doors to these frontier legislators; no gilded halls, with soft carpets and luxurious chairs to receive them." Instead, the Council met in Brookings' cozy cabin and the House went to work in the small office of the *Dakota Democrat*.[44] The *Dakota Democrat*, however, reported that they convened at the "Capital House" on November 2nd.

While they may or may not have met under the same roof, it took four meetings before a quorum was reached. On November 2nd, 3rd, 4th and 5th: no quorum.[45] This gave their enemies ammunition to ridicule them, but once they did meet in sufficient quantity to do business, on November 7th, the legislators went to work with dedication and purpose, just as they did the year before.

The legislature was formed as follows: a Council consisting of six men and a House of Representatives with eleven members. In the Council, Midway and Rock counties were represented by Joseph B. Amidon and W. W. Brookings, the latter named president of the Council; Big Sioux and Pipestone counties by L. B. Atwood and James McCall, and Vermillion and Yankton counties by Joseph Scales and J. B. Greenway. Amidon and McCall were connected with the Dakota Land Company, the latter a Wisconsin man. Atwood and Brookings were with the defunct Western Town Company, while Scales and Greenway were settlers who came in after the town was founded.

Of the group, Greenway stood out among the experimental legislators. He was a Tennessee mountain man, fearless and forceful, rough in his habits and unable to get along with others.[46] By reputation, Greenway had a "mind devoid of either fear or reverence and a gun that spoke quick and earnestly."[47] He was probably as much a mystery to his fellow speculators as he is to the readers of this book.

Greenway was part of a rough group that was typical of other "founding fathers" on the frontier. As all of these men lived in Sioux Falls City, the fact that some were named to represent other counties makes the election itself seem even more questionable.

The House of Representatives consisted of John Rouse, George Freudenreich, R. M. Johnson and S. J. Albright from Big Sioux County; James W. Evans, C. Cooper, J. E. Peters and William Stevens from Midway and Pipestone counties; and William Little, Albert Kilgore and Amos Shaw from Vermillion and Rock Counties. Notice that contrary to the makeup of the Council, the House had no one from Yankton County. Of this group, Evans, Albright and Freudenreich (also spelled "Freidenreich") were members of the Dakota Land Company—the latter was the son of Baron Frederick Freudenreich, a founder of the company. Rouse was a boot and shoemaker who advertised his business in the *Dakota Democrat*. Kilgore, the village blacksmith, was with the Dubuque party. Of the others, only Amos Shaw figured prominently in the future of Dakota.[48]

Officers to serve both houses were appointed and the squatter legislators got down to business as if their plates were full. Over a period of five full-day sessions, a number of bills and memorials were considered and some passed. Greenway introduced a bill to allow McCall to establish a ferry across the Big Sioux River. Peters offered a bill to incorporate the Sioux Falls Library Association. Cooper sought the creation of the Dakota branch of the Pacific Railroad. Little wanted to establish the counties of Buchanan and Douglas, and Evans wanted to create the county of Scott. The proposed towns of Claraville and Thomaston were the subjects of legislation. Stevens wanted a road laid out from Sioux Falls to the Missouri River and McCall introduced bills pertaining to the setting of fires on the prairie, regulating the running of swine and cattle, and for the formation and incorporation of the Sioux Falls Manufacturing Company.

A memorial to Congress asked for the establishment of a semi-weekly mail service from Sioux City to Sioux Falls City. And a measure dealing with the death or resignation of the governor was passed. They even had the nerve to pass a joint resolution instructing the delegate to ask Congress for an appropriation of $6000.00 to defray the expense of running their illegal government.

The lawmakers apparently understood parliamentary procedure and their acts suggest that one or more of them had legislative experience somewhere else. They followed the form used in lawmaking bodies, taking care to read and number bills, to refer them or "lay them on the table," to make motions, form committees and take votes. Records of their proceedings indicate they dealt with one another in a gentlemanly fashion, without fisticuffs or excessive argument. Greenway didn't shoot anyone. Having handled several pieces of lofty legislation, both houses adjourned on Friday, November 18, 1859.[49]

While Sioux Falls City was the scene of extra-legal legislation, the men of Yankton were in a session of their own making. At a "settlers' convention" on November 8th, a small group of men led by Todd, Frost and Armstrong, met to "take into consideration the necessity of an early Territorial organization, and to draft and sign a memorial to Congress praying for a legal form of government." A series of resolutions were drawn up and approved that defined their dilemma and offered a solution. Since Congress created the state of Minnesota, and left much of its former territory outside of the new state, and beyond the reach of laws, the federal legislature was at least expected to grant the people so affected a territorial organization.

This, of course, has a familiar ring; the Sioux Falls City men used the same refrain over and over again. But once again the Yankton men sought to separate themselves from the settlers on the Big Sioux River. While recognizing the need for law and order over the entire area, from Pembina on the Red River of the North, to the Big Sioux River settlements, to the Missouri slope, the Yankton men specifically disavowed any connection with or any support of, any election held in the territory. "We do not approve of any election that has been held, nor will participate in any that may be held in any portion of this Territory for the purpose of electing a delegate to Congress, but we trust to the wisdom and justice of Congress to provide us with a legal form of government at an early day."[50] They had something else in mind.

The Yankton settlers directed Moses K. Armstrong, the secretary of their meeting, to send a copy of their proceedings to the *St. Louis Republican* and the *Sioux City Register*, and to other papers as may be "conducive to our wants," for publication. It is noteworthy that the *Dakota Democrat*, the only newspaper in Dakota, was not mentioned as "conducive" to their wants. So instead of joining with the Sioux Falls City men, the Yankton settlers went their own way with their competing interests and aspirations intact. They too, wanted the capital and all the offices, and the money that went with it. While the Yankton men were largely Republican and the Sioux Falls City men predominantly Democratic, when one looks under the labels this was not a political partisan fight but more like a business rivalry.

The Sioux Falls City men helped to drive a wedge between the two groups by sending Jefferson P. Kidder to Congress, as they were unwilling to wait for the national legislature to act. In Kidder, the squatters had a man of ability and credibility. Born in 1816 in Braintree, Vermont, Kidder made a name for himself before he went west. Well-educated and a lawyer of considerable repute, Kidder served in the Vermont state senate and was elected lieutenant governor in 1854, serving with distinction. He came to St. Paul in 1857 and immediately established himself as a leader amid the angry swirl of controversial, pre-Civil War politics. He was reputed to be a conservative, states-rights Democrat, said to be the "only Democrat who was ever endorsed by a popular vote in Vermont."[51]

He joined forces with the Dakota Land Company and in 1859, went to Sioux Falls City with a view of living there and participating in city building from the ground up. Kidder arrived at Sioux Falls City on horseback in the summer of 1859. If he had any plans to live there, he soon changed his mind. For within two months after his arrival, he was back in St. Paul and would not return to Dakota until 1865. While away, he learned of his "election" as the "delegate" and in the spring of 1860, he was off to Washington.

The *Dakota Democrat* gave Kidder a hearty endorsement, calling him a man of "sterling ability" with "affable manners and gentlemanly bearing." Albright, who knew Kidder well, said he went to Washington "bearing with him the unbroken confidence of his entire constituency."[52] In other quarters, however, his "election" was ridiculed. *The Dubuque Herald* wrote, "Mr. Kidder got his election by taking a dozen good fellows into a wagon and going to a few points in the territory and at each place organizing a poll, naming the precinct and then depositing as many votes as the good fellows thought necessary to show well in the returns."[53]

Historian and journalist George W. Kingsbury had similar

thoughts. When considering the rather large vote Kidder received from Midway County, Kingsbury wrote: ""Medary, the county seat of Midway County, was not a populous town, but it was surrounded by a region capable of sustaining a large population."[54] From Kingsbury's tongue-in-cheek remarks, we can conclude that the ability to sustain a large population was equated to having a large population, and the potential vote became the polled vote. Journalistic satire, however, had no bearing on Kidder's ability and his goals. And all agreed he was imminently qualified to speak on behalf of Dakota.

Kidder delivered a memorial to the House of Representatives, signed by Albright and Brookings, asking for a seat as delegate from Dakota. He delivered his own memorial explaining his reasons for claiming this right. On April 12, 1860, the memorials were referred to the committee of elections and ordered printed. He was given an honorary seat in the House. It seems he made a good first impression.

In his memorial, Kidder launched a series of legal arguments in support of his right to a seat and Dakota's right to representation. Sounding like his predecessor, Alpheus G. Fuller, Kidder covered some old ground, maintaining that a large number of good people, through no fault of their own, had been cut off from law and order when Minnesota was admitted to the Union. These people deserved the protection of law and full representation in Congress no less than folks from the states and territories.

He quoted from the Northwest Ordinance of 1787, which provided "for the government of the territory of the United States northwest of the river Ohio." The purpose of this well-known law was to disseminate all forms of civil government over those who moved out into the frontier. It was an inviolate compact among the people, like the Constitution itself. Kidder insisted that a thoughtful, compassionate government would not continue to deny a segment of its people the security of law and the blessings of liberty that went with it. No matter what other political exigencies were in the fire, fair-minded men must be able to put aside their differences and extend to others those benefits that they and their families enjoyed. Such practices were uniquely American and were what made us Americans.

If passion and precedent were not enough to sway Congress, Kidder put forth a strong rational argument. Referring to the 1849 act that created Minnesota Territory, he argued that a part of that territory still existed. It didn't disappear when the state of Minnesota was admitted; as an entity, it went on uninterrupted. Although people, by common consent, called the area Dakota, it was still a viable, unrepealed territory, fully entitled to representation in Congress.

Returning to gut issues, he pointed out to Congress that the people of Dakota had made considerable material progress against the forces of nature. There were five counties, two fully organized and ready for local government. There were "thousands" of sturdy pioneers engaged in worthwhile pursuits, raising families, plowing and planting, and more folks were flowing in. Why, Sioux Falls City even had a newspaper. And in summation, he told Congress about the depredations caused "by hostile bands of savages" who destroyed "whole towns." If ever there were buzzwords to stir the soul of a congressman, it was talk of the bloody excesses by Native Americans.

Congress was considering the creation of a number of new territories, including Arizona, Nevada, Chippewa, Idaho and Dakota.[55] But on May 11th, the House tabled the bills that would have founded the new territories. This raised the ire of the *St. Paul Pioneer and Democrat*, whose snarling editor laid the blame at the feet of the "Black Republicans" who insisted that no new territories or states be admitted without an anti-slavery clause.[56] While this editorial reflects undue emotionalism, it points accurately to the bone of contention. The national debate over slavery had reached the boiling point in Congress. Each side of the fiery issue had its hardheaded adherents, unwilling to relent. It was dividing the country and there was talk of secession in some southern states. In the face of this furious debate, it is no wonder that Dakota came up the loser. Its concerns were dwarfed by other national issues of the gravest importance.

Kidder made two trips to Washington, but the best he could do was to make a case for reimbursement of his travel expenses in the amount of $1500.00. In Kidder, the Dakota Land Company had inveighed with its biggest gun. If a man of his intellect and background could not sway Congress, then they had no one among them who could. His failure meant the lofty ambitions of his fellow speculators were probably doomed. The fall elections of 1860 were fast approaching and indications were that the St. Paul speculators would not have a friendly Democratic administration to rely on.

But it was, once again, their Yankton rivals who bested them. Todd took a petition with 428 signatures to Washington, in an effort to exploit his political connections and secure legislation favorable to his group. While he was not successful in that regard, he was able to expose Kidder's "certificates." Todd proved that he was not a candidate, and that the Missouri River settlers did not participate in the "election" that sent Kidder to Congress. He was able to produce actual signatures of real settlers, although his figures were probably not reflective of the actual population on the Missouri slope.⁵⁷

There were outside factors to consider, as well. The announcement of the discovery of gold in the Pike's Peak region of extreme western Kansas Territory was something Kidder and his fellow speculators could not overcome. Thousands flocked to the new gold fields from every eastern point in 1858 and 1859, drawn by publicity from newspapers all over the country. Cities and villages in Iowa and Minnesota were drained of much of their populations, and many farm sites were abandoned. No doubt this had a negative impact on the Dakota town sites as well. Gold was something they could not compete with. Despite some editorial skepticism, its lure went unchallenged as the wagon trains bypassed the Dakota prairie town sites in favor of the mountains. It is possible some of the gold fields-bound pilgrims even passed through Sioux Falls City on their way West.

There were no conventions or elections in Sioux Falls City in 1860, and no third session of a squatter legislature. It was a quiet time. Sioux Falls City folk drew back and waited, hoping for good news. There was excited talk in political and journalistic circles about creating a new territory—but not Dakota Territory. The new territory was to be called Jefferson or Laramie, embracing the gold fields of Pike's Peak.

Chapter X

Steamboats on the Big Sioux River

"We understand that two enterprising gentlemen have made arrangements to place on the Big Sioux River, two light draught steamboats."

St. Paul Pioneer and Democrat
May 9, 1858

In the spring of 1858, speculators and their newspapers regularly engaged in optimistic rhetoric, and for good reason. Never mind the hard times following the financial crash of 1857 and the resulting scarcity of money. They succeeded in founding their town sites, and those chosen to remain on the remote venues had survived their first winter in Dakota. Having accomplished the initial phase of their plan, they began thinking about the next steps. It was imperative that they strengthen their commercial ties to other towns, such as Sioux City, if their conquest was to have lasting benefits. A logical way to do this was to utilize the available waterways, especially the Big Sioux River.

During the pre-settlement era, the Big Sioux River was well known to the white man. Eighteenth century mapmakers included the Big Sioux River on their maps. A member of the Lewis and Clark expedition had an understanding of the river, and they were apparently among the earliest white men to explore it and travel on it. In 1804, as the famous expedition made its way into the mysterious northern depths of the Louisiana Purchase, the guide, Pierre Dorion, explained to Lewis and Clark that the Big Sioux River was navigable from its mouth to the Falls.[1] Dorion was one of the first white men to venture into what became Dakota Territory. He lived among the Indians, married a Sioux Indian woman and traveled the river highways in pursuit of furs and adventure.

From early times rivers were looked upon as readymade roads. By 1858 steamboat transportation was well-established on the Missouri River, following the example set by Lewis and Clark. St. Paul had long utilized steamboat traffic on the Mississippi River, and was looking for other watery avenues of commerce.

The Red River of the North was seen as another river of promise. In the spring of 1859, St. Paul was buzzing with news that a company was preparing to run steamboats from that city to the British possessions in Canada. Starting in the Minnesota River, the steamboats would travel to Big Stone Lake, cross a narrow passage to Lake Traverse, and from there, head straight up the Red River of the North. St. Paul merchants were salivating over the money they expected to make from the fur trade from Canada.[2]

The St. Paul to Canada experiment was based on the belief that steamboats could move well on smaller streams if the boats were downsized to fit the contours of narrower banks and shallower beds. The Minnesota River and the Red River of the North were good places to start. The Big Sioux River, which connected Sioux Falls City with Sioux City, Iowa, was another natural place to test the concept.

It wasn't, however, the Dakota Land Company that tried it first. On June 20, 1857, the 75-ton steam ferry, *Lewis Burnes*, plied the Big

Sioux River a distance of 30 miles from Sioux City, without incident. The river channel was declared deep and free of dangerous snags. The successful experiment convinced some men that the river was navigable at least as far north as the Rock River that entered from Iowa.[3]

Actually there were some men who believed it was navigable all the way to the Falls. Lieutenant A. J. Donaldson, a member of a railway survey team, remarked: "It [the Big Sioux River] is about one hundred yards wide at its mouth, and navigable for steamboats to the rapids, and might be made so for a considerable distance by the expenditure of a small sum for its improvement."[4] Others were ready to experiment with steam travel for the sake of adventure.

In September of 1857, a contingent of people from Sergeant Bluff, Iowa, and Dakota City, Nebraska Territory, boarded the steam ferry *Dakotah City*, intending to make a lengthy excursion up the Big Sioux River. They succeeded in traveling four or five miles when they were forced to turn back after their progress was stopped by a "big pile of mud."[5] This may have been the earliest attempt by white people to travel north on the Big Sioux River in something other than a canoe.

Encouraged by these attempts, two men known only as Fanning and Taylor—possibly connected with the Dakota Land Company—announced in May of 1858 that they would run steamboats on the Big Sioux River between Sioux City and Eminija, "a distance of one hundred and forty miles." This made front-page news in St. Paul, and was proudly reported in the *Pioneer and Democrat*. According to the *Pioneer and Democrat*, Fanning thoroughly examined the river during the low-water phase in 1857, and was convinced that the enterprise would be successful. He was satisfied that the river was navigable, for "light draught boats, at all seasons [except, of course, in winter] from its mouth to Eminija," and when the water was at its greatest depth, large boats could traverse those waters with ease and safety. Above the falls, steamboats could travel another one hundred miles. Fanning visited Sioux Falls in the spring of 1858 and returned to St. Paul with news that two boats "were already in the Sioux river trade, each of them having made a trip to Eminija."[6]

But news of the enterprise is scarce, and may be nothing more than Dakota Land Company puffing. In fact, there probably were no attempts to navigate the Big Sioux River by steamboat in 1858. A report in a St. Paul newspaper that steamboats reached Sioux Falls City in the summer of 1858 was quashed by Yankton settler and chronicler, Moses K. Armstrong. He visited Sioux Falls City in October of 1859, and was told by men living there that steamboats had yet to reach the town site.[7]

The year 1859, however, found both the *Lewis Burnes* and the *Dakotah City* gearing up for pleasure trips. At the same time, kindred enterprises were utilizing the waterways in a more practical way. For the traveling pioneer, it was often more important to have a means of crossing rivers than it was navigating them.

In the 1850's, before bridges were built, people crossed the Big Sioux River on horseback, in carriages (assuming the water was not too deep) and on ferries for hire. The best known ferry was run by Paul Pacquette, an eccentric Frenchman, who arrived at the mouth of the Big Sioux River in the mid-1840's and located his ferry at or near the present-day bridge on Interstate Highway 29. His business, and the others like it, operated on water as did the steamboats, but proved to be far more useful and important. They carried settlers, travelers, soldiers and their supplies safely across the river. In the pre-bridge era, their contributions can hardly be under-stressed.

Pacquette was authorized by the U. S. Army, on December 18, 1855, to "put a good ferry boat on the Big Sioux River," for the express purpose of transporting government troops, wagons, and cargo. He was expressly forbidden to "molest friendly Indians," and ordered not to sell them "spirituous liquors."[8] Yet liquor was usually available at the store Pacquette kept beside his ferry.

Pacquette styled himself like many other Frenchmen who came to the great Northwest. He was earthy, colorful and outgoing. He spoke broken English with a peculiar "hissing inflection at the end of each phrase." Early on he took Indians wives. When in 1858, he decided to marry a white woman, he had two Indian wives. He escorted them out West, presumably back to their people. Unfortunately, they returned to the Big Sioux River, much to the annoyance of Pacquette and his new spouse.[9]

In 1859, Pacquette's ferry business was flush with success with little interference from steamboats. A team of horses, mules or oxen could cross the river for fifty cents. A horse with rider paid twenty-five cents. Foot passengers and cattle were charged ten cents each, while hogs or sheep were ferried for a nickel a head.[10] Pacquette's ferry proved to be the most successful of the four located near the mouth of the Big Sioux River. It out-lived the others and ferried goods and people until the first bridge was built.[11]

Another ferry was placed in operation further to the north, at the mouth of the Rock River, where folks had been taking chances at a dangerous ford. In May of 1859, it was learned that a large ferry boat was under construction at the new settlement and would be ready to carry passengers and freight in about three or four weeks. For travelers going from Sioux City to Sioux Falls City, the Rock River crossing would connect them to a good road.[12]

As frontier enterprises, the ferries—while very necessary—were plodding and routine, while the steamboats were exciting and romantic. Taking a cruise on a steamboat was much preferred over sitting, or standing, on a flat platform next to an ox or a couple of pigs while the rope-ferry inched its way across the river. The company was usually unpleasant and the scenery never changed. Although infrequent and unpredictable, the steamboat parties were fun and adventuresome, and never seemed to lack for participants.

In June 1859, the *Lewis Burnes*, with some 40 ladies and gentlemen on board, set out for parts north on an exploratory and pleasure excursion, taking two days' provisions. Accompanying the happy throng was a reporter for the *Sioux City Eagle*. While the reporter neglected to name the excursionists, he left us with a structured and amusing account of their journey that began at six o'clock in the morning under threatening skies.

With the Sioux City band playing "soul stirring and entertaining music," the steam ferry entered the mouth of the Big Sioux without difficulty. They passed a group of men, Indian and white, rafting logs downriver. Opposite Bruyer's farm (probably Brugier's), they stopped on the Dakota side to take on some freight. They passed the Big Sioux ferry landing (probably Pacquette's) and entered a stretch of peaceful water bordered on both sides by open prairie. Further on, the heavily timbered riverbank was augmented with thick underbrush, creating the feeling of being concealed from view.

The reporter obviously enjoyed himself as the natural world revealed its tranquil beauty before his eager eyes. He described with great enthusiasm the lush Dakota bottomland, the high bluffs, the thick woods and the undulating flow of the prairie. The steamboat flushed some ducks from the water and some of the men opened fire, but without success. The ladies gathered wild flowers when the boat docked at Haviland's farm. A lavish dinner was prepared after the excursionists discovered they had brought enough food for a week's stay.

On they went, passing Broken Kettle Creek, Evan's farm and Roudel's farm. Near a group of islands they passed the point where, two years before, the *Lewis Burnes* turned back. The captain and his crew must have felt they reached a milestone. Farm after farm they passed, finally pulling up at the settlement of D. M. Mills for fuel. All hands disembarked and assisted Mills in taking on wood. After leaving the Mills' farm, the *Lewis Burnes* continued its journey, stopping at 6:43 PM for the night, on the "Dacotah" side, about two miles below Westfield, Iowa.

The party disembarked, made camp and after a meal, danced until eleven o'clock, when the call came forth: "every man to his robe." With only mosquitoes to deal with on that particular night, the happy group went to sleep. In the morning, they set out again; their next destination was the mouth of the Rock River. But owing to the late start, the crew turned the steamboat around and headed back. The reporter did not explain the change of plans.

On the return trip, they met with a "slight accident" but no one was injured. And while the small steam ferry lacked the comforts of a large steamer, no one complained. Indeed, all agreed it was a most memorable journey, and all joined in the belief that steamboats could safely traverse the Big Sioux River, at least as far as the Rock River.[13]

It was like everything else on the frontier: someone takes a chance and succeeds and sees no reason why others can't do likewise, or even better.

Following the success of the *Lewis Burnes*, the *Dakotah City* made another run up the Big Sioux, carrying a load of folks to a Fourth of July "Pic Nic."[14] Apparently a reporter was not sent to cover the event, for the *Eagle* reported no details, except that passengers were told to bring their own "food and grogg" since "no refreshments would be sold on the boat."

Eighteen fifty-nine seemed to be the high-water mark for these minor adventures. It was even reported that the "elegant steamer *Omaha*—a wide-wheeler and the largest boat in the Upper Missouri River trade" successfully navigated the Big Sioux River, with passengers and freight, all the way to Sioux Falls City. While this report lacks credibility, all such publicity added to the belief that the navigation of the Big Sioux River by smaller steamers would be readily accomplished.[15]

The successes and the publicity they inspired were doubtlessly well received by the Dakota Land Company. While none of the Sioux City ventures reached Eminija, men of commerce could find encouragement in the attempts. And while the Dakota Land Company never launched a steamboat from either terminus, Eminija was looked upon as the commercial base of the future. The minutes of the 1859 annual stockholders meeting of the Dakota Land Company contain the boast that Eminija was located at the "more practicable head of navigation for large steamers...."[16] A Dakota correspondent from the *New York Times* reported the Big Sioux River was navigable in "some seasons" with "light draft boats" from Sioux City to Sioux Falls.[17]

The Sioux City newspapers make no mention of the *Lewis Burnes*, nor any other steamer for that matter, plying the waters of the Big Sioux River in 1860. The following year, however, the *Lewis Burnes* tried it again—this time with disastrous results.

In July of 1861, the *Lewis Burnes*, with a "crew of one man and a small boy," embarked from Sioux City with a group of pleasure seekers and a newspaper correspondent with a flare for tongue-in-cheek reporting. All was well until the boy, described as near-sighted, spotted dark clouds on the horizon. Soon a thunderstorm was upon them, and despite the "furious winds," the "staunch craft rode the tide." The brave crew and passengers took heart and the craft continued on its voyage until a second "squal" hit. Suddenly the "self-possession of the gallant Capt H.K.C. and his crew....forsook them and the scene that followed may be imagined but not described."

The reporter tied himself to an empty beer keg, hoping it would serve as a life raft in the event of a water evacuation. He heard someone yell from below deck that the bowel of the boat was taking on water. It was then that the Captain made for shore, but the engine shut down. From among the horrified passengers, the reporter spotted a girl with "heavenly eyes." He offered his arm as a life preserver when a "huge wave" struck the boat, causing them to go overboard.

Thinking he was about to meet his maker, he struggled for the shore. Both he and the girl were successful, and once on shore, he cast his "keg to the tide." Later, safely in his Sioux City office, the correspondent wrote of his experience and the fate of the *Lewis Burnes*. It was from a note found in a bottle, he happily explained to his readers, that he learned that the "Lewis is sinking, and may our sales (sp) rest on terra firma." As for he and the girl, "you shall hear anon."[18]

But the *Lewis Burnes* was made of sterner stuff. It did not sink and later undertook what may have been its greatest adventure. In November of 1861, the sturdy little steamer hauled a load of corn from Sioux City to Fort Randall, with Captain C. K. "Charley" Howard at the helm.[19] Howard was considered a "first rate fellow" and an "experienced boatman."[20] Risking high winds and low water, the boat arrived with its cargo—and there it stayed. It was too late in the year to make a return trip and during the winter, ice tore holes in the boat's hull. In April, with the spring thaw, it broke away from its moorings and drifted down river several miles until it became stranded on a sand bar.

A vigorous effort was made to recover and save the vessel because of its vital importance to Sioux City commerce.[21] As the water level rose, however, the *Lewis Burnes* broke free from the sandbar and drifted, entirely on its own, over the fast and perilous waters of the Missouri River, until it beached itself at St. Helena, Nebraska. There Captain Howard and his crew found their beloved steamboat in relatively good condition, having survived a "romantic" one hundred-mile journey, *sans* crew.[22] It was hoped that the gallant *Lewis Burnes* would once again serve on rivers of the frontier.

It is unlikely that it did, however, for Captain C. K. Howard—who also owned and piloted the steam ferryboat *Jane Ritchey*—left Sioux City in November of 1862. With a final and tearful look at his beloved *Jane,* Charley set out for the wilds of the upper Missouri River where he would engage in trade with the Indians at Fort Pierre.[23] Already, Sioux City was too tame for Charley Howard.

Charley Howard went on to become an important figure in Dakota history, a folk hero of sorts.[24] But not so for steamboats on the Big

Sioux River. The project was dropped without fanfare or publicity, doubtless because the river was too shallow and log-infested, and therefore too dangerous in the summer season. Furthermore, by 1862, a well-established wagon road was in operation between Sioux Falls City and Sioux City. Yankton was connected to both towns by overland roads as well. The steamboat experiment sank quietly under the weight of new ideas. On the frontier enterprising men were an impatient lot, with the mental agility to switch quickly from plan to plan. Little time was spent looking back, save for a humorous glance at both the good times and risky adventures. Somebody probably blamed the mosquitoes.

Although the great commercial venture failed, Sioux City ferryboats regularly traversed the Big Sioux River in search of wood for fuel. Also, there remained some interest in occasional "pleasure" excursions. On June 21, 1872, about twenty-five men and women boarded the *Undine* and steamed north for a time. About a month later, a Sunday school group did the same on the *Undine*. How far it went on both occasions is a mystery. There is also some suggestion in the record that a boat called the *Minnehaha* also traveled north from Sioux City for an undetermined duration.[25]

If there was any inclination to revive the goal of steamboat travel on the Big Sioux River, it was made all but impossible by the mid-eighteen seventies. By then the mill owners had built dams at various points on the Big Sioux to run their gristmills. Travel was, of course, limited by the dams. This was apparent to those who rode the steamboat *Lillie* in August of 1878, when its progress up the Big Sioux was halted by a mill dam after it went but thirteen miles upriver from Sioux City.[26]

Thus with these few examples, we can review the history of steamboat travel on the Big Sioux River in a minimum of pages. We may look back upon these events and consider the notion of steamboat travel quaint, outlandish or impractical, but we must surely see it within its proper context: a part of the grand scheme of the Cavaliers of the Dakota frontier. They were bold ones who came to the Dakota frontier in the vanguard of settlement, bringing with them their dreams of fortune and their desire to tame and harness the wilderness and make nature their servant.

Chapter XI

First Newspaper Fight in Dakota

"We have ascertained that it (Sioux Falls) is situated somewhere on the road to the North Pole..."

Sioux City Register
November 19, 1859

Editors of frontier newspapers were a bold and feisty bunch of pioneers. They were humorous, audacious and fearless word-warriors. As intellectual adventurers, they became leaders as soon as they turned out their first sheet of print. Editors voluntarily and unflinchingly carried the banner of the community they represented, boasting of their town's prospects and defending their realm from attacks by outsiders—usually launched by a rival newspaper in a neighboring town, or from another state. The newspaper office became the information center and focal point of the community, and folks rallied around the fearless editor and his staff.

Frontier presses were financially supported by advertisers, subscribers and by those who benefited from the success of the newspaper. Since many frontier newspapers were formed to promote a political or business faction, they were often biased in the extreme, and made no pretense toward being objective. As such, clashes were inevitable, and when newspaper editors fought—get out of the way. Attacks were apt to be a combination of the comic and the caustic, and when the opportunity presented itself—an assault on the jugular.

The first newspaper fight in Dakota kicked off in the fall of 1859, not long after the first issue of the *Dakota Democrat* appeared at Sioux Falls City. As it was the only newspaper in Dakota at the time, an opponent had to be sought from outside the territory. Whether it was by design or by chance, the *Sioux City Register* found itself squared off against the *Dakota Democrat* in what became a colorful, lively battle of several months' duration.

Sioux Falls City was in its second year of existence when the *Democrat* set up shop. Its mission: let the world know about Dakota Territory, a vast wonderland of excitement, natural resources and opportunity. Dakota became a sort of no man's land in 1858, a territory in name only, when Minnesota was admitted to the Union. Yet all knew that there were thousands of envious eyes set on this land, ready to claim it and dig in. The *Dakota Democrat* was created to provide some incentive toward that end, speed things along, and make sure some of the profits went into the pockets of the men from the Dakota Land Company.

While the masthead was new, the press equipment had a storied past that began in 1836, when it was used to print the *Dubuque Visitor*, the first newspaper in that eastern Iowa city. Next, it went to Lancaster, Wisconsin, in March of 1843, to put out the *Grant County Herald*, the first newspaper in western Wisconsin. Moving further west, the press turned up in St. Paul in 1849, where J. M. Goodhue published the *Pioneer Press*, the first newspaper in Minnesota. Then in 1858, the claimant of three frontier firsts was hauled across the prairie in an ox cart, set up in a crude stone building by the river in Sioux Falls City and was put to work again.[1]

As we have seen in another chapter, the equipment arrived in Sioux Falls City in September of 1858, just in time to publish a call for a "mass convention of the people of Dakota Territory." While the convention and subsequent election notices were scattered far and wide, it would be nearly a year before the first number of the *Democrat* was published and placed before the public. During the long, lonesome winter of 1858-59, "a fine stone building, on the corner of Water street and Washington avenue," was completed in anticipation of Sioux Falls City's first newspaper. The press was put in its place and there were cases of type ready for use. They had everything but paper, and when that arrived, folks expected to see newsprint within a short time. Then, with a newspaper to exchange with other cities, Sioux Falls City could truly feel it was within the fraternity of civilized communities.[2]

The publisher and editor was Samuel J. Albright, a Dakota Cavalier who served in the squatter legislature. Albright came to St. Paul in 1853, and on October 4, 1855, he started the *St. Paul Free Press*, and served as its editor and publisher.[3] He was born in Delaware, Ohio in 1829, and was the boyhood friend of Minnesota territorial Governor Samuel A. Medary.[4] Albright, a genial, energetic, short man with a florid complexion and gold-rimmed glasses, was well suited for the new challenges offered by the Dakota frontier. One contemporary made the mysterious assertion that he moved "with the celerity of light."[5] Another called him a Bohemian. He was likeable and had a host of friends.

Albright was associated with the Dakota Land Company and was thoroughly caught up in his company's promotional schemes. He was a veteran of the Mexican war, and had enough adventure left to enable him to handle the throes and woes of a frontier newspaper editor. Albright gained newspaper experience in New Orleans and New York before coming to St. Paul. He apparently had some river piloting experience, as he purchased the steamboat *Wave,* the same vessel that hauled the first load of Dakota Land Company men and supplies from St. Paul to New Ulm in the spring of 1857. "Captain Albright," an article said, "will make a popular commander."[6]

It was, however, in the realm of print that Samuel J. Albright made his mark. In later years, far removed from the frontier, Albright recalled that the Sioux Falls City newspaper venture was originally slated to be handled by Medary and another veteran newspaperman from Detroit, John Harmon. Their vast experience as journalists was counted on to get the newspaper off to a good start and, after Congress created a territorial government, secure the lucrative public printing contract.

This plan never came to fruition, however, and Albright was forced to handle the editorial and publishing chores all by himself on a "smaller scale."[7] He was a still a young man when the first issue of the *Dakota Democrat* came out on July 2, 1859. He was assisted by I. W. Stuart, a St. Paul printer. Stuart recalled that they "flung to the breeze, the *Dakota Democrat* devoted to the organization of Dakota Territory and to the land speculation of its owners," meaning of course, the Dakota Land Company.[8]

The *Dakota Democrat* was issued sporadically, but proudly, in the summer and fall of 1859. But those editions that were printed hold up quite well when compared to the more established newspapers in St. Paul or Dubuque. There was a smattering of national news, a bit of fiction, along with items of local importance, and surprisingly, perhaps, a number of classifieds placed by Sioux Falls City businesses.

Samuel J. Albright and James M. Allen advertised their real estate business, promising to "attend to all business appertaining to a general land agency..." They also listed for sale, four shares of stock in the Dakota Land Company at $150.00 each.

Dr. J. L. Phillips, "physician and surgeon," had a prominent advertisement too. He promised to "make professional visits" in the "town or country," as need may dictate. Albert Kilgore was looking for blacksmith work at his shop on Hill Street, and John Rouse held himself out as a maker of boots and shoes, at prices that were in accord with any other boot maker in the East or West.[9] It all looked very respectable and prosperous. Anyone reading the *Dakota Democrat* would never suspect it originated from a crude and isolated outpost in the Northwest, where the merchants spent most of their time wishing for customers, watching their backs and longing for a future that equaled or exceeded the letter and spirit of their advertisements.

When Albright and Stuart began their duties, there were but a handful of town sites in the Big Sioux Valley, all dominated or owned by the Dakota Land Company. These places looked impressive on a map but had little or no people. The only potential rival to Sioux Falls was the infant town of Yankton on the Missouri River, and it was too new to be considered a serious threat. Besides, it had no newspaper. In order to pick a fight, Albright had to look elsewhere. He found an opponent in nearby Sioux City, Iowa, in the person of F. M. Ziebach, editor of the *Sioux City Register*. The *Register* was a staunch, Democratic, anti-Lincoln, anti-black, pro-slavery newspaper.

Like other newspapers of the era, including the *New York Times*, the *Register's* editorials were often shrill and over-emotional, as if Ziebach wanted to hammer his views into the reluctant mindsets of all those who opposed him. And he took his views to heart, zealously promoting Illinois Senator Stephen O. Douglas, and old-line Democratic principles. He was especially pleased that "Douglas Democrats" had moved into Dakota, as this was proof that the Democratic Party would control the territory's future legislature.[10]

At first the *Register* and Sioux City's other paper, the *Eagle*, treated Sioux Falls City and the rest of Dakota with respect. After all, it was in their best interest to do so, as most of the new settlers coming through Iowa, bound for Dakota, would pass through Sioux City and spend money. In an editorial about Sioux Falls, the *Eagle* said: "...we can but rejoice at the prosperity and advancement which is being made, and the citizens of this place should extend the right hand of fellowship, together with the warmest encouragement to those hardy pioneers, who are making the wilderness around the Falls to blossom with the homes of civilization."[11] When Albright came to Sioux City on business, he was greeted warmly by Ziebach, and sent on his way back to Sioux Falls with good wishes for the success of the *Dakota Democrat*[12]. Everything seemed right for a mutually beneficial relationship.

Prospects were good for Dakota too. During the spring and summer of 1859, a mild form of "Dakota fever" held sway over the Northwest as small parties of immigrants made their slow progress toward the hopeful town sites along the Big Sioux River. By far the greatest number had Sioux Falls City, now freely called the "Capital City," as their destination. One happy correspondent cheerfully warbled that Sioux Falls City was a "loadstone," at the end of a happy, scenic trail. It was also advertised to be a town without hazards, for "all fears of further difficulties with the Indians are dispersed, since the ratification of the treaty with the Yanktons." Even burned-out Medary showed signs of new life with the return of mail service from New Ulm, Minnesota.[13]

In St. Paul, where merchants were still trying to recover from the Panic of 1857, Sioux Falls City-bound pilgrims were most welcome. Suddenly merchants and steamboat companies were making money on the new immigration. Steam vessels such as the *Favorite,* the *Frank Steele* and the *Jeanette Roberts* regularly hauled freight, farm implements, horses, cattle and passengers bound for the "Capital City" of Dakota[14]

The journey took them up the Minnesota River to New Ulm. There they disembarked and traveled overland in prairie schooners on the well-marked government road to Mountain Pass near Lake Benton. From there it was almost straight west to Medary, and turning south, the caravans went on to Sioux Falls City. All along the way, the settlers feasted on the fish and fowl of a bountiful land, while they trained their eager eyes on what many believed was some of the richest farmland in America.

Dakota men who visited St. Paul were greeted by townspeople and the press and pumped for information about the outlying settlements. The Dakotans were free and generous in their praise of the Sioux Valley, especially Sioux Falls City. And upon completing their business they returned to Dakota, often with men who wanted to see this newsworthy place for themselves. When a group of people from Wisconsin showed up in St. Paul, traveling in prairie schooners, they were asked about their destination. One of them unhesitatingly said: "for the Sioux River," as on they went.[15]

Like St. Paul, Sioux City was liberal and free with its Dakota publicity, even though there was some uneasiness when a few of its leading citizens broke for Dakota after the treaty with the Yankton Sioux was approved by the Senate. Nevertheless, a good-natured exchange was carried on between Sioux City and its western and northern neighbors.

Sioux Falls men regularly made trips to Sioux City for mail and supplies, and such visits were duly noticed in the press. On one such occasion, the dignified Henry Masters came down from Sioux Falls City to lecture students in the Sioux City school. Masters, who was personally known and well-liked in Sioux City, was called a "finished scholar" with a "deep interest in the course of education."[16] But later he was gently chided for being a "self-appointed Governor," who delivered his message to "the two imaginary branches of a non-existing Territorial Legislature," and then went back to "tilling the soil."[17]

When the first issue of the *Dakota Democrat* was released, it was welcomed warmly in Sioux City. The *Register* was especially enthusiastic. "The establishment of a newspaper upon the ground which but a few months ago was undisturbed by the industry of the white man, and where the Indian and wild animal held...sway...is evidence of the progressive spirit of the age, and the achievements of a people whose watchword is PROGRESS." Since both newspapers were Democratic in politics, a comfortable sense of ante-bellum camaraderie took hold, and a long, cozy relationship was expected.[18]

This sentiment was echoed by the *St. Paul Pioneer and Democrat* whose editor called Albright's first number of the *Dakota Democrat* "very respectable" and "devoted to the interests of the Democratic Party." Expressing an interest in the progress of democracy, the St. Paul editor said: "Friend Albright, we wish you every success in your undertaking."[19]

"Come To Dakota," implored the *Democrat* in its opening salvo, "one and all—rich and poor, from the farm and from the workshop, from the city and from the country. Right here in the beautiful Sioux Valley there is room and a welcome for you all."[20]

The *Democrat* welcomed just about everyone who was white, including the idle rich, those "broken in fortune," and "pale, effeminate-looking young men." The latter were advised to leave their pills and tonics behind and be returned to health in the "glorious West," where "health rides upon the gale and every breath you draw will insure you a new lease on life." The *Democrat*, of course, was aiming at the crowded East, hoping to attract attention from among the infected, discontented and adventurous. As there were so few people in Dakota, this was the logical way to start. The *Register,* it seemed, would do nothing to stop the flow of immigrants to Dakota.

Not long after the welcoming advances, something happened, and turned the editors sour on each other and their towns. It probably started when the *Register* printed the obituary of Governor Henry Masters who died on September 5, 1859. A traveler from Sioux Falls to Sioux City reported the sudden death of Masters from a "congestive chill." Masters was seemingly in good health, and "attending to his usual business in the afternoon," said the *Register* article, when "he was seized with a chill and died before medical aid could be procured."

If the article had ended there, the fight might not have occurred. But the *Register* went on to say that "considerable sickness prevails at the Falls," among the approximately 30 voters living there. "The people are discouraged and dissatisfied with the prospects at Sioux

Falls, and declare that if the Territory is not organized and the capital located there the coming winter, they will leave in the spring, and settle on the Missouri river."[21]

One wonders if Ziebach simply surmised this, or actually spoke to men from Sioux Falls. Whatever the case, that kind of talk was poisonous to the struggling settlement, especially since new towns were sure to sprout on the Missouri slope, and staffed by men from Sioux City, would assert their capital pretensions. In an article written years later, Albright—who briefly served as "Governor" in place of the deceased Masters—admitted that the Dakota Land Company planned from the outset to make Sioux Falls the capital.[22] Albright probably believed the *Register* had thrown in with the Yankton promoters, and would therefore attack Sioux Falls and its capital aspirations. He immediately went on the offensive; he wasn't about to let the death of one man (Masters) bury the entire town.

Albright was assisted by an angry Henry Masters Jr., who also sought to set the record straight. Writing to the *Dubuque Herald,* the son of the deceased squatter governor said his father did not die suddenly rather his death came in bed, after an illness of eleven days. He denied that sickness and disease had laid the settlement low, for there were only "two cases of chills and fever" at the Falls. The young Masters insisted that the health of the settlement was good, and an equally healthy migration of new people was expected.[23] He had no fear of the remote frontier environment and journeyed back East intending to bring his family to Sioux Falls City, the town so loved by his late father.

The *Dakota Democrat* agreed with this sentiment, advertising Dakota as a place where good health was a result of natural conditions.

In a time when people believed that health was often determined by climate, the *Democrat* proclaimed: "the high elevation, the short duration of the extreme heat of summer, and the pure, dry atmosphere of winter, renders Dakota one of the healthiest of climates...." In fact, it was so dry in the summer of 1859 that the air was characterized as "drier than the parched throat of a wassailer after a night's debauch."[24] Why would anyone want to live anywhere else?

With the deceased governor's son on his side, Albright blasted away, making a big-city type noise. His editorial broadside against his neighbor to the south was printed in the *Register* on November 19, 1859. Albright claimed that a party recently arrived at Sioux Falls from Sioux City, bemoaning conditions at the latter place. The traveler said that men were planning to leave the Iowa river town for "the more flourishing points in Dakota." Sioux City, it seems, was plagued by an early frost that destroyed its crops, and its merchants were losing business to Dakota towns. "Almost every other house [in Sioux City] is said to be tenantless, and of the three hotels, built to improve the surrounding property, not one room is occupied." And if that wasn't bad enough, "chills and fever" prevailed among the people. "We comminserate (sp) with the people in and about our sister city, and hold out to them the glorious Eden of the Sioux Valley as a spot to which they may flee from sickness, stagnation and starvation...."[25]

After Albright rang the death knell over Sioux City, a gasping Ziebach fired back with his own brand of invective. "Whew! What a sensation...the little semi-occasional sheet of the bogus Capital creates when it reaches the haunts of civilization." Here was an opportunity to put Sioux Falls in its place and Ziebach did a masterful job of reminding those who cared that the "bogus Capital" was nothing more than a name beside a dot on a map, lost somewhere in a howling wilderness of eternal winter. "At the expense of much time and labor, by great perseverance, and with considerable difficulty we have ascertained that it [Sioux Falls] is situated somewhere on the road to the North Pole."

Ziebach saved his best barbs for the Dakota politicians who illegally bestowed offices and titles upon themselves. He gleefully rubbed it in, telling the world that the squatter legislature was forced to adjourn for four successive days due to the lack of a quorum. Where were these Dakota "Honorables, Judges and Governors?" "Ah, Mr. Democrat, with the next thaw come down from your winter haunts and leave that little town up there, what you call 'em? Oh! we have it now—Sioux Falls. It makes us aguish to think of it."[26]

A "cotillion" party at Sioux Falls City, and a "protest" by one not invited, gave the *Register* yet another excuse to scorn its neighbor, the "Polar City." This came about after the *Register* was told that a group of men from Sioux City were upset at Ziebach's persistent attacks against the *Dakota Democrat*. A written "protest" by the Sioux City men was sent to the *Democrat* but Albright did not print it. Nevertheless Ziebach was furious that Sioux City men would take Albright's side in the fight; he called them "ninnies" with "puny brains." Thus angered, Ziebach reprinted the *Democrat* article about the cotillion party, and followed it with the "protest" by the uninvited Sioux Falls City man.

The party was reported in the *Democrat,* in lavish detail, as if it had been held in a plush ballroom with sweeping staircases and crystal chandeliers, attended by ladies in formal gowns and gentlemen in tuxedos. "A very pleasant and really enjoyable select Cotillion party, was given by Mr. Cooper, at the Dakota House on Friday evening last [December 30th] at which the beauty and chivalry of Sioux Falls City and Sioux Falls were largely represented. Most excellent music was furnished by Peters' Band, and the *maitre de hote* did himself great credit in the midnight supper which was set by 'mine host' for the refreshment of his guests. The festivities were kept up with spirit until 'the wee sma' hours ayant the twal,' when the party dispersed to respective homes. We hope to see more of these social gatherings."

The "protest" was launched by the Hon. J. B. Greenway, of squatter legislature fame. Feeling slighted because he and his wife were not invited (remember, he was not easy to get along with), Greenway let the *Register* know that the party was not all it was cracked up to be. On January 10, 1860, Greenway penned a crude but satirical letter from "Sioux Falls Citty Dakota Terrytory to the Editur of the Sioux Sitty Register." He called the party a "shindeag" and a "beggar dance," attended by those few folks that Albright could gather together. Greenway said the fancy cuisine was actually lard-shortened pound cake, donuts fried in tallow and coffee unfit to drink.[27]

He said there were only three ladies present for dancing, and only one of them was single, making it a "stag dance." Greenway revealed that Albright published a highly exaggerated report of the party. Albright did so because he feared Ziebach would find out what really happened, and use it to make further fun of Sioux Falls City and its stalwart editor. And with Greenway's aid, this is exactly what happened. The party, probably the first of its kind at the Falls, served as ammunition for furthering Ziebach's attacks on his "Polar City" enemies.[28]

Ziebach fussed over the affair for months, burning over what he considered to be an "unwarrantable attack upon Sioux City." When the opportunity presented itself, he blasted Sioux Falls. Such opportunities were rare, however, as the *Democrat* was put out rather sporadically from its "office" at the "Northeast corner of Bridge and Main Streets."[29] News of the nation and the world was hard to come by when one was isolated and the nearest source of news was the town of one's rival. Information trickled into Sioux Falls no faster than the speed of a man on horseback, and such rarely seen men were, no doubt, pumped for all the outside information they possessed.

In all likelihood men traveling to Sioux Falls passed through Sioux City on their way to the Dakota interior. If the travelers checked in with the editor of the *Register*, they found a man who was at war with Sioux Falls City, only. Ziebach continued to promote Dakota in long, laudatory articles, as if he had something specific in mind. It was only when he came to describing the Falls that he found fault with Dakota Territory. "Near this place is located a small village christened (sp) Sioux Falls City, of independent legislature notoriety."[30]

Albright, if we are to believe his assistant Stuart, was a free swinger, who played fast and loose with his responsibilities. In 1860 he was appointed to conduct a census of Dakota. According to Stuart, "he never left the office but made a thorough canvas and a report showing 4000 people. He gave the names and places of residence of everyone he knew and padded some old city directory to supply the defiency (sp)."[31] One wonders if Ziebach knew exactly what kind of man he was up against.

The free-swinging Albright continued the fight and his punches were summarized in yet another *Register* editorial. Ziebach wrote:

"The editor of the *Sioux Falls Democrat* continues to reiterate his contemptible falsehoods in regard to Sioux City, accompanied by abuse of ourself . When the editor of that paper charges us with endeavoring to misrepresent The Sioux Valley, and retard its settlement and prosperity, he states what he knows to be meanly and contemptibly false."

Ziebach insisted he had never printed anything uncomplimentary or untrue about the Sioux Valley, rather he strived to stress its "natural advantages, beauty and fertility." He nevertheless stuck it to Sioux Falls once again. "It is unnecessary for us to say that the half dozen mud-covered cabins, dignified with the name `Sioux Falls City' from which emanates a semi-occasional sheet called the Democrat, does not constitute the Sioux Valley." Ziebach stoutly denied he was a "tool for Yancton," and proceeded to dispense with his weaker opponent as if, once and for all, the matter was at an end. "We have now done with the goggled dandy and defamer of Sioux City, and shall make no further mention of him in our columns."[32]

The timing of the caustic remark could not have been better. It played right into the hands of the *Sioux City Register*, as the *Democrat* soon folded and Albright left Dakota, under a cloud. While Stuart was in Yankton on business, Albright—impatient at the slow pace of progress in the settlement—made his departure, taking with him the *Democrat* masthead.[33]

He may have also been compelled to leave because of Indian activities in and about Sioux Falls City, as was reflected in the March 31, 1860, edition of the *Democrat*. The stable belonging to Albright and Joseph B. Amidon was raided of its contents one night, and three horses were spirited away. An angry Albright lashed out at Indians and their misguided supporters back East.

Albright published a $50.00 reward for the scalps of thieves and in the same fiery article, scourged the Bostonians who sympathized with the Indians. "We recommend that the Boston sympathizers get up an 'Indian Immigration Society,' and provide funds for the removal of a few thousand of the red-skinned devils to their locality." Echoing the prevailing beliefs, Albright cast the Indian in the role of a thieving beast, a heathen, beyond redemption.[34] It was an appropriate parting shot for a man who had seen enough of Dakota.

After Albright's departure, Stuart stayed on and became the editor of Sioux Falls' next newspaper, the *Northwestern Independent* (also referred to as the *Western Independent*). It, too, was issued infrequently and irregularly, and was short-lived. But it was well received by Ziebach, who was apparently unwilling to carry on his fight with Sioux Falls' second newspaper. Ziebach called the *Independent* a "handsomely printed and ably conducted sheet, and we hope it will meet with that encouragement from the citizens of Sioux Falls which it merits." The fight was over and peace was made with Sioux Falls.

Sioux Falls was dealt a death blow—the kind which the *Register* hadn't the power to deliver—in 1862, following the outbreak of war in Minnesota between whites and Santee Sioux Indians. The town was deserted and, shortly thereafter, ransacked and burned by Indians. This disaster will be chronicled in Chapter XIII. Suffice it to say here that the invaders also destroyed the press used to publish the *Dakota Democrat*. As years went by, parts of the printing equipment were discovered by settlers and put to use, and pieces of the type turned up in Indian pipes.

Albright went to St. Louis where he became the assistant editor of the *Missouri State Journal*.[35] The *Journal* was said to have been a secessionist newspaper and as the Civil War had begun, Albright found himself in hot water. One night a group of Union soldiers prevented the publication of the controversial newspaper. Albright was also associated with another St. Louis newspaper, *Daily Missourian*. This one was pro-Union.[36]

Albight eventually landed in New York where he finally settled down and did very well. When Albright re-visited Sioux Falls in 1887, after a twenty-seven year absence, he was a wealthy man. He liked what he saw in Sioux Falls. He was impressed with the growing city, recalling his days as a frontier editor when he served a mere 32 subscribers with his newspaper. He had one notable criticism, however, saying, "you have spoiled the most picturesque spot West of the Mississippi."[37]

No doubt Albright was referring to the Falls, which had been conquered by railroads, mills and other commercial ventures. To a man who was privileged to see the Falls and the island in their natural, primeval state, the clutter and crass commercialization must have seemed like a wasteful lack of vision.

Albright's erstwhile opponent, F. M. Ziebach, succumbed to Dakota fever, and in 1861 left Sioux City for Yankton. There he launched both a newspaper and political career—which included serving as the mayor of Yankton, and earned a respectable place in Dakota history. Along with John B. S. Todd and William Freney, Ziebach started the *Weekly Dakotian* in Yankton, on June 6, 1961, on a press that had been used to print the first newspaper in Sioux City.[38]

Ziebach remained a Dakotan for life and a popular man with both

Democrats and Republicans. No one ever accused him of trying to subvert Sioux Falls or the Sioux Valley. In addition to being hard-nosed and thick-skinned, frontier "brothers of the quill" were wont to forgive and forget, and would willingly bury the hatchet and fight a common enemy, or jointly promote the turf that supported them and their readers.

Chapter XII

Dakota Territory at Last

"...We hail the intelligence of the organization of Dakota as a harbinger of great joy...and as indicative of a rapid growth and general prosperity of the young Territory..."

Sioux Falls City Resolution in the
St. Paul Pioneer and Democrat, May 1, 1861

After Minnesota became a state, the business of organizing Dakota proceeded quite rapidly. While this is precisely what the speculators wanted, doubtless many of them were surprised at the pace of events leading up to the creation of Dakota Territory. The Dakotans were quick to credit the efforts of Fuller, Kidder, Todd and others—and gave them undue significance—but the record of proceedings in Congress indicates the work of more powerful forces. Indeed Congress, for its own reasons, answered the Dakota question with some expediency, if not just a bit carelessly.

Why should Congress concern itself with the ambitions of a handful of speculators in a far away land, when the nation was moving inexorably toward civil war? The answer, of course, had nothing to do with the speculators. Rather there was a sense of urgency on the part of a battle-weary Congress to dispose of territorial questions along with the thorny issue of slavery. It had come up in the debate over Kansas and Nebraska, and now Dakota—along with Nevada and Colorado—was on the block, and the distasteful question had to be dealt with all over again.

Representatives and senators could ignore or make fun of competing speculators and their false certificates and wordy petitions, but the spread of slavery to newly settled areas was cause for grave concern. While there were some in national legislature who openly or secretly supported either the Sioux Falls or the Yankton speculators, the majority of congressmen were simply reviving old battles over that "peculiar institution." If a new territory were created, would it encourage or impede the spread of slavery? Or would there be another compromise to appease both sides? Knowledgeable Congress watchers from around the country waited for answers.

The anti-slavery element had been forced to watch the legal machinery for prohibiting slavery grow weaker during the 1850's. The great Missouri Compromise of 1820 decreed that slavery be kept out of the Louisiana Purchase north of latitude 36 degrees 30'. Then in 1854, the Kansas-Nebraska Act all but nullified this by permitting slavery in Kansas while prohibiting it in Nebraska. Next, the U. S. Supreme Court in the famous Dred Scott decision ruled that the Missouri Compromise was unconstitutional and further, that the federal government had no right to regulate slavery in the territories. For Dred Scott—a mere slave—was "property" and therefore he had no standing to sue for his freedom. The court said slavery should be decided locally, thus validating "squatter" or "popular sovereignty."

In the midst of all this, the Republican Party was born in a small Wisconsin town in July of 1854. It was a mixture of disgruntled Democrats, ex-Whigs, abolitionists and other independents. Its young and idealistic members turned their attention to fighting the spreading of slavery. Despite gains made by Republicans and anti-Buchanan Democrats in the 1858 election, creating new territories free of slavery was destined to be almost impossible. Dakota had a small role in the struggle.

The work of forming Dakota Territory began in earnest after Fuller was turned down. On December 14, 1858, Representative James Cavanaugh presented a memorial to congress for a grant of land for a railroad from "the southern branch of Minnesota's Root River to Sioux Falls City, on the Big Sioux River...." On the same day, his colleague, Minnesota Senator Henry Rice, introduced a bill for the creation of Dakota Territory.[1] Rice, a Democrat, was a railroad boomer said to be in cahoots with the Sioux Falls City speculators. His effort was derailed, however, by Senator James S. Green of Missouri, chairman of the senate Committee on Territories, and along with it, a number of petitions from Sioux Falls City and Pembina. Green may have been pulling strings for fellow Missourian, David M. Frost, thus protecting the interests of Dakota Land Company rivals. Undaunted, Rice tried again with the same result. Meanwhile, petitions were coming in to Washington from Frost and Todd, lobbying for a territorial bill favorable to them.[2]

With John B. S. Todd at the helm, Yankton men held a "mass territorial" convention on November 8, 1859, at Bramble's store. Among those in attendance were Charles Picotte, J. R. Hanson, H. T. Bailey, Enos Stutsman, George Fiske, Frank Chapel and Moses K. Armstrong, all of whom were founders of Yankton. They passed resolutions rejecting the squatter election held in the Big Sioux Valley, and vowed not to be a part of any future extra-legal elections. Instead, they chose to "trust in the wisdom of Congress to provide us with a legal form of government at any early day." This clearly set them apart from the Sioux Falls City crowd. But they wanted their resolutions sent to other parts of the territory to "invite their cooperation with us." Their memorial contained an astounding 428 signatures.[3]

Todd spent the winter of 1859-60 in Washington urging friendly congressmen to pass a territorial bill he and his group could live with. While there he may have encountered Jefferson P. Kidder who was on a similar mission for the Big Sioux Valley speculators. On April 11, 1860, Kidder submitted a well-reasoned, lawyerly-written petition to the House Committee on Elections, asserting his right to a seat as a delegate from "that portion of the territory of Minnesota not included within the state limits of Minnesota."[4] Kidder was, in essence, stepping into Fuller's shoes, trying essentially the same arguments. He was handed the same negative results. He was not allowed a seat in the House of Representatives and returned to St. Paul disappointed.

On May 11, 1860, after Kidder left for the West, Representative Galusha Grow of Iowa introduced three bills for the creation of Nevada, Colorado and Dakota Territories. The first two were immediately tabled but the Dakota matter was the cause for intense and prolonged debate. Nowhere in the debate was Kidder's name mentioned.

Soon after Grow took up the Dakota measure, the bill's strong, anti-slavery provision was amended to prohibit the territorial legislature from establishing or prohibiting slavery in the territory. This was done, no doubt, to get Southern support, and it immediately drew fire from Representative Eli Thayer of Massachusetts, arguably the most anti-slavery state. A seemingly impatient Thayer abruptly moved to lay the bill on the table. He said he only wanted to "save the public time," but eventually his real motives became known.[5] Throughout the May debate in the House, Thayer took a hard line in opposition to new territories.

Thayer's motion was voted on and upheld. Undaunted, Grow turned his attention to a bill to organize the Territory of Chippewa. The proposed territory consisted of land that now comprises much of North Dakota. It would be formed after adding to the Dakota landmass a large chunk of Nebraska lying north of the Niobrara River. This large territory would then be divided along a north/south line "between the forty-ninth parallels of north latitude," creating two territories. The eastern news media seemed to like the idea, and although it was believed that the "hyperborean territory of Chippewa" was terribly "remote and wintry," it was seen as favorable terrain for agriculture and a transcontinental railroad.[6]

It was another iron in the fire and another attempt to create a new territory—or two—by any name, out of some or all of the unorganized land left behind when Minnesota was admitted to the Union. Soon after the debate began, Thayer moved to lay the bill upon the table. But the desired results were not so fast in coming.

Grow's bill was supported primarily by Representatives Samuel R. Curtis of Iowa, and David W. Gooch, of Massachusetts. They spoke in support of not only this bill, but also others that would organize new territories. Support for Chippewa was, in effect, support for all of the vaguely defined land mass called Dakota. They took a moral high ground, insisting people on the frontier needed, and deserved, good and wholesome laws, consistent with other states and territories. As it is the duty of parents to nurture their infants, so it is up to

Congress to care for and guide new territories through their early and trying years. Without congressional supervision, America might find isolated colonies springing up with alien ideas.

Thayer was chastised for leading the fight to defeat territorial laws summarily, for only laws bestowed by a dutiful Congress would provide the order and legitimacy needed for security and progress. Gooch and Curtis insisted that far too often, Congress had ignored its responsibilities, leaving citizens vulnerable to the outlaw element. And to ignore this duty was to invite anarchy. With a sense of urgency, the pro-Dakota members of Congress wanted to extend the blessings of law a little further into the frontier.

Along with religion, law was the life's blood of an America still in the process of creating itself. It was the universal abstraction that man had long used to carve out safe-havens in the wilderness. It provided the basis for further action, or caused the cessation of action. The imposition of law dispelled chaos and confusion; it simplified animal complexities and de-mystified the mysterious. The law was the means by which light conquered darkness; it was the good sword used to defeat evil. All respectable people wanted law; only outlaws disdained it. Law was direction and authority; it was close to God and based on his word. It was something that everyone recognized even if they didn't agree with it. If a man had to die because the law so decreed, he may have bemoaned his fate but he could find some solace in knowing that he was submitting to a higher, natural authority.

Curtis had a high moral purpose in mind when he asked pointedly: "Shall they (settlers) have no benefit of civil government; and stand day and night in fearful apprehension of the robber and the assassin?"[7] Curtis and Gooch proclaimed their belief in people and progress and neither stated, nor implied, an ulterior motive.

A Southern Representative, Craig from Missouri, had no quarrel with such high principles. While he doubted that there were actually people living in Chippewa, he would vote for all territorial bills if only "my constituents were allowed to take their negroes with them."[8]

It was inevitable that slavery, or "property rights," as others preferred to say, would enter the discourse. Still Gooch and Curtis tried to steer the debate above and beyond that inflammatory issue, trying to reach those who would put principle above partisan politics and provide legitimate governments for territories. In an emotional appeal, Gooch insisted that "every man in all these unorganized Territories is living to-day where he has no law but mob law for his protection," and no courts where he could seek justice.[9] To those who insisted on knowing the population of Chippewa, or Dakota, Gooch said that numbers were irrelevant. Rather it was the duty of Congress to act and provide its moral leadership and support for those who ventured into the new and untested lands.

Finally, however, under constant pressure from Southerners, Gooch admitted he was opposed to the spread of slavery into new territories. Still, he conceded that the definition of "property" was essentially a local issue, and should be decided locally. But he believed this applied to states only. Territories—creatures of the federal government and therefore dependent upon Congress for their legal sustenance—must allow Congress to decide whether slavery should, or should not, be permitted within their borders. (It should be mentioned that no one brought up the Dred Scott decision.)

Gooch and Curtis may have expected more of their Northern

colleagues to support them, but help was not forthcoming. Instead, Representative Thayer turned on them and their principles with theatrical invective and snide humor. Entertaining to some, irritating to others, and impossible to silence, Thayer's oratory barely concealed his motives. For while he was opposed to slavery, he didn't want to confront the issue head-on. For him, the way to keep slavery out of Dakota, and elsewhere, was to stop the creation of new territories. If Congress were to establish governments in the West, people would flock to the standards and the slavery debate would rage once again, perhaps with bloodshed, as in Kansas.

But that was only part of the problem. Organize territories and what do you get? Thayer, of course, answered his own question: Indian discontent and warfare, increased immigration and unnecessary government expense, "damages, pensions and war claims to the end of time." He flayed greedy speculators and their thinly veiled plans. He said people who ventured west were better off with their homemade laws than to be governed by political stiffs sent from Washington. Leave the great western expanses alone, he insisted, and they will remain relatively empty, save for a few extra-hardy souls. Organize new territories and soon Congress will be faced with admitting new states, for population always follows the law.

Thayer put on a great show that day in May. He was a veritable fountain of words, overpowering and unstoppable as a spring flood. His colleagues laughed time and time again as Thayer skewered both North and South with crisp, poetic barbs. With Thayer at the podium, the South needed no help to defeat anti-slavery territorial bills. As if enthralled by Thayer's oratory, most Republicans laughed or kept quiet.

Through it all, however, it is certain that Thayer said whatever he felt was necessary in order to avoid a direct confrontation with the slavery issue. And while he never seemed to run out of clever phrases, it became, even for Thayer, an uncomfortable fence to dance on. Finally, he admitted that he had promised he would not "bring the agitation of the slavery question into the House."[10]

As one examines Thayer's lengthy discourse, one senses there was an urgency about him that his articulate humor could not conceal. He was trying desperately to hold back the tide of disunion that he knew was threatening America. He scolded those who accused him of joining the Democratic Party, saying his position on territories was one that most Americans favored. He won a small victory on May 11, 1860. The House voted to table the Chippewa bill.[11] Thayer had the last word.

Yet all was not lost for Dakota. There were signs that the federal government was quite interested in Dakota notwithstanding Thayer's victory in the House. A federal census revealed 2376 non-Indian people were living on that land, mostly hunters and traders. In October of 1860, it was proposed that a mail route out of Minnesota would be extended to several places in unorganized Dakota, including a weekly run from New Ulm to Medary. Another proposed route would connect Medary, "Flandreau City, Summit City, Sioux Falls City and Eminega, to Sioux City and back," over a two week stretch.[12] Someone from somewhere was asserting his influence.

Along with this, supporters of new territories would not give up. And apparently their persistence finally got to Thayer. For on December 12, 1860, none other than Eli Thayer reported back House Bill No. 611, "to constitute the Dakota land district, and to provide for the Admission to the House of Representatives of a Delegate therefrom..." He recommended immediate passage of the bill.

Why this seemingly strange flip-flop on Dakota Territory? Thayer deftly answered saying, "Mr. Speaker, the bill is a very plain one. It contemplates the survey and sale of the public lands in Dakota. It does not propose to organize any government for the people of Dakota, for they have already organized one for themselves: It provides for the admission of a Delegate from the government to a seat in this House of Representatives." The bill would also give settlers the chance to legally claim land they occupied.[13]

This arrangement displeased Rep. Grow, for it offered "nothing to the people." Thayer's bill contained nothing that established a full territorial government. It provided no organic law, Grow insisted. To create a territory, he said, Congress had to authorize "the people of Dakota to act as a political community under the laws of the United States."[14] Thayer's novel and limited approach failed to do this.

It is not unreasonable to glean from Thayer's proposal that he was siding with the "squatter" government set up by the Sioux Falls City speculators. While he mentioned no one by name, his reference to a "government now in full operation" could only mean the "squatter" legislature of 1859. It was the only "government" in "operation." He drove that point home when he said: "I would therefore recognize the rightfulness and validity of the government now existing in Dakota, by admitting a Delegate from that *political community* to this House."[15] (Emphasis added.)

Thayer's bill was referred to the Committee of the Whole on the state of the Union. It died there, and for all practical purposes, so did the plans of the Dakota Land Company. The fall election saw

Republicans take charge of America's immediate political future. Abraham Lincoln was the new president. There would be no friendly Democratic administration to rely on for the selection of a territorial capital at Sioux Falls City or Medary. Nor would the Dakota Land Company see any of its members appointed to key territorial offices. Having to deal with a nation in peril, a neurotic wife, sickly children and a legion of enemies who attacked him viciously and without mercy, President Lincoln would "little note nor long remember" what he said or thought about Dakota and its ambitious speculators.

W. W. Brookings of the Western Town Company insisted it was not the Republicans, but a serious mistake on the part of the Dakota Land Company men, that wrecked their plans of political conquest. After Minnesota was admitted to the Union in 1858, Brookings said the St. Paul men should have convinced the territorial officers—now without jobs—to simply move to Dakota. There they could have resumed their official positions as territorial officers, since the area was still Minnesota Territory. Buchanan was president and the Democrats were in power, so Brookings reasoned that it should not have been too difficult to obtain official recognition of their right to govern and the existence of a territory, be it Minnesota or Dakota. Having failed to recognize and seize the opportunity, they lost out to the onrushing Republicans.[16]

The astute Charles E. Flandrau of the Dakota Land Company didn't see it that way. He was of the opinion that Congress intentionally delayed passing legislation creating Dakota Territory until after the general election of 1860. This, he said, was the result of a Republican scheme. Knowing the Dakota Land Company was made up of Democrats, the Republicans fought off attempts to create the territory until they were in power, and thus were able to control the territorial government.[17]

There may have been some truth to this, but from the beginning, the Dakota Land Company was in an awkward position. The fulfillment of their goals meant that Congress had to create a territorial government. To accomplish this, the company, dominated by Democrats, had to rely as much on anti-slavery Republicans as Southern Democrats, and they really didn't identify with either group. What they ultimately got was some unholy alliance that finally created the territory, but too late to benefit them.

All this worked to the advantage of their opponents on the Missouri slope. In Yankton, a second "mass territorial convention" was held at Downer T. Bramble's store on January 15, 1861. While immediate prospects seemed bleak, the speculators wanted to do something—anything to keep pressure on Congress. A memorial was prepared and signed by 478 men, an increase of fifty from the prior one. Historian George W. Kingsbury, an early-day Yankton settler, slyly admitted the figure was greatly inflated, saying the total "probably included the entire population of the territory and possibly some of Picotte's kindred..."[18]

Ultimately it was the Senate, not the House, which brought out a bill creating Dakota Territory. On February 15, 1861, Senator James S. Green of Missouri, from the Committee on Territories, reported Senate Bill No. 562 "to provide a temporary government for the Territory of Dakota, and to create the office of surveyor general therein." On the 26th, Green brought it out for a vote, saying passage "will not take five minutes." Indeed the bill drew little resistance and after a third reading it was passed. The real fight—over slavery, of course—took place as the Senate debated territorial bills for Nevada and Colorado.[19]

In the end, all three organic acts were weak on slavery as a concession to the South. To the disappointment of the abolitionists, slavery was not prohibited. Instead, the acts were conciliatory and compromising in nature. The result was deemed another example of "popular sovereignty," which meant that slavery was to be decided by the people of the territory. This was a political aberration to Republicans but sound doctrine to Southern Democrats. For Green, a staunch supporter of slavery, the bill was a compromise he could live with.

In Minnesota, the Senate's action met with happy approval. The pro-slavery *St. Paul Pioneer and Democrat*, mouthpiece for the Dakota Land Company, praised the Senate saying, "Dakota's stock will rise," and provide a promising future for "our surplus of patriotic men who can hardly find berths within our borders."[20]

In the House of Representatives, Senate Bill No. 562 was debated as part of a package along with the Nevada and Colorado bills. On March 1, 1861, with Rep. Galusha Grow taking the lead, anti-slavery House members angrily fought to be heard on the slavery issue, upset that Republican leadership was seemingly laying down to Southern demands. But after Nevada and Colorado were voted in, Grow, like Green in the Senate, quickly moved the Dakota bill to a vote. It contained exactly the same provisions about slavery as did the other two.

There was actually very little discussion about Dakota, itself. Grow mentioned that it contained what was "omitted when the State of Minnesota was admitted into the Union...and also the northern part of the Territory of Nebraska." In this huge land mass, he said, there lived about 3000 people.[21] It passed, and was signed into law on March 2, 1861, by the outgoing President James Buchanan, who did not appoint territorial officers. If there was one, final chance for the Dakota Land Company leaders to land political offices, it was lost when Buchanan—never known for being aggressive—failed to appoint them, leaving the job to the incoming President Lincoln.

It appears that the speculators were successful in convincing Congress to believe the inflated population numbers as stated in the many petitions, certificates and memorials. It may have even been a factor in the outcome. Whatever the truth, the news of the Organic Act was greeted with a great outpouring of joy in Dakota. Three hundred or 3000, Dakotans celebrated.

News was understandably slow in reaching the isolated settlements in Dakota. It was on March 13, 1861 that the Yankton settlement got the word.[22] As it spread up and down the Missouri slope, all paused in their labor to enjoy their moment of triumph. Men smiled, hugged, danced, cracked glasses and shook hands. They gathered around fires, sang songs and talked about their great accomplishments, and more importantly, their future.

I. W. Stuart, publisher of the *Western Independent* in Sioux Falls City, arrived in St. Paul on March 15th. When he learned that Dakota Territory had been in existence for two weeks, he was elated and could hardly wait to get back to Dakota with the good news.[23] Others were ready to depart too. The *Pioneer and Democrat* reported that "several families as well as adventurers are preparing to depart from this and other Districts of the state for the new territory, as soon as the roads are clear."[24]

On March 21, 1861, three weeks after the territory was created, "reliable information of the organization of Dakota was received at Sioux Falls City." That evening a mass meeting of settlers convened at "Independence Hall." The happy throng was treated to energetic speeches by "Acting Governor" Brookings and others. Then the following resolutions were adopted:

> *"Whereas*, the gratifying intelligence has been received of the Territorial organization of Dakota, which took place on the second inst., and
>
> *Whereas*, by said act of organization a new large and fruitful portion of the public domain is thrown open to the active and industrious of all classes, thereby inviting extensive and immediate immigration therefore, be it
>
> *Resolved*, That we hail the intelligence of the organization of Dakota as a harbinger of great joy as the era of the inauguration of a system of wholesome laws and all that goes to make up a sound body politic and as indicative of a rapid growth and general prosperity to the young Territory—the home of our adoption.
>
> *Resolved*, That to the immigrant we extend a hearty welcome, guaranteeing at the same time to all who may come among us, not only a kind reception, but all proper aid and encouragement towards securing for themselves and families happy homes in this fair land, where peace and prosperity are the sure rewards of rectitude and labor.
>
> *Resolved*, That a copy of these Resolutions be forwarded for publication to the St. Paul Pioneer and Democrat, Sioux City Register, North-west Dubuque, and Western Independent, Sioux Falls City, D. T."

That last "D. T." must have been written with great enthusiasm, for this was the validity so many had worked for; this was like the honest coin of the realm delivered up in great quantities as a reward for steadfast, if not heroic, effort. Sometimes the best-laid plans of men do succeed.

Sioux Falls City immediately took on a smiling air of prosperity. Heavy spring rains muddied up the trails but could not slow down by much the pace of work. Farmers planted their crops in anticipation of the demand for staple foods by the "large immigration" everyone expected. Mills were running every day, cutting trees and grinding flour. Plans were made to extend a warm welcome to the influx of newcomers. A weekly stagecoach between Sioux Falls City and Sioux City, and one to Spirit Lake, Iowa, were in the planning stage. Another line from New Ulm, Minnesota, was contemplated.

The "attention of capitalists" was invited to fund and build a large flourmill that would harness the enormous power of the Falls. The gristmill in operation was dismissed as too small to meet the expected new demand. "Real estate is on the rise, and each day the faces of owners seem to assume a more cheerful aspect," despite the "years of blasted hopes and anxieties" caused by congressional inaction.[25]

By late summer of 1861, Byron M. Smith, former explorer for the Dakota Land Company, published a map of the new territory and was selling it in St. Paul bookstores.[26] Smith, an incurable town site boomer, added to the enthusiasm of the times. All kickers, croakers and foot-draggers were forgiven and all obstacles forgotten, however, as Sioux Falls City and the rest of Dakota celebrated their success. Although few and scattered far and wide, a more optimistic group of people would be hard to find anywhere in the West.

As always, ecstasy inevitably gives way to reality—in this case, political reality. While everyone in Dakota was blessed by the creation of the territorial government, only one town would be designated the capital. Other political benefits were certain to be spread unevenly among the aspirants. There was still a great deal to fight over and the rivalry between the Sioux Falls City and Yankton groups was very much alive.

Members of the Dakota Land Company were disheartened by the Republican victory in 1860, but there are indications they had not given up completely. Since Medary was evacuated and destroyed in 1858, all of their efforts were concentrated at Sioux Falls City. There they were bolstered by men from the defunct Western Town Company, a small, irregular, but supportive press, and their organization in St. Paul. Furthermore, the *St. Paul Pioneer and Democrat* persisted in its belief that Sioux Falls City would be the capital city. [27]

While they waited for the names of the new territorial officers, Dakota Land Company diehards undoubtedly considered what might have been had the Democrats managed to capture the presidency. All that was gone, however, lost in the bloody turbulence of secession and civil war. While Dakota was on the remote northwestern frontier, it too, had to feel, and fear, the coming of the awful storm that threatened to rip America apart. The guns fired at Fort Sumter hit targets in distant places.

A sense of gloom and foreboding is reflected in editorials of the *St. Paul Pioneer and Democrat*, a newspaper that did its best to keep Dakota in the news. Scattered among the articles about secession and fighting are occasional pieces about Dakota. There was a generalized fear in Dakota and Minnesota that the Indians might be tempted to turn on the whites now that the bluecoats were busy fighting the

Rebels. Maintaining treaty obligations, along with a sufficient amount of troops at Fort Randall, however, was expected to keep the Indians quiet while the speculators proceeded with setting up a government in Dakota.

The location of the capital of the new territory was a priority. It was the next big thing for the speculators to fight about. Careers and investments in land were at stake. It was also of special concern to Minnesota merchants because of the potential benefit to their business interests.

A writer who called himself "Dacotah" claimed to represent those settlers from St. Joseph and Pembina. He preferred a capital located "some where in the Red river valley, about mid way between the northern and southern limits [of the territory]." This, he said, would benefit the "commercial interest of St. Paul." However, a capital on the Missouri River would draw immigration, and therefore commerce, to that point, too far away to be of any use to St. Paul.[28]

About a week later, the *Pioneer and Democrat* featured a letter from a writer who called himself simply "F_____." He was upset at "Dacotah" and the Red River capital concept. "F", who was probably a member of the Dakota Land Company, reminded everyone that the "nucleus" of the new territory could be found in the Big Sioux Valley. For it was on a strip of land "25 miles wide and 150 miles" long that a "wholesome emigration of civilized people" settled and thereafter drew the attention of Congress. He criticized what he called the "old school skullduggery" of the "Mythical Town Companies of Northern Dakota," and warned that the Yanktonai Indians could, and probably would, drive them out. For him, Sioux Falls City was the logical choice for the capital. Bills presented to Congress even named Sioux

Falls City the capital.[29]

The Organic Act, however, was silent on the matter of the capital. It was something that would have to be worked out by the territorial legislature and whomever the new president appointed to govern Dakota Territory. When news of President Lincoln's appointments reached St. Paul, it was not enthusiastically received by the *Pioneer and Democrat*. Nor was it accurately reported.

The new governor, Dr. William Jayne, was mentioned without explanation except to say that he was the brother in-law of Senator Lyman Trumbull of Illinois. The U. S. Marshall for Dakota was given as Dr. Charles Lieb, "high-priest among border ruffians," and the territorial secretary was John Hutchinson of Minnesota, of "wide shirt-collar fame." The chief justice was S. P. Wilson of Pennsylvania and the surveyor general was "Mr. Hill" of Michigan.[30] It would seem that the *Pioneer and Democrat* was both unimpressed and suspicious, or just suffering from a case of extra-sour grapes.

Whatever the truth, the names of the appointees would not reach Dakota until days later. When the scattered Dakotans finally learned of the men sent to handle their affairs, the inaccuracies of the *Pioneer and Democrat* became apparent. The governor was, indeed, Dr. William Jayne of Springfield, Illinois, a political figure of some prominence in his state. He was the son of Dr. Gershom I., and Sibyl Jayne and the brother-in-law of the powerful Senator Trumbull. Equally interesting, William Jayne was a personal friend and political ally of the president. Thus we see that Lincoln by-passed his wife's cousin, John B. S. Todd, whom many believed to be the logical choice for governor, in favor of his friend and doctor.

Whether Lincoln gave any serious consideration to Todd may

never be known, but it appears he had some misgivings about selecting Dr. Jayne. A memorandum among Lincoln's papers shows that two other names—J. M. North (of Minnesota) and Nathaniel G. Wilson—were deleted and William Jayne inserted.[31]

Lincoln's choice for secretary was John Hutchinson of Minnesota; the U. S. attorney was W. E. Gleason of Maryland; the U. S. marshal was William E. Shafer of Missouri; the surveyor general was George D. Hill of Michigan; the chief justice of the Dakota Supreme Court was Philemon Bliss, of Ohio; and the associate justices were J. P. Williston of Pennsylvania and Joseph L. Williams of Tennessee. These men were not well known to Dakotans and collectively, knew very little about the huge territory they were sent to govern. Their legacy as officials is almost as empty as the great and wild expanses that greeted, and later overwhelmed, them. Both Lincoln and his congressional allies were far too concerned with the impending Civil War to give much thought and care to the selection of Dakota office holders.

All territorial officials were appointed on March 4, 1861, the day of President Lincoln's inauguration, which Dr. Jayne attended. Each man was relatively young, educated and healthy, but not, however, ready for roughing it in the West. All but two were married and all had some background that qualified them for holding office on the frontier. Each one owed his appointment to a Senator or some other influential figure.

Governor Jayne, alone, stands out among the crew. Not for his accomplishments, but because of his intense and heated involvement in Dakota politics for a relatively short time. By temperament, Jayne was not entirely suited to be a governor. He was, by one writer's assessment, a ward politician without statesmanlike ability. The former mayor of Springfield, Illinois, Jayne was a hotheaded man with a sharp, hawk-like nose and piercing eyes that suited his caustic personality.[32]

It was said that Jayne was "truly an intimate of Lincoln," but never used his friendship for personal gain. In his later years Jayne fondly recalled seeing Lincoln for the first time at New Salem, Illinois, when he was a boy and the future president was a gangly, young man.[33] They later met and struck up a friendship that was mutually beneficial and lasted until the Great Emancipator was assassinated.

Jayne graciously accepted his appointment and arrived in Yankton on May 27, 1861[34] with Marshal Shafer. They established their headquarters in a crude log cabin.[35] The 35-year-old Jayne was argumentative and divisive from the outset, and while the titular head of the new Dakota Republican Party, he quickly set about the business of alienating as many men as he attracted.

Another source called Jayne's selection a "wise choice." Noting his "temperate habits and conscientious motives," Jayne proved "equal to the task" of organizing and running a territorial government during trying times.[36]

Most writers attribute Jayne's appointment to Lincoln's friendship, and the president's desire to avoid the charge of nepotism over naming Todd the chief executive of Dakota Territory. But years later, a story in the *Rochelle (Ill.) Register* reveals the strong influence of Senator Trumbull in the appointment. Dr. Jayne was an Illinois state senator in 1861, and it was his vote that ensured Trumbull's re-election to the U. S. Senate. According to the article, "Jayne's vote gave the Republicans a majority of one in the Illinois Senate. Mr.

Jayne's vote gave the election to Mr. Trumbull."

Next, Trumbull went to Lincoln and asked that Jayne be appointed the governor of a territory. Lincoln was opposed because if Jayne left the legislature (to which he had just been elected), the Republicans would lose their majority. Lincoln was depending on a Republican-controlled legislature in Illinois to help implement his war plans. Still Trumbull persisted, and wore down the president's resistance. According to the *Rochelle Register* article, Trumbull got his way and repaid his brother-in-law, favor for favor.[37]

This story is corroborated by a small article in the *Pioneer and Democrat*. Quoting from another source, the *Pioneer and Democrat* said the Illinois legislature opposed naming Jayne governor of Dakota for doing so would turn control of the legislature to the Democrats. Trumbull was denounced for his role, saying he was solely interested in his re-election and was "entirely indifferent to all other interests." The maneuver left both U. S. Senator Trumbull and state Senator Jayne very unpopular in Illinois. So it was probably to Jayne's advantage to leave the state for parts barely known.

When Dakotans learned that their new governor and other federal appointees were on their way to the territory, folks in the Missouri River towns of Vermillion, Yankton and Bon Homme prepared to receive the officials. Each town had capital city ambitions. In Vermillion, a "dignified-looking gentleman" arrived from Sioux City, disembarked from his carriage, and was immediately set upon by welcoming townspeople. He was ushered into a banquet hall, toasted and feasted, and regaled with speeches. As it turned out, he was not the governor, but a man named Bigelow out searching for a place to settle. Nevertheless the newcomer relished the celebration and played his impromptu role to the hilt. Meanwhile, the real governor's carriage passed through Vermillion unnoticed. So impressed was Bigelow that he stayed in Vermillion the rest of his life, known to all as "Governor Bigelow."[38]

It is significant that Governor Jayne set up shop in Yankton, not Sioux Falls City, Vermillion or Bon Homme, a fact that was surely not lost on political watchers. The same could be said for the other territorial officials. All came to Yankton from different states, some by steamboat, some by wagon and some with a military escort. They didn't know each other and had probably never communicated with one another, so it is reasonable to assume that they all received some instructions independently, on where to go and how to get there.[39]

Historian Kingsbury believed that Jayne carried with him, "the seat of government," meaning Yankton was decided in advance of his coming. Indeed, "Yankton appears to have been selected as the rendezvous for the newly appointed federal officials prior to their coming to the territory." It was Todd, the "skillful planner," who had influenced the selection, although Kingsbury insisted that all "unprejudiced people" understood Yankton possessed certain "natural advantages."[40]

Kingsbury failed to elaborate on those features that set Yankton apart from other towns. But it did have a newspaper. The *Weekly Dakotian* set up shop and issued its first sheet on June 6, 1861. Henry Ash and wife established the Ash Hotel that had minimal comforts and good food. It was on the Missouri River and it was close to the Sioux City to Fort Randall trail. Jayne shared a cabin and a bed with Attorney General Gleason. The latter was described as a "delicate" Marylander whose official duties at the outset consisted of walking to the river and bringing back water to the "executive mansion," sufficient for "toilet purposes for himself and the chief executive."[41] For Yankton it was hardly an impressive start, and it would take time before it was anything more than a collection of rude log houses, much like other fledging frontier towns trying to sink roots and grow as fast as possible.

Be that as it may, the men on the Missouri slope had won the opening struggle for Dakota's political destiny. While the Sioux Falls City men could still fight for the capital, the best they could hope for was a fair amount of representation in the new legislature. Of course there were those who recognized which way the wind was blowing and joined hands with the victors.

Dr. Jayne began his duties as if he were serious about governing Dakota. Since there were no laws except the Organic Act, Jayne issued proclamations. One of his first called for a census of the territory. As Dakota then consisted of over 300,000 square miles, it was empire-like in size, especially when transportation was limited to wagon or horseback. But a census was needed if nothing else to properly establish voting precincts for the first legal territorial election to be held in the fall.

While the Civil War increased in ferocity back East, in Dakota, the summer of 1861 was peaceful and promising. As the governor's appointees were busy counting residents, more were arriving from the east, many coming through Iowa. In July, the *Fort Dodge Republican* reported seeing "no less than eleven emigrant teams" in one day, all bound for Dakota. The Dakota-bound traffic that passed through Fort Dodge, Iowa that summer was a boon to the local economy. Fort Dodge found itself on an overland route for western travel, much of it destined for Dakota.[42]

Governor Jayne and Secretary Hutchinson made a trip from Yankton to Sioux Falls on the "good, natural wagon road" between the towns. They had a pleasant stay, visiting with Sioux Falls men and enjoying the magnificent scenery. The governor was undoubtedly impressed with the waterpower, the great abundance of fish, and the large supply of a "kind of red stone," similar to pipestone. He found the town in the caring hands of Brookings, Allen and others, all of whom were prepared to take advantage of both the scenic beauty and natural resources of their town.[43]

The *New York Times* had a correspondent wandering about Dakota that summer, searching for stories. He was apparently impressed with the land and its people and seemed to believe Dakota was off to a safe start. Writing from Vermillion, he mentioned Jayne and Hutchinson's tour of the territory and was quick to conclude that the folks liked their new officials. "The people seem highly pleased with the appearance of these gentlemen," he wrote. Significantly, he also noted that "there can be no doubt that a territorial organization during these times of war will be entirely loyal."[44]

In fact, there was not a hint of disloyalty in Dakota in 1861, among the 2376 people (including mixed bloods) revealed in the census. More than half—1606—lived in Pembina country, far to the north. Among the sparse and scattered population in the southern part of the territory, the Sioux Falls District contained only 50 white males and 10 white females. As there was no mention of Medary, Flandrau or Eminjia, it is probable that any people living in those towns were included in the Sioux Falls total. It is even more probable that no one occupied those town sites. The mythical people no longer showed up on paper. When Dakota Territory was at last created, it contained far less than the ten to fifteen thousand people talked about in Congress.

The Yankton District registered a total of 287 people, along with 265 at Vermillion, and 163 at Bon Homme. It would seem, then, that the bulk of the new settlers were choosing the Missouri slope over the Big Sioux Valley. The Dakota Land Company lost both the political and the propaganda battles.

Another gubernatorial proclamation divided the territory into Council and Representative districts along with voting places within those districts. The Organic Act provided for the election of a delegate to congress and a legislature made up of nine Councilmen and thirteen members of a House of Representatives. To carry this out, it was imperative that elections be held as soon as practicable.

Politically ambitious men needed no urging, however. By the time the governor and his fellow office holders entered the territory, the first political movements were underway. On June 1, 1861, a "mass convention" was held in Vermillion, pursuant to a call for all interested Dakota men. Those in attendance organized a party called the "National Union Party." Its members were all Republicans and, excepting George M. Pinney of Bon Homme, all were from Vermillion. Their short platform contained planks pledging support to the governor, opposing monopolies and those who speculate in large tracts of land, and in support of a "liberal homestead law." They nominated A. J. Bell for delegate and adjourned after "nine hearty cheers" for their candidate.[45]

Bell was said to be a "man of good ability," by Kingsbury. Yet he was not well known in the young territory, having come from

Minnesota in May. In haste, and to the objection of many Dakotans, Bell became a candidate for delegate to Congress after only one month's residency. In St. Paul, where he was known, the *Pioneer and Democrat* reminded its readers that A. Jackson Bell left behind a reputation for "his dodging financial peculiarities."[46]

Two others were nominated for delegate to Congress. On or about September 1st, Charles P. Booge was nominated at a convention in Bon Homme. Booge, formerly a trader at the Yankton Sioux Agency, was better known than Bell.[47] But he, too, had an outsider image to contend with, having been long associated with Sioux City. Yankton's fledgling newspaper, the *Weekly Dakotian*, said without explanation that Booge was backed by the Dakota Land Company.[48]

The third nominee was John B. S. Todd, a true Cavalier of the Dakota Frontier and a genuine Dakotan, although he, too, had a Sioux City background. It was understood that Todd would run for Congress based on his popularity and widespread support. He had the support of the *Weekly Dakotian*, but the *St. Paul Pioneer and Democrat* was not impressed, saying only that Todd "of Fort Randall," was "said to be a brother of Mrs. 'Old Abe' Lincoln."[49] This could not be interpreted as an endorsement.

The thick-skinned Todd needed no protection from any kind of criticism, and required no convention to launch his candidacy. He simply announced he was a candidate. While he was an old-line Democrat, he disdained a party label. Todd was not alone in this philosophy. For although the territory contained more Democrats than Republicans, none of the candidates for delegate or the legislature adhered strictly to national party lines.

Todd's candidacy was adopted by the first formal political

organization to meet in Yankton. A group consisting of both Democrats and Republicans convened on August 24, 1861. The group acted harmoniously, almost joyfully, as nominees for the legislature were named and approved without opposition. But the convention generated some hard feelings because every nominee at the convention was a Democrat, thus many notable Republicans were ignored. As a result, a "rump" group broke free and named its own candidates for the legislature.[50]

As folks prepared for their first election, thoughts of defeating the South, and preserving the Union, were on the minds of everyone. Indeed, all three campaigns made it clear they favored the preservation of the Union. It was the only real political question in Dakota, as elsewhere. Had any man spoken out in favor of secession, his political career in Dakota would have, no doubt, ended abruptly.

The Sioux Falls settlers named their candidates for the legislature too, but Kingsbury's book is silent on the subject (and on Pembina as well.) It is significant however, that no one from the Dakota Land Company was on the ticket. Rather W. W. Brookings, a Republican, and George P. Waldron, an independent Republican, both Sioux Falls originals from the Western Town Company, were in the field for the Council and House, respectively. With no record of proceedings, it is reasonable to think there was some agreement among Sioux Falls men that whoever was selected would lend their support to their home town for capital.

Kingsbury called the short campaign exciting and energetic owing to the "eloquent campaigners." Booge's "resolute activity" was the highlight of a campaign that "passed off without serious disturbance." Votes were cast on September 16, 1861. When all the

George P. Waldron
(Collections of the South Dakota)

counting was done, Todd won the delegate contest, garnering 397 out of 585 votes cast in eight districts. He racked up impressive totals in St. Joseph, Pembina and Yankton, getting all but one vote. The next time Todd appeared in Washington, D. C., he would hand over a *bona fide* election certificate, not a memorial. Booge, the independent, finished a distant second.[51]

For Council in the Sioux Falls precinct, Brookings was the top vote getter with nine. He won thirteen votes from the Big Sioux precinct and twelve from Elk Point, enough to win. Waldron won the House seat, beating James McCall, a Sioux Falls City bootmaker, ten to one. There was no voting at Medary, Flandrau or Eminija. At long last, the actual voting population of the Big Sioux Valley became known. By this time many St. Paul members of the Dakota Land Company had given up on Dakota and turned their thoughts and money to other investments.

Not all, however, had departed, and when the first session of the territorial legislature met in Yankton on March 17, 1862, Franklin J. DeWitt arrived in town and checked into the Ash Hotel. While he was not a member of the legislature, he had business in town. To all appearances, he came to lobby on behalf of Sioux Falls City. DeWitt had been in the Yankton area since the summer of 1861, looking for a ranch. But by the time the legislature was ready to do business, it was believed DeWitt was holding "open house" at his hotel room to lend his influence toward making Sioux Falls City the capital.[52] He was joined by another prominent man from the once high-flying group of speculators that came to Sioux Falls City in 1857, probably Alpheus G. Fuller. Working together with Waldron, they were thought of as the "old guard."[53]

The legislature met in two separate houses located a short distance from one another. The winter had produced considerable snowfall but overall, was not considered severe, and spring was close at hand. This, in part, accounted for the large number of interested people who arrived in Yankton to view the lawmakers in action. Most were there because of the "capital question." Indeed, the location of a permanent capital would determine the location of much of the territory's new business, and some legislators approached the issue with a "do or die" attitude.

This first legislature was quite a sight, judging from the word pictures left behind by Moses K. Armstrong, a member of the House from Yankton. The lively group varied greatly in dress, education and personality. Polished professionals including doctors, lawyers and ministers worked beside "rough frontiersman in buckskin suits, beaded moccasins and long hair."[54] All brought their exuberance and sincerity; some came with their whiskey and weapons.

Armstrong himself was one of the most colorful. Combining wit, humor and writing skill, he wrote a series of newspaper articles roasting the legislature. It was in good fun, of course. But more importantly for Armstrong, it formed the basis for a successful political career in Dakota. His astute mind and facile pen were at the ready when the legislature convened.

Governor Jayne opened the session with a fine speech. He praised Dakota, its pioneers and resources, explaining that here was a land of great promise, a region of tremendous natural resources and a healthful climate. From the fertile river bottom soil to the mineral rich mountains to the west, Dakota was the shining jewel of America. He called upon the territory's first representatives to work honestly and earnestly, passing fair and equitable laws commensurate with their individual integrity and intellect. Speaking, for the most part, in sweeping and complimentary generalizations, Jayne paused and expressed a wish that "the free air of Dakota may never be polluted, or her virgin soil pressed by the footprint of a slave."[55]

Jayne could have mentioned that the Organic Act allowed only "free white males" to vote. For some in the legislature, this restriction was not enough. Showing an attitude that can be described as both anti-slavery and racist, the Council passed a bill "to prevent persons of color from residing in Dakota." The vote was five in favor and three opposed. The House considered the measure and after substantial debate, voted it down.[56]

The legislature did pass an anti-Indian bill. It prohibited an Indian from entering ceded land without a written pass from his agent. Violators were to be arrested and taken back to their reservation. This law was intended to allay the fears of "timid immigrants."[57]

Jayne expressed no preference for the capital site, although he knew it was the biggest issue facing the legislature. When the session opened, Yankton was the favorite with Vermillion a strong second and Sioux Falls a "dark horse." John Shober and George M. Pinney, two Bon Homme men, were named president of the Council and speaker of the House respectively, with the understanding that they would vote for Yankton.[58]

On the eleventh day of the session, a bill to name Yankton "the seat of government of Dakota Territory," was introduced in the Council by Enos Stutsman. After some debate, and an attempt to substitute Vermillion, the bill was voted on and passed, with Shober voting in favor of Yankton in accordance with the arrangement. Among those voting for the Yankton bill was W. W. Brookings. While this may seem surprising in view of the competition between the two towns, Brookings undoubtedly knew Sioux Falls had no realistic chance to win. He pragmatically threw his support toward Yankton, the town that had the greatest immediate potential.

The bill was sent to the House where debate was more prolonged and bitter. The speaker, George M. Pinney, from Bon Homme, was a singularly erratic man of high intelligence, driven by great energy. Originally from Crawford County, Pennsylvania, Pinney had more than a fair amount of education, having studied law and for the ministry. As a teenager, he joined the California gold rush of 1849. One of his colleagues said Pinney was a "scholarly fellow" with "the flashing eyes of genius," proving that young Dakota attracted all types of men.[59]

These traits were much in evidence during the furious debate. In a House almost evenly divided between Yankton and Vermillion, Pinney's help was deemed indispensable, and after all, he was expected to live up to his promise to vote for Yankton. After the discussion began, Pinney's true motives became known: he was not warm on having Yankton as capital and was willing to turn his back on any agreement struck with Yankton's merchants and politicians.

When Armstrong presented the capital bill to the full House, Pinney took charge and moved that "Yankton" be removed and "Bon Homme" inserted. This was voted down. He then moved that "Vermillion" be substituted for "Yankton." This amendment was approved by a narrow margin with Waldron voting in favor. At this point the House found itself at odds with the Council.

The next day Armstrong brought the matter up again and strangely, with Pinney's help, the House maneuvered to strike out

"Vermillion" and insert "Yankton." This outraged the strident anti-Yankton men, including Waldron of Sioux Falls. Waldron, "the man of the waterfalls," made a motion for the appointment of a committee of three to furnish members with knives.[60] The legislators were finding their way, legislating frontier style as there were no experts in parliamentary procedure among them, and no one appeared to care.

So angry was the debate that the governor ordered Company A, of the newly formed Dakota Cavalry, into the hall lest a riot break out. Then, in another bizarre turnabout, the House passed a bill naming Vermillion as capital.

This was sent to the Council, which turned down the amended House bill by a vote of six to two. It was immediately returned to the House by the Council secretary. Kingsbury remembered that the House underwent a strange and "radical change in sentiment," and without undue delay, cast off its amendment and passed the Council bill with but one negative vote. Waldron, who must have been fuming, did not vote. Thus Yankton prevailed, adding yet another feather in Todd's already well plumed hat.[61] Armstrong recalled that the capital bill caused "a little blood to be shed, much whiskey drank, a few eyes blacked, revolvers drawn, and some running done."[62]

The hotheaded Pinney was one of those who tended toward violence. During a political meeting in the rear of a saloon, Pinney was suddenly ejected through a window. Not long after, the seething speaker was seen returning to the saloon with a drawn revolver. He was stopped by concerned citizens before he had the chance to exact vengeance.[63]

The rowdyism was not lost on the governor. Armstrong remembered seeing Jayne and Jesse Wherry, an ex-Kentuckian, formerly of the land office, locked in a "real executive fist fight at the Hotel d'Ash...." "Hair pulling, choking, striking, blood spitting and pugilistic exercises" were "performed with grit and relish."[64] This was a time when politics was a contact sport.

In an effort to ease the tension, the legislature voted to locate a university in Vermillion and a territorial prison in Bon Homme. Sioux Falls City was ignored. The eccentric Pinney resigned the speakership and was replaced by a less volatile personality, but the anger generated by the capital debate meant there were still some soreheads in Yankton. In those days, when a politician was bought he was supposed to stay bought. As Pinney violated this unwritten rule, he lost the respect of his fellow politicians.[65]

One of them, John W. Boyle, Councilman from Vermillion, locked horns with Enos Stutsman at Antoine Robeart's saloon, a favorite watering hole for legislators, lobbyists and other merry-makers. After some words, both men threw bottles and glasses at each other. Then Stutsman, ignoring his obvious physical impairments, lunged across the table at Boyle's throat, seemingly determined to throttle his opponent to death. After a brief struggle, they were separated by their companions.[66]

This incident was conceded by Kingsbury (and no doubt Armstrong too) as appropriate behavior for Dakota's first lawmakers, and no apology was needed. After all, this was the raw frontier. Besides, the legislature completed a great deal of beneficial legislation including a civil and criminal code, laws to live by. George M. Pinney had no future in the new territory but others did. Dakota Territory was given a good send-off.

Chapter XIII

The Great Dakota Stampede

"The people were panic stricken, and in an hour after [John] Bell had come and gone with his false alarm, there was in progress one of the most complete stampedes ever known."

Yankton Daily Press and Dakotaian
April 13, 1876

Not long after the onset of the Civil War, Governor Jayne was notified by the War Department to organize two companies of cavalry from among the able-bodied men of the territory. The Dakota volunteers were to be part of a mighty Union army marshaled to defeat the rebellious Southerners. These soldiers, however, would be confined to Dakota Territory, handling both garrison and patrol duty. It was clear from the beginning, these men would be recruited to face not slave-holding rebels, but warlike Sioux Indians, should the need arise.

This was as it should be, according to the editor of the *Sioux City Register*. "The honor of protecting Dakota should be left to the people of Dakota," not to Iowans, commanded a sword-rattling editorial. Dakotans should be installed at Fort Randall too, so that the soldiers there could be moved to "the seat of the war."[1]

Dakotans needed no lecturing from an Iowa newspaper, however, and the work of organizing the Dakota Cavalry began in short order. Recruiting stations in Bon Homme, Yankton, and Vermillion were established by the governor's proclamation on December 7, 1861. Thereafter, the recruiters seemingly had no trouble finding volunteers from among the farmers and townspeople throughout the scattered settlements. Captain Nelson Miner, of Vermillion, commanded the troops with the assistance of First Lieutenant J. K. Fowler and Second Lieutenant Frederick Plughoff, a German immigrant. The latter had served in both the German and American armies, and was seen by the free-spirited frontiersmen as a strict, and somewhat tiresome, disciplinarian.

Company A, Dakota Cavalry was officially mustered in at Yankton on April 29, 1862. The troops stayed there for a time, waiting for their horses and supplies to arrive.[2] Then on May 20, 1862, Company A was sent to Fort Randall to augment the regulars, Companies A, B, and C of the 14th Regiment of Iowa volunteers, commanded by Captain John Pattee.[3] Fort Randall was considered of utmost importance for defensive purposes, and had the government closed it down, Dakotans would have raised a howl that could have been heard all the way to Washington, D. C.

A year before, amid considerable fanfare, the soldiers of Fort Randall departed by steamboat, having been called to the "seat of the war." They landed at Council Bluffs, Iowa, and prepared to march across the state to fight in a war which, at that time, many still believed would be short, decisive and glorious. At Council Bluffs, the soldiers were treated to a sumptuous dinner by grateful citizens. Then they were given a rousing and patriotic sendoff, complete with cheers from the ladies and a speech by the mayor.[4] All across Iowa, the troops were greeted by flag-waving, cheering crowds.

The Dakota volunteers could not expect star treatment for their mission held out no promise of glory. Not long after they reached Fort Randall, they were split up, with small contingents stationed at Sioux Falls and at Turkey Creek, on the road between Sioux Falls and Yankton. Others were sent to Vermillion and Brule Creek. These volunteers—"the nerve and bone of the west"—were looked upon with pride by the people they were bound to protect.[5]

Despite the apparent state of readiness, no one in Dakota felt particularly threatened in the spring of 1862. In fact, settlers faced the year with more than the usual optimism. President Lincoln signed the Homestead Bill into law on May 20, 1862, and W. W. Brookings made the first filing under that landmark legislation at the land office in Vermillion on October 6, 1862.[6]

Mail was carried regularly between Sioux Falls and Yankton by Marsh and Company. A once-a-week mail was carried from Jackson, Minnesota, a hundred miles to Sioux Falls City, an uncertain journey of two and one-half days.[7] Immigration was steady, encouraged, no doubt, by the recently enacted Homestead Act, and considerable crops were planted. The weather was conducive and a good harvest was expected. Yankton's newspaper, the *Weekly Dakotian*, invited people to come west with frequent one-liners like "Homes for the Homeless in Dakota."

Excursions between Yankton and Sioux Falls were renewed. In June, territorial Secretary John Hutchinson led a group of ladies and gentlemen north, across the prairie. They hunted buffalo, elk and other small game on their way from the capital to Sioux Falls in a seemingly carefree adventure. They fished at the Falls, basking in the splendor of that natural wonder. Their experience was darkened momentarily when one of the ladies nearly drowned after their boat capsized while crossing the Big Sioux River. She was rescued by Secretary Hutchinson. Despite the narrow escape, all agreed that it was time well spent.[8]

That summer politics raised spirits even further as groups of men began to gather around prospective candidates for delegate to Congress. In Sioux Falls, the Minnehaha County Convention was convened on July 6, 1862. The chairman, Joseph B. Amidon, directed a thoroughly harmonious session that included resolutions endorsing the Lincoln Administration, and complimenting Governor Jayne for protecting the frontier settlements against "Indian depredations."[9]

On July 30th, a "mass meeting of the citizens of Minnehaha County" was convened in Sioux Falls City to name candidates for local and territorial offices. W. W. Brookings offered a resolution supporting Governor Jayne for delegate to Congress. It was accepted. Among those nominated for office were Harry Masters for a seat in the House of Representatives, George P. Waldron for district attorney and Joseph B. Amidon for register of deeds. It was reported that "utmost harmony and unanimity prevailed."[10] This was a good start toward the first election under territorial law.

Governor Jayne was supported by most of the Republicans and had the advantage of being a member of the party in power. John B. S. Todd sought re-election and was the favorite of the Democrats, although it was not considered too wise to emphasize one's connection with that party. As the Civil War increased in ferocity, Democrats were more strongly identified with the South. While some viewed Todd as a "dyed-in-the-wool" Democrat, he was more interested in his re -election than in partisan politics, and he had support from anti-Jayne Republicans. He could boast of his long and productive work for Dakota Territory and remind everyone of his relationship with the president's wife. But this claim, no matter how valid, would be hard-pressed to upstage the Republican Jayne whose party was directing the war effort.

Todd was further handicapped by his apparent ties to his erstwhile opponents in the Dakota Land Company. The *Weekly Dakotian* maligned Todd, linking him not only to a familiar ally, Theophile Brugier, but also to Franklin J. DeWitt and Byron M. Smith. They—and others of their ilk—were labeled land-grabbing monopolists, reaping the benefits of a "half-breed scrip" scheme. In support of the land-less William Jayne, Yankton's only newspaper warned the voters to reject Todd and his fellow land-grabbers. If they were not stopped, all the good land would be scripted and beyond the reach of those actual settlers seeking "free" land under the Homestead Act.[11]

Jayne was not above criticism. He, along with other federal appointees, spent so much time away from Dakota that folks were convinced he was seeking a seat in Congress merely to escape the hardships of the frontier. At any rate voters had two distinct personalities to choose from, each with his own special claim to the president's ear.

On July 16, 1862, the Republican and Union Territorial Convention met at Vermillion. These men represented the mainstream Republican Party. In short order, they nominated William Jayne for delegate to Congress. He had only token opposition at the convention. A few days later the People's Union Territorial Convention met, also in Vermillion, and as all expected, nominated John B. S. Todd for Congress. His only opposition was in the form of five votes for DeWitt, the old Dakota Land Company boomer, who was not a candidate.[12] The nominations were locked up so the conventions were mere formalities. Thereafter, the politically inclined Dakotans set in and looked forward to a brisk campaign and their first election under territorial authority. As we have seen, the issues and personalities were significant.

A sense of unease, however, pervaded the vast, young territory. A feeling of uncertainty that strong political rhetoric could not disguise, shaded the thoughts of even the most upbeat Dakotan. Not long after the political conventions adjourned, word reached Dakota that the Santee Sioux of Minnesota were threatening hostilities. All knew that should fighting break out in Minnesota, it would not be kept within state boundaries.

Then in early August, Company "A" troops under Captain Miner came across a "band of pillaging Indians" near Turkey Creek. They had been wandering about southeastern Dakota, lingering, asking for food and otherwise aggravating the settlers. When asked their business, the Indians explained they were Sisseton Sioux from Brown's Valley, Minnesota. Fearing trouble, Miner ordered the Indians out of the territory, and they packed up and headed in the direction of Minnesota.[13]

Not long after, a full-scale war erupted in Minnesota. This was the awful War of the Outbreak, or Dakota War, which cost hundreds of lives, both red and white, and resulted in the expulsion of the Santee Sioux from Minnesota. In 1851, the Santee Sioux ceded a vast tract of land in Minnesota to the U. S. government in exchange for a narrow strip of land for a reservation. The outbreak, and the bloodshed in its wake, was a direct result of the odious and unjust Treaty of Traverse de Sioux.

The war started on August 17, 1862, when a party of four young braves killed a family of three men and two women near Acton, Minnesota. The incident started innocently enough but harassment turned quickly to murder and the four men returned to the camp with a bloody tale to tell. After some discussion the chiefs, led by Little Crow, decided to support the young men rather than turn them in to the agency.

Their decision was based upon years of discontent—hungry and trying times that began almost before the ink was dry on the treaty parchment. First, the Indians were cheated out of their initial payment or "in hand" money. Instead of going into their pockets, it went to pay the phony or exaggerated claims of traders. Thereafter, the agency was consistently slow at disbursing annuities in the form of food, clothing and implements. By August of 1862, the Indians were in a destitute condition, facing starvation, hemmed in by settlers who hated them and agency officials who treated them with contempt.

After Indian guns and arrows gathered in a terrible harvest of death in central and southern Minnesota, the army pushed the warriors onto the prairies of Dakota. Sioux Falls, the town closest to Minnesota, lay in the path of violence and was the first to suffer. Berne C. Fowler, who made a weekly mail run between Yankton and Sioux Falls, noticed "signs" around the "watering places on his route" that told him the Sioux were preparing for hostilities.[14] Fowler reported his findings and the town was on alert, but not overly concerned about trouble from Indians, and was blissfully unaware of the nightmare to come. Peace and prosperity seemed within reach and trouble seemed so distant.

Lieutenant James M. Bacon, who had replaced Lieutenant Plughoff, was stationed just outside of Sioux Falls with a contingent of Company A troops. The soldiers called their base "Camp Jayne," a name that indicates their political preference. When the men weren't drilling, they spent their time listening to political discourses as election-day was drawing near.[15]

Sioux Falls was the scene of considerable political activity that summer, as rival speakers took turns attacking the governor and defending him. Outside of that, the handful of residents was actively involved in the mundane but life-sustaining activities required of pioneers, tending to crops and livestock. Town site speculators like McClellan, Waldron, Evans and Brookings were still encamped in their sylvan valley, along with a few newcomers. The marriage of Eliza Jane Amidon to Harry Masters at the settlement on July 22, 1862, united two pioneer families.[16] Under their second year of territorial rule, Sioux Falls settlers felt relatively safe—until August 25, 1862.

That night Mahala Amidon became frightened and concerned when her husband Joseph B. Amidon, the county probate judge, and her stepson William, a Minnehaha County commissioner, failed to return from a day's work. They had left that morning to cut hay for the government. About four o'clock in the afternoon, Berne C. Fowler, whose claim was nearby, heard gunshots and thought that he was hearing William shooting at blackbirds. Fowler spotted a large flock of blackbirds flying down from the bluff, from the direction of William's claim, and later recalled thinking to himself: "I wish Willie Amidon wouldn't send his blackbirds down to my corn!"[17] Thus thinking, he concluded the incident was no cause for alarm.

But Mrs. Amidon became greatly alarmed as afternoon gave way to evening. After agonizing for several hours that "fearful Monday night," she contemplated going out to search for her husband and stepson herself, but felt it was too dark and the claim too far away. So she went to Lt. Bacon about 10 o'clock that evening and convinced him to conduct a search. Soldiers were immediately sent to the fields on William Amidon's claim located above the bluff, within a mile from the town site, close to where the state penitentiary was later built. The soldiers found the men's empty dinner pail, oxen and wagon in a shed, but no sign of the Amidons. The search was called off because of the darkness of night.

When the soldiers came to Mahala with their findings, she feared the worst. In a letter to her daughter Martha she recalled the tragic incident, saying, "Oh how I longed for morning to come. I could neither sit still nor stand still. All I could do was to cry and groan, I felt almost sure the Indians had killed or wounded them so they could not get home. My dog was all the company I had that fearful night."[18] She paced the floor that night, while the actions of her dog caused her to fear that Indians were lurking nearby. A soldier was detailed to guard the Amidon house.[19]

The next morning the search was resumed. In short order the bodies of the Judge and his son were found. The elder Amidon died of a three gunshot wounds to the chest, and William—about 20 years old—had been killed by a combination of arrows and bullets. Before dying, William removed some of the arrows and placed them by his side.

Based on the positioning of the bodies and Fowler's recollection, observers were able to surmise how the killings took place. It was assumed that William left the hay field with his shotgun after seeing a large flock of blackbirds in his cornfield. The Indian raiding party was hiding in the cornfield, waiting for nightfall when they would attack the settlement. Their plans were spoiled when William happened upon them and they killed him. His father—who never carried a gun—heard the gunshots, entered the cornfield where he, too, was shot and killed.

Lt. Bacon recalled hearing the shots that killed the Amidons. He was fishing at the Falls when shots were fired. Thinking it was his men hunting ducks, the gunfire was of no concern to him.[20]

The Amidons were taken to the settlement in a wagon[21] and presented to their grieving family and friends. Townsmen built two coffins and father and son were buried on the bluff above the town site, beside the grave of squatter governor Henry Masters who was interred there in 1859.[22]

It was said that the Amidons were killed by a war party under the direction of Chief White Lodge, a Sisseton Sioux.[23] White Lodge was a major player in the Minnesota War. On August 20, 1862, his band attacked a settlement at Lake Shetek, Minnesota, killing several people and taking others prisoner, including a former Sioux Falls resident, Mrs. William J. Duley.[24] White Lodge's next assignment was Sioux Falls, where his men fell upon the unsuspecting Amidons.[25]

The widowed Mrs. Amidon was struck by the tragic irony of the incident. She could not fathom why the Indians killed her husband and stepson Willie. Pouring out her grief in a letter to her daughter Martha, she said, "your father always had so much pity for the Indians and used to give them so much and fed them too, and

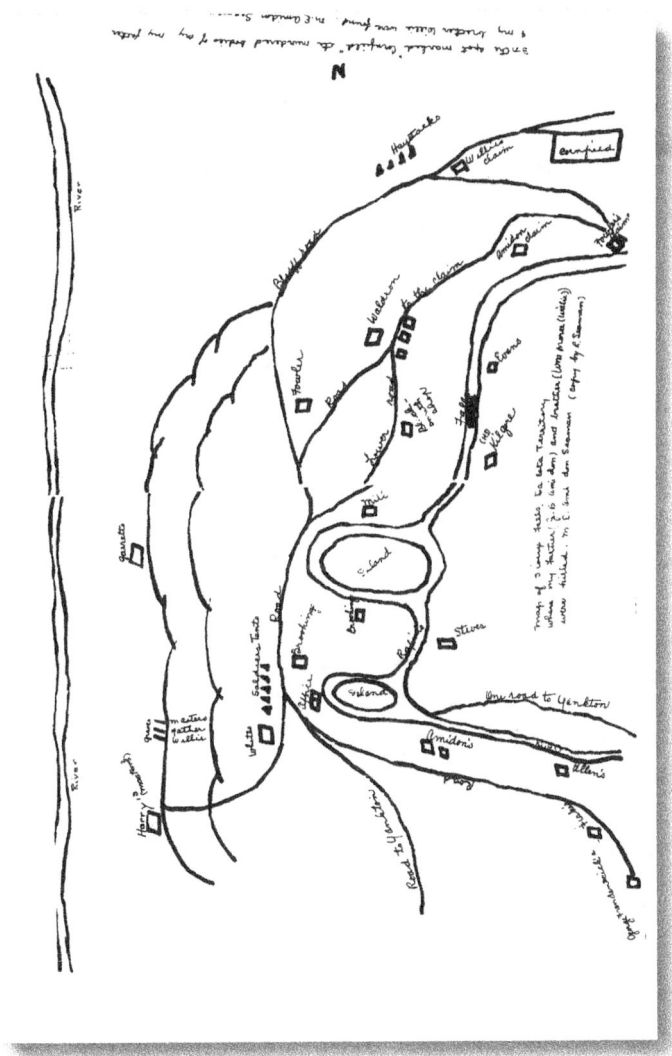

1862 Map of Sioux Falls, Dakota Territory
Courtesy of Mary Doran

then to have them murder him without provocation." It all seemed so senseless and utterly without rational or spiritual explanation.[26] The Amidons apparently had numerous contacts with the Indians as William had learned the Dakota language.[27]

A detail of soldiers scouted the area in an effort to find the Indians responsible for the murders. While they were out, the town was fired upon by a group of Indians from upon the "penitentiary bluff." The rest of the soldiers went in pursuit, only to lose the Indians near a marshy bog west of the town site that was later named Covell's slough. According to Bacon, the Indians returned that night and attempted, unsuccessfully, to drive off the soldiers' horses.[28] It gave the volunteers a taste of action and something to talk about around the campfire.

At this point, Sioux Falls was unaware of the war in Minnesota, but folks were frightened into taking action. According to Waldron, the townspeople gathered in a stone house near the river. Perhaps recalling the Fort Sod incident, they resolved to hold forth, with the help of the soldiers, "whatever the sacrifice." His family had a lot to lose, having built a comfortable house, a barn and a saw- and gristmill on the river.[29]

The next day a courier from Yankton arrived with orders from Governor Jayne to Lt. Bacon, commanding him to return to Yankton with his soldiers. People then learned of the massacre of whites in Minnesota. Thus apprised, they didn't take long to decide it would be prudent to leave. In haste and fear, they packed up necessary belongings and cached other items. As it was raining heavily and would soon be dark, the settlers decided to wait until the morning to leave. After spending another terror-filled night, they fled to Yankton, using the government road. It was a sudden and sad departure as the Sioux Falls pioneers were forced to say goodbye to the thriving settlement where they had cast their lot.

In a strange sense they considered themselves fortunate. For all believed that had William Amidon not came upon the Indians hiding in the cornfield, the settlement would have been attacked that night and all would have been killed. Because of this twist of fate, they were spared.[30]

The number of people occupying Sioux Falls at the time varies among historians and pioneers. Waldron recalled a population of about forty. Kingsbury said the population of Sioux Falls City consisted of W. W. Brookings, William Stevens, John McClellan, Barclay Jarrett, James W. Evans, Amos Shaw, Dr. J. L. Phillips, Harry Masters, the Waldron family, the Charles S. White family, and Berne C. Fowler and his wife.[31] According to Bacon (quoted in Kingsbury), who escorted the settlers to Yankton, only three families lived there, among them the Waldrons, the surviving Amidons and the Foster family (probably the Fowlers). Brookings had departed the day before "the raid."[32]

Mahala Amidon recalled the exodus from Sioux Falls with special sadness, having lived there since 1858. "We saved but little of our goods. We had but one wagon for five people to ride in." Since the Amidons were "living more comfortable than we had before since living in Dakota," leaving their farm, home and its furnishings was especially hard. Harder yet was leaving behind the graves of two family members. Thinking of her late husband, she wrote: "I can't bear to think he lies in that desolate place with no friend to even visit his grave."[33] But she had no choice except to leave it all behind.

Soon people all over southeastern Dakota were on the move. Word of the Sioux War reached Bon Homme and its residents fled to Yankton. Most of Dakota's federally appointed officials left Yankton in fear, seeking shelter in Sioux City. A war party fired upon J. B. Greenway, the former Sioux Falls "squatter" legislator, who operated a ferry across the James River. Greenway was made of stern stuff, however, and instead of running or surrendering, he grabbed his rifle and fired back from inside his log house. A contingent of Company "A" Dakota Cavalry led by Sgt. A. M. English, came to his aid, causing the Indians to withdraw.[34]

English and his Company "A" patrol, known as the "Coyotes," encountered other warriors near a slough where the town of Gayville was later located. The Indians took cover in an abandoned cabin and engaged the soldiers in a gunfight. After an hour of shooting, one Indian was killed. The soldiers had no casualties. The Indians escaped through the tall grass and the relieved soldiers headed for Yankton, their heavier horses unable to match the speed of the Sioux horses. Along the way, the soldiers picked up a number of settlers, including Greenway and his wife.[35]

Additional panic erupted when a soldier, John Bell, raced among the settlements telling people to pack up and leave. Acting entirely on his own, Bell told settlers that the Yankton Sioux joined with the Minnesota hostiles and were bent on exterminating the whites. Bell said the Yanktons, lead by Mad Bull, were destroying the upriver settlements and were on their way to Yankton County. He said Captain Miner was doing his best to keep back the red tide but could not be expected to hold up.

Bell's wholly unexpected and bizarre behavior caused immediate

Moses K. Armstrong
Collections of the South Dakota State Archives

panic. Within an hour after he sounded his false alarm, "there was in progress one of the most complete stampedes ever known." Teams were pulled from fields and hitched to wagons. A few possessions were tossed in with the women and children, and in a flash, a family—or sometimes two or three—was on its way to Sioux City. Livestock was turned loose or in some cases, was tied to the wagons and dragged along. "The exodus began in the middle of the afternoon, and all night long the roads leading out of the territory was (sp) alive with a moving stream of humanity, going, they knew not where only intent upon self-preservation."[36] Along the way, the mass of fleeing humanity grew larger as folks from Clay and Cole Counties joined in.[37]

This became known as the "Great Dakota Stampede" and was long remembered by Dakota pioneers. A number of both serious and amusing incidents took place along the roads leading out of the territory. The judge of the first judicial district, holding court at Vermillion, joined the flock. He was a large fat man who made a funny-looking traveler on the small mule he rode all the way to Sioux City.[38] In another instance, a man told his wife to load up some food as fast as she could. In her terrified state of mind, she thoughtlessly tossed some unbaked loaves of bread into the wagon for her family to eat.[39]

Moses Armstrong, the Yankton humorist, recalled with glee the manner in which Dakota's "loyal" public servants ran for cover. From the governor on down, they fled at the first sign of trouble, "in one wild, panic-stricken express train." Wild-eyed and scared to death, they retreated, "pale and breathless, for the states, [so] that a boy could play marbles on their horizontal coattails." Perhaps thinking of his congressional chances, the governor did come back from his "silken ambush," but only with a military escort. Then after handling some executive business, he left again.⁴⁰ One of the few officials who stayed and provided leadership was territorial Secretary John Hutchinson.

So it was that within hours of Bell's false alarm, most of the settlers between the James and Big Sioux River were gone. The folks at Vermillion, downriver from Yankton, were at first inclined to stay and resist. In response to Jayne's proclamation, the town formed an 83-man militia, armed with muskets sent from Yankton and a "brass six-pounder." The men began creating fortifications on the bluff above the town. They took logs from a church to construct their defenses and started to dig a trench that was apparently intended to surround their stockade. The town's population swelled with the arrival of jittery settlers. Soon after hearing false rumors of fighting in the outlying areas and fearing that Chief Mad Bull's band was about to attack Vermillion, all construction and digging ceased and an evacuation took place with most of the settlers going to Sioux City. Eight men stayed behind and finally they, too, took flight, crossing to an island in Missouri River.⁴¹

For the better part of two days the road to Sioux City was occupied by fleeing settlers. Oxen were urged on at top speed while irrational men tried to calm crying women and children. Attempts to lighten the load meant the road was littered with the possessions of the escapees. So hurriedly did they leave their homes that many were not properly dressed for the emergency.

All were hungry and scared, and when the fearful mass reached the Big Sioux River ferry, panic gave way to chaos. The night air resounded with the bellowing of cattle and the "pitiful cries of children and [their] mothers' lamentations."⁴² Unfortunately for the terror-stricken folks, the ferryman refused to get out of bed and take them across the river to Iowa. He would have his sleep time, "Indians or no Indians."[43] So after a night of fear and dread, the Dakota escapees all crossed into Iowa the next morning, their scalps intact. Most of the people in this bizarre cavalcade of frightened humanity had seen their last of Dakota. Indeed, the fortunes of the young territory had taken a dramatic, downward turn.

A Committee of Safety was organized in Sioux City by those who were moved and saddened by the invasion of terrified settlers from Dakota. On September 6, 1862, a notice was directed "To the citizens of the Missouri slope," advising them that messengers from the Yankton agency brought news of the worst kind: the agency Indians were preparing to join the attack on the settlements. Acknowledging that "women and children along the Missouri are fleeing to Fort Randall or here [Sioux City] for safety," the Committee called upon the "men of Iowa" to stay and defend the frontier, "for two or three weeks until the government troops arrive."[44]

In Yankton, where strength in numbers was soon to take on new meaning, Governor Jayne issued a proclamation, dated August 30, 1862, ordering every male between the ages of 18 and 50 to get their guns, stay in Dakota and join in the defense of their communities. The proclamation also demanded that people in the outlying areas gather in the "main towns" of Yankton, Bon Homme, Elk Point and Vermillion for protection. Citizens were advised to choose their own officers to lead them, and the governor would give the officers commissions.[45] As we have seen, this proclamation was ignored in droves—if, indeed, it was ever made known to those outside of Yankton. As the governor did not set a good example, he would have been hard-pressed to enforce it.

The adjutant of the territory also issued a notice requesting the provost marshal of Sioux City, Iowa, to prevent all "able bodied male citizens of this Territory from going east of Sioux City, unless they have passes from the governor."[46] This too, was useless in view of the panic and besides, by the time it was published in the *Weekly Dakotian*, on September 15, 1862, most able-bodied males, including the governor, were in Sioux City, or east of it. An army officer reported seeing a long, continuous line of settlers on the road south of Sioux City, all irrationally frightened and all "bound to get away from the Indians."[47]

In his absence, and in conformance with the governor's proclamation, the people of Yankton met on August 30, 1862, to discuss their options. Augmented by people from Bon Homme, Sioux Falls, and Yankton County, the town was awash with frightened folks. It was learned by soldiers returning from Sioux Falls that Indians had entered the town, setting fire to a number of buildings, killing chickens and livestock and in general, destroying five years of hard work. The office of the old *Dakota Democrat* was among those torched and the press thrown against the rocks. There was additional fear among whites that the Yankton Sioux would soon join their Santee brethren, and in overwhelming numbers, attack Yankton.

An uneasy Governor Jayne was fully in accord. On September 3, 1862, he sent a letter to Gen. James G. Blunt, commander of the military Department of Kansas, pleading for help, noting the "defenseless condition" of the people. "We are," he said, "a few thousand people at the mercy of 50,000 Indians." Unless troops and guns were soon provided, the entire territory would be depopulated.[48]

Iowa Governor Samuel J. Kirkwood also sounded the alarm. In a letter to Secretary of War Edwin M. Stanton, Kirkwood said settlers were fleeing "by hundreds." He feared that the panic in Dakota could lead to a similar depopulation of northwestern Iowa settlements. Kirkwood demanded action against the Sioux who were threatening "our whole northwestern frontier."[49]

The scope of the panic was truly monumental and way out of proportion to the actual danger. Nevertheless, it spread like wildfire across the prairie, driven by a western wind, affecting much of Minnesota, Nebraska, Iowa, even parts of Wisconsin and Kansas. The scalding fear of Indians had reached new heights.[50]

Although the Civil War kept thousands of troops busy in the East and South, the Lincoln administration did not ignore the emergency in the West. Although sparsely populated, Dakota Territory was deemed worth defending. The Missouri River had become an important artery of transportation, and despite some doubt as to the usefulness of the land for agriculture, Dakota's value was enhanced by the discovery of gold near present-day Bannock, Montana in 1862.

So on September 6, 1862, the president sent Major General John Pope to Minnesota to take charge of all federal troops in the Department of the Northwest, an area that included Minnesota, Iowa, Wisconsin and Dakota and Nebraska Territories. Pope had just been relieved as commander of the Army of the Potomac, after suffering a humiliating defeat at the second battle of Bull Run. He was very unpopular with the army and the administration, so an assignment in the Northwest was like banishment. Nevertheless, he accepted the demotion like a soldier and went west to fight Indians and, perhaps, restore his reputation. It didn't take long before Pope came up with a solution: exterminate the Sioux.

But first Pope had to find the Sioux. He also had to secure the frontier. One of his first decisions was to send troops to Sioux Falls and on September 18, 1862, Pope ordered 300 mounted men to go to that burned out town site. But he soon found that he had very few troops at his disposal and most of them had to be sent east to fight the Confederacy.[51] Sioux Falls would not get any military protection until 1865, when Fort Dakota was established.

The people gathered at Yankton would have welcomed more soldiers. Fearing for their lives, some of them demanded an army escort to Sioux City, which Sergeant English declined to do, lest he violate orders from Captain Miner. So with evacuation out of the question, and after much anxious discussion, the decision was made to stay, form a citizens' militia, and prepare for defense. The former fire-breathing editor of the *Sioux City Register*, F. M. Ziebach, was appointed captain of the militia. Alpheus G. Fuller was placed in charge of Company F.

Within a short time, every white male in Yankton signed a paper pledging his support. Among those on the list were a number of old Sioux Falls boomers including James M. Allen, James W. Evans, John Lawrence, J. B. Greenway, Charles Philbrick, Berne C. Fowler and Williams Stevens. A number of prominent Yankton settlers were also members of Company A, First Dakota Cavalry, including Moses K. Armstrong, George W. Kingsbury, Newton Edmunds, Joseph R. Hanson and William and Samuel Van Osdel. Noticeably absent were the names of any of the federally appointed officials. Apparently their agreement with Lincoln and the Congress did not include defending the territory from an Indian attack.

Those men who were prepared to defend Yankton, decided to build a stockade at the intersection of Broadway and Third Street, near the center of town. Lumber, logs, dirt, rocks, manure and other materials were hastily gathered together and everyone, women included, joined in the building of the fortification. Nearby buildings and fences were raided and other lumber was supplied courtesy of Armstrong and Picotte. The stockade enclosed a number of buildings including the Ash Hotel, Robeart's saloon, a meat market, and the newspaper office. The entire enclosure was approximately 450 feet square, and was considered durable and strong. Blockhouses were built at the northeast and southwest corners. A gate and a bronze gun were situated at the south end that faced the river.[52]

Nor were the Yankton citizens and refugees the only tough-minded settlers who decided to stay and fight, if necessary. At Elk Point in Cole County (now Union County), some citizens also disdained flight and converted the Wixson Hotel into a military barracks.[53] They amounted to but a handful of people compared to the gathering at Yankton.

At peak population, approximately 300 people gathered inside the Yankton stockade, including many women and small children, all trying to keep as safe and comfortable as possible under such crowded conditions. Among those inside were Samuel "Old Spot" Mortimer and James "Limber Jim" Witherspoon, both eccentric but brave and dependable. They were the kind of men who would have stayed at the Alamo.

"Limber Jim" got everyone excited after he left the stockade and set fire to tall grass around Stutsman's cabin, because he was bored and unconcerned about an Indian attack. Picotte spotted the flames and smoke, interpreted it to mean an attack was imminent, and charged through the gates of the compound in a lumber wagon drawn by two large mules. He was excitedly calling the troops to the battlements when Witherspoon appeared and explained that it was he who set the fire. Relieved, most of the men burst into vigorous and prolonged laughter.[54]

Another eccentric was John La Fourve, a Frenchman, better known as "Old Dakota" because of all the years he spent trapping and trading with Indians in the upper Missouri River country. In the mid-1840's, La Fourve drifted into the southeast corner of the territory, along with several other frontier characters including Paul Pacquette and Theophile Brugier. They dug in near the mouth of the Big Sioux River, claiming the distinction of being the first white men to settle in what became Union County.

La Fourve was a not only a frontiersman, but a mountain man who roamed the Black Hills, camped with explorer John C. Fremont in the Rocky Mountains and wandered the West with Kit Carson, fighting Indians. His *bona fides* included working for the American Fur Company, hunting with the Shoshone tribe on the Pacific coast, and fighting the Ree Indians in 1823.[55] Not long before taking up residence in the Yankton stockade, La Fourve and a rancher named Casock Bouret, armed with shotguns, faced down a group of Sioux bent on taking Bouret's ponies. Knowing the legendary "Old Dakota" by reputation, the warriors retreated without the ponies rather than test his marksmanship and iron nerve.[56]

As if entranced by images of the past, "Old Dakota"—known as the "White Bear" to the Indians—would walk within the stockade and nervously watch the horizon with his piercing black eyes. He carried a double-barrel shotgun and muttered to himself: "God dam um, um feared um [Indians] won't come."[57] A man of great passion, numb to fear, he was anxious for a fight and folks were glad to have the quaint old man of at least 60 years with them, knowing he would risk his life in their defense.

Enos Stutsman was equally steadfast and considered an expert marksman. With a rifle strapped to his back, and a revolver hanging from his waist, he set an example for others who lacked his physical impairments. The nose of his revolver scratched the dirt as he scuttled about on crutches, but everyone looked up to him, knowing he was a brave man who would give his life, if necessary, for the defense of the town and its people.

Another man credited with steady nerves during the emergency was Josiah C. Trask, a young man who was simply sojourning in Yankton, employed as a printer, when the crisis erupted. Having no particular attachment to Yankton, he could have easily left as many did, but he stayed and assisted in building the defenses. A year later he was shot and killed by Quantrilll's Rebel raiders at Lawrence, Kansas[58]

Women contributed too, doing more than cooking, serving coffee and quieting the children. One woman, a Mrs. Edgar, who, by chance, just happened to be in Yankton visiting her sister when the trouble started, carried her own gun. She used it one night when it was feared attack was imminent, but not against Indians. Suspecting some men were slackers, she searched the rooms of the Hotel Ash, rooting out "two or three white-livered cowards," who were hiding in the hotel, hoping to remain concealed. When Mrs. Edgar, eyes ablaze with indignation, pointed her gun at the scared rabbits, they reluctantly took their places with the others.[59] She was remembered as the "heroine of the camp."

On the whole, life within the stockade was cramped and crowded, and no one was willing to call it cozy. There were insufficient beds and those that were available, were occupied mostly by women and children. The office of the *Weekly Dakotian* was used as a place of refuge for women and children during the scare, causing staff to skip one week's edition. The saloon was used for storage, not for drinking, and men kept quite sober during those trying times. Despite the inconvenience and constant state of readiness, folks held up admirably. Besides, they were on the frontier as a matter of choice, and any luxury would seem to them to be an unnecessary self-indulgence. And while the *St. Paul Pioneer and Democrat* screamed for extermination of the Indians, the settlers merely prayed for deliverance, ignoring all things pessimistic.

Not everyone was optimistic. A nervous Charles Picotte fully expected an attack at any time. His uncle, Struck by the Ree, was consulted by a committee for his opinion. Old Strike was blunt, and in no uncertain terms advised his white friends to abandon Yankton. He expected the restless young men of his tribe to ally themselves with the Santee Sioux and attack the stockade. Military leaders also favored a retreat, believing Dakota would soon be the theater of an all-out war between the races.

When it was learned that the Yankton Sioux were expected to turn against the whites, the married men held a meeting. It was believed that should they decide to take their families away, the military would have no choice but provide an escort. This, of course, would have been tantamount to a total evacuation. But after a meeting fraught with angry words and threats, the married men voted, by a majority of one, to stay.⁶⁰

Credit was given to Michael Fisher, a Dakota Company A volunteer. He came to Yankton in 1858, in the employ of Todd and Company. Although not a well man, he among the married men was adamant about staying and turned the tide in favor of that decision. Within two years of the siege he was dead, and many veterans of the emergency remembered Fisher, a carpenter by trade, as the man who saved Yankton.⁶¹

On September 6th, it appeared that those who insisted on staying were about to get their just desserts. In the distance, a large body of riders was approaching the stockade. The inmates were thrown into a state of great excitement for it seemed that their luck had run out. Ziebach and English recognized the riders as soldiers and beseeched the settlers to stay calm. Instead, some angry folk gave them a "terrible tongue lashing." English later recalled that at no point in his life had he been subjected to more verbal abuse. He was called a coward, and "all the soldiers were just like me, a lot of cowardly curs." English "choked down" his anger and carried out his duty.⁶² The settlers who could not be placated prepared for an attack, but lowered their guns in great relief when Captain Miner and his men came in view. They had come from Vermillion and were a welcome sight to the siege-weary pioneers.⁶³ Suddenly everyone was happy and abuse heaped on English and Ziebach was replaced by expressions of pure joy.

Miner returned to Vermillion, leaving Lieutenant Bacon in charge of forty soldiers at the stockade. Pickets roamed the hills surrounding the town during the daylight hours, looking for signs of danger. Days passed without an attack, although there were incidents that forced the stockade dwellers to believe that a horde of the "red foe" was about to test their defenses. One night the gun of a picket accidentally discharged, causing the entire contingent of pickets to rush into the stockade. Sleepers were aroused from their tents and wagons. Women and children were rushed to the interior buildings for better protection. A man, in a high state of panic, grabbed one of his children by the hand and another child by the leg and dashed off toward the printing office. With the head of the unfortunate child bouncing off the hard ground, he was dragged crying, along to safety, by his anxious father, oblivious to anything but getting his children under cover.

There were other incidents that sent waves of fear through the community. Washington Reed and his sons Matt and Tom ventured away from their home above the town and into a nearby ravine to cut timber for building purposes. When they failed to return at nightfall, other members of the Reed family were concerned for their safety. They contacted Captain Miner and soon a group of ten men mounted up and went out to search for the Reeds. Among them were A. B. Smith, in a sulky, and "Old Spot" Mortimer on horseback.

During the search Smith and Mortimer became separated from the main body of searchers. When Miner found Smith's empty sulky, it was concluded that he and Mortimer were killed by Indians. The volunteer soldiers continued their search, which now included finding the offending Indians as well as the Reeds. As it was a hot day, some of the soldiers took off their coats revealing their red flannel undershirts. When they came in sight of Smith and Mortimer—both still very much alive—the red-shirted soldiers were mistaken for Indians, causing Smith and Mortimer to mount up and flee. Oddly enough, Miner thought that Smith and Mortimer were Indians and soon he and his men were in hot pursuit. Miner yelled, "Follow me, boys, we must have these Indians." The wild chase took them over the hills, through gulches and ravines, with brush tearing at their clothes. It ended abruptly when their horses got bogged down in "a miry place at the head of a ravine...."

Soon after it came to Miner and his men that they were not chasing Indians, and Smith and Mortimer also came to the profound and happy conclusion that they were not being chased by Indians. When the two groups met, they "enjoyed a hearty laugh over the ludicrous mistakes that all had participated in." Later it was learned that the Reeds had made their way safely to their home, thus ending the exercise.[64]

After about a month with the settlers lodged in the stockade, the siege broke. According to Picotte, signs indicated there would be no attack and that the Indians had left the area. It was learned the decision was made not to attack after Miner arrived with his forty soldiers, and because the Indians had insufficient horses. They were out there, however, in great numbers, about three or four miles from Yankton.

Gradually, the settlers left the stockade and with some trepidation, went out to inspect their claims, many of which had been looted. Farmers who had complained about Indians were now cursing the "roaming bands of cavalry scouts" who helped themselves to garden produce, chickens and pigs for food and rail fences for firewood. It was more misery but from an unexpected source.[65]

For some, the experience inside the stockade, combined with the material losses, was too much to deal with; these people left Dakota. Indeed, it was estimated that about one-half of the population had departed, either with the stampede, or after the siege at Yankton ended.⁶⁶ Yet everyone lived to tell about it; but who did they tell and what did they say or write? The child who was dragged head first through the dirt during the night when it was feared that many would be killed and scalped—where did he go to live out his life? Where did Mrs. Edgar go and what did she do after she concluded her visit to Yankton? What happened to "Old Dakota?" It is unfortunate that historians know so little of the lives of the Yankton stockade people after their ordeal ended.

Among the escapees was Mahala Amidon. After reaching Yankton, she sent a letter to a St. Paul friend to confirm the death of her husband and son at Sioux Falls City. Her goal was to reach St. Paul and get far away from the dreaded frontier.⁶⁷ By mid-October she was in St. Paul where she sent a letter to her daughter Martha, detailing the killing of her husband Joseph and son Willie. It is unlikely that she ever returned to Sioux Falls, apparently satisfied with the burial site of her husband and son.

Another odd feature of this long dilemma was the timing of it all. September 1, 1862, was election-day. It was time for men to shoulder their guns and go to the polls, and yet, as we have seen, on the day voters were to go to the polls, many of them were on the move, scurrying for the safety of Sioux City. Still there was considerable voting, except for the Sioux Falls City precincts where there was none at all. In the far north at Pembina, where peace prevailed, a full round of voting took place. Unfortunately for the Red River folks, their votes did not reach Yankton in time to be counted and all were rejected.⁶⁸

At the Brule Creek settlement in Cole County, anxious voters, not above cheating, opened the polls on the evening of August 30th. After a vigorous round of voting that night, more votes were cast the next morning. Then the voters and their families joined the mass exodus. Eventually, the Brule Creek vote was ruled fraudulent and thrown out, but for a time it counted and most of it went in the Jayne column, making him the eventual winner over Todd. As Dakota's representative in Washington, Jayne could leave the territory and say he had a valid reason for doing so.

But it wasn't over. Todd contested the election. After a territorial investigation, the matter was eventually referred to the U. S. House of Representatives, which reversed the results of the shabby election— due to fraud and gross irregularities—and gave the win to Todd. Due to the timing of the investigation, however, Todd was not sworn in until June 18, 1864, almost two years after the election.[69]

By early November 1862, most folks had recovered from both the Indian scare and the election. Despite the devastation and loss of property, matters could have been much worse. Had the "wild" Lakota Sioux to the west joined with the Santee and attacked full force, the settlers would have suffered many more casualties. As it was, the town sites at Yankton and Sioux Falls had been dealt a deadly blow with the latter getting the worst of it. If Sioux Falls' speculators still harbored dreams of wealth and fame after the 1860 election, the Dakota War of 1862 all but snuffed them out. All the propaganda in the world would not bring another wave of settlers rushing in to Dakota.

With the Civil War in progress, many people believed that the Indians would launch an all-out attack on those settlements that remained. It was even speculated that Confederate agents in Canada were plotting with the Santee and other Sioux tribes, encouraging them to "wipe out all the whites on the Missouri as far down as Sioux City."[70] While it never happened, time was needed for fear to subside and the awful memories to fade.

Still there were some who were willing to tough it out with an eye to the future. Several Sioux Falls men, now settled in Yankton, wanted to return to their town and retrieve some of the belongings that were cached just before their mad departure. The group included W. W. Brookings, Alpheus G. Fuller, George P. Waldron, and J. W. Evans.[71] They were also anxious, of course, to see what, if anything was left of their buildings and other property. Captain Miner was persuaded to lead a contingent of soldiers and former residents back to the deserted town. They camped outside of town and while some men ventured down to investigate, mounted pickets were posted on the hillside.

After the Sioux Falls men recovered some of their possessions and were ready for the return trip, one of the soldiers, Jacob Ludwig, was spotted on horseback, racing toward the camp. Two Indians were right behind him, intent on catching him. Captain Miner and the rest of the soldiers intervened and the pursuing Indians careened away and disappeared. Miner soon discovered a Sioux party of about 40 warriors, just below the Falls. In a moment of caution, the interpreter, Joseph Ellis, went forward and asked the Indians to identify themselves and state their business. One of the Indians said they were from the Minnesota River, and were in Dakota to "kill white men, God damn you."

The part about killing whites was spoken in English, causing Miner to draw his revolver and fire, apparently as a signal to his men.

The Indians were soon off and riding away with the soldiers in hot pursuit. After a long chase one of the Indians was shot and wounded by Charles Wright at a slough just west of town. Sgt Ellis moved in and with his saber, killed the man just as he was trying to explain he was a "good Indian." The rest of the Indians escaped.[72]

According to Kingsbury's account, the Indian was a "giant" who got separated from his fellows and was overtaken by Ellis, Wright and Josiah Gray. A violent struggle took place as the Indian fired his gun and then used it as a club to strike at Ellis. Wright shot the man and brought him to his knees but the wound did not kill him. The desperate Indian then pulled a "long knife" and lunged at Ellis but missed, striking his horse instead. Ellis then dispatched the man with his saber. Among the dead man's possessions, Miner discovered a soldier's jacket and two quilts. At the Indians' camp in a nearby ravine, soldiers found two wagons, one harness and some camping utensils, along with five recently killed hogs. This was all the proof Miner needed to convince him the Indians were hostiles.[73]

It was long believed the dead Indian was one of those who participated in the massacre of settlers in Minnesota, possibly even an Inkpaduta follower or a relative. Recent research and investigation, however, revealed he was not an "unfriendly," but had the misfortune of being caught up the war and became a casualty. His name was Makana Na Ota E'en. He was buried near the site of his death by his companions.[74]

Not long after the incident at the slough, a detail of soldiers encountered Indians again. This time it was at Skunk Creek, southwest of the town site, where they stopped to water their horses. Again it was the Indians riding off with the soldiers in pursuit. After a chase of about twelve miles, the Indians took cover in a buffalo wallow. There the soldiers killed them one by one and returned to Captain Miner with their wild tale. The Captain was reluctant to believe their story, so they returned to the scene of the mass killings, severed a head from the body of one of the slain Indians, and took it back to Miner. He was convinced.[75]

The Miner expedition was not the only visit to Sioux Falls following the stampede. During the winter of 1862-63, a party of 150 men set out from Sioux City, prepared to take back Sioux Falls by force of arms, if necessary. They would avenge the killing of the Amidons. Bad weather, however, forced them to give up the pursuit. They lost six horses and two men from cold and exposure before reaching a place of safety, with tales of terror to tell.[76] Indeed, there were many exploits and deeds to recall with tears and laughter in the years to come as the consequences of the war were far reaching.

With the destruction of Sioux Falls, the Dakota Land Company suffered another serious blow, more economical than political. All of their improvements made over five years were lost. Eventually the federal government reimbursed the company for its losses, thus permitting the company to pay its one and only stock dividend.[77]

The treaties with the Santee were abrogated by the U. S. Senate, and a unanimous Minnesota legislature declared all Indians in the state outside the reservation to be outlaws, unworthy of legal protection.[78] The Indian war in Dakota drug on, moving far to the north and west where major battles took place. Yankton and the southeast were, for the most part, out of the line of fire, although there were a few examples of violence and death to deal with. By 1865 the war was winding down. Fort Dakota at Sioux Falls and Fort James to the west on the James River were established that year, and by 1866, settlers were returning to Minnehaha County to start it all up again.

The 1860's, however, will always be known as wild, precarious times in Dakota, bearing the imprint of audacious, risk-taking people who grew old with memories of their hard work, their triumphs and tragedies, and for a very exclusive group, remembrance of the "Great Dakota Stampede."

It was an uneasy time, when the happy dream of having a large farm in beautiful country was clouded by episodes of desperate, dark anxiety. Yet it was a shared experience, creating memories that lingered in the collective consciousness until the dangerous past became something both exciting and fun to look back on. In time, fear and desperation would give way to nostalgia and romanticism, the stuff that brings out poetry in people who survive a crisis. For example, Joseph Mills Hanson, a Yankton pioneer, had the good bad old days in mind when he penned "The Girls of the Yankton Stockade." This chapter will end with an excerpt:

> "It is strange, do you think, that the women took fright,
> that morning and prayed;
> That men even turned white,
> When over the ridge where the college now looms,
> we caught the first glitter
> Of lances and plumes,
> And heard the dull trample of hoofs drawing nigh,
> Like the rumble of the thunder, low down in the sky?"[79]

Chapter XIV

Fate of the Cavaliers

"Those were times of wild jubilee, mirth and merriment, and as I was then in the prime of life, I enjoyed the exciting events of the frontier."

Moses K. Armstrong

There were some Dakota frontiersmen who went back East to live out their lives, when past their prime. In a tame and stable environment, they spent their latter days in comfortable chairs, smiling through their memories, while looking into the uncomprehending eyes of relatives, friends and neighbors. Moving among mere mortals, they wore their frontier experiences with exalted pride. They had come full circle and returned home safely.

Others stayed in Dakota, believing the best place to live—and die—was on the homesteads they struggled so hard to keep and improve. Here they played out their final roles, as prestigious old-timers, men—and women too—folk heroes who had undertaken the greatest risks and weathered the roughest storms. Old and bent, and worn out by a life of hard work, their last days were observed with respect by the younger generation, and their dying was attended by a sincere outpouring of grief and gratitude. They're out there even now—proudly represented by thousands of weather-worn gravestones in cemeteries throughout the Dakotas.

Of course many Cavaliers died young or died tragically, and

were never able to see how it all turned out. In a social experiment fraught with danger, there were bound to be some casualties. If they were among family or friends, their consolation, if any, was that they did not die among strangers.

For some the frontier experience could not be explained; it could only be experienced. Those who didn't experience it were condemned to be endlessly mystified, for an understanding would always be just out of reach. Very few pioneers tried to write about it. Still, most were happy to talk about it. And while it was a treat for a reporter or a historian to interview someone from the 1860's, the interviewee was often unable to convey the true nature of the times, as if overcome by all the awesome details. Happily, however, a few nuggets of experience do come through.

This last chapter will summarize the lives of some of the Cavaliers of the Dakota Frontier, for whom this book was written. Precious little is known about many of these men, and much less of their wives and families. It seems unfair to history buffs that so many people who lived on the edge, slipped over and away from the record altogether, or were slighted by latter-day historians who recorded the mundane details only. Fortunately, from among the pioneers, Moses K. Armstrong wrote well, revealing the gist of frontier life in vivid word pictures. So we'll start with him.

Moses K. Armstrong, an Ohio native, didn't have a mundane bone in his body. He was not a speculator—which set him apart from most of his fellow pioneers. But lucky for them, he was a good writer and a serious historian—with a sense of humor. He was also a popular, public-spirited man, and a Democrat, who managed to serve two terms as Dakota's delegate to Congress, although the territory was dominated by Republicans. When his second term ended in 1874, he ran for a third term, against his wishes, in order that his party would have a candidate. After losing he left Yankton for St. James, Minnesota. Dakota politics in the 1870's seems to have taken the fun out of the frontier for this frontiersman. Armstrong was broke and tired and needed a new start.

While he never again lived in Dakota, he wrote *Early Empire Builders of the Great West*, which chronicles the events of the late 1850's and 1860's. With fresh and vibrant prose, and colorful attention to detail, Armstrong makes it clear he enjoyed Dakota in the wild, wide-open sixties. The book was published in 1901; he died in 1906, and much about Dakota's past that was unique, exciting and vital died with him.

Some men stuck with Dakota and were well fixed in their middle or golden years. Among them, Dr. Josiah L. Phillips, of the Western Town Company, became one of Sioux Falls' biggest landowners. After the 1862 exodus from Sioux Falls, he served as an assistant surgeon and surgeon with the 16th Iowa Infantry regiment in the Civil War. He was with General William T. Sherman during the Union army's destructive march through Georgia. In 1870, when Sioux Falls was getting a second start, he returned with his wife Hattie and obtained title to a quarter section of land that soon became the heart of the village. The main street of the new town was named Phillips Avenue for Dr. Phillips. He was originally from Farmington, Maine where he was born on June 8, 1835.

As his eyes were damaged during the Civil War, he disdained the practice of medicine, except in extreme cases. Instead he made a comfortable living selling real estate from among the nine blocks

Grave of Dr. Josiah L. Phillips
Mt. Pleasant Cemetery, Sioux Falls, SD
Photo by Author

he owned in the new village. He died suddenly at the age of 47 on June 12, 1882, in Sioux Falls, leaving a widow, six children and large estate.[1] His widow, Hattie Phillips, built a huge and lavish mansion on a prominence overlooking Covell's slough west of Sioux Falls. She became one of the town's most respected ladies with her own frontier credentials. Their mansion is gone.

Phillip's friend and colleague, W. W. Brookings, attained even greater success, lived longer and is the fit subject for a book-length biography. He was born in Woolich, Maine, October 25, 1830, on a farm near Brookings Bay on the Atlantic Ocean, a member of an old colonial family.[2] After graduating from Bowdoin College in 1855, he taught school, read the law and was admitted to the Maine bar. He went to Dubuque, Iowa to establish his law practice, but soon joined the Western Town Company and came to Sioux Fall in 1857.

Although Brookings lost his feet to a cruel accident, his was the steady hand that "rocked the cradle of Dakota." While his enemies were cruel and unrelenting, and his political popularity not as widespread as he would have liked, all remembered him as a true pioneer, never lacking in courage, which was after all, the true measure of a pioneer.

Although he could have been excused for returning to his native Maine after the terrible ordeal in the winter of 1857-58, Brookings was not a man to play it safe. As we have seen, he returned to Sioux Falls and participated in the affairs of the squatter government. He went to Yankton during the great Dakota stampede, and when the crisis was over he stayed there and devoted his energies to politics and business. Brookings served in the legislature and ran unsuccessfully for delegate to congress in 1866. In 1865-66, he supervised the construction of a government wagon road from the Minnesota border, through Fort Pierre, to Montana. In 1869, he was appointed associate justice to the Dakota Supreme Court by President U. S. Grant, and served competently. He handed down the first death sentence in the history of the Dakota judiciary. He married Clara Carney at Dresden, Maine in March of 1869. They were childless.

Brookings hit his peak in 1872, becoming one of the leading political figures in the territory. Brookings County and the town of Brookings were named for him. He was one of a group of men who brought in the Dakota Southern Railroad, linking Sioux City and Yankton in 1872. In his honor, the first locomotive to reach Yankton was named the "Judge Brookings." That same year he ran again for Congress, as a "stalwart" Republican, in a three-way race that featured another Republican (and former friend) Gideon C. Moody. In a campaign marred by bitter personal attacks and vile, acrimonious conduct by all parties, he finished third. The winner was Moses K. Armstrong, the Democrat.

While Brookings had grit, courage and formidable leadership skills, he seemed to lack the charisma needed to win the prize he wanted so badly: a seat in Congress. During a time when political alliances were built on shifting sands, and re-shaped with magical rapidity, he was never able to put together the coalition needed to win. He got a fair measure of respect but never enough votes. But he was a hard, persistent campaigner who, more than once, made points by lashing out at detractors with his cane.

Brookings spoke with a distinctive "nasal whine," that apparently conveyed an unpleasantness that turned off voters. Because he often pleaded for political togetherness, he became known in Dakota as

Grave of Wilmot W. Brookings, Yankton Cemetery, Yankton, SD
Photo by Author

"Old Ha-a-a-monee." When he made his last run for Congress in 1882, as a Democrat, he was merely a figurehead and was easily defeated.[3] Alas, for Brookings. His successes as a politician never came close to his achievements as a frontiersman.

Like Phillips, Brookings also claimed land at the Sioux Falls town site. His quarter section included the Falls of the Big Sioux River and the eleven-acre island at the head of the Falls, taking the name "Brookings Island." He moved back to Sioux Falls in the 1878, sold real estate, engaged in business, banking, and politics. The city named a street for him.

"Judge" Brookings, as he was commonly called, was a leader in the statehood movement, and participated in the Constitutional Conventions. He lived in Sioux Falls until 1897, when he retired to Boston to manage western mining interests. Wilmot Wood Brookings died suddenly in Boston on June 13, 1905, while "riding in the cars."[4] His body was cremated according to his wishes and his ashes carried back to Yankton for interment.

Ezra Millard, who came to Sioux Falls in 1856 in the employ of the Western Town Company, became a pioneer banker in Omaha and mayor of that city from 1869 to 1871. Before that he spent time in Dubuque and Sioux City in the mid-1850's. In 1858, he and his brother Joseph engaged in real estate and private banking in Omaha. In 1866, Ezra Millard organized the Omaha National Bank. From its origin in a small 20 x 40 foot building, the bank experienced steady growth over a long haul. In 1987, it became the FirsTier Bank, housed in the 29-story Woodmen of the World office tower.[5] Scores of people traverse its elevators each day with no knowledge of its originator's pioneer credentials. Millard died August 20, 1886.

Barclay Jarrett was one of the Western Town Company's party of men that arrived at the Falls in 1857. His high-strung brother Jesse Jarrett was in charge of the company until replaced by the astute Brookings. Barclay stayed until 1862, when he went to Yankton. He lived there quietly until March of 1865, operating a saloon. One day at his saloon, he became involved in a fight with a younger man. At first, he was unconcerned as he was just bruised up a bit. Later, he complained of headaches and blindness, and died suddenly, probably of a concussion. He was 50 years old. Those handling his inquest—A. G. Fuller, Byron M. Smith, and J. B. Greenway—were all fellow Sioux Falls pioneers.[6]

George P. Waldron, the flashy young lawyer, Western Town Company official and orator from "the land of rocks and waterfalls," moved his wife and family, and an 18-year-old maid, Margaret Callahan, to Sioux Falls from Dubuque in 1859. Not long after their arrival, Margaret met and married Jacob B. Barnes, a laborer from Iowa, in what was undoubtedly the first marriage in Sioux Falls.[7] Waldron built a comfortable home for his family at the town site.

Originally from New Hampshire, the Waldrons stayed in Yankton after the flight to safety in 1862. Unlike other Sioux Falls refugees, he abandoned the land he claimed in 1859. He built a fine home in Yankton for his wife Lydia and their three children. His daughter Luella "Lulu" Waldron was a talented singer and, along with other family members, entertained frequently.

Following his appointment as provost marshal of Dakota, Waldron's fiery, outspoken personality got him in trouble with the commanding officer of Fort Randall. In June of 1863, Waldron was arrested and sent to Fort Randall for threatening to shoot the commanding officer for not sending troops during the recent Indian crisis.[8] Nothing came of it, however, and he went on to become a prosperous farmer and respected citizen.

In 1877 the Waldrons moved to Fort Pierre on the Missouri River, then a lawless place—a sort of dropping off point for civilization—where everyday life was dominated by the deadly antics of border ruffians. Here he served as U. S. court commissioner until the formation of Stanley County. He then served as county probate judge. Waldron resided in Fort Pierre until his death on August 26, 1896.[9]

John McClellan was another member of the Western Town Company who lived well off his Sioux Falls claim. During the Indian wars following the evacuation of Sioux Falls, McClellan served with distinction and daring in Company A Dakota Cavalry. Returning to Sioux Falls in the early 1870's, he lived rather quietly for the rest of his life. He acquired an interest in the Sioux Falls Brewery, and along with that lucrative business, he made a comfortable fortune selling lots from "McClellan's First and Second Additions" to Sioux Falls. Having been a part of the taming of the wilderness, he cashed in on the royalties.

Very little was known about his antecedents and he was tight-lipped about his past and family. Everyone knew he was born in Ireland. He came to America *via* Canada and lived in New York state and Dubuque, Iowa, before coming to Dakota in May of 1857. He never married. Having proved himself on the frontier, he lived a relatively easy life, coasting into old age. Embodying a friendly mystery, McClellan carried on like a man who had successfully buried his past.

By the time he died on August 2, 1899, he was known as "Uncle

*Grave of John McClellan, Mt. Pleasant Cemetery, Sioux Falls, SD
Photo by Author*

John" McClellan, "the oldest living settler of Sioux Falls," a man who fought Indians in his younger days.[10] He was also known about town as a frequent and heavy drinker. On the night of his death, he was seen out and about with other "genial spirits." He roomed above the Van Eps block in downtown Sioux Falls, and upon taking the elevator to the upper floor, he somehow caught his neck between "the floor of the elevator and the upper casing of the door on the lower floor..." He choked to death and it was believed that drinking was a contributing factor, as he was seen fumbling in the dark near the elevator. McClellan lived through the frontier experience with its multitude of threats only to die in the grasp of some modern contrivance, the likes of which he could never have foreseen when, in 1857, he first looked about the remote, prairie wilderness that was to become the city of Sioux Falls.

McClellan was about 78 years old when he died and left no known heirs. Since he amassed a considerable amount of money, and owned a fair amount of real estate in Sioux Falls, a number of people came forth, claiming kinship, hoping to cash in. His estate was tied up in court for several years as various litigations worked their way through. Eventually, all contestants lost and what was left of McClellan's money went to the state. Strangely, for all his ties to a hazardous frontier past, his name was in the news far more often after his death due to the protracted court proceedings.

Artemus Gale, one of the founders of the Dakota Land Company, probably owned more Sioux Falls property than McClellan, and was one of the few members of his company to profit from land sales. He was a native of Deckerton, New Jersey. Obituaries state that he came to Sioux Falls in 1854 and claimed land where West Sioux Falls was later platted. This is uncorroborated, however, and undoubtedly incorrect. An article published while he was still alive says he located land in Sioux Falls in 1863, but never saw it until 1868, when he made the trip from St. Paul on horseback. He acquired his acreage in St. Paul, using "half-breed" scrip.[11]

Gale was so impressed with the land that he returned in 1870 and laid out a residential addition called "Gales Sioux Falls" on the south edge of the nuclear village. It became known as "Galesburg." He built a home on South Phillips Avenue in 1872, the first house in Galesburg, where he lived with his wife Louisa. The neighborhood he started remains one of the most elegant and stately in Sioux Falls. Like McClellan and Phillips, Gale quietly amassed a fortune from residential development and lot sales. He was also in banking. He was a founding member of the Congregational Church, having hosted the first meeting of the founding church group in his home. He donated five acres of land for construction of the All Saints School. Gale died in Sioux Falls on January 19, 1909 at the age of 84 and was buried in Mount Pleasant Cemetery, as are many other Sioux Falls pioneers.[12] Other members of the Dakota Land Company stayed in Dakota and attained some status and success, although none other than Gale figured prominently in Sioux Falls' future.

James W. Lynd, one of the first Dakota Land Company representatives to arrive at the Falls in 1857, apparently never returned. Lynd became the editor of the *Henderson Democrat* and broke away from both the Democratic Party and the Dakota Land Company in 1859. He was elected to the Minnesota legislature in 1860.

Lynd was living at the Redwood (or Lower) Agency in

Minnesota when the War of the Outbreak erupted. The son of an Illinois minister, he conducted a careful study of the native Dakota people, learned their language, lectured and wrote a comprehensive book about Indian culture. Lynd believed that in order to learn Indian culture, it was necessary to live among them," share their lodges, their food and their blankets." He took his advice to heart and fathered two children by an Indian woman—and left her for another Indian woman. Unfortunately, he worked as a clerk in the store of trader Nathan Myrick, the man most hated by the Santee Sioux. Lynd was killed early in the morning of August 18, 1862, not long after waking up—the first to die at the Redwood Agency.[13]

An Indian woman recalled that he was standing in a doorway facing the flagpole when the fatal shot was fired. She said Lynd was quietly "laboring under some presentiment that morning...."[14] It has been theorized that the family of the deserted woman targeted Lynd for revenge.[15] Gold from a looted safe was stuffed in his mouth.[16]

After he was killed, Lynd's nearly finished and unpublished manuscript that he stored in a trunk was scattered about the store, trampled on and stained with tobacco. It lay neglected for some time and soldiers used some pages for "waste paper." Then an officer recognized that it was a book manuscript and gathered up what remained of it. About 200 pages were recovered and over time, found their way to the Minnesota Historical Society archives.

Many of the Dakota Land Company members remained Minnesotans, or pushed on to other destinations. Some like Parker Paine, a St. Paul banker, probably never came to Dakota. Another Maine native, he was known as a conservative investor, prudent and methodical in his manners and attitude.[17] He was not a frontiersman, and apparently just chalked up his losses. Paine's bank, begun in 1853, survived the Panic of 1857—one of only three St. Paul banks to do so—and became the First National Bank of St. Paul. He was an organizer of the Lake Superior and Mississippi Railroad Company, and he served in the 8th Minnesota state legislature in 1866.[18] Paine lived until January 4, 1875, and lies among the St. Paul pioneers in Oakland Cemetery.

The future of James Liberty Fisk was distinctly western. The man who was among that small group to winter at the Falls of the Big Sioux River in 1857-58, he was appointed a captain in the U. S. Army in 1862, but was not sent to fight the Confederacy. Instead he led a group of immigrants and prospectors consisting of 117 men and 13 women into the western-most reaches of Dakota Territory (now Montana and Idaho), in search of gold in 1862, as ordered by Edwin M. Stanton, Secretary of War.[19]

He led another exploratory expedition in 1863, and in February of 1864, Fisk appeared in Chicago with astounding news of the rich gold fields in Idaho. He told amazed listeners that he saw $900.00 in gold taken from a single pan, and that $25,000,000.00 in gold had already been mined but could not be shipped out of the territory because there was no secure means to ship it.[20]

While he was probably exaggerating, his record of achievement was enough to obtain an appropriation for a third expedition, to lay out "the best route to the new gold country."[21] Starting at Fort Ridgeley with about 175 men, women, children, mules, oxen, wagons and one piece of artillery, the expedition followed the Minnesota River to Big Stone Lake. It entered Dakota Territory, passed Fort Wadsworth (now Fort Sisseton), going due west, crossing the Missouri River at Fort

Rice. The wagon train had a small military escort although Fisk told Charles F. Sims, a man who was invested heavily in the venture, that he had no fear of Indians.

In this regard Fisk was wrong, for a part of his cavalcade was attacked by a contingent of 100 Hunkpapa Teton Sioux led by a young Sitting Bull, in a fight called the Battle of Red Buttes. Trouble started when two of Fisk's wagons broke down while trying to navigate a deep ravine near present-day Dickinson, North Dakota on September 2, 1864. While the rest of the expedition continued on its way, Sitting Bull's Hunkpapas attacked the two wagons left behind. Fortunately for the teamsters a small detail of cavalry accompanied them. A brisk battle ensued and Sitting Bull was wounded and taken away from the site, but the Indians killed and wounded several soldiers and two teamsters. The survivors managed to get away from the Indians and make their way back to the main body of Captain Fisk's circled wagons.

The Indians were apparently satisfied with their deadly work and the two wagons they captured. Cached in one of the wagons was some poisoned bread which was to prove embarrassing to Fisk. More importantly for the victorious Indians, the wagons contained guns and ammunition along with liquor and cigars. During the night the victorious Indians helped themselves to the liquor and cigars, while a burial party from Fisk's group returned to inter their dead.

The next day the Fisk wagon train moved out, with the Indians following it, puffing on confiscated cigars. But having consumed so much booze, they were only able to harass the miners and soldiers with awkward dashes at the slow moving wagons. No one was hurt. Then on the 4th of September, a group of larger and less inebriated

*Grave of James L. Fisk, Oakland Cemetery, St. Paul, MN
Photo by Author*

pursuers appeared and posed a serious threat to the Fisk train. He then pulled his wagons into a circle, erected crude breastworks and accepted the fact that he and his men were in for a prolonged siege. They called their crude fortification "Fort Dilts" in honor of a scout named Jefferson Dilts who had been killed while recklessly attacking Sitting Bull's men two days before.

On September 5th, Fisk found himself surrounded by an estimated 300 to 500 Lakota warriors who fired on the enclosure. Fortunately for Fisk, however, he had a howitzer and it kept the attackers at a distance. Again, there were no casualties. That night a group of soldiers were able to sneak out of Fort Dilts and make their way to east Fort Rice on the Missouri River for help. It would take sixteen boring but tense days before help arrived. Water from a spring and wagon loads of provisions meant that the whites could hold out for a considerable period of time.

During this time the Lakotas tried to negotiate the return of a captured young white woman, Fanny Kelly of Geneva, Kansas. Fisk offered three horses, along with some flour, coffee and sugar, but the Indians turned it down, asking for 40 head of cattle and four wagons. Fisk would not agree to those terms so Kelly remained a captive for several more months before she was ultimately released. Finally, troops from Fort Rice arrived to rescue the beleaguered and would-be miners. By that time most of the Indians had left the area to hunt buffalo so there was no fighting.

While the immediate threat was relieved, there would be no further expedition into gold country. Fisk was informed that his people and their wagons would be escorted back to Fort Rice. He was angry at General Alfred Sully for what he deemed to be an interference with a federally sanctioned expedition, but there was no choice. Eventually, most of the adventurers ended up back in Minnesota, having had enough of the inhospitable Dakota wilderness and its hostile native inhabitants.[22]

A bitter Charles F. Sims called the venture a "miserable failure," because all incurred great financial losses and for some, their lives. He recalled that the Indians made "capital use of the Dakota Hills" from which they struck in ambush. And yet despite his losses and anger, Sims seemed to have a grudging respect for Fisk, whom he called "intelligent, noble-hearted and a good leader."[23]

It was during the September of 1864 expedition that Fisk's reputation became tainted by scandal, however briefly. An eastern newspaper reported that Fisk and his men poisoned and killed more than 100 Indians by putting strychnine on hard tack and bread. While there is no proof that anyone ate any of the toxic bread, it was found on one of the trapped wagons and it was reported that victims included women and children. Fisk was accused of mass murder with genocide on his agenda. The *St. Paul Pioneer* rushed to Fisk's defense saying he knew nothing about the poison and besides, most westerners would go to any extreme to get rid of the "red devils."[24]

The incident faded quickly and did nothing to tarnish Fisk's reputation. He became nationally known as a trailblazer, a status reserved for the boldest of frontiersmen. When he wasn't blazing wilderness trails, he traveled in the states and lectured—he even met President Lincoln in Washington, D. C. He submitted reports of his expeditions to the U. S. House of Representatives and sold maps for 30 cents each. Fisk's work in opening up another chunk of frontier was considered an act of public service. In 1865, the *Washington*

Chronicle interviewed Fisk and declared that his "explorations and expeditionary travels throughout the great prairies and mountains of the Northwest have made his name distinguished among men."[25] His brothers Robert E., Van H. and Andrew also distinguished themselves in the West, making the Fisk family one of the best known on the northwestern frontier.

James L. Fisk died on November 2, 1902, and his bones rest at Oakland Cemetery in St. Paul, beneath a broken-down and neglected grave marker. The shabby marble gravestone with its worn inscriptions foretells that in time most of us will be unsung and forgotten.

The other trailblazing member of the Dakota Land Company, William H. Nobles, returned to New York after the Civil War broke out. In 1862, while in New York, he was appointed Lieutenant Colonel in the 79th New York Infantry Regiment, known as the "Highlanders." He later resigned his commission in South Carolina after some personal difficulties with another officer. After the war ended, Nobles held a number of federal offices, including Cotton Collector for the government in the South, United States Revenue Officer and Master of Transportation of Troops. His health went bad and he sought treatment at the various "hot springs" throughout the country, including Colorado, but to no avail. He returned to St. Paul, where his son, Lemuel Nobles, was living. He checked into the Church Hospital for treatment. He did not, however, recover and died in St. Paul on December 28, 1876.[26]

Nobles' life had been one of adventure, hard work and risk taking. While it wore him down, it had also allowed him to explore his ingenuity and creativity. He patented a number of inventions including those for a heater, a fire escape and a two-engine river and harbor dredge boat. Nothing came of them, however, and like so many men of his time, he did not benefit financially, in a lasting way, from his many accomplishments. While there were times when he was "flush" with money, he died poor, old and worn out before his time. He died a stranger to many, but yet among friends, old-timers and old settlers who remembered him with a special fondness.[27]

Joseph R. Brown emerged as one of the most respected and versatile frontiersmen of his time. Aside from his accomplishments as a trader, explorer and politician—the man who "dreamed a dream of a horseless wagon and steam tractor," invented what was called a "steam wagon."[28] Built by John A. Reed of New York City, this dramatically new but primitive and cumbersome vehicle, was the object of great curiosity, and of course, brought out the skeptics. One man called it a "cross between a sawmill and a locomotive."[29] On a frontier without railroads and just getting accustomed to prairie schooners, the steam wagon seemed totally out of context. But Brown loved his creation, and after its first appearance in Winona in the summer of 1859, "Juggler Joe" came out with an "altered and improved" model in November of 1860, that lumbered across the prairie at five miles per hour. He called this machine "Mazomanie," meaning "Walking Metal."[30]

Moving laboriously across prairie roads, the heavy, three-wheeled steam wagon attracted considerable attention from among the people and the press. People cheered as it moved down the streets of Minnesota towns, pulling two massive carts. With this kind of power and locomotion, the possibilities seemed endless. Someone said it was built to haul freight across the Plains to the Rocky Mountains.

On the Fourth of July, 1860, Brown gave his ponderous machine a trial run at his beloved Henderson, to the biggest crowd that had ever gathered there. One impressed observer predicted that self-propelled machines will one day be built that will "answer every purpose for which wagons or railroad cars are now used, and which will travel with facility over ordinary roads."[31] But the "first automobile" got stuck in deep mud, and there it stayed, rusting away over the years, shot full of holes.[32]

In 1861 the congenial and inventive Brown built a three-and-one-half-story, 19-room stone mansion on the prairie in Renville County, Minnesota, to house his growing family. He called his mansion "Farther and Gay," a take-off on the famous "Fothering Hay" castle in England. The great house was attacked and burned by the Santee Sioux during the Dakota War while Brown was in New York promoting his steam wagon.

Brown's family was captured by the Santee and held prisoner. In time, they were released. Later, at the mass execution of Indians in Mankato, Brown served as the signal officer. After he tapped three times on a drum, the rope was cut, sending 38 men to their deaths.[33] The irrepressible Brown lived a few more years, then died in New York in 1870, while still promoting his steam wagon. His body was returned to Henderson, Minnesota for burial.

Brown's border companion and fellow "moccasin" Democrat Charles E. Flandrau spent some time in Nevada and St. Louis before returning to Minnesota. He topped off a distinguished political career by running for governor of Minnesota in 1867, losing to his Republican challenger. He moved to St. Paul in 1870 and thereafter engaged in the practice of law. Flandrau published a book entitled

*Grave of Charles E. Flandrau, Oakland Cemetery, St. Paul, MN
Photo by Author*

The History of Minnesota and Tales of the Frontier in 1900. While the book contains numerous frontier anecdotes and an extensive treatment of Minnesota politics, it does not include a chapter on the Dakota Land Company. On September 9, 1903, the man others called "the cavalier of the border" died at his home in St. Paul after a long illness. Flandrau lies buried in Oakland Cemetery in St. Paul beneath a large but plain black boulder.

Minnesota Territorial Governor Samuel A. Medary, with limited connections to Dakota, moved back to Ohio after his term of office ended. There he served for a time as postmaster in Columbus. Next it was on to Kansas Territory, where—at the urging of President Buchanan—he was installed as the governor of "bleeding Kansas," thus having the distinction of being a governor of two territories.

In 1859, this die-hard "states rights" Democrat was accused of being in league with the Jayhawkers, a band of pro-slavery, border ruffians, responsible for death and destruction throughout Kansas.[34] Adding fuel to the fire, he vetoed a bill that prohibited slavery in Kansas Territory.[35] Governor Medary resigned in 1860 and returned to Ohio and the newspaper business. As he viewed the impending Civil War with abhorrence, he editorialized constantly, trying to devise peaceful means for settling the sectional differences.[36]

"Old Sam Medary" became known as a "philosopher," "natural dissenter," and a "fanatic protestant." He was a man of great passion, hopelessly wedded to an ante-bellum world that was slipping away from him. Constantly battling against the tide of change, he used his considerable writing skills to strike at his enemies among the Republicans and abolitionists. He could carry on a vibrant conversation and at the same time, write stirring, angry editorials in his weekly *Columbus Crisis*, many of which maligned President Lincoln, whom Medary hated and blamed for the Civil War. Medary was part of an articulate and influential group of "peace Democrats," also referred to as "Copperheads," who supported the preservation of the Union, although they shuddered when they considered the probable consequences of Lincoln's Emancipation Proclamation. Equality for the black race was not on their political agenda.

The conservative Medary was liberal in his attacks on other "Black" Republicans too, calling them "idiots and knavish asses." One night in 1863, a mob attacked and destroyed his printing shop, causing the fearless Medary to blame Union soldiers stationed nearby. His supporters retaliated by attacking the office of an abolitionist newspaper.

His vicious attacks were the cause of his arrest by a federal marshall, on May 20, 1864. He was indicted by a grand jury, but Medary was not one to let up. He was unwilling to accept the fact that the life he longed for—a white, genteel, Jacksonian America—was forever in the past. So he pressed on, and only his death at his home in Columbus, Ohio, on November 7, 1864, shut off the venom from his mind and pen, and saved him from standing trial.[37] As he died the day before the national election, he never got to see how it all ended. But he was spared the disappointment of having to deal with the re-election of Abraham Lincoln, whom he hated above all other Republicans.

A colleague on the staff of the *Ohio Statesman*, of Columbus, remembered the old Democratic War-Horse with fondness and high praise. In an obituary, he praised Medary's independence, courage and single-minded devotion to his ideals. He was remembered as "warm in his friendship and bitter in his hatred, he loved all that was manly and hated all that was mean."[38] The *Statesman* called him "the greatest journalist of the west and the most distinguished citizen of Columbus."[39] In 1869 some of his fellow Democrats erected a monument in Columbus to commemorate Medary's many years of service to his party. It was believed that the "poisoning" incident at the National Hotel in Washington in 1857 contributed to his death.

Medary was a family man with ties to the colonial days, his mother's ancestors having arrived in the New World with William Penn. They settled in what became Pennsylvania where Samuel was born in on February 25, 1801. His family name was originally "Madeira."[40]

Samuel Medary was proud of his common origins. He had a fondness for community service, was interested in farming and was one of the originators of the Ohio State Fair. But his life was dominated by politics and one senses that the political bitterness he felt in his blood and bones overpowered all his relationships and other interests. There was no mention in the *Statesman* obituary about his stint as the last governor of Minnesota Territory, his connection with the Dakota Land Company and the burned out ruins of a town named after him in faraway Dakota Territory. These small accomplishments were overshadowed by his participation in the many larger events of his tumultuous life.

Dr. William Jayne, the contentious first territorial governor of Dakota, returned to his Springfield, Illinois to live out his life. In 1869 he was appointed the pension agent for Illinois by President U. S. Grant and served a four-year term. He served in a variety of other offices, including another stint as the mayor of Springfield, the city he knew and enjoyed from its old whipping post days until the early 20th century. Dr. Jayne—one of the last of the Lincoln men—died at age 89 on March 20, 1916, at his Springfield home.

    Alpheus G. Fuller, best known as the "squatter" delegate sponsored by the Dakota Land Company, fared well and lived a long life, with apparently no interest in re-settling in Sioux Falls. He built a fine home in Yankton and became a beef contractor at Fort Randall. His commodious St. Paul hotel, the Fuller House, burned to the ground on February 3, 1869, long after he had divested himself of all interest in it. He was active in local politics in Yankton but never aspired to high office, perhaps content to have been Dakota's "delegate" during the early days. In the mid-1860's, he was one of a group of men interested in exploring and mining the Black Hills. Fuller moved to Pokomok, Maryland in 1895, and died on April 13, 1900, while on a visit to Scotland, Connecticut.[41] His brothers and sisters also returned to Connecticut to live out their days, except for Abby, who stayed in St. Paul after marrying Samuel Badger Abbe in 1858.

    Franklin J. DeWitt, bold and aggressive as a speculator, disdained both Sioux Falls and Medary, and was attracted instead to the Missouri slope. Like some of his fellow speculators, the break-up of the Dakota Land Company put an end to his town site fever, but not his attachment to the Dakota frontier. Following the evacuation of Sioux Falls in the summer of 1862, DeWitt engaged in Indian trade along the Missouri River. He served two terms as mayor of Yankton and one term in the territorial legislature. He died in Yankton in January of 1898, and is buried there on a prominence and under an impressive tombstone.[42] One senses there was a great deal more to his life than the small samples that emerge from the record.

The same could be said of Samuel J. Albright, editor of the short-lived but feisty *Dakota Democrat*. Not much is known of his life after his departure from Sioux Falls City, the town site he wanted to build into a great city. He went to St. Louis in 1860 and along with a few others, started a newspaper called the *Daily Missourian*. Albright called himself a "Democrat of the most pronounced type." But unlike his friend and contemporary, Samuel A. Medary, however, he strongly favored the Union, and considered those who would secede, or promote secession, to be traitors. Nevertheless, he freely criticized the Union during the Civil War when he saw fit, and because of this, he was ordered to cease publication of his newspaper. He did as ordered and, ending his career as a newspaperman, he went to the front, to Shiloh, Tennessee, where he worked as a "volunteer aid" at one of the bloodiest battles of the Civil War[43]

Another source says he returned to St. Paul in the fall of 1862, after serving in the Union army in the South as a spy and correspondent.[44] Later he lived in New York where he apparently succeeded in some kind of commercial venture. In 1884, he was said to be in Chicago.[45] He visited Sioux Falls in 1887. There is some confusion in the record as to his age, and, in 1912, Albright was a resident of the Ohio Soldiers Home.[46] If this is true, then he could not have been in his mid-fifties when he arrived at Sioux Falls City in 1858, with his printing apparatus.

The life of James M. Allen, who figured prominently in the squatter government at Sioux Falls, took many interesting twists and turns. He was a well-seasoned frontiersman long before he came to Dakota, having lived in Oregon and California.[47] This undoubtedly

Grave of Franklin J. DeWitt, Yankton Cemetery, Yankton, SD
Photo by Author

prepared him for the crises at Fort Sod and at the Yankton stockade.

Allen was appointed receiver of the first land office in Dakota that opened in Vermillion on July 16, 1862. He became mired down in trouble and was criminally charged in connection with his work as a receiver. In October of 1865, he was tried in Vermillion before Judge Kidder on a variety of charges and was acquitted.[48] After that Allen left Yankton, returning to his native Ohio. He got married and spent several years in Toledo and Cleveland, working for the U. S. Post Office. But apparently he still had a longing for the frontier, and the Black Hills gold rush drew him back to the West. In February of 1877, he showed up in Yankton where he prepared for the journey to the Black Hills. He prospected in the Hills for at least a year. Allen was in Denver in 1883.

Ten years later he was again living in the Black Hills. There, on Christmas day of 1893, the man Franklin DeWitt called "one of the truest men" he ever knew, killed himself.[49] When Albright learned of Allen's passing, he said "no truer friend, no braver heart, no honester man, ever has or ever will set foot upon the soil of Dakota."[50] Alas, we are presented with an incomplete sketch of a man who made his mark on the frontier while he endeared himself to his companions, and apparently died in the throes of a terrible personal crisis.

Another true man of the frontier was Jefferson P. Kidder, one of the brightest people associated with the Dakota Land Company. After many productive years in St. Paul as a business and political leader, he left that city and gave Dakota Territory the benefit of his sage counsel. Before he was through evolving, Kidder earned both high office and great respect from his fellow citizens. Indeed, this eloquent, witty man noted for his intellectual bearing, was affectionately called "Dakota's friend." He always seemed to fit in, whether it be in the saloons of Deadwood or the halls of Congress.

In 1863-64 he served Minnesota in the House of Representatives. In 1865 Kidder returned to Dakota, having been appointed an associate justice to the territorial Supreme Court by President Lincoln. He settled in Vermillion with his family, but traveled a circuit, holding court at various towns, including Sioux Falls, presiding over a wide variety of cases. As a judge on the frontier, it was said he "leaned to mercy's side."[51]

His son Lyman S. Kidder enlisted in the U. S. Army and was assigned to the Second Cavalry. On June 29, 1867, while carrying a dispatch from Fort Sedgwick, Nebraska to Col. George A. Custer on the Republican River, Lt. Kidder and his detachment of eleven men were attacked and killed by Cheyenne Indians under the leadership of Chief Roman Nose. On July 11, 1867, while on patrol, Custer discovered the mutilated remains of the soldiers. All were buried in a mass grave. The elder Kidder, deeply saddened by his loss, traveled to the gravesite and exhumed his son's body. It was identified by the checked woolen shirt his mother had made for him. Lt. Kidder was re-buried in St. Paul.[52]

Perhaps under the beguiling influence of his Dakota friends, Jefferson P. Kidder switched to the Republican Party. Then in 1874 and 1876 he was elected to Congress from Dakota by large majorities. He became well acquainted with President Grant and proved to be an effective and popular delegate, and was instrumental in acquiring the Black Hills from the Indians. That alone was sufficient to endear him to white Dakotans.

After he left Congress, Kidder was once again appointed to the Dakota territorial bench. He became involved in the statehood movement, favoring division of the territory and admission of two states. He donated 10 acres of land for the University of South Dakota at Vermillion; the school opened in the fall of 1882.[53] He presided over the first Constitutional Convention held in Sioux Falls in 1883. By then he was a sick man. Jefferson P. Kidder died October 2, 1883, in St. Paul and was buried in Oakland Cemetery.

Long after Judge Kidder died his son Silas W. Kidder found a journal that described in great detail the elder Kidder's journey from St. Paul to Dakota during the squatter days. Understanding its value as a resource for historians, Silas intended to donate it to the South Dakota State Historical Society. Unfortunately, however, it was accidently discarded and burned with other rubbish.[54]

Among the Yankton speculators, Enos Stutsman achieved considerable success and great popularity. Like Kidder, he had the desire, energy, and the convivial personality that attracted admirers. Stutsman always seemed to land a government position, be it by election or appointment. He served in the territorial legislature year after year. The initial civil and criminal codes were drafted thanks largely to Stutsman's legal skills. He would also, on occasion, provide the legislature with some comic relief. For example, in 1864, he introduced a bill "to encourage the cultivation of dogs, and the improvement of the breed thereof...."[55]

In 1867, Stutsman was appointed a "special agent" of the U. S. Treasury Department and worked at the Custom House at the international border in Pembina. In 1870 he was appointed Register of the U. S. Land Office at Pembina. He served for two years and then engaged in law practice. He is remembered in North Dakota by Stutsman County. In the winter of 1873-74, he suddenly took ill, and in the company of friends, Enos Stutsman died on January 31, 1874.

In his obituary, Stutsman's old friend George W. Kingsbury said: "the deceased was very generally known throughout the West, and we believe it can be truthfully said that he enjoyed a wider acquaintance and more personal friends than any other man in the territory."[56] Many old-timers cherished their memories and stories of little "Stuts," a wild man whose zest for life and intellectual prowess far overshadowed his physical limitations. He was long and sorely missed in Dakota.

Other Yankton men left important—although less buoyant—legacies. Throughout the 1860's, John B. S. Todd pursued his political ambitions to the fullest, using Yankton as a power base. When the Civil War broke out, Todd, a native of Kentucky, remained loyal to the Union even though some members of his family did not. President Lincoln gave him the rank of brigadier general on September 19, 1861, and Todd commanded volunteers of the North Missouri District, 6th division of the Army of the Tennessee, until July 17, 1862.[57]

Todd again turned his attention to Dakota, land of his ambitions. Having served as Dakota's first congressional delegate, and part of a second term, he ran again in 1864 and 1868. But competition from others equally ambitious and better connected, kept him away from Washington. He had to be content with service in the Dakota legislature in 1867-68. He died in Yankton at the age of 57, on January 5, 1872.[58]

Todd's former partner in the fur trading business, David M. Frost of St. Louis, threw his lot in with the Confederacy and was given the rank of brigadier general. In 1861 he led a bold but failed attempt to seize the U. S. arsenal in St. Louis. Missouri was a fiercely divided state that the North managed to keep in the Union. This did not bode well for Frost and others who favored the South. It was reported in the spring of 1864 that Frost deserted and fled to Canada, leaving his wife alone in St. Louis, although living in "fashionable style."[59]

Charles Picotte, the man who secured the Yankton Treaty of 1858, lived lavishly on the rewards of the treaty. He was generous with his friends and family, spending his money freely, drinking heavily. He built a fine house in Yankton on Front Street. When he was old and his money depleted, Picotte moved to the Greenwood agency where he was received with honor and respect by his Indian brethren, despite the odious treaty and the many years he spent as a friend to the white man. His old colleague Kingsbury recalled that Picotte reverted to Indian ways, "taking the blanket." He died at Greenwood.[60] Many years after his death, John P. Williamson recalled that Picotte was a "man of good ability" and might have been very successful "if he could have let whiskey alone."[61]

George Pinney, the lightning rod speaker in the first territorial House of Representatives, sought adventure further west. Occasionally news of Pinney's exploits would trickle into Yankton where his former friends and foes could read and shake their heads in amazement. In 1868, he was in Helena, Montana where he managed a newspaper. Once again his partisan personality led to trouble. Pinney's newspaper editorials offended one of Helena's leading citizens, ex-Governor S. W. Beall of Wisconsin. An enraged Beall demanded a retraction, which he backed up by a threat. An altercation followed and Pinney shot and killed Beall. The shooting was determined to be in self-defense.[62] Sometime later Pinney occupied himself in Omaha pursuing the daughter of an actor.[63]

In 1875, he became mired down in political scandal in San Francisco. He was working for the U. S. government when he was charged with "uttering false vouchers." He claimed he was victimized by an unscrupulous political ring consisting of big name California men. Pinney fled the country supposedly in the company of a "notorious woman." who "beguiled" him. He went to South America and then to London. In the meantime his wife divorced him. Pinney finally returned to San Francisco, where, with the aid of his friends, and a repentant ex-wife, he answered to the charges.[64] He popped up again in 1883 in New York, as a defendant in a $50,000.00 libel suit.[65] It would be interesting to know where and how he eventually died, and where his bones lie.

Charles K. Howard, the one-time Missouri River steamboat captain, died in Sioux Falls on November 4, 1918, after a distinguished, unselfish and varied career. He became the sutler at Fort Dakota in 1866, and operated fur trading posts in Sioux Falls and Flandreau. He settled in Sioux Falls operating a general store, among other related businesses.

Howard endeared himself to many settlers by extending credit to those wiped out by the grasshopper plagues of the mid 1870's. He acquired a reputation for public-spirited generosity that has yet to be equaled in Dakota. Many folks owed their survival to Howard, and when talking about the trying times would invariably say, "if not for him...." It was God's truth, people would say.

In the 1880's Charlie headed west and engaged in ranching in the

Black Hills. Eventually he went broke and returned to Sioux Falls, an old man. He was warmly welcomed like the folk hero he was—a generous man who stepped up when his neighbors needed help. The community had not forgotten his kindness and the gruff old man lived comfortably until his death. A large obelisk was placed on his grave at Woodlawn Cemetery in Sioux Falls, by grateful residents for whom memories of C. K. Howard were treasured. He was one of a kind.

It is right that we remember C. K. Howard and his fellow Dakota Cavaliers for their exploits, bravery and accomplishments. These risk takers played major roles in the history of North and South Dakota. The Cavaliers, including the many whose names are not mentioned in this book, made significant, if somewhat unsteady, footprints for others to follow. It was a mission they understood better than we do.

While they built a foundation for the future, they lived in the grip of the present—holding forth against the furies of nature and the opposition of the Native Americans. They took risks but very few of them were headlong, reckless adventurers. The richest and best-placed speculators were willing to hire others to carry the flag of enterprise onto the frontier. Dying young with a nice bank account or a rich claim, and not be able to exploit them, was to miss out on all the much-deserved rewards.

We may admire and thank—even cheer—the Cavaliers, or we can dismiss them as thoughtless, selfish and destructive. Let us keep in mind, however, that they weren't expecting applause, nor would they stand for our condemnation. For no matter how one may look upon their accomplishments and failures, there was no room in their thinking for apology or retreat. People who live on frontiers are never willing to concede anything to those who do not. Those who miss out never fully understand.

The Cavaliers were expecting enrichment and reward, if not for themselves, then for their heirs and offspring. What most of them got, however, was some personal satisfaction, irreplaceable memories, honorable mention in history books and credit for fields plowed and bricks set for the future. The luckiest ones were rewarded with a long and satisfying life, a comfortable retirement and a pleasant exit into the after-life.

The Dakota Cavaliers were the forerunners of a culture that engrafted itself on the wilderness. They made steady, incremental progress for their culture. True, they were the shock troops for the masses yet to come and fodder in a national campaign to destroy Native Americans and their culture. Yet it is wrong to dismiss them as strictly evil agents of a corrupt time. It is better to conclude that they were a hungry and curious people who were joyously overwhelmed by a vast and rich land, believing they had every right to help themselves to it. After all, there was so much of it.

That they tried to grab as much as they could as fast as they could does not automatically make them greedy and thoughtless. Most people come into the circle of life armed with a mixture of both good and bad qualities. For 19th century America, the power of fear and prejudice was great and all pervasive, creating easy suspicions and formidable barriers. It took an intellectual or spiritual giant to overcome them. It was easier and safer to fear and hate than it was to understand and appreciate. The Dakota Cavaliers were far too average to be counted on for that kind of success. And it is unfair to expect it. We owe them an honest evaluation, just as we hope to be judged fairly someday.

While the present is free to howl and harangue, without restraint, the past is voiceless. It is the present deflated and silenced. It is action, intellect and suffering reduced to landmarks, writings and artwork that we gaze upon with envy and wonder. Apart from these timeless forms, a larger part of the past takes its shape in the form of relics and memories disintegrating into dust. This fragile evidence is there to be picked up, studied and preserved, or allowed to blow away and disappear. For many years after it was smashed on the rocks in 1862, Sioux Falls settlers found bits and pieces of the old *Dakota Democrat*. Was any of it saved?

Like Jefferson P. Kidder's journal, far too much of Dakota's early historical record has already disappeared forever. What we have left isn't much; but it's all we've got and it's a pity. But that is the way of all dust. So when we study the record of the Cavaliers of the Dakota frontier, we must remember that future historians will pick through the meager bones of our past for clues of our motives and methods, failures and accomplishments, and judge us based on the scraps we leave behind.

Bibliography

Books

Anderson, Gary Clayton, *Little Crow, Spokesman for the Sioux,* Minnesota Historical Society Press, 1986
Anderson, Gary Clayton, and Woolworth, Alan R., *Through Dakota Eyes, Narrative Accounts of the Minnesota Indian War of 1862,* Minnesota Historical Society Press, St. Paul, 1988
Armstrong, Moses K., *The Early Empire Builders of the Great West,* E. W. Porter, St. Paul, 1901
Bailey, Dana R., *History of Minnehaha County,* Brown & Saenger, Sioux Falls, 1899
Beadle, J. H., *Western Wilds and the Men Who Redeem Them,* Jones Brothers & Co., 1880
Black People in South Dakota History, Bicentennial Committee of Yankton Area, Chamber of Commerce, Yankton, SD, 1977
Bosler, Roy P., Editor, *The Collected Works of Abraham Lincoln,* Vol. VII, Rutgers University Press, 1955
Briggs, Harold E., *Frontiers of the Northwest, a History of the Upper Missouri Valley,* New York, Peter Smith, 1950
Carley, Kenneth, *The Sioux Uprising of 1862,* The Minnesota Historical Society, St. Paul, 1961
Christianson, Theodore, *Minnesota, the Land of Sky-Tinted Waters,* Vol. I, The American Historical Society, Inc., Chicago and New York, 1935
Clodfelter, Michael, *The Dakota War, U. S. Army Versus the Sioux 1862-1865,* McFarland & Co., Publisher, 1998
Coursey, O. W., *Who's Who in South Dakota,* Vol. III, Educator Supply Co., Mitchell, SD, 1920
Flandrau, Charles E., *The History of Minnesota and Tales of the Frontier,* E. W. Porter, St. Paul, 1900
Fletcher, William J., *A History of the City of St. Paul and the County of Ramsey Minnesota,* St. Paul, Published by the Society, 1876
Flood, Renee S., and Bernie, Shirley A., *Remembering Your Relatives, Yankton Sioux Images, 1851-1904,* Marty Indian School, Marty, SD, 1985
Folwell, William Watts, *A History of Minnesota,* Vol. I, II, Minnesota Historical Society, St. Paul, 1922
Gardner-Sharp, Abbie, *History of the Spirit Lake Massacre,* Mill & Co., Des Moines, 1885
Gnirk, Adeline, S., *Epic of the Great Exodus,* Gregory Times Advocate, Gregory, SD, 1985
_____, S., *Epic of the Realm of the Ree,* Gregory Times Advocate, Gregory, SD, 1984
Goodspeed, Weston Arthur, Editor in Chief, *The Provinces and the States,* Madison, WI, The Western Historical Association, Vol. VI, 1904
Hall, H. P., *Observations,* St. Paul, 1904

Haller, Ben Jr., *A History of Banking In Nebraska, 1854-1990,* Nebraska Bankers Association, Inc., 1990
History of Dubuque County, Iowa, Western Historical Society, Chicago, 1881
History of the Red River Valley, Past and Present, Vol. I, Herald Printing Co., Grand Forks, 1909
History of the Spirit Lake Massacre! And of Miss Abigail Gardiner's Three Months Captivity Among the Indians, According to her Own Account, L.P Lee, Publisher, New Britain, CT, 1857
History of Southeastern Dakota, Western Publishing Co., Sioux City, Iowa, 1881
History of Yankton County, Yankton County Historical Society, 1987
Holcombe, Return I., *Minnesota in Three Centuries,* Vol. II, The Publishing Society of Minnesota, 1908
Holley, Frances Chamberlain, *Once Their Home,* Chicago, Donohue and Henneberry, 1891
Jackson, W. Turrentine, *Wagon Roads West, A Study of Federal Road Surveys and Construction in the Trans-Mississippi West, 1846-1869,* University of Nebraska Press, 1979
Jennewein, J. Leonard, and Boorman, Jane, Editors, *Dakota Panaroma,* Brevet Press, 1973
Johannsen, Robert W., *Stephen A. Douglas,* New York, Oxford University Press, 1973
Jones, Evan, *The Minnesota, Forgotten River,* Holt, Rinehart and Winston, New York, 1962
Jones, Robert Huhn, *The Civil War in the Northwest,* University of Oklahoma Press, Norman, 1960
Kelsey, Vera, *Red River Runs North!,* Harper & Brothers, Publishers, New York, 1951
Kingsbury, George W., *History of Dakota Territory,* Vol. I, S. J. Clarke Publishing Co., Chicago, 1915
Lamar, Howard Robert, *Dakota Territory 1861-1889,* New Haven and London, Yale University Press, 1966
Lass, William E., *A History of Steamboating on the Upper Missouri River,* University of Nebraska Press: Lincoln, 1962
Lewis, Lloyd, *The Assassination of Lincoln, History & Myth,* MJF Books, New York, 1994
McKusick, Marshall, *The Iowa Northern Border Brigade,* The University of Iowa, Iowa City, 1975
Meyer, Roy W., *History of the Santee Sioux,* University of Nebraska Press, Lincoln, 1967
Morris, H. S. *Historical Stories, Legends and Traditions, Northeastern South Dakota,* Published by the Sisseton Courier
Neil, Edward Duffield, *History of Minnesota,* Circa 1859
Neil, Rev. Edward O., *History of the Minnesota Valley,* and Bryant, Charles S., *History of the Sioux Massacre,* North Star Publishing, Minneapolis, 1882
Newsom, T. M., *Pen Pictures of St Paul, Minnesota,* Vol. I, Published by the Author, St. Paul, MN, 1886
O'Brien, Frank G., *Minnesota Pioneer Sketches,* H. H. S. Rowell, Publisher, 1904
Oehler, C. M., *The Great Sioux Uprising,* New York Oxford University Press, 1959

Old Rail Fence Corners, The ABC's of Minnesota History, Second Edition, By the Book Committee, 1914
Parker, Donald Dean, Ed., *Pioneering in the Upper Big Sioux Valley, 1967*
_____, *The Recollections of Philander Prescott, Frontiersman of the Old Northwest, 1819-1862,* University of Nebraska Press, 1966
Peterson, William J., *Iowa, The Rivers of Her Valleys,* State Historical Society of Iowa, Iowa City, 1941
Ralph, Julian, *On Canada's Frontier,* Harper & Brothers, New York, 1892
Robinson, Doane, *History of South Dakota,* Vol. I, B. F. Bowen & Co., 1904
Rose, Arthur P., *An Illustrated History of Nobles County, Minnesota,* Northern History Publishing Company, Worthington, MN, 1908
Ross, Alexander, *The Red River Settlement,* Ross & Hanes, Inc., Minneapolis, 1957
Sandburg, Carl, *Abraham Lincoln: the Prairie Years and the War Years,* Harcourt, Brace and Company, New York, 1954
Sanson-Flood, Renee, *Lessons From Chouteau Creek,* The Center for Western Studies, Augustana College, Sioux Falls, SD, 1986
Shell, Herbert S., *Dakota Territory During the 1860's,* Government Research Bureau, University of South Dakota, 1954
_____, *History of Clay County South Dakota,* Clay County Historical Society, Inc., Vermillion, SD, 1976
_____, *History of South Dakota,* University of Nebraska Press, Lincoln, 1961
Smith, Charles M., *Minnehaha County History,* Educator Supply Co., Mitchell, SD 1949
Sprague, William Forrest, *Women and the West, A Short Social History,* Arno Press, NY, 1972
Swisshelm, Jane Grey, *Half A Century,* Jansen, McClurg & Co., Chicago, 1880
Teakle, Thomas, *The Spirit Lake Massacre,* State Historical Society of Iowa, 1918
Trinka, Zena Irma, *Out Where the West Begins, Being the Early and Romantic History of North Dakota,* St. Paul, The Pioneer Co., 1920
Van Nuys, Maxwell, *Inkpaduta, The Scarlet Point,* Maxwell Van Nuys, Denver, CO, 1998
Wills, Jocelyn, *Boosters, Hustlers, and Speculators, Entrepreneurial Culture and the Rise of Minneapolis and St. Paul, 1849-1883,* Minnesota Historical Society Press, 2005

Newspapers

Black Hills Pioneer (Deadwood, D.T.)
Black Hills Times (Deadwood, D. T.)
Canton Advocate (Canton, D.T.)
Chicago Tribune
Cincinnati Daily Commercial
Cincinnati Weekly Gazette
Cleveland Plaindealer
Daily Press and Dakotaian (Yankton, D.T.)
Dakota Democrat (Sioux Falls City, Dakota)

Dakota Herald, (Yankton, D.T.)
Dakota Pantagraph (Sioux Falls, D.T.)
Dickenson Press (North Dakota)
Dubuque Herald
Dubuque Daily Times
Dubuque Daily Tribune
Dubuque Daily Republican
Dubuque Express and Herald
Fort Dodge Republican (Iowa)
Henderson Democrat (Minnesota)
Mankato Independent (Minnesota)
Minneapolis Tribune
Minnesota Free Press (St. Peter)
Monticello Times (Minnesota)
Moody County Enterprise (Flandreau, D.T.)
New York Daily Times
New York Times
New York Independent
New York Tribune
Ohio Statesman (Columbus)
Omaha Nebraskan
Philadelphia North American
Press and Dakotaian (Yankton, D.T.)
Rochelle Register (Illinois)
St. Anthony Express (Minnesota)
St. Paul Daily Minnesotian
St. Paul Daily Times
St. Paul Dispatch
St. Paul Pioneer
St. Paul Pioneer Press
St. Paul Pioneer Press and Democrat
St. Peter Courier (Minnesota)
St. Peter Free Press (Minnesota)
Sioux City Eagle
Sioux City Register
Sioux Falls Argus-Leader
Sioux Falls Independent
Sioux Falls Leader
Sioux Falls Press
South Dakota Record (Sioux Falls)
South Dakota State Forum (Sioux Falls)
The Dakota Bell (Sioux Falls, D.T.)
The Dakotian, (Yankton, D.T.)
The Democrat, (Winona, MN)
The Historian, (Mission Hills, SD)

The Union and Dakotaian (Yankton, D.T.)
The Weekly Dakotian (Yankton, D.T.)
The Yankton Press
Washington (D.C.) Chronicle
Washington (D.C.) Evening Star
Washington (D.C.) Union
Weekly Dubuque Tribune
Yankton Press and Dakotan

Reference Works/Materials/Archives

19th Annual Dakota History Conference, 1988
Abby Abbe Fuller and Family Papers, 1840-1928, Minnesota Historical Society, St. Paul
Amidon Family Bible
Archives of Bowdoin College, Bowdoin, Maine
Archives of the Minnesota Historical Society, Minnesota History Center, St. Paul
Archives of the South Dakota Heritage Center, Pierre
Congressional Globe, First Session of the 35th Congress
Congressional Globe, First and Second Sessions of the 36th Congress
First Annual Report of the Western Town Company, 1857, Siouxland Heritage Museum, Sioux Falls, SD
Green, Edward Baker, *Personal Reminiscences – Past and Present,* Unpublished Manuscript, "Interview with Erhardt Fleitz, Pioneer Soldier"
Journal of the Illinois State Historical Society, Vol. IX, 1916-1917
Memorial and Biographical Record, George A. Ogle & Co., Chicago 1897
Minnesota History, Vol. XIV
Minnesota Historical Society, Vol. VIII, XIV
South Dakota Historical Collections Vol. I, II, V, VI, VIII, IX, X, XI, XII, XIII, XXIII, XXIV, XXVIII,
South Dakota Place Names, Compiled by Workers of the Writers Program of WPA in the State of South Dakota, University of South Dakota, 1941
Territorial Papers of Dakota, Department of State, March 28, 1861 to January 7, 1873
The Monthly South Dakotan, The South Dakotan Company, Sioux Falls and Aberdeen
Upham, Warner, *Minnesota Geographical Names, Their Origin and Historical Significance,* Minnesota Historical Society, 1869

www.famousamericans.net/samuelmedary

Endnotes

Chapter I

1. Parker, Donald Dean, Ed., *The Recollections of Philander Prescott, Frontiersman of the Old Northwest*, 1819-1862, University of Nebraska Press, 1966, PP 133-141. Prescott was praised by contemporaries for his understanding of Indian language and culture. He assisted in the creation of a Dakota dictionary that was published by the Smithsonian Institute. *St. Paul Pioneer and Democrat,* October 24, 1861.
2. *S. D. Historical Collections*, Vol. IX, P 364
3. *S. D. Historical Collections*, Vol. XXIII, 1947, PP 308, 310, & 314
4. Gnirk, Adeline, S., *Epic of the Realm of Ree*, Gregory Times Advocate, Gregory, SD, 1984, PP 285-286
5. Gnirk, Adeline S., *Epic of the Great Exodus,* Gregory Times Advocate, Gregory, SD, 1985, P 15
6. *South Dakota Place Names*, Compiled by Workers of the Writers Program of WPA in the State of S.D., University of South Dakota, Vermillion, SD, 1941, P 421
7. *S. D. Historical Collections*, Vol. IX, P 161; NOTE: While all sources agree that the Bijou Hills were named after a French frontiersman, the spelling of his name is in dispute. Bijaoux, Bessonet, and Bisoton are some of the ways his name is spelled.
8. *The Dakotian*, (Yankton, D.T.), September 15, 1863
9. *The Union and Dakotaian*, (Yankton, D. T.), June 22, 1867
10. *S. D. Historical Collections*, Vol. I, 1902, PP 270-271
11. *Omaha Nebraskan*, January 21, 1856
12. *The Weekly Dakotian*, (Yankton, D. T.), June 27, 1861
13. Meyer, Roy W., *History of the Santee Sioux*, University of Nebraska Press, Lincoln, 1967, PP 76-78
14. *S. D. Historical Collections,* Vol. II, 1904, *History of the Sioux Indians* by Doane Robinson, P 260
15. Meyer, Roy W., PP 80-85
16. Anderson, Gary Clayton, *Little Crow, Spokesman for the Sioux,* Minnesota Historical Society Press, 1986, P 61
17. *Dubuque Express and Herald,* February 29, 1856

Chapter II

1. Briggs, Harold E., *Frontiers of the Northwest, a History of the Upper Missouri Valley*, N. Y. Peter Smith, 1950, P 348
2. *New York Independent,* in the *Dubuque Express and Herald,* May 2, 1856
3. Wills, Jocelyn, *Boosters, Hustlers, and Speculators, Entrepreneurial Culture and the Rise of Minneapolis and St. Paul, 1849-1883,* Minnesota Historical Society Press, 2005, P 54
4. *Henderson Democrat,* (Minnesota) April 3, 1856
5. *Old Rail Fence Corners, The ABC's of Minnesota History,* Second Edition, By the Book Committee, 1914, P 46. NOTE: Parrant's name is also spelled "Passant."

6 Neil, Rev. Edward O., *History of the Minnesota Valley,* and Bryant, Charles S., *History of The Sioux Massacre,* North Star Publishing, Minneapolis, 1882, P 113 and 266

7 Fletcher, William J., *A History of the City of St. Paul and of the County of Ramsey Minnesota,* St. Paul, Published by the Society, 1876, P 248

8 *Henderson Democrat* (Henderson, M.T.), August 21, 1856

9 Neil, Rev. Edward O., and Bryant, Charles S., P 268

10 *St. Paul Daily Times,* January 26, 1857

11 *St. Paul Pioneer and Democrat,* June 17, 1857

12 *Henderson Democrat* (Henderson, M.T.), October 30, 1856

13 *Minnesota Historical Collections,* Vol. 13, 1908, "Lives of the Governors of Minnesota," by J. H. Baker, P 70

14 *Dubuque Express and Herald,* March 8, 1856

15 *Henderson Democrat* (Henderson, M.T.), July 23, 1857

16 *St. Paul Daily Times,* March 16, 1859

17 *Cincinnati Daily Commercial,* November 14, 1861

18 *Dubuque Daily Times,* June 7, 1857

19 Newsom, T. M., *Pen Pictures of St. Paul, Minnesota,* Vol. I, Published by the Author, St. Paul, Minnesota, 1886, P 406

20 Kingsbury, George W., *History of Dakota Territory,* Vol. I, S. J. Clarke Publishing Co., Chicago, 1915, P 109

21 Morris, H. S., *Historical Stories, Legends and Traditions, Northeastern South Dakota,* Published by the Sisseton Courier (no date), P 55

22 Morris, H. S., P 92

23 Anderson, Gary Clayton, *Little Crow, Spokesman for the Sioux,* Minnesota Historical Society Press, 1986, P 107

24 *St. Paul Daily Minnesotian,* May 18, 1857

25 *Saint Peter Courier,* April 28, 1857

26 *St. PaulDaily Minnesotian,* April 23, 1857

27 Johannsen, Robert W., *Stephen A. Douglas,* New York, Oxford University Press, 1973 P 554

28 Folwell, William Watts, *A History of Minnesota,* Vol. I, Minnesota Historical Society, St. Paul, 1922, P 395; It was reported (in *The Democrat,* Winona, MN, December 4, 1858) that Medary actually hated Buchanan and freely and publicly denigrated the president.

29 Christianson, Theodore, *Minnesota, The Land of Sky-Tinted Waters,* Vol. I, The American Historical Society, Inc., Chicago and New York, 1935, PP 277-278

30 Hall, H. P., *Observations,* St. Paul, Minn., 1904, P 12

31 *St. Paul Daily Minnesotian,* May 7, 1857; *Evening Star* (Washington, D. C.), May 4, 1857 and June 17, 1857

32 *St. Paul Pioneer and Democrat* (Supplement) October 27, 1857; *History of Southeastern Dakota,* Western Publishing Co., Sioux City, Iowa, 1881, P 43

33 *Sioux Falls Press,* July 2, 1886

34 *Minnesota History,* Vol. 14, 1933, "Mythical Cities of Southwestern Minnesota," by R. J. Forrest, P 244

35 Hall, H. P., P 13
36 *Henderson Democrat* (Henderson, M.T.), February 5, 1857
37 *St. Paul Daily Minnesotian,* March 3, 1857
38 *St. PaulDaily Minnesotian,* June 12, 1857
39 *Dubuque Daily Republican,* December 6, 1856
40 *St. Paul Daily Minnesotian,* May 20, 1857
41 *St. Paul Pioneer and Democrat,* March 7, 1858
42 *St. Paul Pioneer and Democrat,* November 17, 1858
43 *St. PaulDaily Minnesotian,* June 1, 1857
44 *St. Paul Pioneer and Democrat,* June 11, 1857
45 *Sioux Falls Argus-Leader,* August 22, 1906
46 *St. Paul Daily Minnesotian,* June 12, 1857
47 *St. Paul Daily Minnesotian,* July 14, 1857
48 *Saint Peter Courier,* July 10, 1857. This could refer to the Western Town Company whose expedition was partially made up of Maine men.
49 *St. Paul Daily Minnesotian,* July 14, 1857
50 *Moody County Enterprise* (Flandreau, D.T.), October 9, 1879. Lynd is sometimes spelled "Lynde."
51 *Moody County Enterprise,* October 9, 1879. Eminija is spelled various ways. Clay Bryan spelled it "Em-en-caz-or." In those days Split Rock Creek was known as the "Emenija" River.
52 *Sioux Falls Argus-Leader,* August 22, 1906. Their cabin was located where the Cataract Hotel (NW corner of 9th Street and Phillips Avenue) was later built although most accounts say their first house was built where the Rock Island Railroad depot was later erected. The house of the Western Town Company, the Dubuque House, was constructed on the hillside, beneath the site of the state penitentiary.
53 *Dubuque Express and Herald,* November 28, 1856
54 First Annual Report of the Western Town Company, 1857, Siouxland Heritage Museums, Sioux Falls, SD; *History of Southeastern Dakota,* P 41
55 Smith, Charles M., *Minnehaha County History,* Educator Supply Co., Mitchell, SD, 1949, PP 7-8; *Dubuque Express and Herald,* May 27, 1857
56 First Annual Report of the Western Town Company, 1857
57 *Dubuque Express and Herald,* May 27, 1857
58 *Dubuque Express and Herald,* July 19, 1857
59 *Dubuque Express and Herald,* June 9, 1857
60 *Dubuque Express and Herald,* July 19, 1857
61 *Minnesota Free Press* (St. Peter), July 22, 1857
62 *Minnesota Free Press* (St. Peter), August 5, 1857
63 *St. Paul Pioneer and Democrat,* February 20, 1858
64 *Minnesota Free Press* (St. Peter), July 29, 1857

65 *Sioux Falls Press,* July 2, 1886; *Dubuque Daily Republican,* August 18, 1857. The "negro interpreter" may have been Isaiah, the man who accompanied James W. Lynd and other members of the Dakota Land Company to the Falls in June of that year.

66 *Dubuque Daily Republican,* August 18, 1857; *Sioux Falls Press,* July 2, 1886

67 Kingsbury, George W., Vol. I, P 99

68 *St. Paul Pioneer and Democrat,* in the *Dubuque Express and Herald,* July 19, 1857

69 *St. Paul Pioneer and Democrat,* July 12 & 16, 1857

70 *Sioux Falls Press,* July 2, 1886; *Sioux Falls Argus-Leader,* August 22, 1906

71 *St. Paul Daily Minnesotian,* August 13, 1857

72 Kingsbury, George W., Vol. I, P 99

73 *Dubuque Daily Republican,* October 8, 1857

74 *Memorial and Biographical Record,* George A. Ogle & Co., Chicago, 1897, P 228; *Sioux Falls Argus-Leader,* April 21, 1900; *Dubuque Express and Herald,* July 19, 1857; *History of Dubuque County, Iowa,* Western Historical Society, Chicago, 1880; P 815

75 *History of Southeastern Dakota,* P 44

76 Kingsbury, George W., Vol. I, P 99

77 *Dubuque Daily Republican,* October 8, 1857

78 *Sioux City Eagle,* July 25, 1857

79 *Sioux Falls Argus-Leader,* December 17, 1897

80 *History of Southeastern Dakota,* P 45

81 Parker, Donald Dean, *Pioneering in the Upper Big Sioux Valley,* 1967, P 23

82 *Minnesota History,* Vol. 14, 1933, P 244

83 Krout, John A., and Muzzey, David Saville, *American History for Colleges,* Ginn & Co., 1943, P 354

84 *St. Paul Pioneer and Democrat,* October 1, 1857

85 *St. Paul Pioneer and Democrat* (Supplement), September 11, 1857

86 Neil, Rev. Edward O., and Bryant, Charles S., P 129

87 *St. PaulDaily Minnesotian,* June 23, 1858

88 *Minnesota History,* Vol. 14, 1993, PP 245-259

89 *St. Paul Pioneer and Democrat,* November 29, 1857

90 *History of Southeastern Dakota,* P 45. Those who wintered at the Falls during the winter of 1857-58 were: W. W. Brookings, J. L. Phillips, John McClellan, L. B. Atwood, A. L. Kilgore, Smith Kinsey, Charles McConnell, R. B. McKinley, S. D. Brookings, E. M. Brookings, of the Western Town Company; and James L. Fisk, James McBride, James M. Evans, James M. Allen, William Little and C. Merrill, of the Dakota Land Company

Chapter III

1 *St. Paul Daily Minnesotian,* October 27, 1857

2 *Washington Union* in the *Henderson Democrat,* October 22, 1857

3 *St. Paul Pioneer and Democrat,* December 1, 1857

4 *History of Southeastern Dakota,* Western Publishing Co., Sioux City, Iowa, 1881, PP 45-46

5   *St. Paul Daily Minnesotian*, December 29, 1857
6   *St. Paul Pioneer and Democrat*, December 30, 1857
7   *St. Paul Daily Minnesotian*, December 29, 1857
8   *St. Paul Pioneer Press*, January 29, 1922
9   *St. Paul Dispatch*, January 5, 1928
10 *St. Paul Dispatch*, January 4, 1928; Fort Street was renamed 7th Street
11 *St. Paul Daily Times*, March 16, 1859
12 Fletcher, William J., *A History of the City of St. Paul and the County of Ramsey*, Published by the Minnesota Historical Society, 1876, P 365
13 Newsom, T. M., *Pen Pictures of St. Paul, Minnesota*, Vol. I, Published by the Author, St. Paul, Minnesota, 1886, P 569
14 *Dubuque Express and Herald*, October 2, 1856; *St. Paul Daily Minnesotian*, February 14, 1857 and March 11, 1857
15 *Sioux Falls Argus-Leader*, April 21, 1900
16 *Minnesota Historical Society*, Vol. VIII, 1898, "The First Organized Government of Dakota," by Samuel J. Albright, P 142
17 *St. Paul Pioneer and Democrat*, February 20, 1858.
18 *Dubuque Daily Tribune*, December 11, 1857
19 *Minnesota Historical Society*, Vol. VIII, 1898, P 142
20 *S.D. Historical Collections*, Vol. VI, 1912, "The Settlement at Sioux Falls," PP 141-142
21 *St. Paul Dispatch*, January 9, 1928
22 Holcombe, Return I., *Minnesota in Three Centuries*, Vol. II, The Publishing Society of Minnesota, 1908, P 506
23 Folwell, William Watts, *A History of Minnesota*, Vol. II, Minnesota Historical Society, 1924, P 19
24 *Congressional Globe*, First Session of the 35th Congress, May 27, 1858, PP 2428-2429
25 *Congressional Globe*, First Session of the 35th Congress, June 2, 1858, P 2660
26 Edward M. McCook was later appointed territorial governor of Colorado and served with distinction on the side of the Union in the Civil War, one of the "Fighting McCooks" of Ohio.
27 *Congressional Globe*, First Session of the 35th Congress, June 2, 1858, P 2662
28 *Congressional Globe*, First Session of the 35th Congress, June 3, 1858, P 2679
29 *Henderson Democrat* (Henderson, MN), June 16, 1858
30 *Omaha Nebraskan*, January 20, 1858
31 *Omaha Nebraskan*, June 16, 1858
32 *New York Tribune* in the *St. Paul Daily Times*, December 7, 1858
33 *The Democrat* (Winona, MN), December 4, 1858
34 *St. Paul Pioneer and Democrat*, June 11, 1858
35 *Washington Union* in the *St. Paul Daily Times*, February 13, 1859
36 Abby Abbe Fuller and Family Papers, 1840-1928, Minnesota Historical Society, St. Paul, letter from Abby Fuller to Aaron Francis "Frank" Fuller dated May 22, 1859

Chapter IV

1. Letter from L. P. Leavenworth to his aunt dated September 19, 1857, Minnesota History Center, St. Paul
2. *Henderson Democrat* (Henderson, MT), February 5, 1857
3. *Evening Star (Washington City)*, April 20, 1857
4. *Henderson Democrat* (Henderson, MT), March 12, 1857
5. Rose, Arthur P., *An Illustrated History of Nobles County, Minnesota,* Northern History Publishing Company, Worthington, MN, 1908, P 39
6. *St. Paul Daily Times*, January 26, 1859
7. Jackson, W. Turrentine, *Wagon Roads West, A Study of Federal Road Surveys and Construction in the Trans-Mississippi West, 1846-1869,* University of Nebraska Press, 1979, P 168
8. *St. Paul Daily Times,* October 6, 1858
9. *Henderson Democrat* (Henderson, MT), May 21, 1857
10. *St. Paul Pioneer and Democrat,* July 12, 1857 and July 16, 1857
11. *St. Paul Pioneer and Democrat,* July 16, 1857; Chapter VII is devoted to Inkpaduta and The Spirit Lake Massacre.
12. *St. Paul Pioneer and Democrat* in the *Dubuque Republican,* August 7, 1857
13. *Minnesota Free Press* (St. Peter, MT), August 5, 1857
14. *Evening Star (Washington City),* August 3, 1857
15. *Henderson Democrat* (Henderson, MT), October 1, 1857
16. Jackson, W. Turrentine, P 183
17. *Henderson Democrat* (Henderson, MT), October 1, 1857
18. *Minnesota Free Press* (St. Peter, MT), October 7, 1857
19. *Minnesota Free Press* (St. Peter, MT), October 28, 1857
20. *Minnesota Free Press* (St. Peter, MT), November 18, 1857
21. *St. Paul Pioneer and Democrat,* December 4, 1857
22. *Minnesota Free Press* (St. Peter, MT), December 9, 1857
23. Jackson, W. Turrentine, P 183
24. Da Vere is probably a misspelling of "Davier," a Captain with Nobles' crew.
25. *Minnesota Free Press* (St. Peter, MT), December 16, 1857
26. *St. Paul Pioneer and Democrat,* February 2, 1858
27. *St. Paul Pioneer and Democrat,* February 16, 1858
28. Jackson, W. Turrentine, PP 186-187
29. *Minnesota Free Press* (St. Peter, MT), February 24, 1858
30. *St. Paul Daily Times,* January 26, 1859
31. Jackson, W. Turrentine, P 190
32. *St. Paul Daily Times,* October 8, 1858

Chapter V

1. Goodspeed, Weston Arthur, Editor-in-Chief, *The Provinces and the States,* Madison, Wisconsin, The Western Historical Association, Vol. VI, 1904, P 210
2. *Omaha Nebraskian,* October 14, 1857
3. *St. Paul Pioneer and Democrat,* August 26, 1859
4. *Omaha Nebraskian,* August 26, 1857
5. Sanson-Flood, Renee, *Lessons From Chouteau Creek,* The Center for Western Studies, Augustana College, Sioux Falls, SD, 1986, P 29
6. *S.D. Historical Collections,* Vol. I, 1902, P 115; *S. D. Historical Collections* Vol. 24, 1949, P 180
7. Lewis, Lloyd, *The Assassination of Lincoln, History & Myth,* MJF Books, New York, 1994, Originally published in 1929, as *Myths After Lincoln,* P 111
8. *S. D. Historical Collections,* Vol. XXIV, 1949, P 181
9. Sanson-Flood, Renee, P 33
10. Kingsbury, George W., *History of Dakota Territory,* Vol. I, Chicago, S. J. Clarke Publishing Co., 1915, P 115
11. Smutty Bear's Dakota name was "Mato Sabileya," meaning He Paints Himself Dark Like A Bear. It was corrupted by white Dakotans into Smutty Bear.
12. Shell, Herbert S., *Dakota Territory During the 1860's,* Government Research Bureau, USD, 1954, P 5
13. Kingsbury, George W., Vol. I, P 116
14. *S. D. Historical Collections,* Vol. I, 1902, P 116
15. *Dubuque Daily Express and Herald,* August 7, 1857
16. *S. D. Historical Collections,* Vol. XXIV, 1949, P 181
17. *S. D. Historical Collections,* Vol. XXIV, 1949, P 181
18. Sanson-Flood, Renee, P 19. NOTE: There is some conflict in the record. Other sources indicate that Picotte's mother was a Teton Sioux.
19. Flood, Renee S., and Bernie, Shirley A., *Remembering Your Relatives, Yankton Sioux Images, 1851-1904,* Published by Marty Indian School, Marty, SD, 1985, P 7
20. Holley, Frances Chamberlain, *Once Their Home,* Chicago, Donohue and Henneberry, 1891, P 53
21. Letter from J. R. Hanson to D. W. Robinson dated September 15, 1902, South Dakota Heritage Center, Pierre, SD
22. *S. D. Historical Collections,* Vol. I, 1902, PP 113-114
23. Letter from J. R. Hanson to D. W. Robinson dated September 15, 1902, South Dakota Heritage Center, Pierre, SD
24. Holley, Frances Chamberlain, PP 54-55
25. *S. D. Historical Collections,* Vol. XXIV, 1949, P 185
26. *S. D. Historical Collections,* Vol. XXIV, 1949, P 185
27. Holley, Frances Chamberlain, P 56
28. *S. D. Historical Collections,* Vol. I, P 114
29. Kingsbury, George W., Vol. I, P 116

30 *History of Yankton County,* by the Yankton County Historical Society, 1987, P 3
31 Flood, Renee S., and Bernie, Shirley A., P 4
32 Shell, Herbert S., P 5
33 Kingsbury, George W., Vol. I, P 119; *Yankton Press and Dakotan,* June 6, 1911
34 *Yankton Press and Dakotan,* June 6, 1911
35 Holley, Frances Chamberlain, P 56
36 Sanson-Flood, Renee, P 33
37 Lamar, Howard Robert, *Dakota Territory 1861-1889,* New Haven and London, Yale University Press, 1966, P 36
38 Flood, Renee S., and Bernie, Shirley A., P 8
39 *S. D. Historical Collections,* Vol. XXIV, 1949, P 186
40 Kingsbury, George W., Vol. I, P 120
41 *Sioux City Eagle,* March 5, 1859
42 *St. Paul Pioneer and Democrat,* February 25, 1859
43 *St. Paul Daily Minnesotian,* May 10, 1858
44 *Sioux City Register,* July 29, 1858
45 *Sioux City Register,* November 18, 1858
46 Kingsbury, George W., Vol. I, P 133
47 Kingsbury, George W., Vol. I, P 133
48 *Sioux City Eagle,* October 2, 1858
49 *Yankton Press and Dakotan,* June 6, 1911
50 *Sioux City Register,* November 6 and 13, 1858
51 Kingsbury, George W., Vol. I, PP 136-137
52 Lamar, Howard Robert, P 39
53 *Sioux City Register,* March 5, 1859
54 Shell, Herbert S., *History of Clay County, South Dakota,* Clay County Historical Society, Inc., Vermillion, SD, 1974, P 260
55 Flood, Renee S., and Bernie, Shirley A., P 29
56 *Yankton Press and Dakotan,* June 6, 1911
57 *The Democrat* (Winona, MN), November 26, 1859
58 *Sioux City Eagle,* June 25, 1859
59 *Daily Press and Dakotaian* (Yankton, D.T.), July 17, 1879
60 Kingsbury, George W., Vol. I, PP 141-144
61 Lass, William E., *A History of Steamboating on the Upper Missouri River,* University of Nebraska Press: Lincoln, 1962, P 23
62 *Daily Press and Dakotaian* (Yankton, D. T.), July 17, 1879
63 Lamar, Howard Robert, P 39
64 Kingsbury, George W., Vol. I, P 144
65 *St. Paul Pioneer and Democrat,* August 26, 1859

66 *The Dubuque Herald,* August 11, 1859

67 Holley, Frances Chamberlain, PP 57-58

Chapter VI

1 Kingsbury, George W., *History of Dakota Territory,* Vol. I, S. J. Clarke Pub. Co., Chicago, 1915, P 85

2 Kelsey, Vera, *Red River Runs North!* Harper & Brothers, Publishers, New York, 1951, P 74

3 *St. Paul Pioneer and Democrat,* July 30, 1858

4 *History of the Red River Valley, Past and Present,* Vol. I, Herald Printing Co., Grand Forks, 1909, P 543

5 Ross, Alexander, *The Red River Settlement,* Ross & Hanes, Inc., Minneapolis, 1957 (reprint of 1856 edition) P VI

6 *S. D. Historical Collections,* Vol. I, 1902, P 90

7 *History of the Red River Valley, Past and Present,* P 541

8 Kingsbury, George W., Vol. I, P. 82

9 *S. D. Historical Collections,* Vol. I, P 91

10 Ralph, Julian, *On Canada's Frontier,* Harper & Brothers, New York, 1892, P 176

11 *S. D. Historical Collections,* Vol. I, 1902, P 92

12 Jennewein, J. Leonard, and Boorman, Jane, Eds., *Dakota Panorama,* Brevet Press, 1973, P 64

13 Kelsey, Vera, PP 99-101

14 *Chicago Tribune,* November 6, 1878

15 Kelsey, Vera, PP 100-101

16 *S. D. Historical Collections,* Vol. I, 1902, P 93

17 *History of the Red River Valley, Past and Present,* P 548

18 *St. Paul Pioneer and Democrat,* July 31, 1858

19 *History of the Red River Valley, Past and Present,* P549

20 *St. Paul Pioneer and Democrat,* July 31, 1858

21 Kelsey, Vera, P 123

22 *History of the Red River Valley, Past and Present,* PP 550-551

23 Kelsey, Vera, P 119

24 Neill, Edward Duffield, *History of Minnesota,* circa 1859, P 451

25 *St. Paul Pioneer and Democrat,* August 23, 1859

26 *Dickenson Press,* March 28, 1885

27 *Old Rail Fence Corners, the ABC's of Minnesota History,* Second Edition, by The Book Committee, 1914, P 34

28 Kelsey, Vera, PP 119-121

29 Swisshelm, Jane Grey, *Half A Century,* Jansen, McClurg & Co., Chicago, 1880, P 207

30 Newsom, T. M., *Pen Pictures of St. Paul, Minnesota,* Vol. I, Published by the Author, St. Paul, Minnesota, 1886, P 52

31 Newsom, T. M., P 272

32 *Old Rail Fence Corners, the ABC's of Minnesota History,* P 115

33 Beadle, J. H., *Western Wilds and the Men Who Redeem Them*, Jones Brothers & Co., 1880, PP 379-380

34 Flandrau, Charles E., *The History of Minnesota and Tales of the Frontier*, E. W. Porter, St. Paul, 1900, P 77

35 Kelsey, Vera, P 123

36 *St. Paul Pioneer and Democrat*, June 16, 1860

37 Lamar, Howard Robert, *Dakota Territory 1861-1889,* New Haven and London, Yale University Press, 1966, P 52

38 Flandrau, Charles E., P 129

39 *Weekly Dubuque Tribune,* March 22, 1850

40 *History of The Red River Valley, Past and Present,* P 557

41 *Evening Star* (Washington City), June 29, 1857

Chapter VII

1 Teakle, Thomas, *The Spirit Lake Massacre*, State Historical Society of Iowa, 1918, P 70

2 *S. D. Historical Collections*, Vol. VI, 1912, P 226

3 Teakle, Thomas, P 66

4 *S. D. Historical Collections*, Vol. II, 1904, "History of the Sioux Indians," By Doane Robinson, PP 215-216

5 *S. D. Historical Collections*, Vol. II, 1904, P 209

6 Teakle, Thomas, P 67

7 Van Nuys, Maxwell, *Inkpaduta, The Scarlet Point,* Maxwell Van Nuys, Denver, CO, 1998, P 15

8 Van Nuys, Maxwell, PP 62-64

9 *St. Paul Daily Times,* January 21, 1857

10 Teakle, Thomas, P 69

11 Teakle, Thomas, P 69

12 Van Nuys, Maxwell, P 53

13 Van Nuys, Maxwell, PP 54-55

14 Teakle, Thomas, P 5

15 Teakle, Thomas, P 118

16 Gardner-Sharp, Abbie, *History of the Spirit Lake Massacre*, Mill & Co., Des Moines, 1885, P 71

17 Flandrau, Charles E., *The History of Minnesota and Tales of the Frontier*, E. W. Porter, St. Paul, 1900, PP 105-106

18 *St. Paul Daily Minnesotian,* April 15 and 16, 1857

19 Teakle, Thomas, P 215

20 Gardner-Sharp, Abbie, PP 178-179

21 Gardner-Sharp, Abbie, P 172

22 Teakle, Thomas, P 224

23 Gardner-Sharp, Abbie, P 181; according to *South Dakota Geographic Names,* Brant Lake located near Lake's Madison and Herman was once known as Skunk Lake.

24 Letter from Charles E. Flandrau to Gov Medary, June 1, 1857, Records of Territorial Governor Samuel Medary, Minnesota History Center, St. Paul

25 Flandrau, Charles E., P 107

26 Letter from Charles E. Flandrau to Gov. Medary, June 1, 1857

27 *The Monthly South Dakotan,* Vol. III, May 1900 – April 1901, The South Dakotan Company Sioux Falls, SD, PP 286-287

28 *S. D. Historical Collections,* Vol. II, 1904, PP 238-239. See: Gardner-Sharp, Abbie, PP 181-182. According to Abbie Gardner-Sharp, Mrs. Marble was selected because the Indians would not sell her (Abbie) and Mrs. Noble was rejected because she was German and the Indians hated the Teutons.

29 Teakle, Thomas, PP 226-228

30 Letter from Charles E. Flandrau to Gov. Medary, June 1, 1857

31 *Monticello Times* (Minnesota) June 27, 1857

32 Morris, H. S., *Historical Stories, Legends and Traditions, Northeastern South Dakota* Published by the Sisseton Courier (No Date), P 5

33 Letter from Charles E. Flandrau to Gov. Medary, June 1, 1857

34 Flandrau, Charles E., P 108; Teakle, Thomas, P 233

35 Flandrau, Charles E., P 108

36 Teakle, Thomas, PP 233-234; NOTE: The "Earth Lodges" is undoubtedly a reference to the Dirt Lodges that were the home of the Drifting Goose band of Yanktonais. They were located in Brown County near the James River.

37 Teakle, Thomas, P 236

38 *The Monthly South Dakotan,* Vol. IV, 1901-02, South Dakotan Company, Aberdeen, SD, P 165

39 Teakle, Thomas, P 237

40 Teakle, Thomas, P 239

41 *Monticello Times* (Minnesota), June 27, 1857

42 *Minnesota Free Press,* June 24, 1857

43 *Evening Star* (Washington City), July 28, 1857

44 Teakle, Thomas, P 240

45 *St. Paul Pioneer and Democrat,* in the *Dubuque Express and Herald,* June 26, 1857.

46 *Minnesota Free Press,* June 24, 1857

47 Teakle, Thomas, PP 242-244

48 *Minnesota Free Press,* June 24, 1857

49 *History of the Spirit Lake Massacre! And of Miss Abigail Gardiner's Three Months Captivity Among the Indians, According to her Own Account,* L. P. Lee, Publisher, New Britain, CT, 1857, P 44

50 *St. Paul Daily Minnesotian,* July 24, 1857

51 *Dubuque Express and Herald,* July 9, 1857

52 Teakle, Thomas, P 249

53 Teakle, Thomas, PP 250-251

54 *Dubuque Express and Herald,* August 2, 1857

55 *Evening Star* (Washington City*),* April 29, 1857

56 *New York Daily Times,* September 5, 1857.

57 Teakle, Thomas, PP 252-253

58 *St. Paul Pioneer and Democrat,* August 30, 1857

59 *St. Paul Pioneer and Democrat,* September 10, 1857

60 *St. Paul Pioneer and Democrat,* August 20, 1857

61 *St. Paul Pioneer and Democrat,* September 26, 1857

62 *Dubuque Daily Tribune,* November 10, 1857

63 *St. Paul Pioneer and Democrat,* May 8, 1861

64 *S. D. Historical Collections*, Vol. II, 1904, P 344

65 *S. D. Historical Collections*, Vol. II, 1904, P 266

66 Clodfelter, Michael, *The Dakota War, The U. S. Army Versus the Sioux 1862-1865,* McFarland & Co., Inc., Publisher, 1998, P 26

67 *S. D. Historical Collections*, Vol. II, 1904, P 314

68 *S. D. Historical Collections*, Vol. II, 1904, PP 344-345

69 *S. D. Historical Collections*, Vol. II, 1904, P 324

70 *S. D. Historical Collections*, Vol. II, P 1904, PP 345-346; Teakle, Thomas, P 255

Chapter VIII

1 *Sioux City Eagle*, February 20, 1858

2 *Sioux City Eagle*, April 24, 1858

3 *Sioux City Eagle*, January 9, 1859. It seems unlikely Dr. Phillips would wait two months to operate.

4 *Minnesota Historical Society*, Vol. VIII, 1898, "The First Organized Government of Dakota," by Samuel J. Albright, P 137

5 *Memorial and Biographical Record*, Geo. A. Ogle & Co., Chicago, 1897, P 228; *Sioux Falls Leader,* October 7, 1885

6 *Bowdoin Orient,* January 19, 1906 (From the archives of the Bowdoin College Library.)

7 *Moody County Enterprise*, October 9, 1879

8 *Mankato Independent,* February 20, 1858

9 *Minnesota Free Press* (St. Peter, MT), May 26, 1858

10 *History of Southeastern Dakota*, Western Publishing Co., Sioux City, Iowa, 1881, P 47; *19th Annual Dakota History Conference*, 1988, "Foremothers of Sioux Falls," by Lee N. McLaird, P X.C2

11 Kingsbury, George W., *History of Dakota Territory*, S. J. Clarke Publishing Co., Chicago, 1915, Vol. I, P 111

12 Diary of Frederick P. Leavenworth, Surveyor, Minnesota Historical Society, St. Paul, MN

13 *St. Paul Pioneer and Democrat,* June 9, 1858

14 *St. Paul Pioneer and Democrat*, June 29, 1858 NOTE: "Summit City" is not mentioned in any other source consulted by this writer.

15 *St. Paul Daily Minnesotian,* April 5, 1858

16 *Henderson Democrat*, May 12, 1858

17 *Minnesota Free Press* (St. Peter, MT), April 21, 1858

18 *St. Paul Pioneer and Democrat*, June 9, 1858

19 *Sioux City Eagle*, June 12, 1858

20 *Minnesota Free Press* (St. Peter), June 23, 1858

21 *Journal of Samuel Fisher Corlies, April 27, 1858 to June 14, 1858,* Minnesota Historical Society Archives, St. Paul, MN.

22 *Henderson Democrat*, May 12, 1858

23 Parker, Donald Dean, Dr., *Pioneering in the Upper Big Sioux Valley*, 1967, P 28.

24 Parker, Donald Dean, P 24

25 *S. D. Historical Collections*, Vol. X, 1920, P 398

26 Parker, Donald Dean, P 23. The estimated number of Indians at Medary ranged from 1500 to 6000.

27 *S. D. Historical Collections*, Vol. X, 1920, P 398

28 *Sioux Falls Press,* July 26, 1907

29 *Dubuque Express and Herald*, July 9, 1858

30 *St. Paul Daily Minnesotian*, June 21, 1858

31 Parker, Donald Dean, P 29

32 *St. Paul Pioneer and Democrat*, June 24, 1858

33 *St. Paul Daily Times,* July 15, 1858

34 *St. Paul Pioneer and Democrat*, June 26, 1858

35 *Mankato Independent,* June 26, 1858

36 *St. Paul Daily Minnesotian,* August 28, 1858

37 *Minnesota Free Press,* July 14, 1858

38 *Monticello Times* (Minnesota), July 10, 1858

39 *St. Paul Pioneer and Democrat*, June 24, 1858

40 *Minnesota Free Press,* June 23, 1858

41 *Journal of Samuel Fisher Corlies;* He may have taken photographs of his Dakota adventure for after returning to Philadelphia, Corlies was an organizing member of the Photographic Society of Philadelphia in 1862

42 *St. Paul Pioneer and Democrat*, June 24, 1858

43 *Minnesota Historical Society*, Vol. VIII, St. Paul, MN, 1898, "The First Organized Government of Dakota," by Samuel J. Albright, P 139. In present day Sioux Falls, the Dakota House would be located at the foot of 9th Street at the bank of the river.

44 *Minnesota Historical Society*, Vol. VIII, P 140

45 Bailey, Dana R., *History of Minnehaha County*, Brown & Saenger, Sioux Falls, 1899, P 15

46 Bailey, Dana R., P 15

47 *Dubuque Daily Times* in the *St.Paul Daily Minnesotian,* July 10, 1858
48 *19th Annual Dakota History Conference*, Herbert W. Blakely, Director, 1988, "Foremothers of Sioux Falls," by Lee N. McLaird, P X.C2
49 *Dubuque Express and Herald,* August 5, 1858
50 Bailey, Dana R., P 14
51 *Sioux City Eagle*, July 17, 1858
52 *Sioux City Eagle,* July 31, 1858
53 *Dubuque Express and Herald,* August 11, 1858
54 *St. Paul Pioneer and Democrat*, August 6, 1858
55 *St. Paul Pioneer and Democrat,* September 30, 1858
56 *St. Paul Pioneer and Democrat*, October 19, 1858
57 *St. Paul Pioneer and Democrat*, August 3, 1858
58 *St. Paul Pioneer and Democrat,* October 29, 1858
59 *St. Peter Free Press* in *The Democrat* (Winona, MN), December 4, 1858
60 *St. Paul Daily Times,* January 11, 1859
61 *The Democrat* (Winona, MN), in the *St. Paul Pioneer and Democrat,* December 16, 1858
62 *St. Paul Pioneer and Democrat,* January 11, 1859
63 *Sioux City Eagle*, January 9, 1859
64 Robinson, Doane, *History of South Dakota,* Vol. I, B. F. Bowen & Co., 1904, P 464
65 *Dubuque Daily Times,* January 3, 1859
66 *St. Paul Pioneer and Democrat,* January 9, 1859
67 Sprague, William Forrest, *Women and the West, A Short Social History*, Arno Press, NY, 1972, P 114
68 *Dubuque Daily Times,* May 25, 1859
69 Thank you, Leonard Cohen.
70 *St. Paul Daily Times,* May 27, 1859
71 *Central City (NY) Courier* in the *St. Paul Daily Minnesotian,* September 10, 1859
72 *St. Paul Pioneer and Democrat,* August 25, 1859
73 *The Democrat* (Winona, MN), August 6, 1859
74 *The Democrat* (Winona, MN), December 3, 1859
75 *St. Paul Daily Minnesotian,* September 15, 1859
76 Robinson, Doane, P 179
77 *St. Paul Pioneer and Democrat*, August 6, 1859
78 *St. Paul Daily Minnesotian,* September 28, 1859

Chapter IX

1 *St. Paul Pioneer and Democrat,* November 25, 1858
2 *St. Paul Pioneer and Democrat,* August 28, 1858
3 *Sioux City Eagle*, September 18, 1858

Cavaliers of the Dakota Frontier

4 *History of Southeastern Dakota*, Western Publishing Co., Sioux City, Iowa, 1881, P 48

5 *St. Paul Pioneer and Democrat*, October 29, 1858

6 *St. Paul Pioneer and Democrat*, October 19, 1858

7 *Minnesota Free Press* (St. Peter, MN), October 20, 1858

8 Goodspeed, Weston Arthur, Ed. in Chief, *The Province and the States*, Vol. VI, The Western Historical Association, Madison, Wisconsin, 1904, P 214

9 *St. Paul Pioneer and Democrat,* November 4, 1858. Aside from Pierce and Albright, this writer has been unable to discover the names of the other squatter legislators of 1858.

10 *St. Paul Pioneer and Democrat*, October 29, 1858

11 Goodspeed, Weston Arthur, P 214

12 *St. Paul Daily Minnesotian,* January 5, 1858

13 *S. D. Historical Collections*, Vol. XI, 1922, P 440

14 *St. Paul Pioneer and Democrat,* December 1, 1858

15 *The Monthly South Dakotan*, Vol. II May 1899 – April 1900, The South Dakotan Company, Sioux Falls, S. D. P 143

16 *The Democrat* (Winona, MN), December 4, 1858

17 *The Democrat* (Winona, MN), December 4, 1858

18 *Minnesota Free Press* (St. Peter, MN) October 20, 1858

19 Robinson, Doane, *History of South Dakota,* Vol. I, B. F. Bowen & Co., 1904, P 178

20 Robinson, Doane, Vol. I, P 176

21 *St. Paul Pioneer and Democrat*, October 29, 1858

22 *St. Paul Pioneer and Democrat*, November 11, 1858

23 *St. Anthony Express* in the *St. Paul Pioneer and Democrat,* December 15, 1858

24 *St. Paul Pioneer and Democrat,* January 11, 1859

25 *Dubuque Express and Herald,* January 21, 1859

26 *Sioux City Eagle*, October 30, 1858

27 *Sioux City Eagle*, November 25, 1858

28 *St. Paul Daily Times,* December 7, 1858

29 *Sioux City Eagle*, February 26, 1859; *The Democrat* (Winona, MN), February 26, 1859

30 *Dubuque Daily Times,* June 23, 1859

31 *Dakota Democrat,* August 26, 1859

32 *Sioux City Eagle*, December 11, 1858.

33 *S. D. Historical Collections*, Vol. VI, 1912, P 145. NOTE: The "Dakota House" was located at the foot of 9th Street in Sioux Falls.

34 *Minnesota Historical Society,* Vol. VIII, 1898, "The First Organized Government of Dakota," by Samuel J. Albright, P 141

35 *S. D. Historical Collections*, Vol. XI, 1922, P 440

36 Albright, Samuel J., P 144

37 *Dakota Democrat,* August 26, 1859

38 Albright, Samuel J., P 145

39 *S. D. Historical Collections,* Vol. VI, 1912, P-147

40 *The Monthly South Dakotan,* Vol. IV, 1901-1902, South Dakotan Company, Aberdeen, S. D., P 109

41 *The Democrat* (Winona, MN) December 3, 1859

42 *S. D. Historical Collections,* Vol. VI, 1912, P 146

43 Robinson, Doane, Vol. I, P 180; *Sioux City Register* in the *Dubuque Herald,* September 28, 1859; *The Monthly South Dakotan,* Vol. IV, 1901-02, South Dakotan Company, Aberdeen, S. D.

44 Albright, Samuel J., P 146

45 *S. D. Historical Collections,* Vol. VI, 1912, P 160

46 *S. D. Historical Collections,* Vol. VI, 1912, PP 161-162

47 *The Monthly South Dakotan,* Vol. IV, 1901-1902, South Dakotan Company, Aberdeen, S. D., P 216

48 *S. D. Historical Collections,* Vol. VI, P 162. A man named Williams Stevens lived in Sioux Falls in the late 1860's, after the Fort Dakota days. He died there in 1869 and was buried on the bluff. He was re-buried in Mt. Pleasant Cemetery. He was probably the William Stevens who served in the second squatter legislature of Dakota.

49 *S. D. Historical Collections,* Vol. VI, 1912, PP 160-167

50 *St. Paul Pioneer and Democrat,* December 6, 1859

51 *St. Paul Pioneer and Democrat,* November 3, 1858

52 *S. D. Historical Collections,* Vol. VI, 1912, P 149

53 *Dubuque Herald,* October 27, 1859

54 Kingsbury, George W., *History of Dakota Territory,* Vol. I, S. J. Clarke Publishing Co., Chicago, 1915, P 103

55 *Sioux City Register,* May 19, 1860.

56 *St. Paul Pioneer and Democrat,* May 15, 1860

57 Schell, Herbert S., *History of South Dakota,* University of Nebraska Press, Lincoln, 1961, P 76

Chapter X

1 Peterson, William J., *Iowa, The Rivers of Her Valleys,* Published at Iowa City, Iowa, by the State Historical Society of Iowa, 1941, P 235

2 *Dubuque Daily Times,* May 16, 1859

3 *Sioux City Eagle,* July 4, 1857

4 *Dubuque Express and Herald,* May 27, 1857

5 *Omaha Nebraskan,* September 23, 1857

6 *St. Paul Pioneer and Democrat,* May 9, 1858

7 *The Democrat (*Winona, MN*),* December 3, 1859

8 *S. D. Historical Collections,* Vol. XXIII, 1947, P 323

9 *S. D. Historical Collections,* Vol. XXIII, 1947, P 313

10 *S. D. Historical Collections,* Vol. XXIII, 1947, PP 335-336

11 *S. D. Historical Collections,* Vol. XXIII, 1947, P 311

12 *Sioux City Eagle,* May 21, 1859
13 *Sioux City Eagle,* June 25, 1859
14 *Sioux City Eagle,* July 2, 1859
15 *St. Paul Daily Minnesotian,* July 22, 1859
16 *S. D. Historical Collections,* Vol. VI, 1912, P-171
17 *New York Times,* July 23, 1861
18 *The Weekly Dakotian* (Yankton, D.T.), July 13, 1861
19 *Sioux City Register,* November 9, 1861
20 *The Weekly Dakotian* (Yankton, D.T.), September 11, 1861
21 *Sioux City Register,* April 12, 1862
22 *Sioux City Register,* April 19, 1862
23 *Sioux City Register,* November 29, 1862
24 There is a large monument to mark his grave at Woodlawn Cemetery in Sioux Falls, SD
25 Peterson, William J., P 241
26 *Canton Advocate,* August 6, 1878

Chapter XI

1 *S. D. Historical Collections,* Vol. I, 1902, P 118. The origin and history of the *Dakota Democrat* hand press has been disputed by the Minnesota Historical Society. Based on contrary evidence, it is claimed that the hand press taken by Albright to Dakota was actually the one used to print the *Minnesota Democrat,* not the one used by Goodhue to print the *Minnesota Pioneer.*
2 *St. Paul Pioneer and Democrat,* January 11, 1859
3 Williams, J. Fletcher, *A History of the City of St. Paul and the County of Ramsey,* Published by the Minnesota Historical Society, 1876, P 359
4 *The Monthly South Dakotan,* Vol. II, May 1899 – April 1900, the South Dakotan Company, Sioux Falls, S. D., PP 143-144
5 Newsom, T. M., *Pen Pictures of St. Paul, Minnesota,* Vol. I, Published by the Author, St. Paul, Minnesota, 1886, P 536
6 *St. Paul Daily Minnesotian,* June 1, 1857
7 *The Monthly South Dakotan,* Vol. II, P 143
8 *Daily Press and Dakotaian* (Yankton, D.T.), September 1, 1879
9 *Dakota Democrat,* August 26, 1859
10 *Sioux City Register,* July 21, 1860
11 *Sioux City Eagle,* June 26, 1858
12 *Sioux City Register,* July 7, 1859
13 *St. Paul Daily Minnesotian,* May 21, 1859
14 *St. Paul Daily Minnesotian,* August 1, 1859
15 *St. Paul Daily Minnesotian,* June 21, 1859
16 *Sioux City Eagle,* January 15, 1859
17 *Sioux City Eagle,* July 16, 1859

18 *Sioux City Register*, August 6, 1859

19 *St. Paul Pioneer and Democrat*, August 9, 1859

20 *Dakota Democrat* quoted in the *Sioux City Register*, August 6, 1859

21 *Sioux City Register*, September 15, 1859. It was also reported (*St. Paul Daily Minnesotian*, September 28, 1859) that Masters died as a result of overeating melons and other garden produce on some "public" occasion.

22 *Minnesota Historical Society*, Vol. VIII, 1898, "The First Organized Government of Dakota," By Samuel J. Albright, P 136

23 *Dubuque Herald*, September 30, 1859

24 *Dakota Democrat,* August 26, 1859

25 *Sioux City Register*, November 19, 1859

26 *Sioux City Register*, November 19, 1859

27 *The Monthly South Dakotan,* Vol. IV, 1901-1902, South Dakotan Company, Aberdeen, S.D., P 217

28 *Sioux City Register*, January 21, 1860; *Sioux Falls Argus-Leader*, May 27, 1901

29 *Dakota Democrat*, Aug. 26, 1859

30 *Sioux City Register*, March 3, 1860

31 *Daily Press and Dakotaian* (Yankton, D.T.), Sept. 1, 1879

32 *Sioux City Register*, April 21, 1860

33 *Daily Press and Dakotaian* (Yankton, D.T.), Sept. 1, 1879

34 *Dakota Democrat* quoted in the *St. Paul Pioneer and Democrat,* April 15, 1860

35 *The Monthly South Dakotan*, Vol. II. P 144

36 *St. Paul Pioneer and Democrat,* August 3, 1861

37 *The Dakota Bell*, April 16, 1887

38 *Yankton Press and Dakotan,* June 6, 1911

Chapter XII

1 *St. Paul Pioneer and Democrat,* December 23, 1858

2 Lamar, Howard, *Dakota Territory 1861-1889*, New Haven and London, Yale University Press, 1966, PP 55-56

3 Kingsbury, George W., *History of Dakota Territory*, Vol. I, S. J. Clarke Publishing Co., Chicago, 1915, PP 166-168

4 *S. D. Historical Collections*, Vol. VI, 1912, P 152

5 *Congressional Globe*, First Session of the 36th Congress, May 11, 1860, P 2069

6 *Philadelphia North American* in the *Henderson Democrat,* May 12, 1860

7 *Congressional Globe*, First Session of the 36th Congress, May 11, 1860, P 2070

8 *Congressional Globe*, First Session of the 36th Congress, May 11, 1860, P 2070

9 *Congressional Globe*, First Session of the 36th Congress, May 11, 1860, P 2071

10 *Congressional Globe*, First Session of the 36th Congress, May 11, 1860, P 2076

11 *Congressional Globe*, First Session of the 36th Congress, May 11, 1860, P 2077

12 *Henderson Democrat,* July 7, 1860

13 *Congressional Globe*, Second Session of the 36th Congress, December 12, 1860, P 80
14 *Congressional Globe*, Second Session of the 36th Congress, December 12, 1860, P 80
15 *Congressional Globe*, Second Session of the 36th Congress, December 12, 1860, P 81
16 Kingsbury, George W., Vol. I, P 111
17 *Daily Press and Dakotaian* (Yankton, D. T.), September 18, 1879
18 Kingsbury, George W., Vol. I, P 169
19 *Congressional Globe*, Second Session of the 36th Congress, February 26, 1861, PP 1207-1208
20 *St. Paul Pioneer and Democrat*, February 27, 1861
21 *Congressional Globe*, Second Session of the 36th Congress, March 1, 1861, P 1334
22 Kingsbury, George W., Vol. I, P 169
23 *St. Paul Pioneer and Democrat*, March 15, 1861
24 *St. Paul Pioneer and Democrat*, March 16, 1861
25 *St. Paul Pioneer and Democrat*, May 1, 1861
26 *St. Paul Pioneer and Democrat,* August 3, 1861
27 *St. Paul Pioneer and Democrat,* August 25, 1861
28 *St. Paul Pioneer and Democrat*, March 19, 1861
29 *St. Paul Pioneer and Democrat*, March 23, 1861
30 *St. Paul Pioneer and Democrat*, March 26, 1861
31 Bosler, Roy P., Editor, *The Collected Works of Abraham Lincoln,* Vol. VII, Rutgers University Press, 1955, PP 294-295
32 Lamar, Howard Robert, P 68
33 *Journal of the Illinois State Historical Society,* Vol. IX, 1916-1917, "Dr. William Jayne," PP 82 & 89
34 Territorial Papers of Dakota, March 28, 1861 to January 7, 1873, Dept. of State, William Jayne letter to William H. Seward, May 30, 1861
35 Kingsbury, George W., Vol. I, P 176
36 Goodspeed, Weston Arthur, Ed. In Chief, *The Provinces and the States,* Vol. VI, Madison Wisconsin, The Western Historical Association, 1904, P 223
37 *Rochelle (Ill.) Register*, July 27, 1872
38 Robinson, Doane, *History of South Dakota,* Vol. I, B. F. Bowen & Co., 1904, P 189
39 *Yankton Press and Dakotan,* June 6, 1911
40 Kingsbury, George W., Vol. I, PP 176-177
41 *Yankton Press and Dakotan, June 6, 1911*
42 *Fort Dodge Republican* in the *Sioux City Register*, July 13, 1861
43 *The Weekly Dakotian* (Yankton, D.T.), June 27, 1861
44 *New York Times*, July 23, 1861
45 Kingsbury, George W., Vol. I, P 184
46 *St. Paul Pioneer and Democrat*, June 27, 1861
47 Kingsbury, George W., Vol. I, P 184

48 *The Weekly Dakotian* (Yankton, D.T.), September 11, 1861

49 *St. Paul Pioneer and Democrat*, June 27, 1861

50 Kingsbury, George W., Vol. I, PP 185-186

51 Kingsbury, George W., Vol. I, P 187

52 Kingsbury, George W., Vol. I, P 195

53 *Yankton Press and Dakotan,* June 6, 1911

54 Armstrong, Moses K., *The Early Empire Builders of the Great West*, E. W. Porter, St. Paul, MN, 1901, P 52

55 Kingsbury, George W., Vol. I, PP 197-204

56 *Black People in South Dakota History*, Bicentennial Committee of Yankton Area, Chamber of Commerce, Yankton, SD, 1977, P 3. The word "white" was deleted by legislation in 1868.

57 Armstrong, Moses K., P 75

58 *Yankton Press and Dakotan,* June 6, 1911

59 *Yankton Press and Dakotan,* June 6, 1911

60 Armstrong, Moses K., P 61

61 Kingsbury, George W., Vol. I, PP 206-207

62 Armstrong, Moses, K., PP 63-64

63 Kingsbury, George W., Vol. I, P 209

64 Armstrong, Moses K., P 73

65 Robinson, Doane, *History of South Dakota,* Vol. I, B. F. Bowen & Company, Publishers, 1904, P 193

66 Kingsbury, George W., Vol. I, P 209

Chapter XIII

1 *Sioux City Register*, October 12, 1861

2 Kingsbury, George W., *History of Dakota Territory*, Vol. I, S. J. Clarke Publishing Co., Chicago, 1915, PP 191-192

3 *Sioux City Register*, November 30, 1861. NOTE: Pattee is also referred to in other sources as "Major" or "Lt. Col." Pattee.

4 *Daily Omaha Nebraskian*, May 5, 1861

5 *Sioux City Register*, February 22, 1862

6 Kingsbury, George W., Vol. I, P 216

7 *St. Paul Pioneer Press and Democrat,* January 14, 1862

8 *The Dakotian* (Yankton, D.T.), June 17, 1862

9 *The Dakotian* (Yankton, D.T.), July 15, 1862

10 *The Dakotian* (Yankton, D.T.), August 5, 1862; Masters was most likely the son of Henry Masters, the late "squatter" Governor.

11 *The Dakotian* (Yankton, D.T.), August 19, 1862

12 Kingsbury, George W., Vol. I, PP 219-221

13 Kingsbury, George W., Vol. I, P 233

14 *S. D. Historical Collections,* Vol. X, 1920, P 400

15 *The Dakotian* (Yankton, D.T.), August 26, 1862

16 Amidon Family Bible, Record of Marriages

17 *South Dakota Record* (Sioux Falls), December 22, 1893

18 Letter from Mahala Amidon to Martha Amidon, dated October 12, 1862

19 *South Dakota Record* (Sioux Falls), December 22, 1893

20 Kingsbury, George W., Vol. I, PP 106-107

21 Robinson, Doane, *History of South Dakota,* Vol. I, B. F. Bowen & Co., 1904, P 204

22 Green, Edward Baker, *Personal Reminiscences – Past and Present,* Unpublished Manuscript, "Interview with Erhardt Fleitz, Pioneer Soldier"

23 *S. D. Historical Collections,* Vol. II, 1904, P 30

24 Her husband swore eternal vengeance against Indians, vowing to spend the rest of his life carrying out his vendetta. He was given the "honor" of cutting the rope at the execution of 38 Santee Sioux at Mankato (*St. Paul Pioneer,* January 21, 1863).

25 *S. D. Historical Collections,* Vol. II, 1904, P 305

26 Letter from Mahala Amidon to Martha Amidon, dated October 12, 1862

27 *South Dakota Record* (Sioux Falls), December 22, 1893

28 Kingsbury, George W., Vol. I, P 107

29 *Sioux Falls Independent,* June 25, 1874

30 *South Dakota Record* (Sioux Falls), December 22, 1893

31 Kingsbury, George W., Vol. I, P 106

32 Kingsbury, George W., Vol. I, P 107

33 Letter from Mahala Amidon to Martha Amidon, dated October 12, 1862

34 *S. D. Historical Collections,* Vol. IX, PP 245-247

35 *S. D. Historical Collections,* Vol. IX, P 248

36 *Yankton Daily Press and Dakotaian,* April 13, 1876; Another source (*S. D. Historical Collections,* Vol. X, 1920, P 513) said Bell was a Sunday School Superintendent who lived on the bank of Brule creek.

37 Cole County is now Union County

38 *Dakota Pantagraph,* December 11, 1878

39 *Yankton Daily Press and Dakotaian,* April 13, 1876

40 Armstrong, Moses K., *The Early Empire Builders of the Great West,* E. W. Porter, St. Paul, Minnesota, 1901, P 82

41 Schell, Herbert S., *History of Clay County South Dakota,* Clay County Historical Society, Inc., Vermillion, SD, 1976, P 23

42 *S. D. Historical Collections,* Vol. XII, 1924, P 317

43 *S. D. Historical Collections,* Vol. X, 1920, P 514

44 *St. Paul Pioneer and Democrat,* September 12, 1862

45 *The Dakotian* (Yankton, D.T.), September 15, 1862; *S. D. Historical Collections,* Vol. VIII, 1916 P 101

46 *The Dakotian* (Yankton, D.T.), September 15, 1862

47 McKusick, Marshall, *The Iowa Northern Border Brigade,* The University of Iowa, Iowa City, 1975, P 11

48 *S. D. Historical Collections,* Vol. VIII, 1916, P 102

49 Jones, Robert Huhn, *The Civil War in the Northwest,* University of Oklahoma Press: Norman, 1960, P 29

50 McKusick, Marshall, PP 7-8

51 Jones, Robert Huhn, P 142

52 *The Dakotian* (Yankton, D.T.), September 15, 1862

53 *S. D. Historical Collections,* Vol. X, 1920, P 511

54 Kingsbury, George W., Vol. I, P 243

55 *The Historian,* Mission Hills, SD, September 2, 1910

56 *Yankton Press and Dakotan,* June 6, 1911

57 *S. D. Historical Collections,* Vol. IX, P 249. His name was also spelled "LaFevre."

58 *The Dakotian* (Yankton, D.T.), August 25, 1863

59 *S. D. Historical Collections,* Vol. IX, 1918, P 256

60 Kingsbury, George W., Vol. I, P 237

61 *The Dakoti*an (Yankton, D. T.), August 23, 1864

62 *Yankton Press and Dakotan,* June 6, 1911

63 Kingsbury, George W., Vol. I, P 242

64 *Yankton Press and Dakotan,* June 6, 1911

65 McKusick, Marshall, P 15

66 Kingsbury, George W., Vol. I, PP 245-246

67 *St. Paul Pioneer and Democrat,* September 17, 1862

68 Kingsbury, George W., Vol. I, P 232

69 Kingsbury, George W., Vol. I, P 272

70 *New York Times,* December 21, 1862

71 Kingsbury, George W., Vol. I, P 113

72 *S. D. Historical Collections,* Vol. IX, 1918, PP 254-255. The slough was later named Covell's Slough after a settler. It is now known as Covell's Lake and is part of Terrace Park.

73 Kingsbury, George W., Vol. I, P 113

74 On June 13, 1993, the Minnehaha County Historical Society dedicated a historical marker in memory of the slain man.

75 *Sioux Falls Argus-Leader,* April 2, 1898

76 *Dakota Pantagraph,* October 2, 1878

77 Kingsbury, George W., Vol. I., P 109

78 *St. Paul Pioneer,* January 16, 1863

79 Coursey, O. W., *Who's Who in South Dakota,* Vol. III, Educator Supply Co., Mitchell, SD, 1920, PP 429-430

Chapter XIV

1. Smith, Charles M., *A Comprehensive History of Minnehaha County*, Educator Supply Co., Mitchell, SD, 1949, PP 113-114

2. *Sioux Falls Leader,* October 7, 1885. A biographical compendium published in 1897 says he was born on October 3, 1830.

3. *Black Hills Times*, October 14, 1882

4. *Memorial and Biographical Record*, George A. Ogle & Co.,Chicago, 1897, P 228; *Yankton Press*, August 23, 1871; *Sioux Falls Press,* June 17, 1905; *S. D. Historical Collections,* Vol. X, 1920, P 399

5. Haller, Jr., Ben, *A History of Banking in Nebraska, 1854-1990*, Nebraska Bankers Association, Inc., 1990, PP 9, 29, 30, 46, 47 and 75

6. *The Union and Dakotaian* (Yankton, D.T.), March 18, 1865

7. *S. D. Historical Collections,* Vol. X, 1920, PP 398-399. NOTE: this article on the 1860 census of Dakota contains many errors and must be used with caution.

8. Armstrong, Moses K., *The Early Empire Builders of the Great West*, E. W. Porter, St. Paul, MN, 1901, P 94

9. Robinson, Doane, *History of South Dakota*, Vol. II, B. F. Bowen & Co., 1904, P 1441

10. *Sioux Falls Argus-Leader*, August 3, 1899

11. *Sioux Falls Leader,* October 7, 1885

12. *S. D. State Forum*, January 22, 1909; *Sioux Falls Press,* January 19, 1909; *Sioux Falls Argus-Leader*, January 19, 1909

13. Holcombe, Return I., *Minnesota in Three Centuries*, Vol. III, The Publishing Society of Minnesota, 1908, P 94

14. Anderson, Gary Clayton and Woolworth, Alan R., *Through Dakota Eyes, Narrative Accounts of the Minnesota Indian War of 1862,* Minnesota Historical Society Press, St. Paul, 1988, P 47

15. Carley, Kenneth, *The Sioux Uprising of 1862,* The Minnesota Historical Society, St. Paul, 1961, P 20

16. Oehler, C. M., *The Great Sioux Uprising,* New York Oxford University Press, 1959, P 39

17. Newsom, T. M., *Pen Pictures of St. Paul, Minnesota*, Vol. I, Published by the Author, St. Paul, Minnesota, 1886, P 730

18. Hubbard, Lucius F., and Holcombe, Return I., P 432

19. Trinka, Zena Irma, *Out Where the West Begins, Being the Early and Romantic History of North Dakota,* St. Paul, The Pioneer Co., 1920, P 80

20. *Cincinnati Weekly Gazette,* February 17, 1864

21. O'Brien, Frank G., *Minnesota Pioneer Sketches,* H. H. S. Rowell, Publisher, 1904, P 101

22. Clodfelter, Michael, *The Dakota War, The U. S. Army Versus the Sioux, 1862-1865,* McFarland & Co., Inc, publisher, 1998, PP 193-197

23. O'Brien, Frank G., PP 102-107

24. *St. Paul Pioneer,* November 30, 1864

25. *Washington Chronicle* in the *St. Paul Pioneer,* June 8, 1865

26. Upham, Warner, *Minnesota Geographical Names, Their Origin and Historical Significance,* Minnesota Historical Society, 1869, Reprint Edition, P 376

27 *St. Paul Pioneer Press,* December 29, 1876

28 Morris, H. S., *Historical Stories, Legends and Traditions, Northeastern South Dakota* Published by the Sisseton Courier, (No date) P 91

29 *St. Paul Daily Minnesotian,* July 7, 1860

30 *St. Paul Daily Minnesotian,* November 10, 1860

31 *Henderson Democrat,* July 14, 1860

32 Jones, Evan, *The Minnesota, Forgotten River,* Holt, Rinehart and Winston, New York, 1962, P 124

33 O'Brien, Frank G., P 269

34 *Dubuque Times,* March 12, 1859

35 *Cleveland Plain Dealer,* February 29, 1860

36 Christianson, Theodore, *Minnesota, The Land of Sky-Tinted Waters,* Vol. I, The American Historical Society, Inc., Chicago and New York, 1935, PP 277-278

37 Sandburg, Carl, *Abraham Lincoln; the Prairie Years and the War Years,* Harcourt, Brace and Company, N. Y., 1954, PP 371-372; *Yankton Union and Dakotaian,* November 19, 1864

38 *Ohio Statesman* (Columbus), November 8, 1864

39 *Ohio Statesman* (Columbus), November 11, 1864

40 www.famousamericans.net/samuelmedary

41 *S. D. Historical Collections,* Vol. V, 1910, P 279; *Sioux Falls Argus-Leader,* April 21, 1900; *Minnesota Historical Society,* Vol. XIV, 1912, Published by the Society, St. Paul, P 247

42 *Memorial and Biographical Record,* George A. Ogle & Co., Chicago, 1897, P 569; *Minneapolis Tribune,* January 26, 1898

43 *The Monthly South Dakotan,* Vol. II, May 1899 – April 1900, The South Dakotan Company, Sioux Falls, S. D., PP 144-145

44 *St. Paul Pioneer,* September 30, 1862

45 Newsom, T. M., P 536

46 *S. D. Historical Collections,* Vol. VI, 1912, P 133; *Sioux Falls Argus-Leader,* May 4, 1898

47 *The Dakotian* (Yankton, D.T.), October 18, 1863

48 *S. D. Historical Collections,* Vol. XIII, 1926, PP 98-99

49 *S. D. Historical Collections,* Vol. VI, 1912, P 134; *Black Hills Pioneer,* January 16, 1878; *Dakota Herald,* February 24, 1877 and August 25, 1883; *Sioux Falls Argus-Leader,* January 3, 1894

50 *The Monthly South Dakotan,* Vol. II, P 144

51 South Dakota State Archives, Cultural Heritage Center, Pierre, SD, SC 2, J. P. Kidder Papers, Biographical Material, Folder One

52 Robinson, Doane, *History of South Dakota,* Vol. I, The American Historical Society, Inc., Chicago and New York, 1930, P 550

53 *S. D. Historical Collections,* Vol. XXVIII, 1956, P 42

54 *The Monthly South Dakotan,* Vol. III, May 1900 – April 1901, The South Dakotan Company, Sioux Falls, S. D., P 59

55 *Daily Press and Dakotaian* (Yankton, D.T.), September 16, 1885

56 *Press and Dakotaian* (Yankton, D.T.), February 5, 1874

57 Warner, Ezra J., *Generals in Blue, Lives of the Union Commanders*, Louisiana State University Press, Baton Rouge and London, 1996, P 507

58 *The Yankton Press*, January 10, 1872

59 *New York Tribune*, April 16, 1864

60 Kingsbury, George W., *History of Dakota Territory,* Vol. I, S. J. Clarke Publishing Co., Chicago, 1915, P 257

61 South Dakota Heritage Center, Pierre, Letter from Rev. John P. Williamson to D. W. Robinson, September 19, 1902

62 *St. Paul Pioneer,* October 11, 1868

63 *Dakota Herald*, June 16, 1877

64 *Daily Press and Dakotaian* (Yankton, D.T.), May 10, 1877

65 *Black Hills Times*, June 10, 1883

Index

Abbe, Samuel Badger, 394
Acton, MN, 333
Adams, at the Falls of the Big Sioux River in 1856, 38
Adams, Austin, 34, 37
Albright, Samuel J., 215-216, 224, 227-229, 232, 237, 247-248, as squatter governor, 250 in squatter legislature of 1859, 252; 255-256; brings press to Sioux Falls City, 275; 276-278, 280, fights with Ziebach, 282-287; leaves Dakota, 288; 289, newspaperman in the Civil War, 395, 398
Alexander, Colonel, 170
Allen, James, Captain, 4
Allen, James M., 47, 58, at Fort Sod, 210-211, 223, 246, 248, 277, 315, in Dakota militia, 349, 395, kills himself, 398
Amidon, Eliza Jane, 334
Amidon, Joseph B., 251, 287, 330, 334, the killing of 335-336, 357, 361
Amidon, Mahala, 334-336; 339-340, 357
Amidon, William, 334, the killing of, 335-336; 339-340, 357, 361
American Fur Company, 4, 6, 351
Armstrong, Moses K., 121-122, 222, 249, 253-254, 264, 293, elected to legislature, 322; 324, writes about legislature, 325-326, describes mass exodus, 344-345, in Dakota militia, 349; 350, 363-364, writes book, 365; 369
Ash, Henry C., 120, 313
Ash Hotel (Hotel d'Ash), 120, 313, 321, 326, 350, 352
Assiniboia, 133, 138
Assiniboine Indians, 136
Aston, SD, 171
Atkinson, Edward, 112
Atwood, L. B., 251

Back, H. L., 199, 202
Bacon, James M., 334-336, 339, 354
Bad Lands, 181
Bad River, 107
Bailey, Horace T., 118, 293
Baird, W. R., 34
Balcom, Henry, 118
Balcom, Myrom, 118
Barnes, Jacob B., 373
Beadle, J. H., 147
Beall, S. W., 402-403
Bell, A. J., 316-317

Bell, John, 327, 341, 345
Beusamy, Joseph, 81
Bee, Barnard E., 160-161
Big Driftwood Lake, 179
Big Mound, battle of, 181
Big Sioux County, 48, 56, 58, 71, 214, 229, 244, 247-249, 251-252
Big Sioux Falls Colony, 29-31
Big Sioux River, 4, 5, 11, 15, 28-33, 37, 39, 40, 43, 46, 52-53, 56, 66, called "Big Blue River," 72; 75, 82-86, 95, 99, 101, 116, 128, 150, 156, 162-164, 168, called "Crooked River," 177; 187, 189, 194, 197, 204, 208, 212-215, 218, 220-221, 223, 225, 227-228, Master's poem, 236; 237, 240, 246, 254, 261, steamboats on, 262-263; ferries on 264-266; and the *Lewis Burnes,* 267-269; 271-272, 278, 293, 330, 345, 351, 380
Big Sioux Valley, 14, 39, 42, 91, 143, 168, 209, 216, 222, 226-228, 248, 277, 279, 283, 290, 293-294, 308, 316, 321
Big Stone Lake, 40, 180, 242, 262, 380
Bigelow, "Governor," 312-313
Bijou Hills, 6-7
Bissonette, Joseph, 7
Black Hills, 7, 28, 52, 351, 394, 398, 399, 404
"Black Republicans," 55, 258, 392
Bliss, Philemon, 310
Blunt, James G., 347
Bon Homme town site, 312-313, 316, convention in, 317; 324, 326, 328, 341, 346-347
Booge, Charles P., 317-318
Bouret, Casock, 351
Bowdoin College, 188-189
Boyle, John W., 326
Bramble, Downer T., 302
Brawley, D. F., 223
Breckinridge, John C., 20, 195
Broken Kettle Creek, 267
Brookings County, SD, 369
Brookings Island, 372
Brookings, S.D., 218-219, 369
Brookings, Wilmot W., 44-46, 58; tragic accident, 186-192; 196, 218-220, 248, 250, in squatter legislature of 1859, 251; 256, 301, acting governor, 305; 315, 318; elected to legislature, 321; 323-324, 329-330, 334, 340, 359, 368, on Dakota Supreme Court, 369; death of, 372 Brown County, MN, 56, 89-90

Brown County, SD, 196
Brown, Joseph R., 20, described 21-23; 31, 40-41, 47, 51, the "Juggler," 58; 59, 72-73, 78-79, 206, 212, invents steam wagon, 387; builds prairie mansion, 388
Brown, N. R., 27, 51
Brown, Samuel F., 21, 27
Brown's Valley, MN, 332
Brugier, Theophile, 5, 110, 266, 331, 351
Brule Creek, 329, 357-358
Brule Sioux, 101
Bryan, Clay, 30-32, 44
Buchanan, James, 23-24, 27, 59, 110, 221, 245, 293, 301, signs bill creating Dakota Territory, 304; 391
Buffalo, 4, 15, 43, 82-83, 101, 138, 143-146, 148, 164, 171, 195-197, 213, 240, 329
Buffalo Bill's Wild West Show, 182
Burns, Peter P., 13, 31, 34, 38, 41-42, 44
Burr, Aaron, 21

Callahan, Margaret, 373
"Camp Jayne," 335
Campbell, A. J., 177-179
Campbell, Thomas, 27
Carney, Clara, 36,
Carrier (steamboat), 123
Carson, Kit, 351
Catlin, George, 8
Cavanaugh, James M., 67, 243, 293
Central City (New York) *Courier,* 222
Chapel, Frank, 106, 122, 293
Cheyenne River, 143
Chippewa Indians, 134
Chouteau Creek, 120
Chouteau, Pierre, 7-8
Churchill, William, 34
Clay, Cassius, 235
Cleveland Herald, 223
Cochrane, Clark B., 72
Columbus Crisis, 392
Columbia Fur Company, 107
Commerce City town site, 215
Cooper, C., 252, 285
Cooper, James Fennimore, 235
Corlies, Samuel Fisher, 197, 199, 208
Coteau des Prairies, 31, 85, 242
Coteau Percee Creek, 214
Cottonwood County, MN, 27, 51
Cottonwood Lake, 199
Cottonwood River, 82-83, 85-87, 90
Covell's slough, 339
Craig, Representative, 297
Crazy Horse, 182
Cree Indians, 136

Cullen, William J., 176-179
Curtis, Samuel R., 295-297
Custer, George A., 399

D. M. Frost and Company, 104
Daily Minnesotian, (St. Paul) 29-31, 44, 51, 55, 58-59, 116, 161, 202, 205, 207, 224
Daily Missourian, 395
Dakota Cavalry, 325, 327-328, 341, 349, 374
Dakota Democrat, 227, 236, 248, 251-252, 254, 274-278, first issue released, 280-281; fights with *Sioux City Register,* 282-287; publication ends, 288; 347, 395, 406
Dakota House at Sioux Falls City, 209-210, 246, 285
Dakota Land Company, 13-14, 19-23, created 27; 29, town site expedition, 30-33; 38, called Dacotah Land Company, 39; criticized, 40-44; 46-48, accused of voting fraud, 51; 52, political plans of, 56; 60, 62, 66, 69, 74-76, attacked by W. C. Dodge, 77; 81-83, 87, 90-96, 100, 105, 126, 132, 148, 150, 168-169, 189, 192-193 stock price raised, 194; 197, attacked by the press 205-208; 209, 211, annual meeting, 213; 220-221, 223-224, 226, brings press to Sioux Falls City, 227; 229-232, 240, 245, 247, 249, 251-252, 254, 258, 262-264, 268, starts newspaper in Sioux Falls City, 274-275; 276-277, 282, 293, 300-302, 304, 306-307, 316-317, 321, 331-332, 361, 377-379, 386, 393-394, 398
Dakota Southern Railroad, 369
Dakota Territory, (also Dacotah) 27-28, 31, 52, 55-56, 60, 62, 65, 71-72, 75, 116, 122, 126, 128, 150, 203, 221, 227-229, squatter legislature in, 237-239; 241, territorial bill in Congress, 243-245; 259, 262, 275-276, 291, 293-294, 300-301, another territorial bill introduced, 302; created March 2, 1861, 304; capital fight in, 309; 311, 314; population in 1861, 315; 316, 318, 321-324, 326, 327, 332, 341, 346, gold discovered in, 348; 380, 393, 398
Dakotah City (steamboat), 263-264, 268
Davier, William, 81
Dead Buffalo, battle of, 181
Democratic Party, 13, 23, 27, 87, 90, 94, 206, 232, 245, 278, 280, 299, 378
Des Moines River, 156
De Smet, Peter Father, 107
De Vere, Captain, 93

Devil's Lake, 145
DeWitt, Franklin J., 27, 46, 193, 199, 202-203; argues for damages, 207; 209, 211-212, 227, 249, 321, 331-332, dies in Yankton, 394; 398
Dickenson, ND, 381
Dickson, Robert, 136-137
Dilts, Jefferson, 384
Dodge, W. C., 39-41, 77-78, 81, 83-84, attacks Nobles, 87-95; 96, 232
Dog's Claw, 113
Donaldson, A. J., 263
Donaldson, H. S., 242
Dorion, Pierre, 262
Douglas, Frederick, 235
Douglas, Stephen, 20, 24, 278
Dred Scott Supreme Court Decision, 292, 297
Drifting Goose, 42, 46
Dubuque Daily Times, 211
Dubuque Herald, 126, 255, 282
Dubuque Express and Herald, 37, 39, 241
Dubuque House at Sioux Falls City, 45, 220
Dubuque, Ia., 14, 20, 32-33, 37, 44-45, 47, 126, 175, 185-186, 188, 212, 219-220, 231, 252, 276, 374
Dulac, Perrin, 5
Duley, W. J., 205-206, 212
Duley, Mrs. William J., 336

Eagle Woman Who All Look At, 107
Earth Lodges (Dirt Lodges), 170, 196
Edgar, Mrs., 352-353, 357
Edmunds, Newton, 349
Election of October 13, 1857, 55, 67-68, 70
Election of September 12, 1859, 247-249
Elk Point town site, 321, 346, 350
Ellis, Joseph, 359-360
Elm River, 196
Eminija town site, 34, 52-53, 71, 187, 189, 192, 194, 208, 214, 217, 229, and steamboats 263-264, 268; 299, 315, 321
End of the Snake, 170
English, A. M., 341, 354
Evans, James W., 47, 58, 252, 334, 340, in Dakota militia, 349; 359
Evening Star (Washington, D. C.), 84, 150, 177

Falls of the Big Sioux River, 1-2, 4-5, 29, 31-33, 37, immense water power; 38, called "Great Sioux Falls," 39; 45, 99, 122, 186, 188, 194, 196, 208, 212, described, 215-216; 218, 228, 235, Master's poem, 236; 241, 250, 262-263, death of Masters at, 281-282; 329, 359, 372

Fanning and Taylor, 263-264
Faribault, MN, 193
Farwell, James, 38
Favorite (steamboat), 222, 279
Ferris, Jacob, 1, 37
Fire Cloud, 157
"First Organized Government of Dakota," 247
Fish, Ross, 81, 83
Fisher, Michael, 354
Fisk, George D. (also Fiske), 106, 113, 293
Fisk, Andrew, 386
Fisk, James L., 34, 38, 42, 47, 56, 58, the trailblazer, 380; wagon train attacked, 381-384; poisoning incident, 385; death of, 386
Fisk, Robert E., 386
Fisk, Van H., 386
Flandrau, Charles E., 20, described, 21-23; 78, pursues Inkpaduta, 160-162; 164-165, 168-170, speaks to Indians, 173-174; 175, 177, 301, runs for governor in 1867, 388; death of, 391
Flandrau town site, (also Flandreau), 31, 46, 48, 53, 194, 203, 205, 209, 213-215, 229, 240, 299, 315, 321, 403
Foote, Obed, 120
Fort Abercrombie, 145
Fort Daer, 134
Fort Dakota, 349, 361, 403
Fort Dilts, 384
Fort Dodge Republican, (Iowa) 314
Fort Douglas (Kildonan), 134-135, 138-139
Fort James, 361
Fort Lookout (Old Fort Lookout), 23, 85, 223
Fort Pierre, 7, called "Fort Desolation," 8, 100, 104, 110, 120, 270, 369, 374
Fort Randall, 8-9, 101, 104, 110, 115, 118, 120, 194, 212, 269, 308, 313, 317, 327-329, 346, 373, 394
Fort Rice, 381, 384
Fort Ridgely, 23, 78-79, 82, 85-86, 89, 156, 160, 162, 164, 170, 380
Fort Snelling, 21, 138
Fort Sod, 210-213, 223, 339, 398
Fort Sumter, 307
Fort Tecumseh, 107
Fort Union, 105
Fort Wadsworth (Fort Sisseton), 380
Fowler, Berne C., 333-335, 340, in Dakota militia, 349
Fowler, J. K., 328
Fox, Kate, 235
Fox, Maggie, 235
Frank Steele (steamboat), 279
Fremont, John C., 351

Freney, William, 289
Freudenreich, George, 252
Freudenreich, Frederick, 27, 39, 252
Frost, Todd and Company, 105-106, 113-114, 118, 127, 132, 223, 293
Frost, David M., 104-105, 253, 293, 401, joins Confederacy, 402
Fuller, Abby, 60, 76, 394
Fuller, Albert, 60
Fuller, Alpheus G., 27, 30, 39, 46, 55, "elected" delegate to Congress, 57; background of, 60; St. Paul alderman, 61; goes to Washington, D. C., 62; in Congress, 65-76; 226-227, 231-232, 242-243, 248-249, 256, 291, 294, 321, in Dakota militia, 349; 359, 373, death of, 394
Fuller, David Luce, Jr., 60
Fuller, Elizabeth, 60
Fuller, Frank, 76
Fuller, George, 60
Fuller House, 30, 47, built in 1856, 61-62; 172-173, 194, destroyed by fire in 1869, 394
Fuller, Jane, 60
Fuller, Sarah, 60

Gale, Artemus, 27, 377-378
Galesburg, 378
Gardner, Abigail "Abbie," 159-160, 163-164, 170, rescued, 171-172; 173-175
Gardner, Rowland, 159
Gay, Joseph, 213, 215, 221
Gayville, DT, 341
Gilmer, John A., 68, 70
Gleason, W. E., 310, 313-314
Gooch, David W., 295-297
Goodrich, J. D., 81
Goodwin, Rebecca, 193, 210-211
Gorman, Willis A., 23, 85
Granger, Henry W., 7
Grant, U. S., 269, 393, 399
Gray Foot (Si Ha Hota), 165, 168
Gray, Josiah, 360
Great Dakota Stampede, 344, 362
Great Father, 9, 105, 110, 173, 185
Great Oasis town site, 214
Greeley, Horace, 235
Green, James S., 293, introduced Dakota Territory bill, 302; 303
Greenway, J. B., 251, 253, 285, 341, in Dakota militia, 349; 373
Greenwood Agency, (Yankton Sioux Reservation) 116, 119, 123, 127, 249, 346, 402

Grow, Galusa, 294-295, 300, 303
Grow, William, 82

Haseloh, Frederick, 219
Hanson, Joseph Mills, 362
Hanson, Joseph R., 107, 118, 293, in Dakota Militia, 349
Harmon, John, 276
Harney, William S., 8, 101, 104, 110
Harris, Thomas L., 67-70, 72-73
Henderson Democrat, 73, 78, 84-85, 198, 245, 378
Henderson, MN, 22, 85, 388
Henry, Alexander, 134
Hetherington, Henry S., 34, 37
Hill, George D., 309-310
Hisayu, 198
Holman, C. J., 112
Holman, W. P., 112-113, 118-119
Homestead Act, 192, 329, 331
Howard, Charles K., 269-271, Sioux Falls beloved merchant, 403; death of, 404
Hudson Bay Company, 132-133, 135, 139-140
Hughes, James, 71-72
Hutchinson, John, 309-310, 315, 329-330, 345

Inkpaduta, 31, 82-83, 153, birth of, 154; described, 155; 156-158, in flight 161-164, releases one captive, 165; 169-171, 175-179, rumors and reputation about, 180-181, death of, 182-183, 360
Iron Hawk (Che-tan-maza), 169
Isaiah, 33, 42

Jackson, Andrew, 24
Jackson County, MN, 27
Jacques, or James, River, 15, 43, 85-86, 95, 99, 112, 116, 122, 156, 164, 171, 181, 194, 197-198, 220, 223, 246, 345, 362
Jacques, John A., 87-91, 95
James River Valley, 170
Jane Ritchey (steamboat), 270
Jarrett, Amanda, 45
Jarrett, Barclay, 38-39, 340, killed in a fight, 373
Jarrett, Jesse T., 34, 38, 45, 373
Jarrett's Hill, 228
Jayne, Dr., Gershon I., 309
Jayne, Sibyl, 309
Jayne, Dr. William, described 309-310; relationship with Lincoln, 311-312; 313-314, goes to Sioux Falls City, 315; addresses legislature, 322-323; 325, 327, nominated for Congress, 330; 331, 339, 345-347, returns to Illinois, 393; death of, 394

Jeanette Roberts (steamboat), 222, 279
Johnson, R. M., 252
Johnston, Albert Sidney, 145

Kansas-Nebraska Act, 244, 292
Kelly, Fanny, 384
Kelsey, William H., 70
Kennerly, Lewis, H., 112
Kidder, Lyman, 399
Kidder, Jefferson P., 248-249, goes to Congress, 254-259, 291, lobbies for seat in the House, 294, 398, appointed to Dakota Supreme Court, 399; death of, 400; 406
Kidder, Silas B., 400
Kilgore, Albert L., 58, 252, 277
Killdeer Mountain, battle of, 181
Kingsbury, George W., 111, 131, 255-256, 302, 313, 316, 318, 325-326, 340, in Dakota militia, 349; 360, 401-402
Kingsbury, William W., 48, in Congress, 66-74, 76, 242-243
Kinsey, Smith, 44-45, 186-189, 192, 210-211, 219
Kirkwood, Samuel J., 348

LaBarge, Joseph M., 5
LaBarge, Pelacie, 5
Lac Qui Parle, 168
La Fourve, John "Old Dakota" and "White Bear," 351-352, 357
La Framboise, Joseph, 160
Lake Como, 19
Lake County, SD 164
Lake Benton, 31, 43, 85, 214, 279
Lake Herman (Skunk Lake), 164-165, 177
Lake Heron, 160
Lake Madison, 164, 171
Lake of the Woods, 137
Lake Okoboji, 158, 162
Lake Preston, 221
Lake Shetek, 336
Lake Traverse, 132, 136, 143, 262
Lake Winnipeg, 132
Lakota Sioux, 358
Lamb, Curtis, 155
LaPaire, Francis, 202
Lawrence, John, 349
Lean Dog, 199
Leavenworth, Frederick, P., 193
Lewis Burnes (steamboat), 262, 264, 266-270
Lewis and Clark, 3, 100, 112, 261-262
Lieb, Charles Dr., 309
Lincoln, Abraham, 104, 301, 304, appoints territorial officers, 309-310; 311, signs Homestead Bill, 329; 330, 348-349,
385, 392, 399, 401
Lincoln, Mary Todd, 104, 317
Little Big Horn, battle of, 182
Little Crow, pursues Inkpaduta, 176-179; 180, leads Santee Sioux, 333
Little Sioux River, 156
Little, William, 58, 193, 252
Long, Edward, 62
Long, Stephen, 62
Lord Selkirk (Thomas Douglas), 132-137, death of, 138; 139
Lovell, Charles S., 118-119
Lowell town site, 220
Ludwig, Jacob, 359
Lyman, William P., 106
Lynd, James W., 27, 33-34, 245-246, 378, killed in War of the Outbreak, 379
Lynd town site, 214

Mad Bull, 341, 345
Mahoney, Dennis A., 34, 37
Makana Na Ota E'en, 360
Mankato Independent, 204-205
Marble, Margaret Ann, 159, rescued, 165-168; 169-170; 172, 174
Marble, William, 159-160
Martha (steamboat), 6
Martin County, MN, 27
Masters, Henry, 193, 230, squatter governor, 230-232; 235-236, message to squatter legislature, 237-240; 241-242, 248, death of 250; 280, obituary of, 281; 336
Masters, Henry, Jr. (also Harry), 250, 282, 330, 334, 340
Mass execution at Mankato, 388
Massacre of the Red River, 135-136
Maxwell, Captain of the steamboat *Wave*, 30
Mazakutamani, Paul, 169, 174
McAboy, William, 94
McBride, James, 34, 38, 42, 47, 56, 58
McCall, James, 251-252, 321
McClellan, John, 38, 42, 44, 46, 220, 334, 340, the mystery man, 374; 377
McClure, Charles, 66
McCook, Edward M., 69
McGrath, W. M. F., 78
McKinley, J. M., 34
Mdewankaton Sioux, 9, 176
Medary, Samuel A., described 23-24; 27, 41, 48-49, 51, 58-60, 62, 69, 78, 83, 164, 169, 172, speech to Indians, 173-174; 175, 195, 206, 230; leaves Minnesota, 231; 275-276, as governor of Kansas Territory, 391; newspaperman in Civil War, 392; death of, 393

Medary, Jr., Samuel A., 24, 81-82
Medary town site, 31-32, 41-44, 46, 48, 53, convention at, 56; 71, 82, 85, 131, 185, gets new settlers, 193; 194-195, burning of, 197-204; 205-206, 207-209, 213-215. 219, 221, 229, 240, 244, 246, 256, 279, 299, 301, 307, 315, 394
Metis (Red River "Half-Breeds"), 131, 134-135, 140, 146, 149-150
Midway County, 48, 56, 62, 70-71, 248, 251-252, 256
Millard, Ezra, 37-38, starts Omaha National Bank, 372
Mills, David M., 37-38, 267
Miner, Nelson, 328, 332, 341, 349. 354-356, 359-361
Minneapolis, 15, 19, 145
Minnehaha County, 330, 334, 362
Minnehaha (steamboat) 271
Minnesota Free Press, 39, 77, 83, 87, 174, 206-207, 232
Minnesota Historical Society, 379
Minnesota River, 10, 18, 22, 30, 116, 160, 262, 279, 359, 380
Minnesota Territory, 9, 13, 15, 19, 27-28, 30, 55-56, 60, 65-66, 69, 71-72, 75, 136, 145, 147, 149-150, 156-157, 160-161, 164, 231, 257, 294, 301, 393
Mississippi River, 15, 18, 62, 136-137, 145-146, 262
Missouri Compromise of 1820, 292
Missouri River, 5-9, 11, 14, 23, 27-29, 40-41, 52-53, 69, 74, 84-86, 95, 99-100, 104-105, 113, 115, 121, 126, 150, 154, 170, 178, 180, 189, 194, 215, 217, 223, 226, 240, 246, 252, 258, 262, 268, 277, 282, 308, 312-313, 345, 348, 351, 359, 374, 380, 394
Mix, Charles M., 114, 116
Moccasin Democrats, 22, 149, 388
Monticello Times, 206
Moody, Gideon C., 369
Mortimer, Samuel "Old Spot," 112-113, 350, 355-356
Mountain Pass ("Hole-in-the-Mountain") town site, 31, 43, 44, 48, 82, 85, 197, 214, 222, 279
Mud Creek, 197
Murray County, MN, 51
Myrick, Nathan, 379

National Union Party, 316
Neal, Daniel, 197
Nebraska Territory, 71, 101, 194, 263, 304
New York Times, 268, 277, 315

New York Tribune, 73, 243
New Ulm, MN, 30-31, 43, 87-88, 181, 194. 217, 246, 276, 279, 299, 306
Nicollet County, MN, 90
Nicollett, Jean, 38
Nicollett town site in Sioux County, IA, 212, 220
Nobles County, MN, 27, 90, 214
Nobles, Mrs. Alvin, 159, 168, 170, death of, 171; 172
Nobles, Lemuel, 386
Nobles Pass in the Sierra Mountains, 23
Nobles Road, 23-24, 31, 41, 43, 77-81, 83, described, 86; 87, 90-91, 96-97, 169, 194, 199, 206, 214
Nobles, William H., 23, 41, 43-44, 77-79, early life of, 80-82; confronted by Yankton Sioux, 83; criticized by Washington D. C. newspaper, 84; in a street fight, 85; 86, fights with John A. Jacques, 87-94, 95-97, 169, 206, serves in Civil War, 386; death of, 387
North, J. M., 310
Northwest Fur Company, 134-135
Northwest Ordinance of 1787
Northwestern Independent, (also *Western Independent*), 288, 304

Omaha (steamboat), 268
Omaha Indians, 156
Omaha Nebraskan, 73
Ohio Statesman, 24, 392-393
Oakes, ND, 181
Oleson, Halvor, 38
Organic Act, creating Dakota Territory, 304; 309, 314, 316
Other Day, John, 169

Patterson, John, 118
Panic of 1857, 47, 172, 245, 279, 380
Pacquette, Paul, 264-265, 351
Parker, Paine, 27, 224, 379-380
Parrant, Pierre, 18
Pattee, John, 328
Pembina County, 149, 242
Pembina town site, 51, 59, 131-132, 134, 138-139, 143, 148-150, 232, 242, 247-248, 254, 293, 308, 315, 318, 321, 357
Pembina, River, 134
Pemmican, 144-146
Penn, William, 393
Peters' Band, 285
Peters, J. E., 252
Philbrick, Charles, 349

Phillips, Hattie, 365, 368
Phillips, Dr. Josiah L., 44, 56, 58, 188, 213, 220, 277, 340, serves in Civil War, 365; 372
Picotte, Charles F., 106, years of his youth, 107; goes to Washington, D. C., 110-112; 114-116, 122, 127, 293, 302, 350-351, 353, 356, dies at Greenwood, 402
Picotte, Honore F., 107
Pierce, Ephraim, 230
Pierce, Franklin, 21
Pike's Peak, 259
Pinney, George M., 316, 323, described, 324; 325, goes to Montana, 402; California scandal, 403
Pipestone Creek, 214
Pipestone County, MN, 27, 51, 56, 244, 252
Pipestone Quarries, 4, 115, 158, 197
Plughoff, Frederick, 328
Polk, James K., 24
Pope, John, 348-349
Prescott, Philander, 4, 160
Presho, George, 106, 122

Ramsey, Alexander, 9-10, 28, 48, 149
Randolph, Evan, 197
Rattle Strike, 157
Red Buttes, battle of 381
Redfield, Alexander H., 118-119, 123, 127
Redfield, Tom, 127
Red River of the North, 15, 28, 52, 131-134, 137, 139-140, 143, 145, 148-151, 195, 254, 262, 357
Red River Ox Cart, 140, 143, 145-148
Red River Valley, 134, 136, 143-144, 148
Redwood town site, 214
Redwood Agency (Lower), 10, 176, 378-379
Redwood Centre town site, 214
Ree Indians, 351
Reed, John A., 387
Reed, Matt, 355
Reed, Tom, 355
Reed, Washington, 355
Rencontre, Zephyr, 110
Renshaw town site, 214
Republican Party, 13, 48, 245, 292, 331, 399
Rhine Creek, 113
Rice, Henry M., 19-20, 80, 293
Richardson, Lilliore, 60
Riggs, Stephen R., 168, 174, 198
Roaring Cloud, 157, 171, death of, 175
Robinson, Doane, 10, 181
Rochelle (Ill.) Register, 311-312
Rock County, MN, 27, 56, 244, 248, 251-252
Rock River, 187, 208, 212, 343, 265-267

Roman Nose, 399
Rouse, John, 252

St. Anthony Express, 240
St. Anthony Falls, 38
St. Anthony, MN 144, 147
St. Joseph town site, 131, 149, 242, 308, 321
St. Louis Republican, 254
St. Paul, 13-14, early days of 15-19; known as "Pig's Eye," 18; 24, 27, 30, 38-40, 42-44, 47, 54-55, 58, 60, 80-81, 83, 85, 93, 116, 132, Ox-Cart trade in 145-149, 168, 171, 175, 185-186, 204, 206, 215, 217, 224, 227, 231-232, 241, 255, 262-263, 274, 276, 279, 294, 304, 306-309 317, 321, 357, 394
St. Paul Light Cavalry, 175
St. Paul Daily Times, 18, 97, 203
St. Paul Pioneer and Democrat, 39, 40, 51-53, 55, 58-59, 75, 80-81, 91, 100, 116, 131, 144, 153, 179, 185-186, 195, 204-207, 217, 225, 227, 230, 237, 258, 261, 263, 280; 291, 303-304, 307, 309, 312, 317, 353
St. Paul Pioneer, 385
St. Paul Pioneer Press, 274
St. Paul speculators, 40, 48, 90, 205, 207, 225, 232, 258
St. Peter, MN, 39, 77, 83, 94, 193, 206, 232
Santee (Eastern) Sioux 9, 10, 31, 100, 114, 154, 198, 288, 332, 347, 353, 358-359, 361, 379, 388
Santee Sioux Reservation, 44
Saratoga town site, 214
Scales, Joseph, 251
Schoonover, B., 221
Selkirkers, 134-135, 139-140, 143
Shado Utonwahe, (Yankton Village) 105, 112, 115, 118, 123, 189, 192, 227
Shafer, William E., 310-311
Shakopee, MN, 61
Shaw, Amos, 252
Sheehan, T. J., 180
Sherman, William T., 365
Shober, John, 323
Sibley, Henry H., 48, 51, 68, 71, 80, 181, 204
Sims, Charles F., 381, 385
Sioux City Eagle, 46, 99, 116, 117-119, 122, 186-187, 196, 228, 241-242, 266, 278
Sioux City, IA, 15, 37, 42, 45, 99, 101, 104, 106, 112, 115, 117-119, 122, 155-156, 185-186, 188, 194, 212, 218, 227, 241-242, 253, 261-263, 266, 268-271, 277, 279-281, 289, 299, 306, 312-313, 317, 341, 344, 346-349, 357, 359, 361, 369

Sioux City Register, 117, 121, 254, 273-274, 277-278, 280, Master's obituary in, 281-282; fights with *Dakota Democrat,* 282-287; 327. 349
Sioux Falls City (also Sioux Falls), created, 34; 38-39, 41-43, 45-46, 48, described, 52; population of, 53; 54, mass meeting at, 56; 58-59, 71, 76, 82, 117, 126, 128, 131, 181, 185-187, gets new settlers, 193; 194, 196, 199, 202, 208, prepares for defense, 209-212; 213-222; described in 1859, 222; 223, 227, mass convention at, 228-230; 231-232, 238-239, 241-243, capital city, 244; convention at, 246; holds election 247-249; 250, 252-254, 257, 259, 262, 266, and steamboats, 268-271; 274; first newspaper in, 275; 276, 278-281; cotillion party at, 284-285; 286-287, 289-290; 292, 294, 299, 301, celebrates, 304-305; 306-307, and fight for capital, 308-309; 313, population in 1861, 315; 321, 323-326, 328, 330, and the War of the Outbreak, 333-339; evacuated, 340; Indians destroy, 347; 349, 357-359, 361, 373, 394-395, 403
"Sioux Falls City, Iowa," 122
Sioux Falls Library Association, 252
Sioux Falls Manufacturing Company, 253
Sioux Falls Press, 13
Sisseton Sioux, 9, 178, 180, 202, 204 332
Sitting Bull, 182, 381
Skunk Creek, 360
Slavery, 13, 244, 258, 291-292, 297-299, 302-303, 323
Smith, A. B., 355-356
Smith, Byron, 27, 33, 189, 192, 202, 215, 223, 306, 331, 373
Smithland, IA, 156-157
Smutty Bear, 105, 114-115, 122, 197, 199
Smutty Bear's Bottom, 105
Snake Creek, 171, 178
Sounding Heavens, 165
South Dakota Heritage Center, 249
South Dakota Historical Collections, 248
South Dakota State Historical Society, 202, 400
Spirit Lake, 31, 82, 158, 160, 172, 180, 306
Spirit Lake Massacre, 159-161
Spiritualism, 235-236
Split Rock River (Creek), 4, 34, called Eminija River, 53; 189, 208, 214
Springfield (Jackson), MN, 160-162, 329
Squatter Legislature of 1859, 251-253
Staples, Dr. George M., 34, 37, 44-45

Stafford, Ben, 99, 112
Stanton, Edwin M., 348, 380
States and Territories of the Great Northwest, 1, 37
Stevens, William, 252, 340, in Dakota militia, 349
Stillwater, MN, 80-81
Stony Lake, battle of, 181
Struck By The Ree, 99, 107, goes to Washington, D. C., 111-112; 115, 118, 122, 353
Stutsman County, ND, 401
Stutsman, Enos, 112, 120-122, 293, in legislature, 323; 326, 352, moves to Pembina, 400; death of, 401
Stuart, I. W., 276-277, 286, 288, 304
Sully, Alfred, 181, 384
Summit City, 71, 194, 299

Tackett, Charles L., 120-121
Taylor, J. W., 34
Taylor, Zachary, 28
Teakle, Thomas, 154
Territory of Chippewa, 295
Teton Sioux, 100, 107, 180, 202, 381
Thatcher, Mrs. Joseph, 159, 162, death of, 163; 169
Thayer, Eli, 294-296, 298-300
The History of Minnesota and Tales of the Frontier, 391
The Spirit Lake Massacre, 154
Thompson, Jacob, 81
Todd, John B. S., 69-70, 74, 76, described, 101; 104-108, goes to Washington, D. C., 110-112; 114-116, 118-123, 126, 248, 250, 253, 258; 289, 291, 293, lobbies in Washington, 294; 309, 313, candidate for Congress, 317-318; elected delegate, 321; 325, 330-331, nominated for Congress, 332; 358, serves in Civil War, 401
Transit Railroad Company, 30, 214, 216
Trask, Josiah C., 352
Treaty of Mendota, 9
Treaty of Traverse de Sioux, 9-10, 28, 156-157, 176, 198, 204, 333
Trumbull, Lyman, 309, 311-312
Turkey Creek, 329, 332
Turrentine, W. Jackson, 95
Tuttle, A., 87-89, 91, 95

Undine (steamboat), 271
Union County, DT, 350-351
Upper Missouri Land Company, 112, 126

Van Osdel, Samuel, 349

Van Osdel, William, 349
Vermillion County, 214, 248, 251-252
Vermillion town site, 154, 244, 312-313, 315, mass convention at, 316, 323-326, 328-329, 331, 344-346, 354, 398

Wabashaw County, MT, 28
Wahpekute Sioux, 9, 82 153-156
Wahpeton Sioux, 9, 204
Waldron, George P., 34, 318, 321, 325, 330, 334, 339-340, 359, re-settles in Yankton, 373; death of, 374
Waldron, Luella ("Lulu"), 373
Waldron, Lydia, 373
Walker, G. G., 221
War Eagle, 5
War Eagle That May Be Seen, 155
War of the Outbreak, (Dakota War of 1862), 10, 180, 332-336, 358, 379, 388
Wamdisapa (Black Eagle), 154
Washburn, Representative, 70
Washington Chronicle, 386
Washington Union, 55-56, 220
Watonwan River, 154
Wave (steamboat), 30, 276
Weekly Dakotian, 289, 313, 317, 329, 331, 347, 353
West Lake Okoboji, 159
Western Town Company, 32-33, created 34; town site expedition of 37-38; 39, 44-45, 48, 100, 105, 186, 188-189, 192, 196, 210, 212, 219, selling out, 220; 224, 231, 251, 301, 307, 318, 365, 368, 372
Westfield, IA, 267
Wherry, Jesse, 325
White, Charles and family, 193, 340
White Lodge, 336
Whitestone Hill, battle of, 181
Williams, Joseph L., 310
Williamson, Dr. John, 168, 198-199, 203, 402
Williston, J. P., 310
Wilson, James, 70
Wilson, Kerwin, 118
Wilson, Nathaniel G., 310
Wilson, S. P., 309
Winona, MN, 30, 122
Winona Democrat, 222, 231-232
Winona Republican, 205
Wiseman, Hansen, 181
Witherspoon, James "Limber Jim," 121, 123, 350-351
Whitney, A. J., 81
Wright, Charles, 360

Yankton County, 341, 347

Yankton Land and Town Company, 126
Yankton Sioux, 5, 43, 53, 69, 74, 82-84, 99-101, 106-107, 110, 114-115, 117, 120, 122, leave their village, 123; 126-127, 156, 164, 170-174, 176, 178, 180, 185, 192, 196-197, 211, 216, 221, 223, 246, 347, 353
Yanktonai Sioux, 15, 42, 136, 164, 176, destroy Medary, 196-198; 204, 221; 229, 308
Yankton town site, 76, 99-100, 113-114, 116, 120-123, town created, 126; 127-128, 131, 181, 202, 243-244, 247-249, 251-254, 271, 277, 289, 292, mass convention at, 293; another mass convention at, 302; celebration in, 304; 307, officials arrive in, 311-312; named temporary capital, 313-314; population in 1861, 316; 318, 321, legislature meets in, 322-324; named permanent capital, 325; 328-329, 331, 339-341, 345, settlers gather in 346-349; stockade in, 350-356; 358-359, 369, Brookings' ashes buried at, 372; 373, 394, 398, 401-402
Yankton Treaty of 1858, 114-115, 120, 196, 223, 246, 279, 402
Yellow Medicine Agency (Upper), 10, 83, 165, 168, 171, 175-177, 204
Yellow Medicine River, 180

Ziebach, F. M., 120-121, 277, fights with Albright, 282-287; 288, moves to Yankton, 289; 349, 354

ABOUT THE AUTHOR

WAYNE FANEBUST was born in Sioux Falls, South Dakota, and raised "out in the country" always living near Sioux Falls, except for a short stay in Iowa. His early years were entirely rural and his elementary education was attained in small, wooden country schoolhouses. Living out in the country instilled in him a love of birds and animals and an appreciation of the natural world. To this day, a walk in the wooded hills along the Big Sioux River brings him great pleasure. A strong environmental ethic shows up in all of his books, sometimes in subtle ways and at other times, very direct.

He graduated from Washington High School in Sioux Falls, joined the United States Marine Corps and was sent to San Diego for boot camp. He was stationed at Camp Pendleton, California. After his military time was served, Fanebust returned to Sioux Falls for one year. In 1965 he moved to Los Angeles to chase his dream, pursuing a career as a rock 'n roll musician and songwriter. As a guitar player he sang and performed in bands in Los Angeles in the mid-and late 60's. He also worked as an "extra" in a few movies and TV shows, while living a Hollywood lifestyle.

It was while he was a student at the University of California, Santa Barbara, that Fanebust acquired an interest in writing history. He took a course called "History of the American West" and found himself fascinated with the frontier experience and how it shaped the American character. Fanebust graduated with a degree in history from UCLA in 1973. He started the research for his first book, *Where the Sioux River Bends*, in the mid-1970's. It was just the beginning. Separating truth from myth and enjoying both has kept him busy, taking up most of his spare time over the years.

Fanebust attended law school at Western State University College of Law in San Diego and was admitted to the California Bar in 1980. He entered into private law practice in San Diego and maintained a law office in that city until 1993 when he returned to Sioux Falls, looking for a career change. He is now a corporate lawyer for a nationwide financial services company.

Fanebust's books include: *Where the Sioux River Bends*, *Tales of Dakota Territory* (*Volumes I* and *II*), *Echoes of November: The Life and Times of Senator R. F. Pettigrew of South Dakota*, and *The Missing Corpse, Grave Robbing a Gilded Age Tycoon*.

His mother and his four sisters and two brothers, and their families, all live in South Dakota. He has one lovely daughter, Danae Howell, who is the mother of his first and only grandchild, the beautiful Angelina Howell.

www.ingramcontent.com/pod-product-compliance
Lightning Source LLC
Chambersburg PA
CBHW071222230426
43668CB00011B/1270